W9-BIY-099

ARKANSAS ROADSIDES
A GUIDEBOOK FOR THE STATE

BY BILL EARNGEY
WITH EDITORIAL ASSISTANCE FROM ROSS SACKETT

East Mountain Press
in Association with
August House / Little Rock
PUBLISHERS

Cover Design: Bill Womack, Memphis, Tn.

Front Cover Photograph: by John Jackson, Courtesy of Arkansas Highway and Transportation Department

Back Cover Photographs: Courtesy of Arkansas Parks and Tourism

State Highway Maps: Courtesy of Arkansas Highway and Transportation Department

Historical Maps: Courtesy of Special Collections, University of Arkansas, Fayetteville, Ar.

Black & White Photographs: Courtesy of Special Collections, University of Arkansas, Fayetteville, Ar.

Black & White Photographic Processing, Reproduction and Technical Assistance: Rick and Carol Green, Johnson, Ar.

Copy Editors: Pat Sims and Gary Green, Tivoli, N.Y.

Linotronic Typesetting: Aptos Post, Aptos, Ca.

Copyright © 1987 Bill Earngey. All rights including reproduction by photographic or electronic process and translation into foreign languages are fully reserved by the publisher. Reproduction of this book in whole or in part — including format, text and illustrations — without written permission of the publisher is strictly prohibited.

East Mountain Press
9 Steel Street
P.O. Box 446
Eureka Springs, Arkansas 72632

Library of Congress Catalog Card Number 87-08304
ISBN 0-9619592-0-7

This Book Is Dedicated To
Blacktop Highways And Mary Sims

Both Have Brought Charm
And Wonder To An Ordinary Life

CENTRAL ARKANSAS LIBRARY SYSTEM
JACKSONVILLE BRANCH
JACKSONVILLE, ARKANSAS

TABLE OF CONTENTS

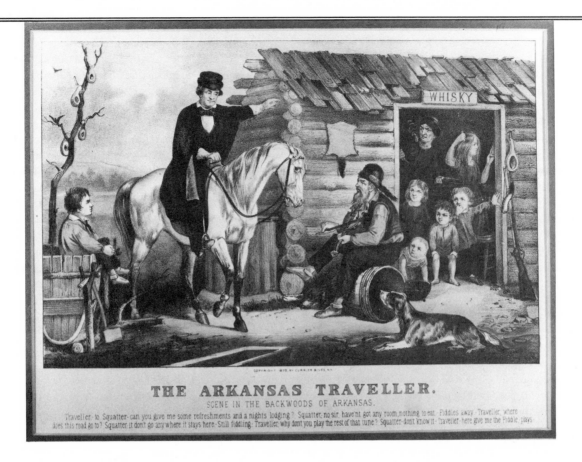

THE ARKANSAS TRAVELLER.
SCENE IN THE BACKWOODS OF ARKANSAS.
Traveller: to Squatter-can you give me some refreshments and a nights lodging? Squatter; no sir, have'nt got any room, nothing to eat. Fiddles away. Traveller, where
does this road go to? Squatter: it don't go anywhere it stays here. Still fiddling. Traveller: why dont you play the rest of that tune? Squatter: dont know it. traveller: here give me the Fiddle, plays

ACKNOWLEDGEMENTS

With sincere apologies for inadvertent omissions: Arkansas Archaeological Survey Commission, Arkansas Game and Fish Commission, Arkansas Geological Commission, Arkansas Highway and Transportation Department, Arkansas Historical Commission, Arkansas Museum Services, Arkansas Parks and Tourism, Arkansas Natural Heritage Commission, Arkansas Nature Conservancy, Arkansas Tourism Development, Corps of Engineers, Eureka Springs Post Office, Historical Report of the Secretary of State (1968), Quapaw Quarter Association, Afak Haydar, Affrida Bristow, Al Brown, Alan Clack, Amelia Martin, Ann Early, Anna Jordan, Barbara Caffee, Barbara Haynes, Bette Vogel, Betty Ann Grove, Betty Friddle, Betty Sloan, Bill Albright, Bill Jackson, Bill Looney, Bill Pich, Billy Thompson, Bob Besom, Bob Bounds, Bob Boyd, Bobbie McNeely, Buddy Garrett, Buddy Hoelzeman, C. Bruce Tanner, Carolyn Magruder, Carolyn McLean, Carolyn Shipman, Catherine Robinson, Chalmers Clark, Charlean T. Etter, Charlena Malone, Charlotte Jones, Clyde McGinnis, Connie Echols, Craig Hilburn, Craig Ogilvie, Dan Dennington, Darlene Cree, Dathine Thomas, David A. Saugey, David Caldwell, David G. McNully, David G. Meador, David Gill, Dean Walls, Debbie Baldwin, Dewey C. Faught, Dick Warner, Don Kunath, Don Lambert, Don Montgomery, Don R. Simons, Don Venhaus, Donald L. Waterworth, Donna D. Gallaher, Donna Kennedy, Doris T. Thurman, Doris West, Dorothy W. Whitaker, Doug Fairley, Drew Alexander, Earl B. Adams, Ed Smith, Edith Stoval, Edra Lumsden, Edward J. Wenner, Edwin Luther, Ellen Stern, Elsie Minton, Emy McCool, Eva V. Evans, Evelyn Erwin, Evelyn Flippo, Francis Harper, G.W. Watkins, Gary F. Blythe, Gaye K. Gland, George Phillips, Geraldine Petree, Gladys Baldwin, Glen T. Ruff, Gloria Green, Gloria Sisk, H. McCollum, H.G. Alvarez, H.W. Hammersla, Harry Nielwald, Helen Stell, Hershel Eaton, Hugh B. Carruth, J.D. Humphrey, J.J. Sheffelin, J.M. Buffington, J.R. Boise, Jack Beeson, Jack McCormick, Jake Commer, James R. Young, Jane D. Pittman, Janice Y. Clark, Janie Glover, Jason Rouby, Jean Quinn, Jeff Testerman, Jerome Rosewater, Jerry C. Sanders, Jessie Jones, Jim Sumpter, Jimmy King, Jo Claire English, Joan E. Cook, Joanie Morris, Joe Mouton, Joe Powell, John Little, John T.

Bowen, John Swink, John Teeter, Joyce Hyde, Joyce Lindsey, Juanita Gibson, Juanita Rees, Julie Wiedower, K.C. Drew, Karen Czaplicki, Kathy P. Johnson, Kay Hester, Keith H. Johnson, Ken Eastin, Kenneth Hunter, Kenneth Poindexter, Kerry Kraus, King O'Neal, Kit Bakker, Kitty Crawford, Larry W. Goodson, Laura Findley, Lee and Beatrice Hearn, Lillian Tucker, Lillie Fuhrman, Linda Tucker, Lisa Wolfe, Liz Burks, Lorene Chambers, Louie Graves, Lucille Westbrook, Mrs. Henry Morris, Marianne Woods, Marie Hillyer, Marilyn Hiatt Hudgens, Marion M. Stroud, Martha S. Lessenberry, Mary Coles, Mary Dillingham, Mary Francis Harold, Mary Gay Shipley, Mary Yates, Mason E. Miller, Maxwell Nelson, Michael Dabrishus, Michelle Dickey, Mike Dumas, Mike Mills, Mike Polston, Mrs. A.R. Meacham, Mrs. J. B. Kittrell, Mrs. J.C. Ross, Mrs. James L. Moore, Mrs. Noel Baker, Mrs. Otis A. Blackwood, Mrs. P. Glenn Smith, Mrs. S. Jemiolo, Mrs. C. Mullis, Mrs. T.A. Gilbert, Ms. Jimmy, Nancy DeLamar, Nancy Dugwyler, Nelda Archer, Nick Shivley, Nina Waters, Orilla Pinkston, P.J. Spaul, Pat Donat, Pat McCaughan, Patty Kay Elliott, Peg N. Smith, Phil Chudy, Polly Burkeen, R.H. Segraves, Ray Appleget, Ray C. Culver, Jr., Reece Hogins, Richard E. McCamant, Richard L. Shelton, Richard Wegner, Robert G. Winn, Robert Williams, Jr., Robert Zirkle, Roger Giddings, Ron Magness, Rosalie S. Gould, Roy Renfrow, Rufus Buie, Rufus D. Wolf, Russell Lyn Gurley, Ruth Eichor, S.C. Cooke, Sam A. Weems, Sharon K. Arnold, Sharon Marrs, Sibyl Hightower, Sue A. Wynne, Sue Chambers, Sue Trulock, Suzy Keasler, T.J. Spencer, Thaddeus Fox, Theresa Spragins, Theta Shipman, Thomas Bridgeman, Thomas E. Jackson, Thomas J. Crowson, Tim Erwin, Tim V. Scott, Tom O'Connor, Tommie Crawford, Toni Snow, Trixie Finn, Tyler Hardeman, Vance Phillips, Violet Hankins, Virgil Spruill, W.D. Beseau, Walter M. Adams, Wausita Hinton, Wayne Boren, Weldon Ramey, Wendy Richter, William M. Shepherd, Worth Matteson, and Zoe Medlin Caywood.

Special Thanks: My mother, Ada Sue Thomas Overman, who has given me a lifetime of support and encouragement, Lisa Bradley and Joe Rice for sources and material, Dan Morse for research advice, John D. McFarland for research advice, Russell P. Baker for research advice, Marie Betzold-Riley and Steven Grisham for computer technical support, René Diaz for architectural advice, Michael Acklin for Civil War and Trail of Tears research, University of Arkansas' Special Collections for research assistance, Babby Lovett for her good sense, W.J. Lemke (Butterfield Overland Mail Through Northwest Arkansas), DeForest Sackett for technical design assistance, Norman Muse for regional research, Ellen Shipley for source material, Jerry Dupy for design assistance, Jo Luck Wilson for source material, Wesley Creel for research assistance, MEGABYTE for computer technical support, Billy Ray McKelvy for regional research, Elwin Goolsby for regional research, Helen Lindley for regional research, John and Marjem Gill (On The Courthouse Square), Mary Humphrey for regional research, John F. Ferguson and J.H. Atkinson (Historic Arkansas), Patricia L. Curry for regional research, Ranny and Charmayne Cullon (Arkansas Outdoors), D.W. Powell for regional research, Skip Sackett for good advice, William E. Leach for regional research, Emma Earngey and Ron and Lyn Jerit, who helped explore the highways, Tommie Webb for Civil War editing, Hester Davis and Charles McGimsey (Indians of Arkansas),Orville McInturff for regional research, Verna P. Reitzammer for all of Arkansas City, W.J. Lemke for Butterfield Stage material, Cone Magie for source material, Ted R. Worley (Butterfield Overland Mail – Memphis to Fort Smith Branch), Marylea Vines for regional research, Roger and Nancy Menzies for good designs, Carol Van Pelt for photo research, Harold K. Grimmett for Natural Heritage Areas, Jo Eveld for regional research, Tom Foti (Natural Divisions of Arkansas), Ann B. Carroll for regional research, Bryan Keller for trails information, Mara Leveritt for source material, and Charlie and Sally Davis, who wish to remain anonymous.

ABOUT THIS BOOK

Arkansas Roadsides is not about restaurants or motels. Other guides have thoroughly covered those subjects. What this guide offers is the spirit of adventure and a practical reference for Arkansas' attractions. More important, the book was written to satisfy curiosity, to answer familiar questions like What was _that_? – and What's down _that_ road? Listed alphabetically are towns and their place-names (like Smackover and Greasy Corner), as well as their histories, architecture, points of interest, oddities and events and festivals. Also included is Arkansas' ever-present natural beauty: Its prairies, mountains, river valleys, forests and swamps that provide habitats for wildlife like black bears, cougars, bald eagles and blue herons. These areas – along with state and national parks, lakes and streams, and outdoor recreation like camping, hiking, canoeing, hunting and fishing – are located and described. And, as a thread of continuity, topics about what helped to create Arkansas are indexed in the main text. Not just commentaries, these topics are as real as the Indian mounds, Civil War battlefields and railroads found throughout the state.

My introduction to Arkansas' roadsides began with the only book on the subject, Arkansas: A Guide To The State (American Guide Series, Hastings House, 1941). Thoroughly entertaining and informative, this Works Projects Administration (WPA) guide was also thoroughly out of date, which meant that my information had to rely on original research. Besides city, state and federal agencies, hundreds of Arkansawyers contributed to this book. It is to their credit that this guide has more varied detailed information about the state than any other single source. My part in the project was to accumulate suggestions, cross-check facts, and then organize the material. The content is actually a consensus of what local residents think is most interesting about their towns and counties.

By way of apology I need to point out that not everyone who should have been included in the "Home of entries" was, nor were the towns always their birthplaces. For example, Bill Clinton claims both Arkadelphia (where he was born) and Hot Springs (where he grew up) as home, and, while Sam Walton claims Bentonville as home, he was neither born nor reared there. The idea of these entries is to give a sense of the cross section of personalities who call Arkansas home.

Another entry that might need explanation is "Records," which is located in the Index. It lists a range of topics with modifiers like largest, smallest, only, etc. When not qualified (America's largest, World's only, etc.), it may be assumed that the record is for Arkansas.

As a footnote, a caution about place-names is necessary. Pioneers were not aware they were making history. Babies were born, children reared, and a generation would pass. Most often, no official public records were left behind to explain the sentiments or hopes or heroes that named Arkansas' towns. Family possessions like Bibles, diaries and letters are what helped preserve their histories, as did newspaper accounts and memories that often added and dropped stitches while weaving a good story. These stories are called legend, tradition or "it is said." Where more than one account is equally disputed, all are mentioned here. As for the truth, well, we live in a democracy; let the majority rule.

Arkansas Roadsides was a pleasure to write. I hope you find it entertaining and useful. In fond memory of the 1941 WPA guidebook I would like to close with an excerpt from it that is still good advice for those exploring the open road: "Motorists attentive to the variety of fauna encountered on Arkansas roads may remember that wild birds invariably get out of the way, hens make two or three false starts but usually escape unharmed, a litter of pigs will parade soberly across with no monkeyshines, horses ordinarily stick to the shoulders and ditches, mules are unpredictable but know how to take care of themselves, dogs dart from under the wheel at the last moment, and only cows are completely oblivious; a herd of cattle on the road is the signal to slow down to five miles an hour or to come to a full stop."

—Bill Earngey

Because this book already has a wide range of facts about Arkansas, there is no special section listing them as a whole. For those few not included – like state symbols, motto and nickname – space has been made available here.

STATE SYMBOLS, MOTTO AND NICKNAME:
Flower: ....Apple Blossom, 1901
Bird: ....Mocking Bird, 1929
Tree: ....Pine, 1939
Gem: ....Diamond, 1967
Mineral: ....Quartz Crystal, 1967
Rock: ....Bauxite, 1967
Musical Instrument:.....Fiddle, 1985
Drink: ....Milk, 1985
Motto: ....Regnat Populus (The People Rule)
Nickname: ....The Land of Opportunity, 1953
State Song: ...."Arkansas"

ARKANSAS FACTS:
Population: 2,285,500
Area: ....51,945 square miles (27th in U.S.A.)
Capital: ....Little Rock
Time Zone: ....Central, Daylight Savings Time
Age For Drivers: ....16 years old
Extreme Length: ....240 miles
Extreme Width: ....275 miles
Water Area: ....605 square miles
Climate: ....Average Annual, 61.4°F

ARKANSAS BEVERAGE LAWS:
No Sunday sales. Legal age 21. Sold by package and by the drink; subject to amendment by local option.

Arkansas State Flag

Field: red
Diamond Border: blue with white stars
Diamond: white
ARKANSAS: blue
Diamond Stars: blue

25 Stars: 25th state admitted to the Union
4 stars: 3 bottom stars indicate the nations that
governed it: Spain, France and the United States.
The top star commemorates the Confederacy.
The Diamond Shape: signifies Arkansas as the only
diamond-producing state in the United States.

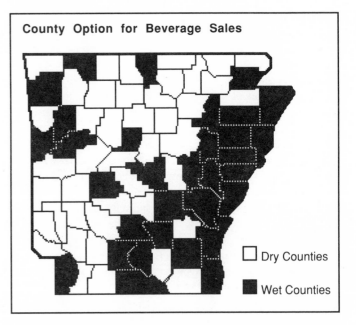

County Option for Beverage Sales

☐ Dry Counties
■ Wet Counties

The following Arkansas counties have voted to sell alcoholic beverages. Those not listed are "dry"; however, the laws might have changed; inquire locally: Arkansas, Baxter, Calhoun, Carroll (liquor by the drink, Eureka Springs), Chicot, Cleveland, Conway, Crittenden, Cross, Drew, Dallas, Desha, Franklin (liquor by the drink, Wiederkehr Village), Garland (liquor by the drink, all), Greene, Jackson, Jefferson (liquor by the drink, Pine Bluff), Lee, Logan (beer and native wines), Miller, Mississippi, Monroe, Ouachita, Phillips (liquor by the drink, Helena), Poinsett, Prairie, Pulaski (liquor by the drink, all), St. Francis, Sebastian, Union, Washington and Woodruff.

THE ARKANSAS CREED:
I believe in Arkansas as a land of opportunity and promise.
I believe in the rich heritage of Arkansas, and I honor the men and women who created this heritage.
I believe in the youth of Arkansas who will build our future.
I am proud of my State. I will uphold its constitution, obey its laws and work for the good of all its citizens.

Remember, to use this book effectively, that subjects are in alphabetical order, and that all *italicized* words are subjects, too, and should be thought of as *see also*. Although the book is divided into sections, *italicized* words refer to additional information about subjects listed throughout the guide.

Scanning the table of contents will show that the book is divided into alphabetical sections: Arkansas Roadsides (towns, countryside and related subjects) which is followed by recreation and recreational facilities (Arkansas Campgrounds, Float Streams, Lakes, National Forests, State Parks, Trails, etc.). Unless specifically noted, these sections are also divided into alphabetical order.

Also keep in mind that the Index is a quick source of reference, particularly for smaller, more specific subjects like Corps of Engineers parks and campgrounds or national forest recreation areas. Finding these by name (with their page numbers) in the Index is faster and easier than thumbing through the book for its section and then finding it alphabetically.

In addition to the traditional index there is a special index, the Mini-Finder, which lists subjects by map coordinates. For example, C-2 lists all the subjects (with their page numbers) found in that one graph square of the book's highway map. The Mini-Finder is useful for seeing at a glance what is in the immediate area or what can be found along the way.

Along with the state highway maps are historical maps, which range in date through the 19th century. They are particularly helpful when reading the histories of Arkansas towns, tracing roads and railroads or just trying to get an idea of why anyone would build a town where they did.

Below is a listing for Altus, showing terms used in this book. Notice that the *italicized* words can be subjects, parts of subjects and even in parentheses. No matter how the *italicized* word is used, it is an internal index referring to additional information.

HOW TO USE THIS BOOK

Map Locater (❑ NW Quarter, ●General Location of Subject) _____

Subject (Altus) _____

Population, Altitude & Map Coordinate _____

Arkansas River Valley = See Also Arkansas River _____

Little Rock & Ft. Smith *Railroad* = See Also Railroad (History) _____

Coal Hill = See Also Coal Hilll _____

Wineries = Point of Interest _____

(BELOW) = Additional Information Follows _____

WIEDERKEHR'S = Subheading _____

National Historic Register = U.S. Government-Designated Landmark _____

NOTE: All Directions and Mileage Are From the Subject:

US 64, E of Downtown = On Federal Hwy 64 East of Downtown Altus _____

St. Mary's Catholic Church = Point of Interest _____

(Subiaco) = See Also Subiaco _____

N of US 64 on SR 186 = Located North of Federal Hwy 64 on State Road 186 _____

Events/Festivals = Special Occasions (Usually Held on Weekends) _____

Early Aug = Sometime in the First Two Weeks of August _____

ALTUS
POP. 441   ALT. 471   MAP C-2

Settled in 1875, "the village known for its wines" was the highest (altus) point surveyed in the *Arkansas River* Valley by the Little Rock & Ft. Smith *Railroad*. A minor American melting pot, its original settlers were the Swiss and Germans who worked the vineyards, and the Slavic and Irish coal miners of nearby Alix, Denning and *Coal Hill*.

Wineries. Noting the similarities of climate and terrain between Altus and their previous homes, Swiss and German immigrants began growing grapes in this area c.1880. All but Mt. Bethel are grouped around St. Mary's Catholic Church (BELOW); all offer tours/tasting. WIEDERKEHR'S: Founded in 1880 by Swiss immigrant Johann A. Wiederkehr, it claims the only gold medals won so far by Arkansas wines. The original wine cellar is on the National Historic Register. POST: (1880) German immigrant Jacob Post began this award-winning winery by serving wine to passengers when trains stopped for fuel and water. SAX: (1880) August Kuehnis, stepfather of the Sax family, built the basement wine cellar that is now a salesroom. MT. BETHEL: Jacob Post's great-grandson, Eugene Post, owns this small family business, one of the last Arkansas wineries to be established (1956). US 64, E of Downtown.

St. Mary's Catholic Church. National Historic Register. This basilica-style structure, visible for miles, was built by the Benedictine Order *(Subiaco)* in 1901 using sandstone quarried at the site. A 120-foot tower rings four bells whose aggregate weight is 6,393 pounds. During WWI German painter Fridolin Fuchs created gold-leaf murals, using local residents as models. Highlighting his work are 29 stained-glass windows. N of US 64 on SR 186.

Events/Festivals. Early May: Springtime Gala. Music. Auction. Arts & Crafts. Early Aug: Grape Festival. Music. Food. Tours & Tasting.

WHY THERE IS AN ARKANSAS

About 500 million years ago Arkansas lay underwater. Across its breadth stretched a deep basin, the Ouachita Trough, where nearly 30,000 feet of sediment would accumulate. To the north, in east-central Missouri, the St. Francis Mountains were an island that would rise, forming the Ozarks. Far to the south was a land mass called Llanoria that would drift north until eventually colliding with what would later be most of the continental United States.

In Arkansas, along the Ouachita Trough, this collision squeezed millions of years of sediment, compressing it from a width of 120 miles to about 60, which caused the tilting, twisted, torn and wrinkled rocks seen in roadcuts throughout the Ouachita Mountains today. This odd geological formation, running east-west (as opposed to the more common north-south pattern), was ground down by erosion as fast as it was squeezed together, eventually losing 18,000 feet. During this period, to the north at the St. Francis Mountains, a large area of ocean bottom, a mass of limestone and dolomite rock formed from the skeletons of marine life, was thrust straight up, forming the Ozarks. Between these two newly created mountain ranges stretched what is today the Arkansas River Valley.

Approximately 135 million years ago the land in southwestern Arkansas, Oklahoma and Texas began to rise, draining away the sea that had once washed across southern Arkansas just below Hot Springs. Beginning about 63 million years ago the Gulf of Mexico began its final retreat across the eastern and southern portions of Arkansas. Although the water was never very deep, evidence of its effects can still be seen in the sand and gravel of the Gulf Coastal region. Also around this period the Ozarks and Ouachitas began to take today's shapes of relatively flat-topped mountains of about the same height.

The last great geological event in Arkansas (beginning about a million years ago) was perhaps its most unusual – the

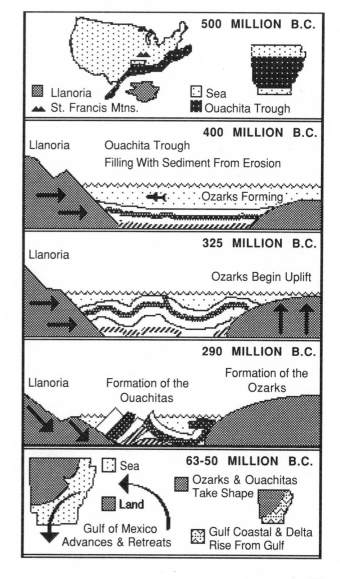

forming of *Crowley's Ridge*. This ridge is an erosional remnant, a highland between two valleys formed by the Mississippi River flowing to the west of it and the Ohio to the east (the Arkansas River flowed east, then south). While creating this ridge, these huge rivers (formed from glaciers melting in central Missouri as late as 20,000-13,000 years ago) carried away ocean-bottom sand and gravel, replacing them with the sand, silt and clay characteristic of the Delta today. Diversion of these rivers to their present courses may have been caused by a tectonic uplift in southeast Missouri about 18,000 years ago, during the same time that people first began immigrating across the land bridge between Asia and North America.

In Arkansas, about 8,500-7,900 B.C., there lived people referred to as Dalton. Although little is known about them, they had a complex culture that included cemeteries with exotic artifacts. These people were followed by hunter-gatherers, who were in turn followed by mound builders *(Trail of Tears)*. When the first Europeans arrived in 1541 *(De Soto)* they found a complex society of people joined by loose confederations. Journals kept by men of this Spanish expedition searching for gold record continual encounters with people who were mostly farmers living in communities grouped around large mounds. However, when the next explorers, Marquette and Joliet, arrived 131 years later (1673) these "temple mound builders" had vanished *(Blytheville,* Chickasawba Mound), replaced by the historic Quapaw, Osage and Caddo *(Trail of Tears)*.

Nine years later, in 1682, La Salle claimed for France all the land drained by the Mississippi River and its tributaries, naming the area Louisiana in honor of King Louis XIV. Later, De Tonti (1686) established the first European settlement in the lower Mississippi River Valley (Arkansas Post, *National Parks)*. Subsequent explorers like La Harpe (1719-22) continued to penetrate deeper into Arkansas, and by 1799 it had an estimated European population of 386 *(Arkansawyer)*.

Arkansas, as a small part of this vast Louisiana, was passed back and forth for political reasons between France and Spain in secret treaties until Napoleon, emperor of France, sold Louisiana in 1803 to America (Louisiana Purchase, *State Parks)*. At first a part of the newly created Territory of Louisiana, it became the District of Arkansas (Territory of Missouri) when Louisiana became a state (1812), and then the Territory of Arkansas in 1819 when Missouri applied for statehood.

Even with a population of 14,000 and status as a territory, Arkansas still did not have its present shape *(Boundary Lines)*. Its eastern and southern borders were established but the northern and western ones remained to be fixed. Missouri's statehood in 1821 set the northern boundary, leaving the western one as a political problem that was not resolved until 1829. Between 1817-1828 Arkansas had within its borders Indian nations whose sovereignty was recognized by the federal government *(Trail of Tears)*. After these nations were relocated, the western boundary was established *(Boundary Lines)*.

On June 15, 1836, by an act of Congress, Arkansas was admitted to the Union, becoming the 25th state.

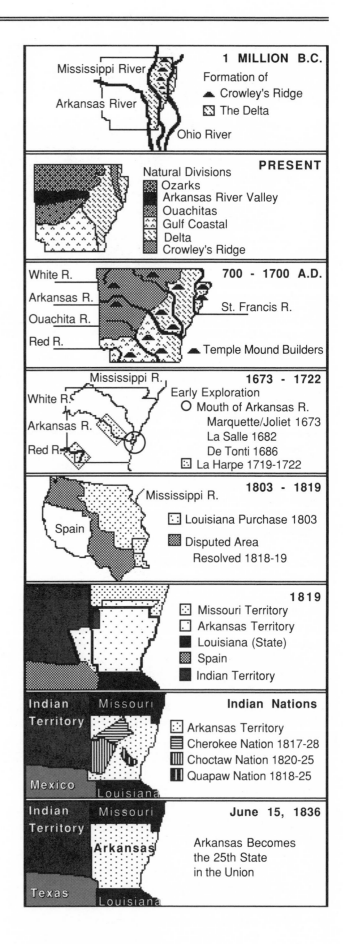

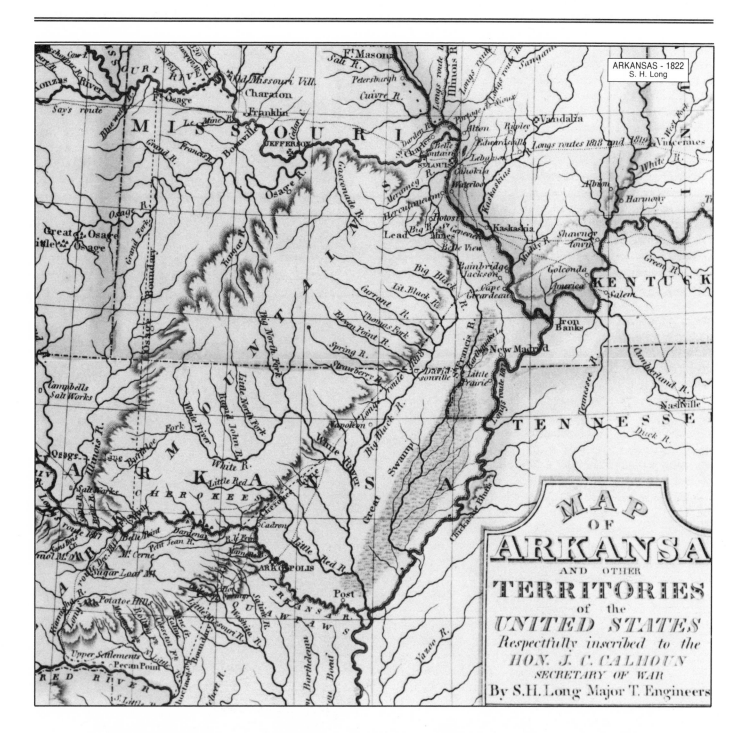

MODERN AND HISTORICAL MAPS

While reading the historical maps, keep in mind that cartographers were likely to misplace or misname towns, and that often dates (establishment of county seats, founding of towns and disappearances of both) were not always immediately reflected on them, because the map had already been drawn or the cartographer was late in receiving the information. What is interesting is to see the ebb and flow of towns; how they were affected by reorganization of counties, rerouting or recent addition of roads and the coming of the steamboat and the railroad. Some towns literally moved – taking houses and buildings –

to establish new ones with different names. Others ignored the new competition and are now suburbs of their upstart rivals, while quite a few simply vanished. But most often towns did not move, were not incorporated into larger ones and did not wither. These communities today seem isolated when in fact they may once have been mainstream, prosperous towns. Finding and exploring these "out-of-the-way" places is always an adventure. More than likely they have some remnant of their past, and nearly always they have a nostalgic location that sets them apart from the ordinary.

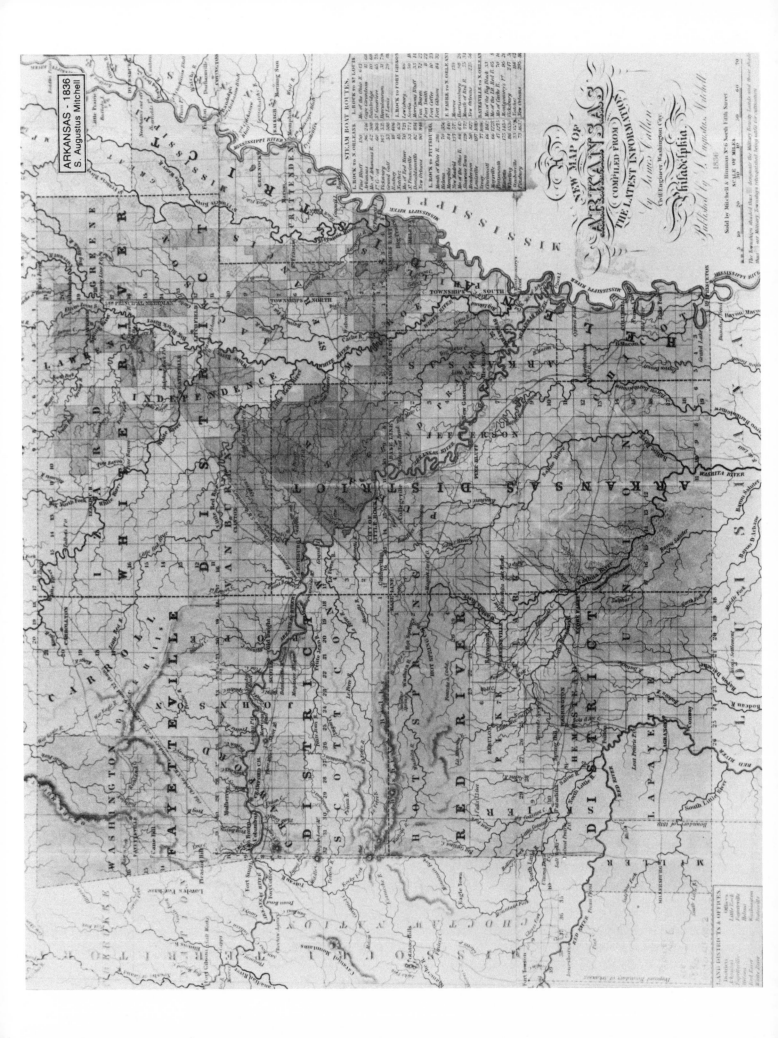

ARKANSAS - 1836
S. Augustus Mitchell

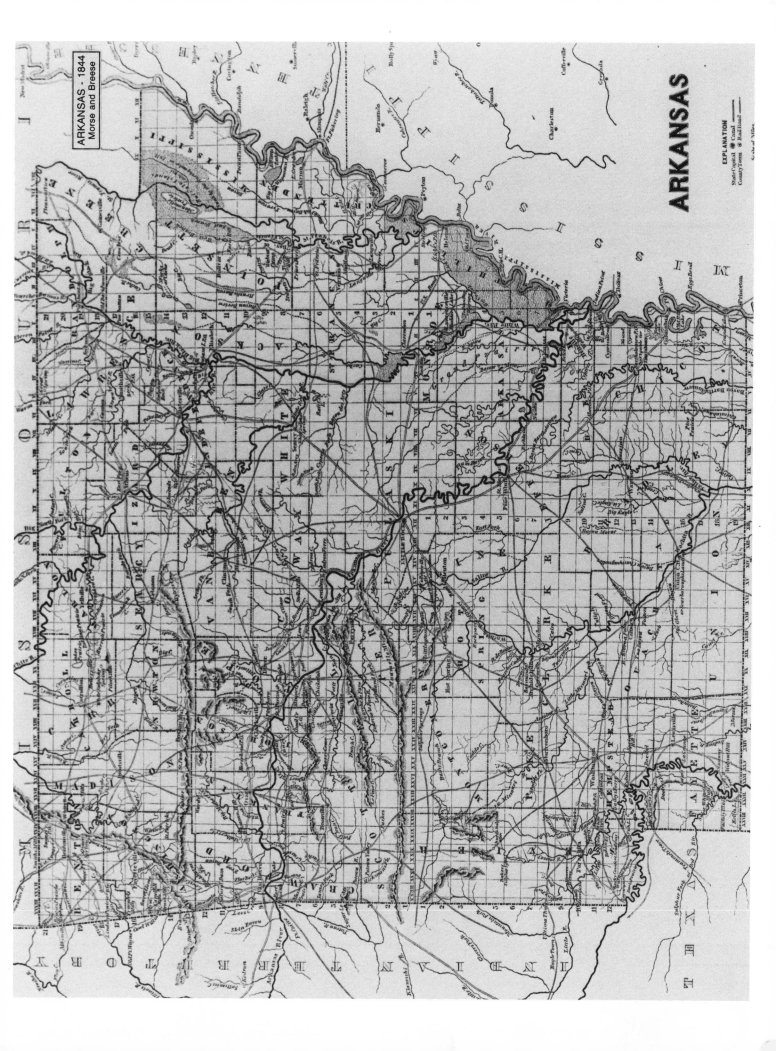

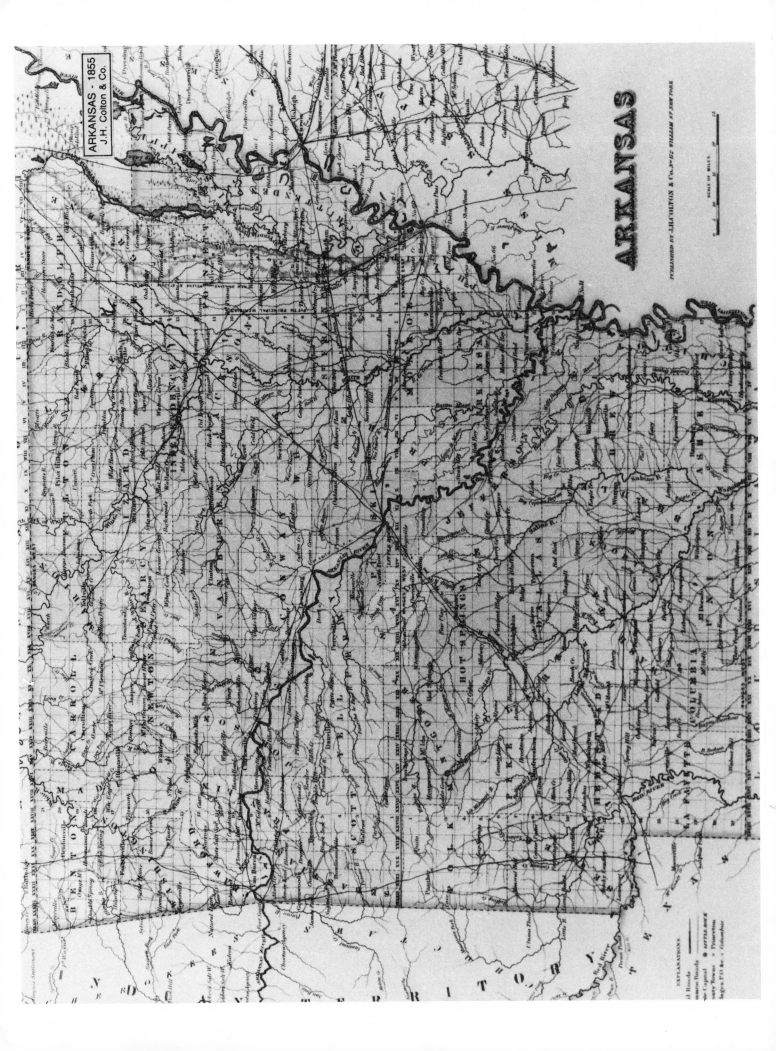

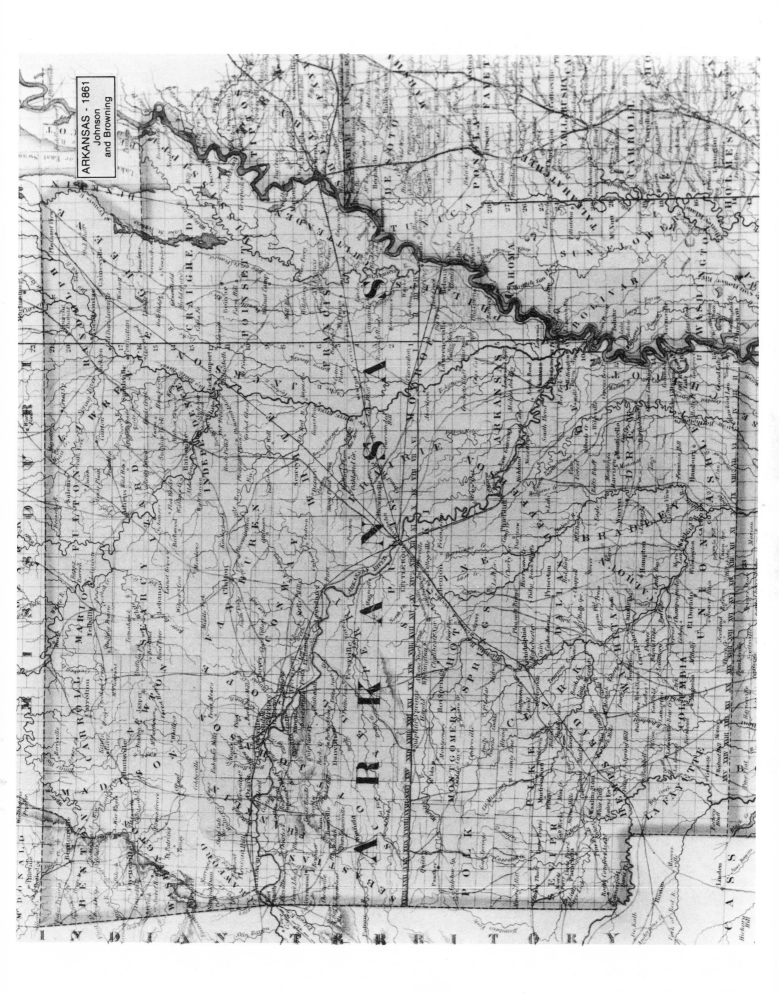

ARKANSAS - 1861
Johnson
and Browning

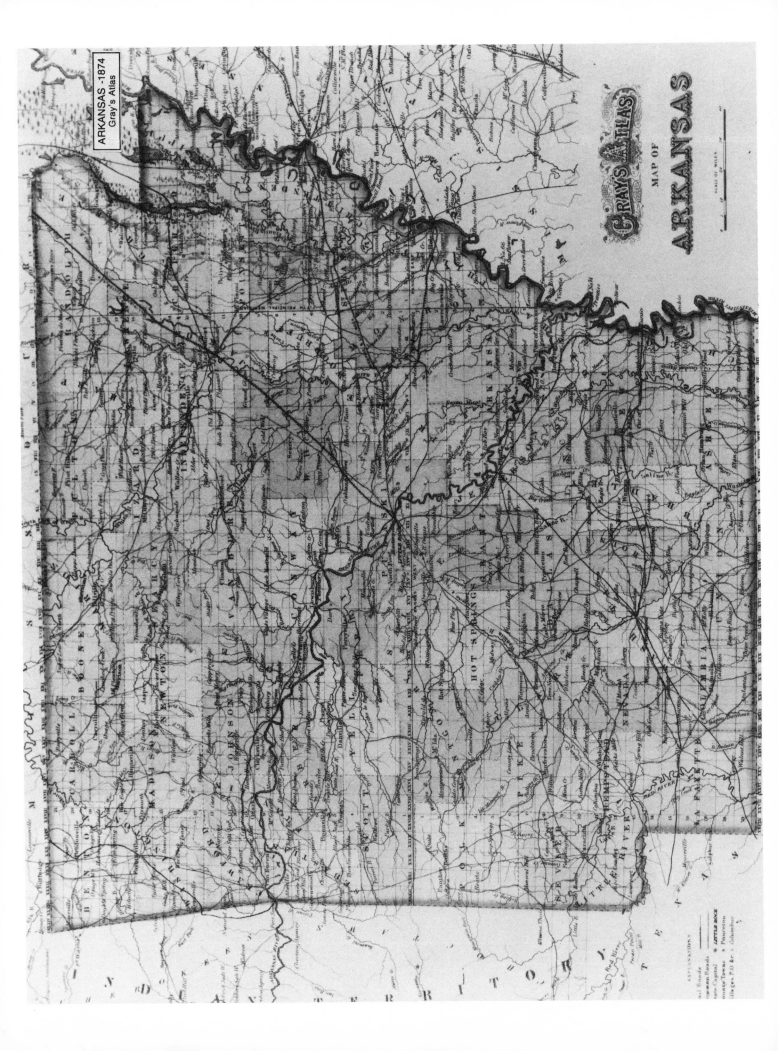

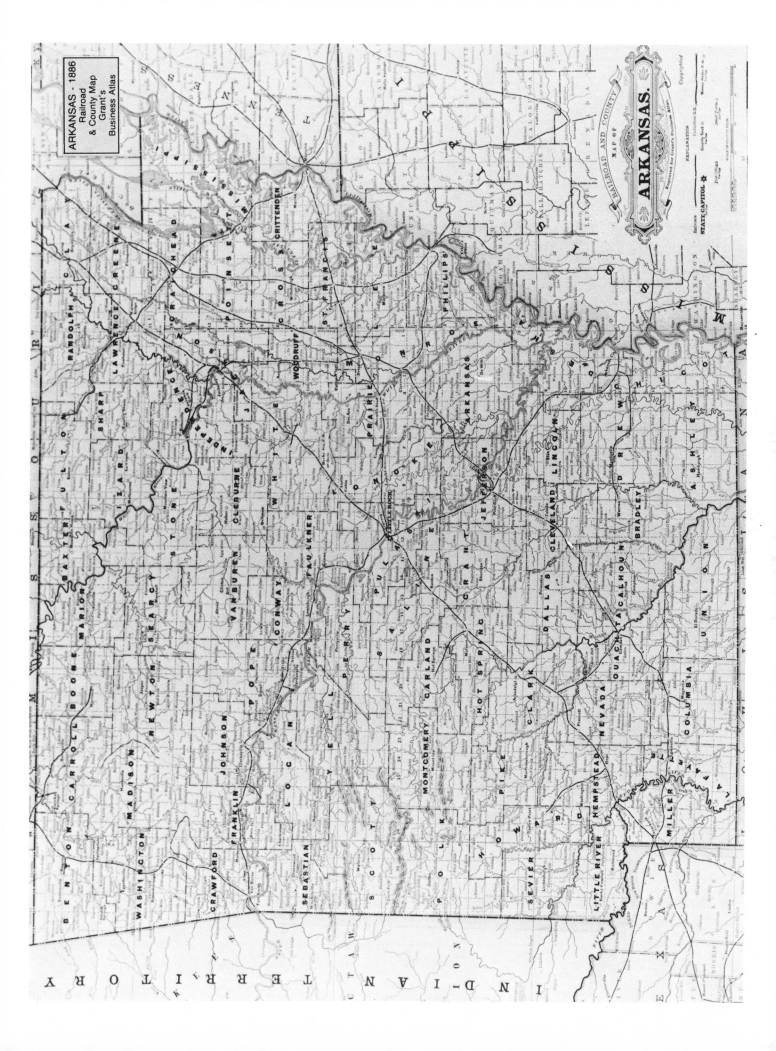

ARKANSAS - 1886
Railroad
& County Map
Grant's
Business Atlas

RAILROAD AND COUNTY MAP OF
ARKANSAS.

Engraved for Grant's Business Atlas.

EXPLANATION
STATE CAPITOL ☆
County Seat ○

MAP 1 NORTHWEST QUARTER

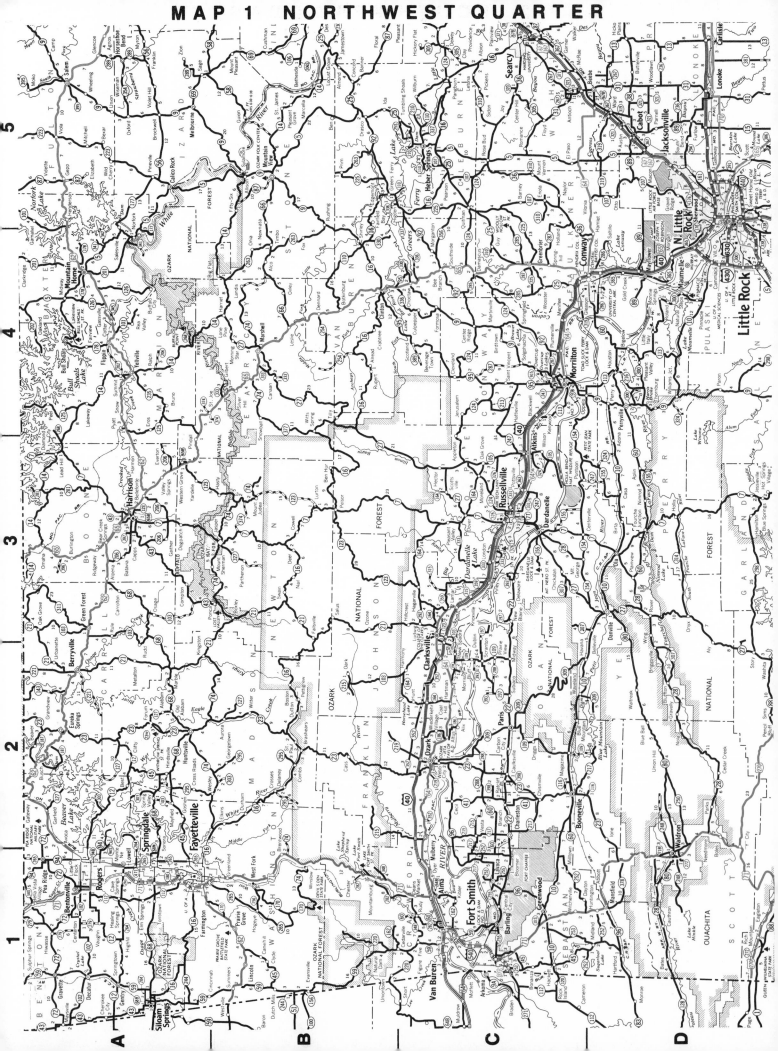

MAP 3 NORTHEAST QUARTER

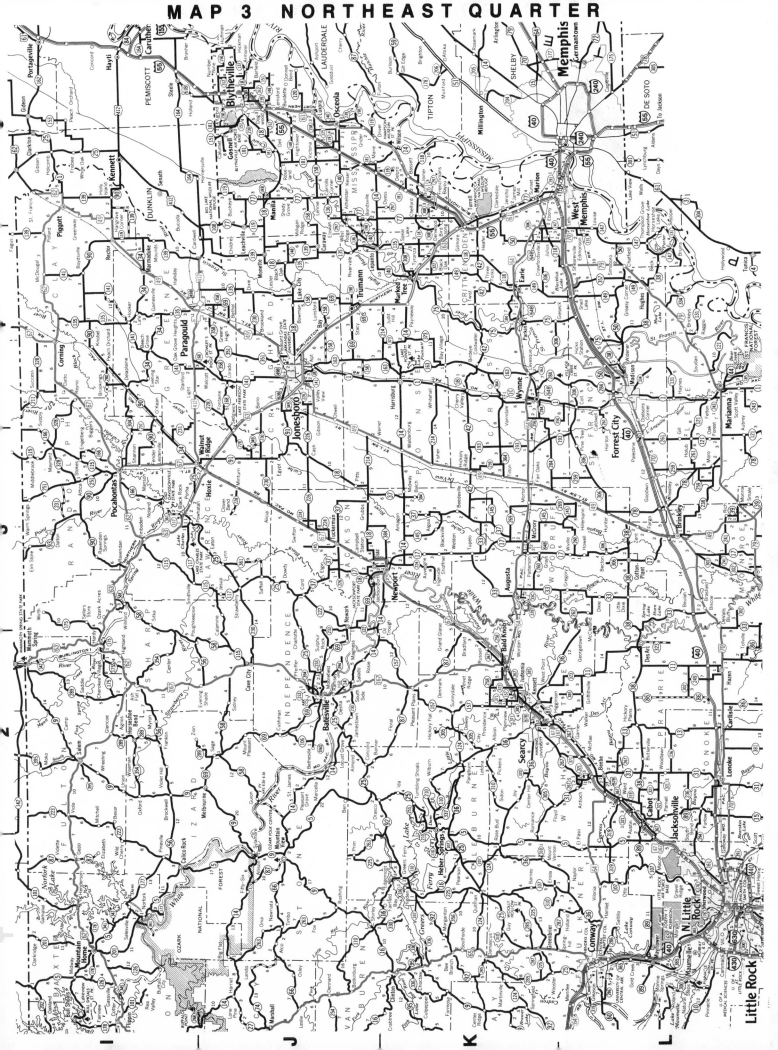

MAP 2 SOUTHWEST QUARTER

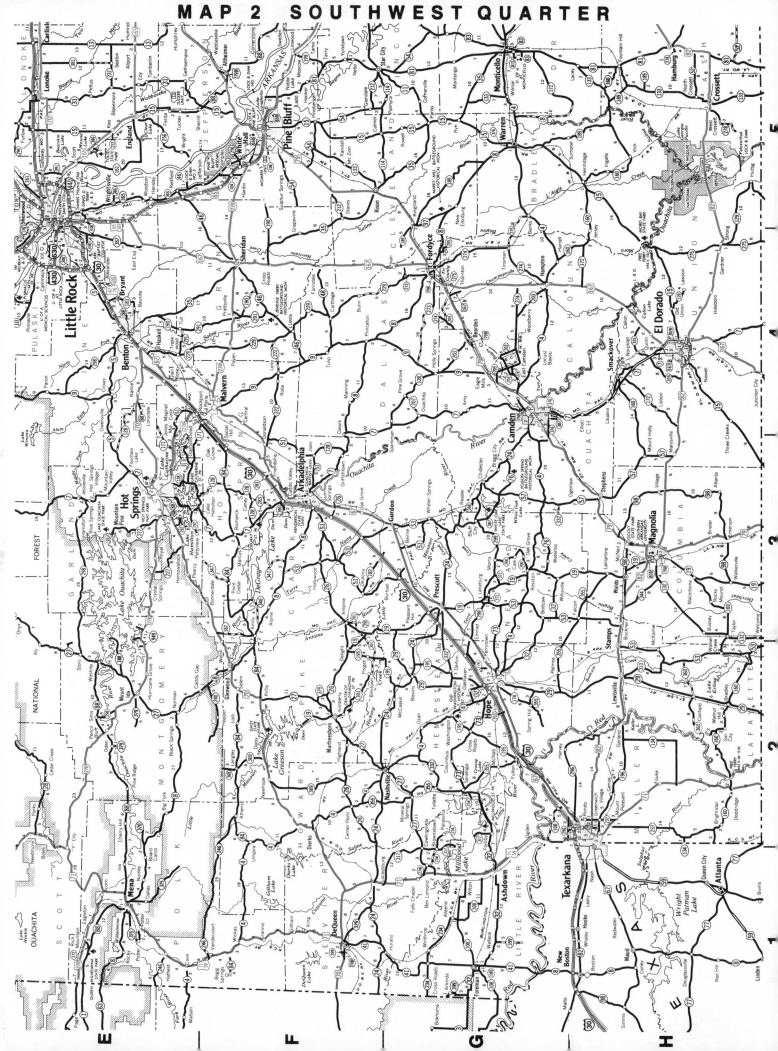

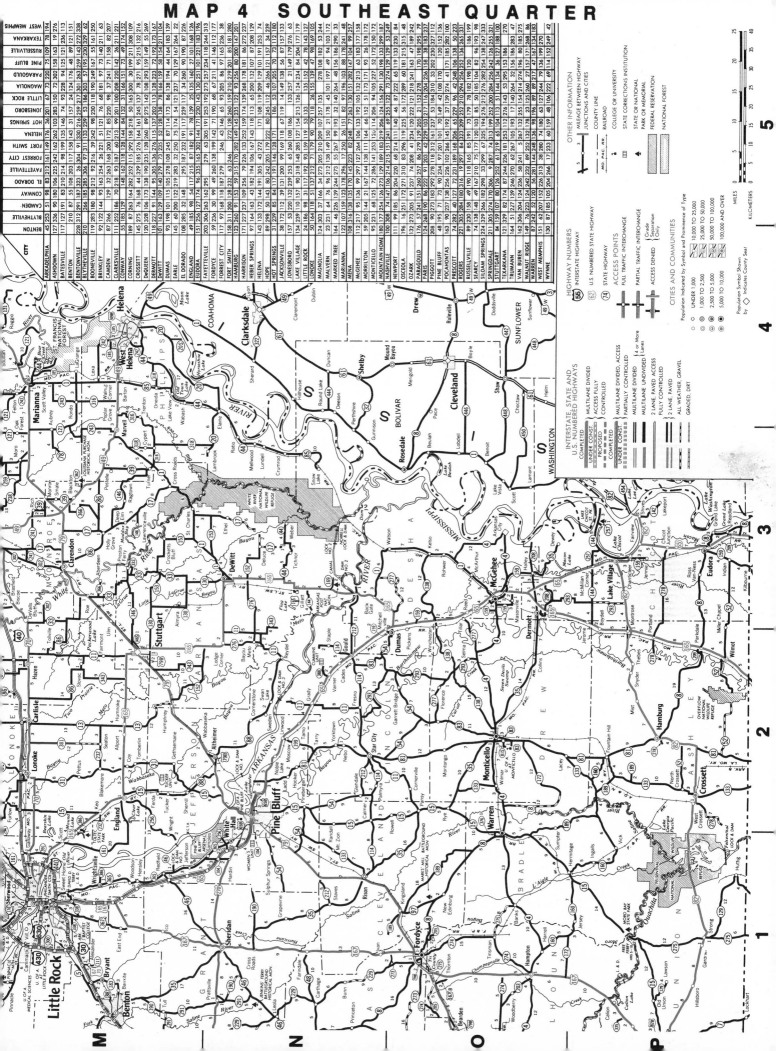

ARKANSAS ROADSIDES

ALLEENE
COMMUNITY   ALT. 330   MAP G-1

An antebellum post office, Minneola, served the area until the present site was created by the Texarkana-Ft. Smith *Railroad* (Kansas City Southern) in 1892. Ben Lawrence donated the land, attempting to call the town Lawrenceville, but railroad officials named it (reason unknown) Alleene. Home of Chester Lauck, who portrayed Lum Eddards of "Lum 'N Abner," the 1930s radio comedy *(Pine Ridge)*.

Will Reed Log House. National Historic Register, 1895. The dogtrot of this restored cabin divides a kitchen/living room and bedroom/storeroom that have typical furnishings of the late 1880s, including a spinning wheel, pump organ, woodstove and feather bed. In Town.

ALPENA
POP. 344   ALT. 1,135   MAP A-3

Created by the St. Louis & North Arkansas Railway (Missouri & North Arkansas *Railroad)* in 1901 as Alpena Pass, it was the final blow to the struggling town of *Carrollton*. Today's line of stone storefront buildings faces the vanished tracks. Although the origin of its name is unknown, there is also an Alpena, Michigan, whose name, "the Indian word for partridge," was suggested in 1857 by Henry Rowe Schoolcraft, who had explored the White River and northern Arkansas in 1818-19.

SR 206. Originally (c.1836), the portion of this state highway from *Harrison* to Batavia continued to *Carrollton* as a part of a major *road* system in North Arkansas. Today, older homes and barns reflect its past. US 62, E 3 m.

ALTUS
POP. 441   ALT. 471   MAP C-2

Settled in 1875, "the village known for its wines" was the highest (altus) point surveyed in the *Arkansas River* Valley by the Little Rock & Ft. Smith *Railroad*. A minor American melting pot, its original settlers were the Swiss and Germans who worked the vineyards, and the Slavic and Irish coal miners of nearby Alix, Denning and *Coal Hill*.

Wineries. Noting the similarities of climate and terrain between Altus and their previous homes, Swiss and German immigrants began growing grapes in this area c.1880. All but Mt. Bethel are grouped around St. Mary's Catholic Church (BELOW); all offer tours/tastings. WIEDERKEHR'S: Founded in 1880 by Swiss immigrant Johann A. Wiederkehr, it claims the only gold medals won so far by Arkansas wines. The original wine cellar is on the National Historic Register. POST: (1880) German immigrant Jacob Post established this award-winning winery by serving wine to passengers when trains stopped for fuel and water. SAX: (1880) August Kuehnis, stepfather of the Sax family, built the basement wine cellar that is now a salesroom. MT. BETHEL: Jacob Post's great-grandson, Eugene Post, owns this small family business, one of the last Arkansas wineries to be established (1956). US 64, E of Downtown.

St. Mary's Catholic Church. National Historic Register. Visible for miles, this basilica-style structure was built by the Benedictine Order *(Subiaco)* in 1901, using sandstone quarried at the site. A 120-foot tower rings four bells whose aggregate weight is 6,393 pounds. During WWI German painter Fridolin Fuchs created gold-leaf murals, using local residents as models. Highlighting his work are 29 stained-glass windows. N of US 64 on SR 186.

Events/Festivals. Early May: Springtime Gala. Music. Auction. Arts & Crafts. Early Aug: Grape Festival. Music. Food. Tours & Tasting.

ARKADELPHIA
POP. 10,169   ALT. 200   MAP F-3

Although a colorful local legend claims that in 1800 the first settlers "came in riding on buffaloes" to the campgrounds of the Caddo, this city marks its beginnings as a river landing established c.1809 on a bluff overlooking the Ouachita *River (Float Streams)* by blacksmith Wm. (some say Adam) Blakeley. Blakeleytown (also Blakeley Bluff), about four miles south of the Southwest Trail *(Roads)*, grew steadily because of the John Hemphill salt works (Arkansas' first industry, 1814) and Jacob Barkman's enterprises: trade with New Orleans beginning in 1815, common pleas judge in 1820, first postmaster in 1823, owner/builder of the first steamboat on the Ouachita (The Dime, 1830), and proprietor of a stagecoach stop in 1831. The town was first surveyed and divided into lots in 1839. In 1842, at a legendary barbecue much like the one at *Pocahontas*, Clark County voted to move the county seat from Greenville (present-day Hollywood), making Arkadelphia permanent county seat in 1843. The present town name was first spelled with a "c" – Arcadelphia – appearing in court records as early as 1839 (and on maps well into the 1870s). Origin of this one-of-a-kind town name (both with the "c" and the "k") is disputed; conclusive evidence is not available. One version relies on a combination of arc and a portion of Philadelphia to translate as a circle where love dwells, or an arc (as a rainbow) of brotherly (friendly) love. The second uses the "k" to combine Arkansas and Philadelphia in the same sense: a city of brotherly (friendly) love. Home of Henderson State University and Ouachita Baptist University. Possible *De Soto* Route.

Local legend claims that the first settlers of Arkadelphia "came in riding on buffaloes"

Henderson State University Museum. Established 1949. A 30-room Victorian mansion containing "the best collection of interior wooden fretwork" in the state, shares space with the Arkansas Archaeological Survey Station. With an outstanding exhibit of Caddo artifacts it also features an excellent collection of minerals and fossils, birds and animals, lamps and lanterns. HSU campus, Henderson & 10th.
Clark County Courthouse. Romanesque Revival, 1899. National Historic Register. Nine-foot windows, 18-foot ceilings and original furnishings make it an excellent example of 19th century courtroom architecture. Features: five-story clock tower. Downtown, 4th & Crittenden. *(County Profiles)*
National Historic Register. James E.M. Barkman House (c.1860), 406 N. 10th. Bozeman House (c.1847), Hollywood Rd. W of town on SR 26 & 51. Clark County Library (1903),

609 Caddo St. Flangin Law Office (1855), 320 Clay St. Magnolia Manor (1854), 6 m. SW of Jct. I-30/SR 51 on I-30.

ARKANSAS CITY
POP. 668   ALT. 140   MAP O-3

A steamboat landing as early as 1834, a community in 1850, Arkansas City was incorporated in 1873 by refugees from nearby Napoleon, Arkansas (BELOW), which was destroyed by two disastrous floods. County seat in 1881, by the 1890s it was a prominent *river* port town of 15,000. Today its old houses and buildings sit in the shadow of the world's tallest levee. Home of John H. Johnson, publisher of Jet and Ebony.
Napoleon. In the 1820s it was a port town of cardsharps, rivermen and cargo heading up the Arkansas and White Rivers as well as an alternate route in the late 1850s for the *Butterfield Overland Mail* (using either the Arkansas or White Rivers). Plagued by severe floods *(Flood of 1927)*, Napoleon was completely washed away in 1874. Mark Twain said he saw the town disappear in 15 minutes. With four-wheel drive and patience the townsite and two tombstones can be found. Inquire Locally.
Levee. A good vantage point for seeing crop duster aerobatics and Mississippi River traffic is from the world's tallest (32 feet high) and longest levee (Venice, La., to Cairo, Il., or 1,608 miles). An unbroken span runs 650 miles (the mouth of the *Arkansas River* to Venice, La.). Gravel and sometimes blacktop, with a few detours, it is possible to drive from Venice to Cairo without losing sight of the river.
Arkansas City Museum. Opened on request, it displays artifacts from the town's river days. The red brick building (1882), as others, is set high to keep dry, underscoring the danger of floods like the *Flood of 1927*, which brought waters 30 feet deep. Capital & Kate Adams.
Methodist Church. Built in 1889 facing Kate Adams Ave., the building was later turned around by a tornado to face its present position on Capital St. Across from the museum.
Indian Mound. Locally called Indian Temple, the top of this prehistoric mound was used as a settlers' cemetery. Surrounding the base is a later cemetery, Garden of Memories. Most of the early markers were swept away by the *Flood of 1927.* Avalon, N of town at the levee.
Docks. Steps on the side of the levee are all that remain where steamboats like the Kate Adams, Robt. E. Lee and Arkansas City once tied up. S end of Sprague. Marker.
St. Clement's Episcopal Church. Built 1901, the original furnishings, Bible and altar hangings are still intact and in use. Natchez Ave., N of the courthouse.
Desha County Courthouse. Italianate, 1900. National Historic Register. It is the second smallest county seat *(Ash Flat)* and the only one with a separate location *(McGehee)* for court only. Features: five chimneys, a four-story clock tower and red tile roof. Grounds: a clapboard building (c.1880s), the city's first school. Robt. S. Moore Ave. *(County Profiles)*
National Historic Register. Thane House, Levy & First.

For other houses and buildings inquire at the Arkansas City Museum, corner of Capital & Kate Adams.

ARKANSAS RIVER
MAP BEGINS C-1 & ENDS O-3

The river begins at Tennessee Pass (Rocky Mountains) on the eastern side of the Continental Divide in West Central Colorado and then wends its way 1,450 miles across Kansas, Oklahoma and Arkansas, ending just north of *Arkansas City,* where it empties into the Mississippi River. The Arkansas River is the 36th longest river in the world and the third longest in America (Missouri first, Mississippi second). Also see *Rivers* for the historical uses of the rivers of Arkansas. Incidentally, in Kansas they pronounce it the Ar-KANSAS River *(Arkansawyer)*. WARNING: no swimming or wading (strong currents, undertows, unstable and crumbling banks, sinkholes, suctions and whirlpools).

ARKANSAWYER
MAP ALL QUARTERS

Some archaeologists believe the Quapaw, for whom Arkansas is supposedly named, developed from already existing cultures in the lower Mississippi River Valley similar to the "Nodena Phase" at Chickasawba *(Blytheville)*. However, oral tradition of the Quapaw Nation claims that they migrated with other tribes of the Ohio River Valley, separating near a "stream," possibly the confluence of the Missouri and Mississippi Rivers. Some of the tribes, like the Kansa and Osage, went to the Missouri, "going upstream or against the current" (Omaha in their language); while the Quapaw and possibly others went to the Mississippi, "going downstream or with the current" (Ugakhpa). Ugakhpa (Oo-gaq-pa, "downstream people") was translated to French by Algonquian interpreters as Oo-ka-na-sa ("south wind people"), and is considered to be the root word for their later European name, which has been spelled (among many ways) Akansea, Akansa, Arkanscas, Acansa or as La Harpe wrote it: Arkansas. As late as 1824 American maps carried the name as Arkansa. Although admitted to the Union in 1836 as Arkansas, it took state legislation in 1881 to prescribe the pronunciation: AR-kan-SAW. Presumably, people from AR-kan-SAW should be called AR-kan-SAWYERS, but Ar-KANSANS can't seem to agree. Incidentally, the original confusion about pronunciation is said to have stemmed from the Arkansa (or Quapaw) being referred to in the plural, Arkansas, like Kansas (people from the Kansa Nation). Some say the final "s" should be omitted as it is in Wichita, Omaha, etc.

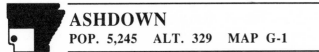

ASHDOWN
POP. 5,245   ALT. 329   MAP G-1

A farming area since 1835, the present townsite was locally known as Turkey Flats, a natural crossing point for railroads (three crossed here between 1889 and 1906). Lawrence Alexander Byrne, a railroad lawyer and land speculator, recognized the opportunity in 1888 and bought 80 acres on which a sawmill community and post office, Keller, grew along the tracks of the arriving (1889) Texarkana & Ft. Smith *Railroad* (Kansas City Southern). A sawmill fire there in 1890 prompted the legend that Byrne said "It was all burned down to ashes" and his new town would be Ashdown. It is also said that his native Scotland has a town with the same name. Incorporated in 1892 as Ashdown; county seat in 1905.

Caddo Mound & White Cliffs. *(Lockesburg)*

Peytonville. Ornate tombstones are all that remain of this 1850 farm town. SR 32, 5 m. E of Jct. 71/32, Peytonville Rd. N then W.

Little River County Courthouse. Neo-Classic, 1907. National Historic Register. Features: an octagonal copper-domed skylight. Downtown, Main & 2nd. *(County Profiles)*

ASH FLAT
POP. 524   ALT. 856   MAP I-2

Settled prior to the Civil War, it is said to have been named for "a level place on which grew a stand of ash trees."

Sharp County Courthouse. Sixties Modern, 1967. Despite Ash Flat's size, it settled the argument over *dual county seats* between *Evening Shade* and *Hardy* by taking both their places in 1967 and becoming Arkansas' smallest county seat. *(County Profiles)*

ATKINS
POP. 3,002   ALT. 357   MAP C-3

The town began in the early 1870s three miles east of its present location as Perry Station because that's where money for construction of the Little Rock & Ft. Smith *Railroad* ended. The town's name centers around Boston, Ma., a man named Elisha (some say Andrew) Atkins and the funds necessary to continue the line: Atkins either went to Boston to raise the money or he was from Boston and financed its construction. Platted in 1873, it was incorporated in 1876, attracting German immigrants and residents of nearby Galla Rock. Today, city hall is in the train depot.

Galla (Galley) Rock. First settled by Cherokees from Tennessee c.1819 *(Trail of Tears)*, among whom were John Jolly (brother of Tollantusky, *Cadron*) and Sequoya (Dwight, *Russellville*). Established as an Arkansas town and post office in 1837, it was platted in 1860, continuing to prosper (population 1,163 in 1870) as a steamboat landing and trading center linking the *Arkansas River* to the Ozark Mountains until the Little Rock & Ft. Smith *Railroad's* arrival in Atkins (1873) took away its business. A large cemetery, overgrown with vines, overlooks the vanished townsite. Possible *De Soto* Route. S of Atkins, SR 105, at the river.

Lake Atkins. Owned by the Game and Fish Commission, it is stocked with bluegill, crappie, catfish and bass. Primitive camping facilities. SR 105, S 5 m.

AUGUSTA
POP. 3,496   ALT. 224   MAP K-3

Originally Chickasaw Crossing, an Indian village built high on a bluff of the White *River (Float Streams),* Augusta was established as a trading camp for lumbermen in 1852 by Thomas Pough (a wealthy Quaker from Maryland), who named the site for his niece.

The Augusta Railroad. Faced with the same fate as other detoured river ports like Jacksonport *(State Park),* the town laid its own mile of track to join the St. Louis, Iron Mountain & Southern *(Railroad),* nicknaming the train "Little Dummy" in honor of the mule-drawn streetcar used at first *(Paragould).* No evidence remains.

Quantrell/Crocker Grave. Legends of Woodruff County maintain that Quantrell, notorious Confederate guerrilla whose men included the James and Younger brothers, did not die in but escaped from a Federal prison hospital (1865). In 1867 Capt. L.J. Crocker (a man with no history, a bag of gold and the same battle scars and appearance as Quantrell) settled in Gregory, near Augusta. (His wife, Gabrellia, was an aunt of the Younger brothers. The Youngers, along with the James boys, visited often.) Eyewitnesses identified him. Seven years before his death in 1917, he admitted being Quantrell to his best friend, state Sen. W.E. Ferguson. US 64B, Augusta Memorial Cemetery. Flagpole to 1st left, 1st plot on right past 1st intersection.

White River Bottoms/Levee Road. Once used throughout the Delta to cross marshes, swamps and backwater, levee roads are less needed now due to extensive flood control programs *(Flood of 1927).* US 64, Augusta to Wordan.

Woodruff County Courthouse. Romanesque Revival, 1902. National Historic Register. Unusual because it is set in a residential neighborhood, the courthouse features a four-story clock tower and multicolored ceramic-tile floors with a tile mural. US 64B (3rd St.). *(County Profiles)*

National Historic Register. Ferguson House (1866), 416 N. Third.

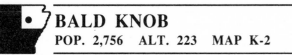

BALD KNOB
POP. 2,756   ALT. 223   MAP K-2

Established on the tracks of the St. Louis, Iron Mountain & Southern *(Railroad)* in 1878, nearly all of its early population came from nearby Stevens Creek. Named for a large outcropping of rock (later quarried; no remnants) on the northeast side of town.

Business District. This district, which still conducts everyday business, is said to be representative of early 20th century America's small towns. Downtown.

BATESVILLE
POP. 8,447   ALT. 365   MAP J-2

This geographical site (a radius of one and a half miles) has had four names. First settled by the Trimbles and Laffertys c.1810, the settlement's location on Poke Bayou was its name until establishment in 1820 of nearby Poke Creek post office at the home of Charles Kelly (or Kelley), the first sheriff of newly formed Independence County (1820). Although Poke Bayou had been described in 1814 by land speculator Wm. Russell *(Little Rock, Helena)* as a "promising young settlement," Kelly's house was designated temporary county seat in 1820 and was carried on maps as a town, Napoleon, as late as 1824. While Batesville was recorded as a town name as early as 1821 on a deed locating the property as the permanent county seat, the post office name was not changed to Batesville until 1824. Reportedly, its namesake is for James Woodson Bates, who was the first Territorial delegate to Congress in 1821. Defeated by Henry W. Conway *(Walnut Hill)* for a second term, Bates moved in 1823 to Batesville, where he practiced law and served as a Territorial judge until 1830, when he moved to Crawford County. The settlement's early prosperity was based on its location by the White *River (Float Streams)* and its proximity to the Southwest Trail *(Roads).* Arrival of steamboats (The Waverly, first to ascend the White River in 1831) and the St. Louis, Iron Mountain & Southern *(Railroad)* in 1882 helped establish the town as a center of commerce. Home of Arkansas College, Gateway Vocational Technical School and three governors: Thomas S. Drew (1844-49), Elisha Baxter (1873-74) and Wm. R. Miller (1877-79). Possible *De Soto* Route. Maps: chamber of commerce: 409 Vine St., US 167, 8 blks. W on SR 69.

Lock & Dam No.1/Riverside Park. Built in 1903 by the Corps of Engineers as the first of three locks and dams on the White River for navigation past Batesville. No longer used but still in place. Picnic tables and a white sand beach. In town, E on Chaney Dr. off US 167 at the bridge.

Arkansas College. A private Christian college established in 1872, its new campus (College & 22nd) has the Grigsby Log Home (1860s dogtrot) and the Regional Culture Center, which includes the John Quincy Wolf folk music collection (mainly Ozark, 1940-60). Old Campus, College & 7th.

Commercial District. The lower two blocks of Main St. are on the National Historic Register; the entire downtown is a participant in Main Street Arkansas, part of a national preservation program. US 167, W on Main St.

Residential District. During the Batesville home tours, nearly 30 houses are shown in an area bounded by Water and Boswell Streets, 10th and 4th. US 167, W on Main St.

Pioneer Cemetery. The oldest recognized and preserved cemetery in Arkansas (1820s-1882) has a few eloquent tombstones remaining in a small park in the middle of downtown but most were moved to Oaklawn Cemetery. 3rd & College.

Oaklawn Cemetery. Platted in 1882, replacing Pioneer Cemetery, it was laid out in an oval with footpaths and has some fine examples of 19th century carved limestone. Sidney & Lawrence, US 167, E on Lawrence.

Spring Mill. One of the oldest *grist mills* in mid-America (1867), it was built by the same contractor as the Jacksonport *(State Parks)* courthouse. Little used today, it serves as a small museum. 8 m. NW of town on US 69.

K & W Sorghum Co. Part of the process, crushing, begins with five 30-inch cast-iron rollers. Like the few remaining commercial sorghum mills in the country, this one uses only sorghum cane juice as a sweetener. Mr. Wilson, sole owner, tends it all: from planting to production to packaging and selling a pint or 24 pounds. Tours. Bethesda, 8 m. W of Batesville on 106S.

Events/Festivals. Mid-Apr: Ozark Scottish Festival & Highland Games at Arkansas College. Scottish music, dancing, games & feast. Early May: Spring Tour of Homes. Early Aug: Annual White River Water Carnival. Music. Arts & Crafts. Catfish. Hot Air Balloon Races. 10K Run. Gun Show.

Independence County Courthouse. Moderne, 1940. The exterior is Batesville white marble. Features: a 6-by-18-foot-high marble monument to Confederate veterans. 2nd & Main.

National Historic Register. All those listed are in the Commercial or Residential Districts. Maps: chamber of commerce. *(County Profiles)*

 BAYOU BARTHOLOMEW
MAP N+O+P-2

As glaciers melted during the last Ice Age, modern rivers began forming. This bayou was once the bed of the *Arkansas River* (the Mississippi ran down the present Arkansas; the Ohio down today's Mississippi). Approximately 300 miles long, it is reportedly the world's longest bayou (BUY-you, French for a sluggish creek). From *Pine Bluff* it flows W of US 65/165 past the Louisiana border. *(Crowley's Ridge)*

 BEAVER
POP. 81 ALT. 980 MAP A-2

Established by Squire W.A. Beaver c.1850 as a ferry crossing on the White *River (Float Streams),* it also served as a stagecoach stop and finally as a depot for the newly arrived Missouri & Arkansas *Railroad* (Missouri & North Arkansas) in 1881. Incorporated 1949. Used as a location for the TV miniseries "The Blue And The Gray".

Little Golden Gate Bridge. This 528-foot steel cable suspension bridge is even painted golden. Built using twin towers and cables in 1947 to replace a 1926 cement bridge destroyed by a flood in 1945, it is best seen when approaching from the S on SR 187.

The Beaver Store. Built by the Swope family in 1901, this two-story brick building is still intact. In Town.

Beavertown Park. Leased from the Corps of Engineers in 1982, the park has 30 campsites, a boat ramp, trailer/marine dump station, electrical hookups and restrooms. Attractions: towering bluffs, *trails,* swimming beach and fishing. In Town.

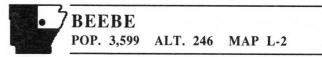 **BEEBE**
POP. 3,599 ALT. 246 MAP L-2

Established in 1872, when merchants moved their stores five miles east from the 1849 post office settlement of Stoney Point to be on the new Cairo & Fulton *Railroad.* Named for Roswell Beebe, first president (1853) of the Cairo & Fulton, whose name was also used for the first steam locomotive (The Roswell Beebe) to run from the Red River to Little Rock. Downtown has several stores and homes built in the 1880s. Home of Arkansas State University (Beebe Branch).

Holiness Campground. South of town a grove of oaks marks where camp meetings have been held since the 1880s.

National Historic Register. Beebe Depot (1915), Downtown.

 **BELLA VISTA**
COMMUNITY ALT. 1,250 MAP A-1

This summer resort, established in 1917 because of the beautiful views, grew its own wine, advertised horseback riding, swimming, tennis, and even had "nationally known orchestras" playing dance music in Wonderland Cavern. Bought by Cooper Communities and made a part of Bella Vista Village in 1963, the old part of the main resort is just off US 71 about four miles south of the Missouri border.

Bella Vista Historical Society Museum. Mostly a community cultural and educational center, it does have occasional traveling exhibits such as IBM's, which featured models of Leonardo da Vinci's inventions. US 71. In Town. Signs.

Events/Festivals. Late Oct: Annual Bella Vista Arts & Crafts Fair. "Circus-Style Tents."

 **BELLEFONTE**
POP. 393 ALT. 1,062 MAP A-3

A local spring gave the town its name and its livelihood as a layover for ox-drawn freighters hauling goods to and from Springfield, Mo. The town (pronounced BELLA-font) lost the election for county seat to *Harrison* by 18 votes in 1873.

Museum of the Ozarks. This collection, begun at church rummage sales and auctions in 1952, is as serious and authentic as it is varied. Housed in buildings ranging from barns to log cabins (a dogtrot and a former tavern) are, among the many artifacts: maps (1833, 1872 and Indian Territory, 1873), a Springfield wagon, pioneer kitchen, school room, general store, primitive paintings of S.E. Moore (also collected by the Smithsonian), Civil War relics, Indian pottery, a 1902 Chandler Price printing press in working condition, a 1910-20 telephone exchange and the old Bellefonte post office. US 65,

4 m. S to Valley Springs, 3 m. E to Rally Hill. Signs.

BENTON
POP. 17,717   ALT. 291   MAP E-4

First known as Lockhart Crossing when Wm. Lockhart used it as a ford for the Saline *River (Float Streams)* on the Southwest Trail *(Roads)* in 1805, it was later called Saline Crossing. Platted in 1836, subdivided and sold on the installment plan, Benton is one of the oldest (1839) incorporated cities in Arkansas *(Little Rock, Helena),* and was named for Missouri politician Thomas Hart Benton *(Bentonville).* The town and county are said to supply 97% of the nation's bauxite (raw material for aluminum), discovered in the area c.1887. Possible *De Soto* Route.

Gann House/Museum. National Historic Register, 1893. Built by patients unable to pay Dr. Dewell Gann (a railroad and bauxite industry doctor), it reportedly is the only house in the world made of bauxite. Now a museum, it exhibits Indian artifacts, pioneer tools and a history of bauxite in Saline County. Also displayed is niloak pottery, a collector's item today, which was made locally from the area's naturally colored clay (swirls like a shooter's marble) and shipped worldwide from 1909-44. Incidentally, niloak spelled backward is kaolin, a white Chinese clay used in ceramics and medicine. 3 blks. S of the courthouse.

Collegeville. Named in 1823 as a site for a proposed state college that was never built. A sign erected here in 1936 by the Daughters of American Colonists states: "The Geographical Center of Arkansas Is A Few Steps North of This Highway." If plans are made to take those few steps, pack a lunch *(Mayflower).* I-30, Alexander exit, SR 5S for 2.5 m. to Pine Crest Cemetery.

Shoppach House. National Historic Register, 1852. Three bricks wide, the small L-shaped house on the Southwest Trail *(Roads)* served as headquarters for both Confederates and Federals. Main at Military Rd., 2 blks. N of the courthouse.

Events/Festivals. Early Oct: Annual Old-Fashioned Day. Arts & Crafts. Music. Auction.

Saline County Courthouse. Romanesque Revival, 1900. National Historic Register. Used by moviemakers because of its "Southern" look, it features: a four-story clock tower, two-story towers and colored, round floor tiles. SR 35, business district, S on Market.

National Historic Register. Dr. James Wyatt Walton House (1903), 301 W. Sevier. Old River Bridge (1889), River Rd. & Saline River. *(County Profiles)*

BENTONVILLE
POP. 8,756   ALT. 1,370   MAP A-1

First known by its 1836 post office name, Osage, a town was later (1837) named for Thomas Hart Benton (Missouri politician responsible for carving Arkansas Territory from the new state of Missouri, 1819). Although destroyed by both sides after the battle of Pea Ridge *(National Park)* in 1862 (rebuilt and reincorporated in 1873), the town's worst blow came in 1881 when the St. Louis & San Francisco *(Railroad)* bypassed it, building *Rogers.* Home of Sam Walton, founder of Wal-Mart, richest man in America (1986).

Centerton State Fish Hatchery. Begun in 1941, today's output is .5-2.5 million fish for public lakes and reservoirs. Gravity fed by a 1,500 gal/min free-flowing spring, the pond's principal species are catfish, crappie, sunfish, walleye and bass, although some special-purpose ones like Israeli and Chinese carp are stocked. SR 102, 4 m. W.

James H. Berry's Grave. The nephew of B.H. Berry *(Berryville)* was governor (1883-85) and a U.S. senator for 22 years (1885-1907). US 71B, W on 4th SW St. to "F" SW St.; then N 1/2 blk.

The Gann House in Benton is said to be the only house in the world made from bauxite

---

Events/Festivals. Early May: Annual Governor Berry's Sugar Creek Days. Arts & Crafts. Entertainment. Children's Games.

Benton County Courthouse. Italian Renaissance, 1928. An architectural aspect of the courtroom, called egg-carton construction by some, is actually pressed-block cardboard that creates a dramatic effect. Features: limestone and marble. Court Square, N. Main & US 72. *(County Profiles)*

National Historic Register. The town has many historic homes. Some are listed in the Register. Maps: chamber of commerce, 122 S. Main, 1 blk. E of Jct. US 71B & US 72.

BERRYVILLE
POP. 2,966   ALT. 1,246   MAP A-2

Although the site was first settled by the Plumlee brothers in 1836, the town was founded in 1850 by and named for B.H. Berry, the uncle of Gov. (1883-85) James H. Berry *(Bentonville).* It became county seat (1875) before being incorporated (1876) because of its central location *(Carrollton).*

Town Square. Both the Confederates and Federals used it as an assembly area. Skirmishes, reprisals and attrition destroyed all but two of the buildings. Rebuilt in brick and stone, today it is an old-fashioned version of a shopping center and the focus of community life.

Saunders Memorial Museum. This high-caliber display "is rated as the best collection of small arms in the United States." Collected by "Col." C. Burton Saunders (1863-1952), international award-winning sharpshooter and the son of Judge L.B. Saunders *(Eureka Springs),* it includes a complete line of Colts, a 500-year-old Chinese pistol and guns belonging to the famous and infamous. Along with the firearms are an Arabian sheik's tent, 400-year-old carved teakwood furniture, Persian rugs, Bowie knife, lacework, totem scalps, Indian blankets and headdress and a lot more. US 62 at the Square. Signs.

Cosmic Caverns. Discovered in 1845, "The Cave That Has Guides" also has one of the Ozarks' largest underground lakes (with trout), a petting zoo topside and a very unassuming setting. One-Hour Tours. SR 21N, 6 m.

Heritage Center Museum. National Historic Register, 1881. This three-story, red-brick building was the Carroll County Courthouse until 1977. Now it has hundreds of historical items, good archives, a moonshine still, pioneer school room and pioneer funeral home. US 62, town square.

Pioneer Memorial Park Cemetery. A monument to the unmarked graves of the original settlers and slaves (1844-99) and a tombstone for B.H. Berry's wife, Eliza (died 1854), designate the city's first cemetery. Also on the grounds: a 150-year-old restored log cabin, picnic tables and basketball court. Church St., 2 blks. W of town square.

Iron Bridges. Once the only two bridges across the Osage and Kings Rivers *(Float Streams)* in Carroll County, these plank-bottom, iron-truss structures are still safe and offer a romantic ride through Ozark farmland. US 62W, 3.2 m. to a westward blacktop near the *WPA* bridge, then stay right. Rejoins US 62 in 4 m.

Carroll County Courthouse. *(County Profiles)* Modern, 1947. *Dual County Seat (Eureka Springs).* Located in the former Carroll County Electric Co-Op building, it is the only courthouse in Arkansas not originally built for its purpose. Church St., 1 blk. W of town square.

BIG FORK
COMMUNITY   ALT. 1,000   MAP E-2

Named for the Big Fork of the Ouachita River and listed on maps in the late 1800s, it is famous for the abundance of wildflowers that give an annual spring show throughout the Big Fork Natural Area. Inquire Locally.

Womble-Silver Road. On this noteworthy 18-mile stretch of gravel road are the Crystal Mountain Scenic Area (100-acre stand of virgin pine and hardwood), a fire tower offering long views of the Ouachitas and the largest white pine in Arkansas (Crystal Campground, Ouachita *National Forest*). SR 8, 19 m. E to Norman, appx.1 m. N on SR 27 to FS 177 E.

BIGGERS
POP. 363   ALT. 285   MAP I-4

Part of the town is located on 800 acres given c.1830 to Thomas Drew (Arkansas' fourth governor, 1844-49) and his bride, Cinderella, as a dowry by Dr. Ransom Bettis, founder of *Pocahontas*. In 1889 B.F. Biggers established a distillery and ferry here on the Current *River (Float Streams)*.

Hite Cemetery/Cabin. The first school and church in the Cherokee Bay area, this c.1860s log cabin is located in the Hite family cemetery in Biggers.

BINGEN
COMMUNITY   ALT. 380   MAP F-2

First settled by Dr. J.R. Wolff in 1859, the Ozan Post Office (1859), not to be confused with present-day Ozan (est. 1889) near Washington, changed its name in 1880 (for Bingen-on-the-Rhine in Germany) because of mail mix-ups with Ozone in the Ozarks. Dropped from some maps, it is just off SR 27, appx. 9 m. S of *Murfreesboro*. Incidentally, Ozan is a French family name; Emily Ozan was mother of Charles McDermott *(Dermott)*.

The Wolff Store. Opened in 1871 by the first of three generations, it is a combination general store-museum filled with everyday items from another era.

BLACK ROCK
POP. 848   ALT. 249   MAP I-3

Although cleared for farming by 1850, nearby *Powhatan* was the area's trading center until the arrival of the Kansas City, Ft. Smith and Gulf *Railroad* in 1882. In 1884 this newly created Black *River* town was named Black Rock (for the colorful black rocks in the vicinity) by the Lawrence County court, was incorporated with a population of 277, and had begun the lumber and shipping industry (steamboat and railroad) that resulted in an estimated population of 3,000 by 1897, the same year a 14-grain pink pearl was found in a Black River mussel. A short-lived pearl boom ($310,000 in 1901) led to the establishment of what is claimed to be Arkansas' first (1900) button factory, a business that for 70 years made "blanks" from mussel shells. After the timber had been stripped out and the button industry declined, the town faded away.

National Historic Register. PORTIA, AR. (US 63, 2 m. S): Portia Schoolhouse (1914), City Park.

BLYTHEVILLE
POP. 23,844   ALT. 254   MAP J-5

In 1853 Henry T. Blythe, a Virginia-born Methodist preacher, founded a community, Blythe Chapel, using it as a base for his circuit camp meetings. An 1880 post office, Blytheville, incorporated in 1891 as a lumber town, later grew into a cotton production and trading center. Home of Mississippi County Community College.

Chickasawba Mound. This prime example of a major 16th century Indian culture (Nodena Phase, Central Mississippi Valley, *Wilson*), may have been part of Pacaha as described by *De Soto's* expedition. Subsequent French explorers and later American pioneers found no evidence of contemporary habitation of any mounds in Arkansas. Archaeologists propose that European disease decimated 80% of the population, shifting the political configuration "from paramount chiefs to a council of chiefs which characterized [later] Quapaw politics." This undeveloped 13-acre site has been occupied since 700 A.D. Incidentally, it briefly served as a German POW camp during WW II. SR 151, immediately NW of town.

Mississippi County Community College. This community college gets its total energy requirements from the sun, and has been described as "the world's largest and most comprehensively practical alternate-energy application based on solar cells." The state-of-the-art plant is a work of art itself. MCCC Campus: I-55 exit US 61S. Signs.

Ritz Civic Center. Originally built in the early thirties, purchased and renovated by the city in 1980, it still reflects an Art Deco design. Along with displaying local and regional art, the center sponsors local and road-show theater and concerts. Downtown.

Events/Festivals. Early May: Springtime On The Mall. Downtown. Arts & Crafts. Bands. Family-Oriented.

Mississippi County Courthouse. Neo-Classic, 1919. *Dual County Seat (Osceola).* Features: white marble floors, walls and stairs. *(County Profiles)*

BOONEVILLE
POP. 3,718   ALT. 511   MAP C-2

Settled in 1828 by Walter Cauthron as a trading post that was later selected temporary county seat (1833-36, *Waldron*) of newly created Scott County. The same year (1837) that town lots were advertised in the Arkansas Gazette, Cauthron established a post office, naming it Bonneville in honor of his good friend Capt. Benjamin Bonneville of *Fort Smith,* but for unknown reasons (possibly a spelling error), it was recorded officially as Booneville. Incorporated in 1878; reincorporated in 1899 on the tracks of the Chicago, Rock Island and Pacific *Railroad.* In 1901 this former temporary county seat of Scott County was made a *dual county seat (Paris)* of Logan County (created in 1871 from part of Scott County). Incidentally, Logan County was organized as Sarber but changed names in 1875 supposedly because county constituents disapproved of the honor being bestowed on a former Union soldier.

Arkansas Tuberculosis Sanatorium. Now the Arkansas Human Development Center, a training center for mentally retarded young adults, these buildings once housed "the finest sanatorium of its kind in the world," which could accommodate 1,100 patients in a totally self-sufficient environment. SR 23S; 3.6 m. E on SR 116.

Golden City. This gold mining town boomed and fizzled (1886-87) in newspaper reports. First it was gold at $440 per ton. Miners came from the West; investors from the East. The next news release stated that along with having very little (and very low-grade) ore, the state geologist's report claimed that the main veins had been "salted" with the likes of iron pyrite and copper percussion caps. A church and cemetery remain today. Inquire at Arkansas Human Development Center.

General John Paul McConnell Memorabilia. USAF Chief of Staff, 1965-69. Along with a miniature flag carried to the moon on APOLLO 10 (1969) is a unique collection of mementos from heads of state. Also displayed: extensive documents, photographs and pieces of spacecraft. Booneville Library, 419 N. Kennedy St.

Buffalo Hole. Reportedly it is a large watering hole named for the buffalo that used it. Both elk and buffalo had mostly disappeared by 1828. 8 m. W, SR 10/60 at Barber on the Petit Jean River.

Events/Festivals. Early Mar: Annual Arkansas Marathon (26 miles). Late Apr: 5th Annual Booneville Open "Cow Pasture Pool" (a 12-hole golf pasture). MAGAZINE, AR. (SR 10, 7 m. E): Mid-Apr: New Shiloh Arts & Crafts Fair.

Logan County Courthouse. Renaissance Revival, 1928. *Dual County Seat (Paris).* Features: gray and white terrazzo floors; high, arched windows. *(County Profiles)*

National Historic Register. Dunn Insurance Building, 1 W. Main.

BOUNDARY LINES
MAP ALL QUARTERS

Centerlines of rivers and surveys (latitude and longitude) mark boundary lines. Historically, Arkansas' southern border of Louisiana, eastern border of the Mississippi River and northern border of Missouri (the "bootheel" occurred because influential Missouri Territory farmers did not want to be included with Arkansas Territory in 1819) have caused few problems, although the Mississippi River "swapped" five square miles of Arkansas for 25 square miles of Tennessee in 1876.

Most of Arkansas' western boundary line was set by the Choctaw and Cherokee

Like the Mississippi River, Arkansas' western boundary has wandered, changed courses and swapped property. Beginning as a territory in 1819, it was defined by today's eastern edge of the Texas panhandle. However, for early Arkansas settlers, the western border was the Cherokee and Choctaw Nations' eastern boundary, a limit to western expansion that was pushed against with treaties as well as acts of Congress and the territorial and state legislatures *(Trail of Tears).* A short-lived act of Congress in 1824 dropped a straight line from 40 miles west of SW Missouri to the Red River (then down the river to Mexico's (present-day Texas') border and then due south to Louisiana). Another act/treaty (1828) moved the Cherokee *(Trail of Tears)* to Indian Territory (Oklahoma), establishing the present line north from near Fort Smith to the SW border of Missouri *(Three Corners).* A Choctaw Treaty of 1825 set the present boundary south from Fort Smith (disputed until 1877). The surveyor, James S. Conway (first state governor, 1836-40), certified the line, a U.S. attorney general's opinion confirmed it (1829), but the final survey of 1877 showed it "shorted" the Choctaws (some say intentionally) 136,204.02 acres for which they were paid 50 cents an acre. Since 1877, with minor adjustments *(Fort Smith,* Belle Point), Arkansas' western border has remained as defined today.

LOVELY COUNTY: *(County Profiles)* As an added confusion to the western boundary, a "ghost county" (Lovely) came and went in less than a year (1827-28). The circumstances involved wishful thinking and hasty legislation. In 1816 Major Wm. L. Lovely had bought land for the federal government from the Osage that included parts of Crawford County and extended as far west as the Verdigris River near Ft. Gibson, Ok. The government, by treaty, in 1817 set aside most of that same land for the Cherokee Nation. However, in 1824 Henry W. Conway (brother of James S.) used the "Lovely Purchase" as a basis for having Congress extend the boundary of Arkansas 40 miles further west (1824 Boundary Act, ABOVE), hoping to open it for settlement. But this extension ran contrary to the original 1817 U.S. treaty giving the Cherokee a portion of northern Arkansas and part of the Lovely Purchase in present-day Oklahoma. Nevertheless, in 1827 Territorial Governor George Izard approved state legislation creating Lovely County (including the "40-mile strip" in present-day Oklahoma), but the following year's 1828 Treaty (ABOVE), relocating the Cherokee *(Trail of Tears),* dissolved the "40-mile strip." Lovely County was then incorporated in Washington County with the present-day western boundary.

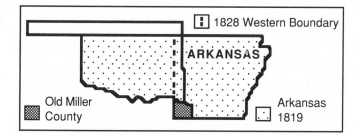

OLD MILLER COUNTY: *(County Profiles)* Although created from part of Hempstead County in 1820, its boundaries weren't defined until 1831; then the western border was surveyed so as to include the present-day "bite" out of the SW corner of the state, extending about 25 miles further west than today's line (James S. Conway, then living at *Walnut Hill,* surveyed this line). The Republic of Mexico complained that the survey violated its border, but took no action. Later, in 1838, the Republic of Texas (founded in 1836) without complaining "usurped full jurisdiction," dividing most of the Arkansas county into two Texas counties (Red River and Fannin) thereby creating today's "bite." *Arkansawyers* in this region had supported the Texas Revolution and were said to be more inclined to (and directly affected by) Texas' jurisdiction. Arkansas' first governor, James S. Conway, recognizing the incorrigible circumstances, reported to the Arkansas General Assembly of 1838: "The easiest and most effectual remedy that presents itself to my mind, is the abolition of Miller County and the attachment of her territory to some other possessed of more patriotism." That same year Miller County was disorganized, and the undisputed remainder was attached to Lafayette County, whose western line then paralleled today's western

Miller County line. To end the story, in 1874 Miller County (New) was reestablished as a county (present boundaries) out of Lafayette County, and *Texarkana* was made county seat.

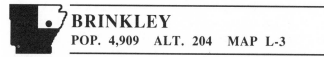

BOXLEY
COMMUNITY   ALT. 1,210   MAP B-3

Situated high in the Boston Mountains, its 1851 post office, Whiteley, was named for a pioneer family who (along with the Villines family) settled this area c.1838. After the Civil War a merchant, D. Boxley, moved to the site and later (1883) established another post office.

Boxley Baptist Church. Built c.1900 in a pastoral valley setting, the two-story white clapboard church could be an illustration by Norman Rockwell. In Town.

Villines Cabin. This hand-hewn double-pen log cabin is a partial skeleton with half-dovetailed corners and a chimney. SR 43, 5 m. W.

Grist Mill. Built in 1870 to replace an 1840 *grist mill,* the three-story clapboard structure has a foundation of unmortared, stacked stone. The mill, pond and spring highlight a spectacular setting. Closed since 1960; now a part of the Buffalo National River *(National Park).* Restoration planned. SR 43, 1 m. N. Inquire Locally.

Ponca. Now canoe outfitters and shuttle service for the Buffalo River *(Float Streams),* it was once a turn-of-the-century lead mining town established and platted by the Ponca City, Oklahoma Mining Company. SR 43, 5 m. W.

Upper Buffalo Wilderness. Natural Heritage Area. Over 10,000 acres (Forest Service property) encompass much of the Buffalo River's headwaters. Oak (some 10 feet in diameter), beech, hickory and black gum as well as pine comprise old stands with little undergrowth in places. The terrain also has ridgetops, rocky bluffs, steep slopes and 19 waterfalls. SR 21, 20 m. S to Fallsville. Inquire Locally.

BRINKLEY
POP. 4,909   ALT. 204   MAP L-3

First called "Lick Skillet" (licking a skillet clean, meaning to do a thorough job) for hardworking Irish immigrants building the Memphis & Little Rock *Railroad,* it was laid out beside the tracks in 1869-70 and incorporated in 1872 as Brinkley, honoring the president (Robt. C.) of the line. In 1909 this town of more than 1,600 was struck by a tornado that killed 60 people, leaving only a church and "six or eight homes" standing.

Burrows Taxidermy. Some people claim the largest taxidermy in Monroe County will even stuff butterflies. The building is stuffed with creatures both common and extraordinary. SR 17, 7 m. S of town.

Lake Greenlee. Built in 1962, it is primarily a crappie and bream fishing lake (300 acres). Fairly shallow during the summer, aquatic vegetation becomes dense. No camping facil-

ities. SR 238, just S of US 70.
National Historic Register. Maj. Wm. Black Family House (1895), 331 W. Ash. Gazzola & Vaccaro Building, 131-33 W. Cypress. Lo Beele House, 312 New York Ave.

BULL SHOALS
POP. 1,312   ALT. 695   MAP A-4

Settled prior to the Civil War and known as Newton Flat, the land was passed back and forth (mostly for taxes) until 1945 when land developer C.S. Woods discovered that the Corps of Engineers was building a dam (Bull Shoals *Lake)*. He bought land, advertised it as resort property, paid for paving three miles of SR 178 and established a post office, Bull Shoals, at the base of Bull Mountain. With construction completed in 1952, the lake was filled by 1953, helping to create the tourist boom in NW Arkansas.
Mountain Village/Bull Shoals Caverns. The village, set on a green, is laid out and restored like one from the 1890s, including a general store, church, school house and log cabin. The cavern, billed as "The Cadillac of Caves," uses concrete trails and electric lights to show off natural formations said to be about 350 million years old. In town, SR 178. Signs.
Bull Shoals State Park. (Bull Shoals *State Park)*
Events/Festivals. Late May: Arts & Crafts Fair.

BUTTERFIELD OVERLAND MAIL COMPANY

The Overland Mail Company was organized by John Butterfield of New York in 1857 when he was awarded a six-year U.S. mail contract for $600,000 a year with rates of 10 cents a letter. Using more than 100 Concord coaches, 1,000 horses, 500 mules and nearly 2,000 employees, it made two trips weekly each way from Memphis and St. Louis to San Francisco (via Fort Smith), averaging 120 miles per 24 hours (they ran night and day) for 2,800 miles with more than 141 stations spaced every 20 miles. The coaches could carry nine scheduled passengers (40 lbs. of free baggage each) for a fare of $200, or "wayside" passengers for 10 cents a mile. Interrupted by the *Civil War,* the line finally faded and was never reestablished as a whole.
NW Arkansas (St. Louis Route). The St. Louis branch entered NW Arkansas paralleling today's US 62 from the state line to *Fayetteville* with stops at present-day *Rogers* and *Shiloh (Springdale),* then south near SR 265 to Hogeye and Strickler (elevation 1,560 feet) on the Boston Mountain Road, beyond which lay "the roughest 10 miles between St. Louis and San Francisco" (a New York reporter said: "I might say the road was steep, rugged, jagged, rough and mountainous and then wish for more impressive words"). After crossing Lee's Creek, the route approximated SR 220 to Cedarville, where it intercepted the Cane Hill Road (US 59) to *Van Buren* and then proceeded by ferry to *Fort Smith*.

Butterfield Mail Route

Central Arkansas (Memphis Route). Originally proposed as a steamboat route from Memphis to Fort Smith, the *Arkansas River's* unpredictability forced the line overland in a crazy quilt transportation system by boat, train, stage and often foot through sections of eastern Arkansas' jungles, swamps, unimproved *roads* and bridgeless streams. Not as well-defined as the northwest route, this one did its best to reach *Clarendon* or *Des Arc* by river from Napoleon *(Arkansas City),* or by the Memphis & Little Rock *Railroad* from Hopefield *(West Memphis)* to *Madison*. Initially Little Rock was only a "feeder line" stop (later a main stop) connecting at Old Austin *(Cabot)* where the stage from Des Arc (appx. SR 38) then proceeded west to *Cadron* (near Conway), Lewisburg *(Morrilton)* and *Pottsville,* crossing the river at Norristown *(Russellville)* to *Dardanelle* where it mostly followed today's SR 22 through present-day *Paris* and *Charleston* to *Fort Smith*.

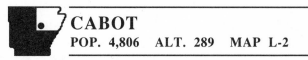

CABOT
POP. 4,806   ALT. 289   MAP L-2

Settled in the early 1870s and probably named for a railroad engineer, the town was the product of a refused right-of-way for the Cairo & Fulton *Railroad* (Old Austin, BELOW).
Old Austin. (Ghost Town) Although cartographers carried its 1830 post office's name of Oakland Grove through the 1870s, the town was officially Austin by 1858 after briefly being known as Sandersville (for a nearby farm) and Atlanta (probably for the Atlanta Hotel, a stopover for the *Butterfield Overland Mail)*. The area, an historical crossroads supported by stagecoaches between Searcy and Little Rock as well as White River freight from *Des Arc,* prospered until the Cairo & Fulton *Railroad* was refused right-of-way in the early 1870s, and bypassed it, creating Austin Station and Cabot. 3 m. N to Austin; 1 m. E.
Camp Nelson Confederate Cemetery. First gathered up and reburied in 1906-7, this second restoration (1982) was rededicated to the memory of those 430 Confederates who died near Old Austin during a measles epidemic. S of Cabot, SR 89 to SR 321E. Signs.

Events/Festivals. OTTO, AR. (SR 89, 6 m. E; SR 107, 5 m. N): Annual Memorial Day Weekend Festival of Gospel Music at the Lester Flat Memorial Park. Early July: Mountain Music Festival. Bluegrass. Early Aug: The Annual Southern Gospel Sing. Mid-Sept: Annual Arts & Craft Show. For all events/festivals contact Kuykendall Corp, #1 Beth Dr., Gravel Ridge, 72072.

CADDO GAP
COMMUNITY   ALT. 619   MAP F-2

The narrow pass of the same name supposedly marks the *De Soto* expedition's most western advance from Florida. First settled at the gap before 1850 on the Fort Smith-Washington *Road,* the town was later moved to its present site when the gap was widened in 1907 by the Gurdon & Ft. Smith Northern *Railroad* (St. Louis, Iron Mountain & Southern).

Indian Statue. Four metal markers, surrounding a life-sized bronze statue of a Tula Indian, tell the story of the area. SR 8, in town.

Architecture. Facing what was once "downtown" are excellent representatives of 19th century residential structures.

The Gap. Ground out of the Ouachitas by the Caddo River (later widened by the railroad), this narrow pass gives long views of pines, pastures and steep mountains. SR 8.

Womble-Silver Road. On this noteworthy 18-mile stretch of gravel road are the Crystal Mountain Scenic Area (100-acre stand of virgin pine and hardwood), a fire tower offering long views of the Ouachitas and the largest white pine in Arkansas (Crystal Campground, Ouachita *National Forest*). SR 8, 19 m. E to Norman, appx.1 m. N on SR 27 to FS 177 E.

CADRON (GHOST TOWN)
FEDERAL PARK   ALT. 375   MAP D-4

National Historic Register. Although an 1817 St. Louis mail route came through Cadron to Arkansas Post *(National Park)* without stopping at *Little Rock* , this former French trading post (1770s) lost the election for Territorial capital to Little Rock in 1821. An *Arkansas River* town located on the Memphis-Ft. Smith Military *Road,* the coming of the Little Rock & Ft. Smith *Railroad (Conway)* in 1872 signaled its decline. *Butterfield Overland Mail* route. Picnic areas overlook the river. W of Conway, I-40 exits 118 or 125 to US 64; S on SR 319 (appx. .5 m.).

Cadron Blockhouse. An excellent replica of the original 18th century fort has been built from rough-sawed cypress using weather-notched corners, a cantilevered second story and slit windows. Its shake roof is set at 45 degrees between two free-standing chimneys. A loft ladder leads to the second story and a nice view.

Tollantusky Trail. Foster father of Sam Houston (Old Washington *State Park)*, Tollantusky led 300 Cherokees from Tennessee to settle the Arkansas River Valley in 1809. This

trail leads through a woods along the Arkansas River. Various historical spots are identified, including pioneer *roads,* a *grist mill* site and the Cadron Section Corner (1819), which defined land grants for veterans of the War of 1812 (Louisiana Purchase, *State Parks)*. A leisurely 45-minute walk. Benches.

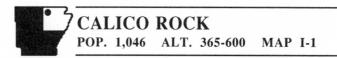

CALICO ROCK
POP. 1,046   ALT. 365-600   MAP I-1

Although a steamboat landing and one of the older settlements *(Mount Olive, Norfork)* along the White *River (Float Streams)*, two disastrous fires and numerous floods have wiped away the evidence. A briefly established post office (1857-59) and several buildings faded away to appear again in 1879 as the beginnings of a 1902 *railroad* town (White River Railway Company of the St. Louis, Iron Mountain & Southern) that was incorporated in 1905.

The Calico Rock. Some of the rocks that named this town have mostly regained their color after portions were blasted away by the railroad in 1902. Both the rocks and the steep grade that causes downtown to have three levels can be seen best from the south bank of the river on SR 5.

Downtown. State Historical District. Moviemakers use it for a 1930s set. Right down at the river, still intact and standard storefront, the one- and two-story buildings face each other (one side stone, the other brick) on three different levels divided by SR 5.

CALION
POP. 638   ALT. 93   MAP H-4

Historically a crossing point on the Ouachita *River,* even the name is a crossing (CAL-houn and Un-ION Counties). Indian trails crossed on the high bluffs. According to one historical report, *De Soto,* retreating from *Caddo Gap,* might have wintered here (1541-42) at an Indian village, Utiangue. Called El Dorado Landing and used by *El Dorado* as a port until the Camden & Alexander Railway joined El Dorado to the St. Louis, Iron Mountain & Southern *(Railroad)* in 1891, the landing shrunk away then reappeared as Calion when the Little Rock Southern (Chicago, Rock Island & Pacific) crossed the river in 1903. US 167 followed in 1930, and a shipping terminal was established two years later, making old El Dorado Landing a port city again.

Champagnolle Landing. Legend claims that the town's name was carved in beech trees as early as 1818. In 1840 the name was changed to Union Courthouse when it became the county seat, then changed back to Champagnolle Landing in 1840 when it lost the county seat to *El Dorado.* No remnants. S of Calion Lake.

Calion Lake. This 600-acre lake was originally built next to a high bluff in 1936 using wheelbarrows and shovels to dam a creek. Fishing: bluegill, crappie, catfish and bass. Swimming. Picnic Areas. S of town. Signs.

Calion Lock & Dam. Recently completed (1985), the facility is a part of the Ouachita River Basin System to improve navigation and flood control. The 84-by-600-foot lock can accommodate pleasure boats or barges by raising or lowering the water 12 feet inside the lock, working in stair-step fashion to match the level where river traffic is entering or exiting. Proposed facilities: picnic areas, pavilion, restrooms, water, boat ramps and playgrounds. US 167, N of town; S on access road past Calion Lake. Signs.

Iron R.R. Bridge. (1903). They could tear the track up but not the bridge. It is still turned crossways over the Ouachita.

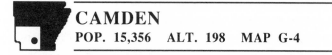

CAMDEN
POP. 15,356   ALT. 198   MAP G-4

Ecore á Fabre (Fabre's Bluff) was reportedly a French trading post in 1783 that was later settled by John Nunn in 1824 and platted in 1839 using that name (dropping the "á"). The first county seat of Union County (1829), it was later selected county seat of newly created Ouachita County (1842). Local tradition claims the name Ecore Fabre was so susceptible to corruption (an 1830 post office spelled it Corea Fabre) that when incorporated in 1844, it was changed to Camden, a change influenced (some say unpopularly) by Gen. Thomas Woodward in honor of his former hometown, whose location, Alabama or South Carolina, is still disputed. The townsite has always been literally a crossroads. Two Indian trails, six pioneer *roads*, three *railroads* and steamboats have met here (in some cases, simultaneously). *De Soto* might have passed by (possibly wintering here) in 1541 on his way from *Caddo Gap* to *Calion*. Today SR 4 and 7 cross US 79, three railroads and the Ouachita Navigational System. And it has an airport. Home of Southern Arkansas University Tech at Camden.

---

*Ecore á Fabre (today's Camden) was
reportedly a French trading post in 1783*

Fort Lookout. One of a semicircle of earthen forts with rifle trenches and redoubts, cannon and field guns, its rifle trenches and cannon pits remain much the same today as when built in 1864. Off US 79B at the end of Monroe Ave. on a high bluff overlooking the Ouachita.

Confederate Cemetery. At once ornate and austere, it features a tall marble shaft marking the graves of nearly 200 unknown soldiers. Buried in the same cemetery is a child who died suddenly on board ship and whose only marker at hand was four wooden posts and part of an anchor chain. Off US 79B on Adams at Maul.

McCollum-Chidester House. National Historic Register, 1847. Col. John T. Chidester, three years after buying the house in 1857 for a reported $10,000 in gold, formed a mail company covering 1,560 miles (from Arkansas to Arizona) requiring 2,000 horses, 300 men, 60 Concord coaches and a de-

tachment of the U.S. Army. The house is virtually unchanged and includes furnishings, jewlery, pictures, books and mementos. 926 Washington St. NW, off US 79B.

Events/Festivals. Late Sept: Annual Barn Sale. Entertainment. Arts & Crafts.

Ouachita County Courthouse. English Neo-Classic, 1933. Called the best example of 18th century English architect John Sloan's style, it features: tall arched windows and a cupola with four clocks. Grounds: a monument to Confederate women and a sesquicentennial time capsule dated 1974 (to be opened 2024), commemorating their settlement's founding in 1824. E of US 79B on Washington. *(County Profiles)*

National Historic Register. There is a long list of houses and buildings (eight from the 1850s). Tour Homes. Maps: chamber of commerce, off 79B at 221 Washington St. NW.

CANE HILL
COMMUNITY   ALT. 1,691   MAP B-1

First called Hillsboro, it was renamed Cane Hill (post office, 1830) for the dense growth of cane in the area. Boonsboro (post office 1843) replaced the community's name after Maj. Wm. Boone (said to be a relative of Daniel Boone) "proclaimed the town Boonsboro" during a passionate political speech. Although the Cane Hill post office was reestablished twice (1867 and 1870), the townsite continued as Boonsboro until the turn of the century. Mostly burned after the Battle of Prairie Grove *(State Parks),* today's structures don't reflect its reputation as the oldest settlement in NW Arkansas or its founding date of 1827. Establishment in 1835 of Cane Hill Collegiate College, an institute for young ministers, is said to have led to the founding of Cane Hill College (chartered 1852), which is now College of the Ozarks at *Clarksville*. Incidentally, while some maps spell the town name "Canehill," the town and its newspaper spell it "Cane Hill."

Truesdale-Pyeatt & Moore Mill. Built in 1840, it was moved to its present site in 1866. One of the first steam-and-water-powered mills *(Grist Mills)* in the country, it used a 36-foot overshot wheel that is all that remains today. SR 45, roadside park.

CARLISLE
POP. 2,567   ALT. 299   MAP L-2

Laid out by Samuel McCormick on his property beside the tracks of the Memphis & Little Rock *Railroad* in 1872 (incorporated 1878), legend assigns the name to either his previous residence in Carlisle, Pa., or to a "friend who was a state senator in another state." At first a dairy center, it switched to agriculture, harvesting Arkansas' first rice crop in 1904. Humorist Opie P. Read began his career here. His first newspaper (1876), The Prairie Flower, had as its masthead motto: "If you have to walk, be sure to start in time."

Grand Prairie Remnant. Natural Heritage Area. Along the

Rock Island Railroad/US 70 right-of-way is a 13-mile stretch of the original prairie that was once roughly bounded by the Lower White and Arkansas Rivers, and was named Gran Maris by early French explorers. US 70, Carlisle, east to *DeValls Bluff. (Hazen)*

Smoke Hole. Natural Heritage Area. This two-mile course of the Two Prairie Bayou is made up of a tupelo swamp and mixed bottomland forest, both of which are representative of some of the area's former appearance. SR 86, 12 m. SE, at Two Prairie Bayou.

CARROLLTON
COMMUNITY   ALT. 1,202   MAP A-3

Platted in 1834 and named for county namesake Charles Carroll *(County Profiles),* it was county seat until 1875 when reductions (from 1836-69) in county size affected its previous central location *(Berryville).* This town of 1,000 faded when bypassed in 1901 *(Alpena)* by the St. Louis & North Arkansas Railroad (Missouri & North Arkansas *Railroad).*

Roadside Park. Remnants of a chimney mark the old town site. Historical Marker. SR 68.

Lodge Hall. (1876). A two-story white clapboard structure, once a church, sits on a hill overlooking the countryside. Unmarked road, first turn S of the community park; W 1 blk. to join US 62W, drive W; keep right.

CASS
COMMUNITY   ALT. 1,100   MAP B-2

Settled by Elias Turner and called Turner's Bend until the 1850s, it was the terminus (1915-1924) for Phipps Lumber Company's Black Mountain & Eastern *Railroad* (a spur of the St. Louis & San Francisco from Combs to Cass) and for five years (1915-20) reportedly produced more wooden wagon wheels than any place in the world. Today, the Civilian Conservation Corps Center (CCC) and canoe outfitters (Mulberry River, *Float Streams)* produce income for the community.

Mountaincrest Academy. Second Empire, 1915. Built by the Home Board of the Presbyterian Church, this three-story native stone structure was a coeducational boarding (and day) school (1915-1931). Depletion of the hardwood forest by 1924 and the Depression combined to close it. Derelict, but still intact on top of a 2,362-foot plateau, it is an impressive sight. COMBS, AR. (SR 23, N 11 m.; SR 16, W 3 m.): FR 1007, S 6.5 m. (Or from between Bee Rock and White Rock on unimproved road FR 1509 N appx. 8 m. to FR 1007 S appx. 3 m.) Inquire Locally.

White Rock. Called the Grand Canyon of the Ozarks, it provides spectacular views, picnic sites and access to the Ozark Highlands *Trail.* Thirties-style housekeeping cabins. 8 Campsites. First gravel road S of the CCC, 12 m. W. Signs.

Bee Rock. This rugged rock formation is a home for millons of honey bees, which were reportedly placed there as a swarm

in 1935 by members of the railroad construction crew. First gravel road S of the CCC, 2 m. W. Signs.

Lost Mines. There are two in the area. For a price you can hunt for treasure. Incidentally, one of the owners has a house-broken pet chicken and makes banjos. His personal banjo has a maple neck; the belly is a drum from a 1950s Dynaflow transmission. N of Cass, SR 215, 4 m. E, 1st house on the south side of the 1st cement bridge.

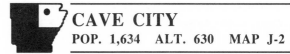

CAVE CITY
POP. 1,634   ALT. 630   MAP J-2

In 1889 Loyal Post Office was moved a mile south to Horn's Cave and renamed Cave City. A "two-story" town, the cave below has literally supported the town: as a water supply and as one of the older tourist attractions (1933) in the state.

The Mysterous Crystal Cave/Cave Courts. Nostalgically old-fashioned, the tourists' courts and cave are a thirties' set piece. Hubert Carpenter collected "foam geodes," quartz and fossils to build his house and office. Other rocks, "from across the nation," were used in making bas-reliefs (mostly crosses). Although designed by Carpenter, these buildings (like many less flamboyant ones in the area) were built by farmer-turned-stonemason Charles Prince Matlock. The cave, steeped in Indian legend and apocryphal pioneer stories, is one large room leading down to crystal-clear water. Carpenter claimed to have used a boat and a mile of rope without finding the end. It is said that fluctuations in the Mississippi River affect this stream's depth. In Town.

Maxville Church/Cemetery. Originally two stories (second floor Masonic Lodge), Maxville Methodist Church (Watson's Chapel) is a 28-by-32-foot hand-hewn log building erected c.1867 as a community church, school and lodge. Today it is used sometimes for elections, funerals and weddings. The cemetery (c.1851) is nicely situated on a hill with shade trees and a pine pew. 4 m. N on US 167, just S of SR 58, down a gravel driveway. Sign.

Events/Festivals. Early Aug: Annual Watermelon Festival. Carnival. Camp Meeting.

CENTER POINT
COMMUNITY   ALT. 600   MAP F-2

Settled in 1837, it became Center Point (post office) in 1849 as a central trading point and crossroads west of *Washington,* then later county seat of newly created Howard County (1873) until replaced as county seat by *Nashville* in 1905.

Ebenezer Campground. National Historic Register. One of the oldest Methodist camp meetings in the South began here in 1837, and has been held at this site since c.1854. August. SR 4, 1.5 m. N. Marker.

National Historic Register. Adams Boyd House (c.1848), SR 26 E of town. Clardy-Lee House (c.1873), SR 26, in town. Russey-Murray House (c.1851), SR 4, S.

CHARLESTON
POP. 1,748   ALT. 510   MAP C-2

Founded c.1843 on an important east-west *road* (later the *Butterfield Overland Mail* route) and named Charles Town by Massachusetts Free Will Baptist preacher Charles Kellum, it changed its name in 1874 when the preacher's businesses failed and the town was incorporated.

Cherokee Prairie. Natural Heritage Area. Very much like presettlement Arkansas prairies, these 280 acres make up the largest remaining tallgrass prairie in the state. From March to October flowers of every description are in bloom, including rare yellow puccoon and grass pink orchid. 3 m. N on SR 217 at SR 60.

Potato Hill. Poking up out of the prairie, rising to a point, this pioneer landmark west of town is now used for artillery target practice by soldiers at Fort Chaffee.

Budweiser Advertisement. Near the junction of SR 96 and 22 is what could be the world's largest Budweiser beer can, but is actually an advertisement (an empty silo that could hold 8,734,902 ounces of the brewer's art). SR 22, 10 m. W.

Franklin County Courthouse. Renaissance Modern, 1921. *Dual County Seat (Ozark).* Grounds: a Fourth of July flag that flew over the U.S. Capitol during America's bicentennial. *(County Profiles)*

CHESTER
POP. 139   ALT. 842   MAP B-1

Although first settled in 1839, it was Capt. J. C. Wright who pioneered the area in 1853, maintaining a subsistence farm here for 34 years before another building was erected. Arrival of the St. Louis & San Francisco *(Railroad)* in 1882 helped establish a town reportedly named for survey engineer (first name unknown) Hepburn's hometown (some say in Iowa). Construction of a roundhouse and repair shop in 1887 brought a short-lived prosperity. Incorporated in 1889, its population of 500-600 evaporated about a year later when the roundhouse was moved to Fort Smith.

Wright's Log Cabin. Capt. Wright's restored dogtrot cabin (1853) can be seen from the road. First right after Yoes Building, midway up the hill. Private.

Col. Jacob Yoes Building. National Historic Register, 1887. The "Colonel" (discharged as a sergeant after the Civil War), was a U.S. marshall from 1890-93, and one of the so-called "men who rode for Parker" (Judge Parker, *Fort Smith*). Among other buildings along the path of the railroad *(Mountainburg)*, he built this two-story brick building as a mercantile store and a 17-room hotel to accommodate the boom. In the same year a saloon was added to the north side. In Town.

Swinging Bridge. One of four built across this creek, it is a classic. Typically, these bridges are "homemade," and usually are built across creeks, using two wooden platforms joined by rope webbing with a plank bottom. City Park.

CHISMVILLE
COMMUNITY   ALT. 511   MAP C-2

The Ozark-Waldron and Ft. Smith-Little Rock *Roads* probably crossed here, inspiring its first name, Cross Roads, which was changed to Chismville (c.1854) for Dr. Stephen H. Chism, who was the son-in-law of county namesake James B. Logan *(County Profiles)*.

Chism House. This double-block dogtrot (now enclosed) of hand-hewn logs was built by slaves c.1845. Behind it, the old drummer's hotel led to legends that the house was a tavern/way station. In Town. Private.

Metcalf House. It is believed this log house was built by Metcalf about 1845. SR 41, 1 m. S.

CIVIL WAR 1861-1865
MAP ALL QUARTERS

After the bluster and the sword rattling of emotional tirades and grandstand gestures like the first battle of Bull Run, a few sober-thinking Northerners began to confront the overwhelming evidence that no one single contest would bring the South back into the Union. It would be necessary to begin a protracted siege against a like-minded and determined enemy on his home ground. The general idea was an historical anaconda plan to encircle and squeeze. In order to succeed, the Federals needed control of the coastlines and, to Arkansas' misfortune, the Mississippi River.

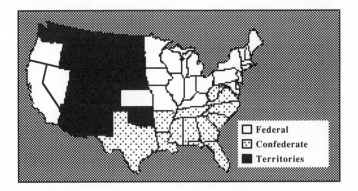

The first years of the Civil War were action and reaction. Communication and general planning were ragtag affairs left to the passions and pressures of the moment, creating the impression at times that anyone with the money for a costume could be a general. It was not until the later years, 1863-65, that practical ("born of the fire of battle") men came forward, then the Federals began to methodically pull the constricting circle tighter and tighter until a hopelessly surrounded and outnumbered General Robert E. Lee symbolically surrendered the South, offering his sword to General Ulysses S. Grant at Appomattox Court House on April 9, 1865.

Arkansas' popular vote concerning secession involved approximately 75,000 citizens. The proposition to secede lost by

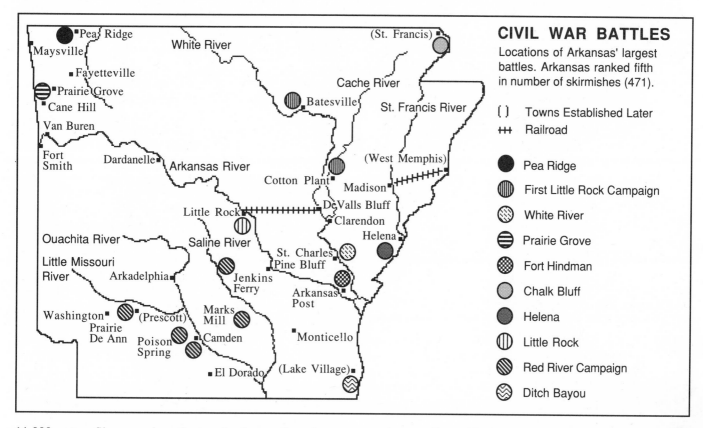

CIVIL WAR BATTLES

Locations of Arkansas' largest battles. Arkansas ranked fifth in number of skirmishes (471).

{ }   Towns Established Later
╫╫   Railroad

● Pea Ridge
▥ First Little Rock Campaign
▨ White River
▤ Prairie Grove
▦ Fort Hindman
◯ Chalk Bluff
◍ Helena
▥ Little Rock
▨ Red River Campaign
▨ Ditch Bayou

11,000 votes. Slave-owning planters in the south and east found their influence offset by homestead farmers in the Ozark and Ouachita Mountains, who, although former residents of Alabama, Tennessee, Georgia, Kentucky and the Carolinas, had left home to avoid just such social and political confrontations. They wanted to be left alone. But when Washington, D.C., called for troops after the fall of Ft. Sumner, these first- and second-generation Arkansas highlanders aligned themselves with the families and friends left behind in the deep South; not with moral or political interests. By an act of the state legislature on May 6, 1861, Arkansas voted to secede with but one dissenting vote (Isaac Murphy, pressured to make the vote unanimous, refused to compromise his principles, *Huntsville).*

In 1861, Arkansas was still largely a frontier with little strategic value other than the status of enemy territory poised on the border of a vacillating Missouri. Later it became vital that the Mississippi River be secured. To accomplish their objectives in Arkansas, the Federals would have to engage toughened frontiersmen defending homes situated in rugged mountains and vast wetlands where roads were nonexistent or nearly impassable and food for large numbers of men was scarce. The best that can be said about either side's war efforts here is that Arkansas was neutralized. Divided loyalty in the Confederate camp and long Federal supply lines kept troops, for the most part, garrisoned in larger towns held by their respective partisans.

As an overall view (a chronology is outlined below), the war in Arkansas began in 1862 with its most violent engagement of the Civil War, Pea Ridge *(National Park),* after which Federal troops tried and failed to move on Little Rock by

staging near Batesville. Retreating down the White and Cache River basins, harassed all the way, they finally retired to Helena in 1862 but regrouped in 1863 to take Little Rock without opposition. In fact, Arkansas Federalists then petitioned President Lincoln for readmission. Although endorsed by him, Congress blocked it because the "new"1864 state constitution did not allow blacks to vote or hold office. After the fall of Little Rock (the capital was removed to *Washington,* Ar.) and after the Red River Campaign in 1864, no significant strategy was acted upon by either side for the consolidation of Arkansas. Generally, skirmishes and battles continued until 45 days after Lee's surrender but for the most part all lands north of the *Arkansas River* were Federal and those below, with the exception of a Southern stronghold in extreme SW Arkansas, were a no-mans-land roamed by hit-and-run Confederates who had no means of regaining control of the state. It should be noted here that renegades (Northern jawhawkers and Southern bushwhackers) are said to have caused more suffering and destruction in Arkansas than did the "regular" troops. These outlaws continued preying on the countryside well after the war had ended, and while romanticized by legends like those surrounding Jessie James, were actually hardcore criminals.

From the period of Isaac Murphy's 1864 appointment in occupied Little Rock as a "loyalist antislavery" governor under a "Federal state constitution" until years after Arkansas' readmission to the Union in 1868, politics was determined by "light-horse" brigades and vigilantes as well as by Southern resentments focused on injuries both real and imaginary: conveyance of land to "officers of the occupation" *(Searcy,* Judsonia), disenfranchisement of Confederate veterans *(Garland)* and interparty hostilities over the benefits of cooperating with Re-publicans *(Sheridan)*. Reconstruction ended in 1874 with a hotly contested election wherein two Republicans fought both politically and militarily for the office of governor. This Brooks-Baxter War resulted in Elisha Baxter succeeding as governor, drafting a state constitution and becoming the last Republican governor until Winthrop Rockefeller in 1966.

Any civil war is a result of drastic and irreconcilable differences. The American Civil War so totally saturated the nation with emotional and physical violence that its traces still endure in monuments, songs, stories and regional politics. The following are major events that affected the war in Arkansas. Casualties and troop strengths are taken from reliable sources that readily admit that the figures are, at best, estimates.

The three-day battle at Pea Ridge resulted in combined casualties of approximately 2,600

Battle of Pea Ridge—Loss of Missouri. (Pea Ridge *National Park*) The war was 10 months old in December of 1861 when Federal General Samuel R. Curtis assumed command of the Southwestern District of Missouri and began an aggressive campaign to clear it of pro-Confederate forces. In February of 1862 General Sterling Price, Confederate commander of the Missouri State Guard, crossed into Arkansas, joining forces with General Ben McCulloch in the Boston Mountains. These combined Confederate forces of 16,000 under General Earl Van Dorn then turned north with St. Louis as their goal. Curtis, with 10,500 Federal troops, dug in at Sugar Creek near Pea Ridge (Elkhorn Tavern) and waited. Van Dorn, realizing a frontal attack was suicide, skirted to the north to attack from the rear on March 7, 1862. Curtis recognized the tactic, pulled his men away from Sugar Creek and "faced about" to meet the Confederates in the open. What followed was typical of Civil War engagements, a kind of dumb luck and perseverance of savage, bloody combat that culminated three days later in no clear victory for either side, but can, with historical hindsight, be pointed to as having secured Missouri for the Union. Casualties were about equal at approximately 1,300 each. Van Dorn made an orderly withdrawal east down the Huntsville *Road*. Later he and his troops were ordered east of the Mississippi River, leaving Arkansas virtually defenseless. Curtis set out for Batesville and the first attempt to capture Little Rock.

First Attempt to Capture Little Rock. Following the Battle of Pea Ridge, Federal General S.R. Curtis with 20,000 troops occupied Batesville on May 3 in preparation for an assault on Little Rock but lost nearly half his forces to orders for duty east of the Mississippi River. Still commanding 12,500 men (Confederate Arkansas had no effective troops), and with outposts only 35 miles from Little Rock, he waited for the White River to be freed for supplies. Meanwhile, Confederate General Thomas C. Hindman, in two months, miraculously organized 20,000 men to confront Curtis. Now threatened by

Missouri Confederate guerrillas breaking his supply line in the north and Hindman's impending offensive from the south, Curtis was forced to retreat down the White and Cache River basins (swampland), struggling with short supplies, disease and nearly impossible transportation while suffering substantial casualties from hit-and-run Confederate tactics and General Albert Rust's attempt to hold the Cache River crossing near *Cotton Plant*. Joining Federal forces already occupying Helena on July 13th, the attack on Little Rock was left for another time (1863) and a different general (Steele).

Loss of the White River and Railroad. In 1862 the unfinished Memphis & Little Rock *Railroad* was the only rail transportation in the state. The White River divided the RR line that was completed from Memphis to Madison and from Little Rock to DeValls Bluff (tracks parallel today's I-40). Federal gunboats gained control of the river on June 17, 1862 with the capture of *St. Charles*. Later a major supply depot was established at DeValls Bluff that collected an estimated population of 35,000 civilians and military personnel.

Battle of Prairie Grove–Loss of N Arkansas River. (Prairie Grove Battlefield *State Park*) Confederate General Thomas C. Hindman, who in September of 1862 had been gathering forces for another attempt at invading Missouri, inherited during November the position of having to protect Ft. Smith and Van Buren against a Federal attack from Missouri by General James F. Blunt, who was massed at *Cane Hill* (appx. 20 m. SW of *Fayetteville*) with about 8,000 men while waiting for 6,000 reinforcements led by General Francis J. Herron in a forced march from Springfield, Mo. Hindman left Van Buren with 11,500 men on December 3 to intercept Herron's reinforcements eight miles NE of Cane Hill on December 7, 1862 at Prairie Grove, hoping to keep the two Federal forces divided in order to dispose of them singly, but Blunt (upon "hearing the guns") arrived unexpectedly that afternoon. Fighting broke off at dark leaving a nearly equally divided total of 2,500 casualties. Although Hindman claimed to have routed the Federals, he was forced to give up the field because of a shortage of supplies and ammunition. Withdrawing to Van Buren, he was pursued and forced to retreat to Little Rock. Hindman's campaign practically destroyed his army, leaving the upper Arkansas River area defenseless and eliminating once again the threat of Confederate influence in the "border state" of Missouri.

5,000 Confederates at Fort Hindman held off eight successive assaults by 32,000 Federals

---

Battle of Ft. Hindman—Loss of S Arkansas River. (Arkansas Post *National Park*) On January 11, 1863, Federal General J.A. McClernand with a force of 32,000 attacked Ft. Hindman at Arkansas Post. General T.J. Churchill's 5,000 Confederates reportedly held off eight assaults (140 Confederate casualties, 1,061 Federal) before surrendering more men than ever previously captured during any battle in Arkansas. With the fall of Arkansas Post, the lower Arkansas River had been secured and another Mississippi River access point was denied Confederates for the defense of Vicksburg, Ms.

Battle of Chalk Bluff. *(St. Francis,* Chalk Bluff Park) Little noted in war histories, this May 1 & 2, 1863, engagement was another Confederate attempt to invade Missouri. General John S. Marmaduke, leading a force of 5,000, swept across the state line about six miles north of present-day *St. Francis,* intending to recruit and generate enthusiasm to aid in the capture of the state, but he was turned back by 8,000 Federals. Taking a defensive position at Chalk Bluff, Marmaduke lost 130 men while contemporary Federal reports called their own participation "disastrous." On the following day Marmaduke "effected a leisurely withdrawal." Years afterward, loggers had to carefully saw around lead still lodged in the trees.

Battle of Helena. *(Helena)* July 4, 1863, (the same day Federal General U.S. Grant captured Vicksburg, Ms.) Confederates were assaulting Helena's three closest of four fortified hills. Said to have been an attempt at restoring confidence in the Arkansas army, it was a disaster; moreover, had the Confederates taken the city, Federal gunboats on the Mississippi would have retaken it in less than 24 hours. Confederate General T.H. Holmes with 8,000 men attacked General B.M. Prentiss' 4,000 Federals. Although Graveyard Hill was captured by General Sterling Price, the remaining two were successfully defended and (along with gunboat support) bombed the Confederates off the captured one before noon. Withdrawing, they suffered 1,636 casualties to the Union's 239. Holmes fell sick on July 23 and turned over command of the District of Arkansas to Price, who immediately began preparations for the defense of Little Rock.

The first bridge across the river at Little Rock was built by Federals attacking the city

The Capture of Little Rock. After the fall of Vicksburg, Ms. (which coincided with the South's defeat at Gettysburg, Pa.), the Union could now commit more troops to Arkansas. Federal General Fredrick Steele moved from Helena on August 5, 1863, arriving in *DeValls Bluff* on Aug. 18 with an aggregate force of 14,500 men and 57 pieces of artillery. There was no Battle of Little Rock. Confederate General Sterling Price had 8,000 troops, of which about 1,250 were on the south side of the Arkansas River to prevent a crossing. The rest, dug in on the north side, were "turned" on September 10, 1863, by Steele, who built a pontoon bridge (the first bridge at Little Rock) and crossed below town, advancing up both sides. Skirmishes along Bayou Fourche and around Little Rock resulted in 64 losses for the Confederates and 137 for the Federals. Price withdrew first to Benton and then to Arkadelphia (appx. paralleling today's I-30), where Holmes resumed command on Sept. 25, establishing himself at *Camden* on Oct 7. In the meantime Steele had easily secured both Pine Bluff and Benton. Federals now controlled all land north of the Arkansas

River while Confederates held a stronghold in SW Arkansas around the new capital of *Washington* and a general hit-and-run dominance south of the Arkansas River.

The Red River Campaign mired 13,000 Federal troops deep in enemy territory

The Red River Campaign. *(Prescott, Camden* and *State Parks:* Poison Spring, Marks Mill and Jenkins Ferry) The expedition was a Federal strategy to consolidate the Southwest (Louisiana, Texas and Arkansas) in the spring of 1864. Federal General Nathaniel P. Banks was to proceed from New Orleans, ascend the Red River and, joined by General Fredrick Steele marching south from Little Rock, assault Shreveport, La. Legendary poor transportation in the area by both road and river compounded problems of troop movement, supply and communication. On April 8, 1864, Confederate General Kirby Smith forced Banks to retreat at Sabine Crossroads, La. ("two marches from Shreveport"), while Steele was just approaching Prairie De Ann (BELOW). Unknown to Steele at the time, his participation in the Red River Campaign would be limited to fighting his way into and back out of South Central Arkansas from April 9 to April 30. PRAIRIE DE ANN: Advancing down the Southwest Trail *(Roads),* Steele (still believing he was to rendezvous with Banks at Shreveport) fought through skirmish lines to meet and combine forces south of the Little Missouri River with General John M. Thayer from Ft. Smith on April 9. With 13,000 troops the Federals arrived at present-day *Prescott,* where for three days Confederates under General Joseph O. Shelby defended what was considered an advance on nearby *Washington.* After the third day (on April 16), Steele turned or was "turned" and withdrew to occupy *Camden* without a contest (Confederate troops had left to defend Washington). Here he learned of Banks' retreat, the failure of the Red River Campaign, and the truth of his predicament: deep in enemy territory with no means of resupply. POISON SPRINGS: Short of supplies, Steele on April 17 sent 200 wagons guarded by 1,000 men to secure a storehouse of corn 12 miles west of Camden. On April 18, Confederate General Sterling Price, waiting until the wagons were loaded, blocked their return and routed the Federals, inflicting 301 casualties to his 114 and capturing all the wagons. MARKS MILL: Certain that Confederate General Kirby Smith's reinforcements marching from the Shreveport area were closing in, Steele made one last attempt at resupply, this time from Pine Bluff. On April 25, 10 miles east of *Fordyce,* Confederate General James F. Fagan routed the 240-wagon supply train, capturing more prisoners (Federal casualties of 1,300) and military equipment than in any other Arkansas battle. JENKINS FERRY: No longer in a position to hold off the threat from a combining strength of Confederate Generals Smith and Price, Steele left Camden for Little Rock. Blocked by a rain-swollen Saline River about 13 miles SW of present-day *Sheridan,* hotly pursued by Smith and Price, Steele threw up pontoon bridges but was caught there.

The half-day battle ended with Steele escaping to Little Rock, suffering 700 casualties to Smith's 1,000. Badly mauled, the Confederates did not pursue, but with the failure of the Red River Campaign they continued to control southwest Arkansas without challenge until the end of the war.

Battle of Ditch Bayou. *(Lake Village)* Not particularly significant in the war, it did typify the hit-and-run tactics of the Confederates and particularly those of General J.S. Marmaduke. By 1864 Federals had developed a plan to trap annoying raiders like Marmaduke. Patrolling the Mississippi River on transports, the Federals would wait to draw fire, then dispatch mounted troops. At Ditch Bayou on June 6, charging the sound of the guns, Federal General A.J. Smith found himself mired in a mile-wide swamp and pinned down by crossfire that cost him 250 casualties. Marmaduke, with only 37 casualties, withdrew in "almost parade-like fashion."

The "Price Raid" — Surrender of the West. After the Red River Campaign (spring 1864), no other Federal offensive in Arkansas was attempted. Most of Federal General Fredrick Steele's troops were ordered east to help General Wm. T. Sherman's "March to the Sea." Seizing the opportunity, Confederate General Kirby Smith ordered General Sterling Price and 15,000 men to invade Missouri in vain hope of recovering Arkansas and diverting Federal troops from Sherman's campaign. Price forded the Arkansas River at Dardanelle in early September of 1864 and marched northwest to enter SW Missouri, eventually assaulting the outskirts of St. Louis. Turned back, Price tried and failed at Jefferson City and then again at Kansas City. Severely beaten, he reentered Arkansas at *Maysville* in late October with about 5,000 of the original troops (the rest either killed, captured or deserted). No other significant battles took place in Missouri or Arkansas. After the East surrendered in April of 1865, Smith tried to make a military alliance with Maximillian, the French-backed emperor of Mexico, but his officers revolted, surrendering the Trans-Mississippi on May 24, 1865. Legend claims that General Joe Shelby's "Iron Brigade" crossed the Rio Grande and buried their battle flag, never giving up.

CLARENDON
POP. 2,361   ALT. 176   MAP M-3

This prehistoric Indian site, first sold as a Spanish land grant to Elijah McKinney in 1803, was bought by land speculator Sylvanus Phillips *(Helena)* for a White *River* ferry crossing (c.1827) on the Memphis-Little Rock Military *Road*. The name of its 1828 post office, Mouth-of-the-Cache (sometimes called White River Crossing), was changed in 1837 to Clarendon possibly for the Earl of Clarendon (it is not known why). County seat in 1857 (moved from 1838 Lawrenceville), incorporated in 1859, this important steamboat landing also served nearby Rock Roe from 1858 to 1871 as a "shuttle station" for the Memphis & Little Rock *Railroad* and *Butterfield Overland Mail*. Reduced to "weeds and ashes" during the *Civil War* as a reprisal for sinking the Federal ironclad, Queen City, it was reincorporated in 1898.

Rock Roe/Cemetery. This ferry crossing/steamboat landing sprung up on the west side of the river about seven miles south of Clarendon and by 1838 was a connecting point for mail service (also stagecoach/riverboat for the Great Western U.S. Mail Line in 1842) between Little Rock and the mouth of the White River; then later for the railroad and the Butterfield Stage. A ferry operated until the US 79 bridge was completed in 1931. The cemetery is old and large with markers dating from the 1840s. US 79, 7 m. S to Roe; SR 33, 2 m. S to SR 366, E appx. 2 m. then N on gravel 1 m. Also nearby is Aberdeen (Ragan's Bluff), an 1830s-1860s river port.

Town Square/Architecture. Historical preservation here results more from benign neglect than design. Used as a movie set for "A Soldier's Story" and "Summer's End." There are 22 structures listed in the National Historic Register, including: MONROE COUNTY JAIL, 1892: This unique example of an early correctional facility had a modern water system 22 years before the town did. 2nd & Kendall. US 79 BRIDGE, 1930: The 720-foot steel bridge together with its cement approach and "dirt fills" over Old River and Rock Roe Bayou spans three miles. NEW SOUTH INN, c.1903: It and the adjacent building have been used in two movies. 132-164 2nd. CUMBERLAND PRESBYTERIAN CHURCH, 1869: Built from heart-cypress with wooden pegs, it remains basically unchanged. 120 Washington. METHODIST EPISCOPAL CHURCH, 1912: Classic Revival, its sanctuary is two stories high; the clay tile roof supports a large dome. Stained-glass. Ionic Columns. 121 3rd.

Bounds Building/"Museum." National Historic Register, 1917. Not actually a museum or advertised as one, it does have enough artifacts to be one. 105 2nd.

Monroe County Courthouse. Italianate, 1911. National Historic Register. Conical roofs cap four bays at each corner. The seven-story clock tower has a copper weather vane. Inside, the marble and arches, oak and wrought iron, stained-glass dome skylight and chandeliers are still intact after the disastrous *Flood of 1927* brought water so high that boats were rowed through the hallways. Most of the records, beginning in 1829, have been preserved. Town Square. *(County Profiles)*

National Historic Register. Town Square and Architecture (ABOVE).

CLARKSVILLE
POP. 5,237   ALT. 379   MAP C-2

Selected as a county seat location and once known as Johnson County Court House, it was named for either pioneer settler Gen. Lorenzo Clark or for Abram Clark (who is said to have donated land in exchange for the honor). Made county seat in 1836 (Spadra, BELOW). Incorporated in 1848. Once third in coal production (1937-38) in Arkansas *(Greenwood)*, it also has natural gas reserves. Home of the Clarksville Institute (first school for the education of the blind, 1850), John W. Woodward (Arkansas' first teacher of the deaf, 1851) and the College of the Ozarks *(Cane Hill)*.

Spadra (Park). A Spanish pun for broken sword, it was a coal mining town, delivering its first shipment to Little Rock in 1841, but its original beginnings were in 1817 as an Indian trading post (Federal Fur Trading Factory, 1819). The first (1819) agent, Matthew Lyon, as representative from Vermont cast the deciding vote in the U.S House of Representatives (the 16 states had been deadlocked for 36 ballots) in 1800 that elected Thomas Jefferson president instead of Aaron Burr when the two had tied in the Electoral College. Its post office was moved a few miles north to the recently selected county seat and then changed to Clarksville in 1841. Picnic shelters overlooking *Lake* Dardanelle *(Arkansas River Parks and Campgrounds).* SR 103S to the river.

Arkansas River Bridge. At 8,537 feet (1.6 miles), it is the longest bridge in the state. SR 109.

Events/Festivals. Early Apr: Spring Arts & Crafts Gala. Late June: Annual Johnson County Peach Festival. Parade. Greased Pig. Horseshoes.

Johnson County Courthouse. Renaissance Revival, 1936. Called one of the most impressive and best preserved courtrooms in Arkansas, it has tintype portraits of Confederate veterans on display. Grounds: an eternal flame for Johnson County veterans, and a bell from Lone Pine School (1921-53). *(County Profiles)*

National Historic Register. Davis House, 212 Fulton. Dunlap House, 101 Grandview. Capt. A.S. McKennon House (1868), 215 N. Central. McKennon House, 155 Grandview.

 # CLINTON
POP. 2,080 ALT. 550 MAP B-4

A post office, presumably named for DeWitt Clinton *(DeWitt)*, was established in 1823 where the Archery River meets the Little Red *River (Float Streams)* in the foothills of the Ozarks. Located almost in the center of the state, postal *roads* from all directions crossed here. In 1844 the county seat was moved here from Bloomington (10 m. E on the Little Red). Incorporated 1879.

Natural Bridge. Actually used as a bridge, this sandstone formation is set in an old-fashioned tourist atmosphere. The steep ride down (no trailers) is as spectacular as the scenery. On the grounds are a restored log cabin, moonshine still and rocks as round and smooth and large as beach balls. US 65, 4 m. N. Signs.

Halls of History. Along with wax figures, musical instruments and a stage-set Victorian village, there is (advertised as "one of the largest in existence") a model railroad with 390 feet of track winding through replicas of Indian villages, frontier towns and modern cities in the Ozark Mountains. US 65, 5 m. S. Signs.

Sugar Loaf Mountain/Trail. Rising 560 feet above Greers Ferry *Lake,* this game refuge is a flat-top island capped by massive limestone and pine trees. Arkansas' first (1971) designated National Recreational *Trail* begins at the lake and winds up the mountain, ending on top at 1,001 feet. The 1.3-mile trail has rest stops along a route that includes abundant wildlife (from deer to turtles), sandstone with vertical fractures measuring 100 feet deep, banzai English elms, ferns and wildflowers. The views are panoramic and spectacular. Shuttle service or boat rental available at local marinas. SR 16, 15 m E.

Events/Festivals. Late May: Clinton Arts & Crafts Fair. Fourth of July: Fireworks Spectacular. FAIRFIELD BAY, AR. (SR 16, 11 m. E): Easter: Spring Festival. Sunrise Service. Entertainment. Arts & Crafts. Late June: Annual Fairfield Bay – Ozark Folk Center *State Park* Crafts Fair.

Van Buren County Courthouse. Moderne, 1934. This sandstone building, in terms of square feet of covered ground, is the smallest courthouse in Arkansas. *(County Profiles)*

National Historic Register. CHOCTAW, AR. (SR 9, .5 m. S.): Stobaugh House (1850s).

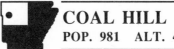 # COAL HILL
POP. 981 ALT. 471 MAP C-2

It is said that one of the first sit-down strikes in America occurred at this coal mining town *(Clarksville,* Spadra) in 1886. Mining contractors "leased" state prisoners without pay or regulations. Reportedly, protesting convicts barricaded the tunnels, made pipe-cannons and killed mules for food. Over two weeks later their terms were met, and after an investigation the lease system was first modified, then later abolished *(Varner).* Evidence of the mines still remains. Inquire Locally.

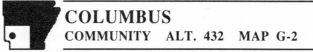 # COLUMBUS
COMMUNITY ALT. 432 MAP G-2

Although settled by Reuben and Abner Maurin (blacksmiths, *grist mill* operators, traders) in 1801, the structures today are mostly turn-of-the-century: three stores (of them, one was originally a saloon, the other a bank), two churches and a pre-Civil War house. While Christopher Columbus is the inspiration for most American towns of that name, it is not known if this were the case here or if another town named Columbus (Columbus, Ohio, etc.) was meant to be honored.

 # CONWAY
POP. 20,375 ALT. 387 MAP D-4

A.P. Robinson, chief survey engineer for the Little Rock-Ft. Smith *Railroad,* took a mile-square parcel of land just north of *Cadron* in lieu of salary. With the arrival of the train in 1870 he deeded a small tract back to the railroad for a depot and platted a town around it in 1871, reportedly naming the site after the famous Conway family *(Walnut Hill).* Designated county seat of newly created Faulkner County in 1873, incorporated 1875. Home of the University of Central Arkansas, Hendrix College and Central Baptist College. Possible *De Soto* Route. NOTE: While I-40 signs read east-west, this portion of the highway runs nearly due north-south.

Cadron Settlement Federal Park. *(Cadron)*

Toad Suck. Passed from *river* ferry/tavern/settlement to the lock and dam of today, the name supposedly originated (there are variations) when a traveler remarked about the heavy drinking at a riverside tavern: "Those fellows suck at a bottle 'till they swell up like toads." The first *Arkansas River* crossings here c.1820 (a boatman poling a skiff large enough for a horse and rider) operated for the postal route to Hot Springs. Continuously "modernized" into the 20th century, it continued as a ferry until 1970. A picnic park on the river displays a metal tow-craft (c.1939) powered by an 85 h.p. Ford V-8 engine. US 60 at the Arkansas River.

Toad Suck Ferry Lock & Dam. Completed in 1969 as a part of the 445-mile McClellan-Kerr *Arkansas River* Navigation system (from near Tulsa, Ok., to the Mississippi River), the 110-by-600-foot lock can accommodate pleasure boats or barges by raising or lowering the water 16 feet inside the lock, working in stair-step fashion to match the level where river traffic is entering or exiting. Recreation: *Arkansas River Parks and Campground,* Little Rock-Dardanelle. US 60, 4.6 m. S.

Missouri Pacific Railway Tunnel. Convict labor leased from the state *(Coal Hill)* built this tunnel, an engineering feat in 1903. US 64, 2 m. W of I-40.

Greathouse Home/Museum. The reconstructed dogtrot log house (c.1830) is furnished as an 1870s pioneer home and includes a loom, spinning wheel, cannon-ball bed and hooked rugs. Courthouse Square.

Faulkner County Jail. National Historic Register, 1896. Since 1936 it has been the public library. Features: a pyramidal roof, a pointed corner tower and exposed earthquake rods. Courthouse Square.

Beaver Fork Lake. Besides boating, skiing and picnicking, this 900-acre city-owned lake has fishing for bluegill, catfish, crappie and bass. I-40 Exit US 65 or SR 25, appx. 2 m. N.

Brewer Lake. City-owned and operated, this 1,165-acre lake offers fishing for bluegill, crappie, catfish and bass. I-40, 13 m. W to Plumerville Exit; SR 92, 6 m. N.

Faulkner County Courthouse. English Regency Revival, 1936. Interior: The courtroom has a 20-foot ceiling; the fourth floor is the county jail. Grounds: a time capsule (2073) and a 20-foot granite monument to Confederate soldiers. US 65B, W on Main, just across RR tracks. *(County Profiles)*

National Historic Register. Many sites. Maps: chamber of commerce, US 65B, W on Oak, S on Parkway at Main.

CORNING
POP. 3,650   ALT. 291   MAP I-4

Hecth City was founded in 1872 (post office in 1873) by the Hecth brothers on the new grade of the Cairo & Fulton *Railroad,* but most people called it by the depot agent's name, Carpenter's Station. To further muddle recognition, the town divided. The southern half incorporated in 1873 under the name Corning, honoring the civil engineer who built the line; the

northern part joined the "new" town in 1878.

Meteorite. Around 1887 a two-foot piece of fallen star was unearthed in a farmer's field near Palatka. Courthouse Lawn.

Donham State Fish Hatchery. A federal hatchery since 1938, budget cuts closed it in 1983. Newly reopened by the state, two 110-foot wells provide warm water (50°–90°F) for raising catfish, crappie, bream, bass and other species for public and private purposes. US 62, 1 m. W.

Clay County Jail. This early 1900s jail stands deserted. The original cells and prisoners' graffiti are still intact. Next to the courthouse, 3rd St.

Events/Festivals. Annual Fourth of July Homecoming: Picnic, Barbeque, Carnival Rides.

Clay County Courthouse. Modern, 1966. *Dual County Seat.* This courthouse and its counterpart in *Piggott* were built in the same year by the same architect. Corning's burned; it requested building funds. Piggott tore its down, then requested the same. *(County Profiles)*

National Historic Register. Oliver House (1880), 203 W. Front. Sheeks House, 502 Market. SUCCESS, AR. (SR 328, NW of Clay Co.): Baynham House (1911) and Waddle House (1909), S. Erwin.

COTTER
POP. 920   ALT. 440   MAP A-4

"Trout Capital of the World" today, it was settled in 1868 and named Lake's Ferry (or Landing) in 1883. Bought in 1892, and then conveyed to the Red Bud Realty Company (1903), which laid it out for the arriving White River Railway Company's division point *(Mount Olive).* When incorporated (1905), 1,500 lots were sold. The downtown buildings, mostly stone, reflect the era, while the highway bridge, a cement "rainbow-arch," is from 1930. Named for either the railroad manager or for a local farmer.

Events/Festivals. Late May: Annual Craft Festival. Entertainment. Games.

COTTON PLANT
POP. 1,323   ALT. 192   MAP L-3

Richmond (formerly on the east side of present-day Cotton Plant) was said to have been settled as early as 1836 by P.P. Hill on Turkey Creek (and a later branch of the Memphis-Little Rock *Road* that ran to *Batesville).* In 1846 Wm. D. Lynch built a store and house. Local tradition claims cotton seeds brought with him from Mississippi accidentally sprouted next to his new home, prompting him to name it Cotton Plant. Application for a Richmond post office in 1852 was refused by Washington, D.C. (one already existed), but the suggestion of "Cotton Plant" was accepted.

Cotton Plant Cemetery. This cemetery records an interesting history, ranging through one Mexican War soldier and seven Civil War veterans to include one Wing Bow Gee ("Born in Canton, China; died June 13, 1945").

Civil War Skirmish. A large skirmish (July 7, 1862) took place at a crossroads on the P. P. Hill plantation during the first attempt to capture Little Rock *(Civil War)*. Near Town. Inquire Locally.

 COUNTY PROFILES
MAP ALL QUARTERS

The American model for counties was patterned after territorial divisions of Great Britain and Ireland (formerly Anglo-Saxon shires) that were used for administrative, judicial and political purposes.

In 1813, while still part of Missouri Territory, Arkansas' first county was established by the Missouri Territorial Legislature when it changed the District of Arkansas into Arkansas County. This county (extending into parts of present-day Oklahoma) included all of what is now Arkansas except for the northeast and extreme north, which were later filled in when Lawrence County was added in 1815 by the Missouri Territorial Legislature. Three other counties were established before Arkansas became a territory in 1819: Clark, Hempstead and Pulaski (all in 1818).

Today, Arkansas has 75 counties (with 85 county seats, *Dual County Seats)*. The following list of counties, which includes dates created, namesakes, progeny counties and county seats, was compiled by the Arkansas Historical Commission.

Arkansas County. Created December 13, 1813, from the District of Arkansas, Missouri Territory, it was named for the Quapaw Nation *(Arkansawyer, Trail of Tears)*. County Seats: *DeWitt, Stuttgart.*

Ashley County. Created November 30, 1848, from Chicot, Drew and Union Counties, it was named in honor of Chester Ashley, a U.S. senator who died in office in April of 1848. County Seat: Hamburg.

Baxter County. Created March 24, 1873, from Fulton, Izard, Marion and Searcy Counties, it was named in honor of Elisha Baxter, last Republican governor (1873-74) of Arkansas until Winthrop Rockefeller in 1966 *(Civil War)*. County Seat: *Mountain Home.*

Benton County. Created September 30, 1836, from Washington County, it was named for Thomas Hart Benton *(Bentonville)*. County Seat: *Bentonville.*

Boone County. Created April 9, 1869, from Carroll and Madison Counties, it was supposedly named for Daniel Boone (1734-1820), the legendary frontiersman. NOTE: Others claim that the county name was formerly spelled "Boon" for the boon its formation would cause for the new residents. County Seat: *Harrison.*

Bradley County. Created December 18, 1840, from Union County, it was named for Hugh Bradley, an early settler, a member of the Arkansas Territorial Legislature and a prosperous local farmer at the time the county was formed. County Seat: *Warren.*

Calhoun County. Created December 6, 1850, from Dallas,

Ouachita and Union Counties, it was named in honor of the outspoken Southern U.S. congressman (later vice-president under James Monroe) John C. Calhoun, who died in 1850. County Seat: *Hampton.*

Carroll County. Created November 1, 1833, from Izard County, it was named for Maryland resident Charles Carroll, last surviving signer (1832) of the Declaration of Independence, whose signature on that document read: Charles Carroll of Carrollton. County Seats: *Berryville, Eureka Springs.*

Chicot County. Created October 25, 1823, from Arkansas County, it was named for Point Chicot *(Lake Village)*. County Seat: *Lake Village.*

Clark County. Created December 15, 1818, from Arkansas County while still a part of Missouri Territory, it was named in honor of William Clark, governor of Missouri (1813-21) and a member of the Lewis and Clark expedition that explored the Northwest (1804-06). County Seat: *Arkadelphia.*

Clay County. Created March 24, 1873, as Clayton County (changed to Clay on December 6, 1875). Formed from Randolph and Greene Counties, it was named for John M. Clayton, a member of the Arkansas Senate when the county was created and brother of Powell Clayton *(Eureka Springs)*, who was the first Reconstruction governor of Arkansas (1868-71). NOTE: Some say the name was changed because of political disapproval of Powell Clayton, and that Clay was adopted for the noted Southern statesman, Henry Clay. County Seats: *Corning, Piggott.*

Anglo - Saxon shires were used as the political models for American counties

---

Cleburne County. Created February 20, 1883, from Independence, Van Buren and White Counties, it is the youngest county in Arkansas and was named for Patrick R. Cleburne, noted Confederate major-general who was killed in the Battle of Franklin in Tennessee. County Seat: *Heber Springs.*

Cleveland County. Created April 17, 1873, from Bradley, Dallas, Jefferson and Lincoln Counties, and first named Dorsey for Stephen W. Dorsey, a U.S. senator from Arkansas when the county was organized, the name was changed March 5, 1885, to honor President Grover Cleveland (1885-89; 1893-97). It is said that Dorsey so politically discredited himself that the county voted to change the name. County Seat: *Rison.*

Columbia County. Created December 17, 1852, from Hempstead, Lafayette, Ouachita and Union Counties, it was reportedly named for "a poetical appellation in honor of Columbus," the explorer who is credited with discovering America in 1492. County Seat: *Magnolia.*

Conway County. Created October 20, 1825, from Pulaski County, it was named for Henry W. Conway, Territorial representative to the U.S. Congress (1823-25-27) and brother of James S. Conway, first (1836-40) governor of Arkansas *(Walnut Hill)*. County Seat: *Morrilton.*

Craighead County. Created February 19, 1859, from Mississippi, Greene and Poinsett Counties, it was named in honor of State Senator Thomas B. Craighead. County Seats: *Jonesboro, Lake City.*

Crawford County. Created October 18, 1820, from Pulaski County, it was named for William H. Crawford, American statesman and U.S. secretary of the Treasury when the county was formed. County Seat: *Van Buren.*

Crittenden County. Created on October 22, 1825, from Phillips County, it was named for Robert Crittenden who, as an influential Territorial politician, was Arkansas' first Territorial secretary in 1819 (and acting governor much of his first eight years in office). County Seat: *Marion.*

Faulkner County's namesake originated the fiddle tune, "The Arkansas Traveler"

Cross County. Created November 15, 1862, from Crittenden, Poinsett and St. Francis Counties, it was named for David C. Cross, a local landowner and Confederate colonel in 1862. NOTE: Some say the county's namesake is Edward Cross, Territorial judge, U.S. congressman (1939-45) and Arkansas Supreme Court judge (1845-46). County Seat: *Wynne.*

Dallas County. Created January 1, 1845, from Bradley and Clark Counties, it was named in honor of U.S. Vice-President George M. Dallas (James K. Polk administration, 1845-49). County Seat: *Fordyce.*

Desha County. Created December 12, 1838, from Arkansas County, it was named in honor of Benjamin Desha, an Arkansas Territory politician and wealthy landowner. County Seat: *Arkansas City.*

Drew County. Created November 26, 1846, from Bradley County, and named for Thomas S. Drew *(Pocahontas),* governor (1844-49), who resigned after two months into his second term as governor because the salary was "insufficient". County Seat: *Monticello.*

Faulkner County. Created April 12, 1873, from Conway and Pulaski Counties, it was named for Sanford C. (Sandy) Faulkner, a "colorful character" and storyteller who is credited with originating the dialogue and fiddle tune of "The Arkansas Traveler" (Norristown, *Russellville*). County Seat: *Conway.*

Franklin County. Created on December 19, 1837, from Crawford County, it was named for noted statesman and inventor Benjamin Franklin. County Seats: *Charleston, Ozark.*

Fulton County. Created December 21, 1842, from Izard County, it was named for William S. Fulton, secretary (1828) and then last governor (1835-36) of Arkansas Territory, and U.S. senator (1836-44). County Seat: *Salem.*

Garland County. Created April 5, 1873, from Hot Spring, Montgomery and Saline Counties, it was named in honor of Augustus H. Garland, governor (1874-77), U.S. senator (1877-85) and U.S attorney general (1885-89, *Garland*). County Seat: *Hot Springs.*

Grant County. Created February 4, 1869, from Hot Spring, Jefferson and Saline Counties, it was named for former Union general, then president (1869-77), Ulysses S. Grant *(Sheridan).* County Seat: *Sheridan.*

Greene County. Created November 5, 1833, from Lawrence County, it was reportedly named for Revolutionary War hero Nathaniel Greene. County Seat: *Paragould.*

Hempstead County. Created on December 15, 1818, from Arkansas County, while still a part of Missouri Territory, it was named for Edward Hempstead, an influential Territorial lawyer and politician, who died in 1817. County Seat: *Hope.*

Hot Spring County. Created on November 2, 1829, from Clark County, it was named for the hot springs *(Hot Springs)* that once were included in this county (see Garland County, ABOVE). County Seat: *Malvern.*

Howard County. Created April 17, 1873, from Hempstead, Pike, Polk and Sevier Counties, it was named for James H. Howard, who was a state senator from that district when the county was formed. County Seat: *Nashville.*

Independence County. Created October 20, 1820, from Lawrence County, it is said to have been named in honor of the independence won by the American Revolution. County Seat: *Batesville.*

Izard County. Created October 27, 1825, from Independence County, it was named in honor of George Izard while he was serving as second governor of Arkansas Territory (1825-29). County Seat: *Melbourne.*

Jackson County. Created November 5, 1829, from Independence County, it was named for President Andrew Jackson (1829-37). County Seat: *Newport.*

Jefferson County. Created on November 2, 1829, from Arkansas and Pulaski Counties, it was named for President Thomas Jefferson (1801-09). County Seat: *Pine Bluff.*

Johnson County. Created November 16, 1833, from Pope County, it was named for Benjamin Johnson, a member of the Arkansas Territorial Supreme Court at the time the county was formed. County Seat: *Clarksville.*

Hot Spring County was named for the hot springs now included in Garland County

---

Lafayette County. Created October 15, 1827, from Hempstead County, it was named for the French marquis LaFayette, who became an American folk hero during the Revolutionary War. County Seat: *Lewisville.*

Lawrence County. Created January 15, 1815, from New Madrid County, Missouri, it was named for James Lawrence, a Naval captain during the War of 1812 who, when fatally wounded in a sea battle in 1813, is credited with originating the now-famous battle cry: "Don't give up the ship." County Seat: *Walnut Ridge.*

Lee County. Created on April 17, 1873, from Crittenden, Monroe, Phillips and St. Francis Counties, it was named for the commanding general of the Confederacy, Robert E. Lee. County Seat: *Marianna.*

Lincoln County. Created March 28, 1871, from Arkansas,

Bradley, Desha, Drew and Jefferson Counties, it was named for Abraham Lincoln, one of America's most honored presidents (1861-65). County Seat: *Star City*.

Little River County. Created on March 5, 1867, from Hempstead and Sevier Counties, it was named for the Little River, which forms the northern and eastern boundaries of the county. County Seat: *Ashdown*.

Logan County. Created March 22, 1871, as Sarber County (changed to Logan, December 14, 1875), it was formed from Franklin, Johnson, Scott and Yell Counties. J. Newton Sarber, a state senator and former Union soldier, reportedly lost the honor of having the county named for him to James Logan (an influential pioneer settler who died in 1859) because county constituents disapproved of the honor being bestowed on a Yankee *(Booneville)*. County Seats: *Booneville, Paris*.

Lonoke County is the only Arkansas county whose name corresponds with its county seat

---

Lonoke County. Created April 16, 1873, from Prairie and Pulaski Counties, it was named in honor of the city of Lonoke (and county seat), which was named for a lone oak tree used as a survey marker *(Lonoke)*. Lonoke is the only county seat in Arkansas whose name corresponds with its county's. County Seat: *Lonoke*.

Lovely County. Created October 13, 1827, from Crawford County and the Lovely Purchase, it was named for Major Wm. L. Lovely, Indian agent and the negotiator for the land bought from the Osage Nation that was used as part of the county. Abolished October 17, 1828 *(Boundary Lines)*.

Madison County. Created on September 30, 1836, from Washington and Carroll Counties, it was named for President James Madison (1809-17), who died June 28, 1836. Incidentally, the original settlers of the area came from Huntsville, Madison County, Alabama. County Seat: *Huntsville*.

Marion County. Created on November 3, 1835, as Searcy County but changed to Marion, September 29, 1836. Formed from Izard County, it was initially named for Richard Searcy, an early pioneer and Territorial Supreme Court judge, but was changed (no recorded reason) to honor the Revolutionary War hero, Gen. Francis Marion ("The Swamp Fox"). In 1838 Marion County was divided east-west, and the new southern part was named Searcy. Traditionally, the two counties have had conflicting political philosophies. Today, Marion is predominantly Democratic while Searcy is mostly Republican. County Seat: *Yellville*.

Miller County (Old). Created April 1, 1820, from Hempstead County, it was named in honor of James Miller, first governor (1819-25) of Arkansas Territory. Abolished in 1838 *(Boundary Lines)*.

Miller County. Created December 22, 1874, from Lafayette County, it was named in honor of the former ("Old") Miller County. County Seat: *Texarkana*.

Mississippi County. Created on November 1, 1833, from

Crittenden County, it was named for the Mississippi River. County Seats: *Blytheville, Osceola*.

Monroe County. Created November 2, 1829, from Arkansas and Phillips Counties, and named in honor of President James Monroe (1817-25). County Seat: *Clarendon*.

Montgomery County. Created on December 9, 1842, from Hot Spring County, it was named in honor of Richard Montgomery, a general killed during the Revolutionary War. County Seat: *Mount Ida*.

Nevada County. Created March 20, 1871, from Columbia, Hempstead and Ouachita Counties, it was named for the state of Nevada, although locally it is pronounced knee-VAY-dah. County Seat: *Prescott*.

Newton County. Created December 14, 1842, from Carroll County, it was named in honor of Thomas W. Newton, whose careers ranged from carrying the mail between Arkansas Post *(National Parks)* and *Cadron* to serving in the Territorial and state legislatures.

Ouachita County. Created on November 29, 1842, from Union County, it was named for the Ouachita River, which flows north-south through the county, and forms its southeastern boundary. County Seat: *Camden*.

Perry County. Created December 18, 1840, from Conway County, it was named in honor of Naval officer Oliver H. Perry (American Revolution and War of 1812), who, after destroying a British squadron during the Battle of Lake Erie in 1813, sent the now-famous message: "We have met the enemy and they are ours." County Seat: *Perryville*.

Phillips County. Created on May 1, 1820, from Arkansas County, it was named for Sylvanus Phillips, land speculator and founder of Helena. County Seat: *Helena*.

Poinsett County's namesake, Joel R. Poinsett, is also namesake of the plant, poinsettia

---

Pike County. Created on November 1, 1833, from Clark and Hempstead Counties, it was named in honor of Zebulon Pike, famous explorer (Pike's Peak) whose western expeditions and adventures from 1805-10 cover three volumes. Killed in 1813 during the War of 1812. County Seat: *Murfreesboro*.

Poinsett County. Created February 28, 1838, from Greene and St. Francis Counties, it was named for Joel R. Poinsett *(Fort Smith)*, U.S congressman and diplomat who, while U.S. minister to Mexico in 1828, discovered the plant that was named (poinsettia) for him. County Seat: *Harrisburg*.

Polk County. Created November 30, 1844, from Sevier County, it was named for newly elected President James K. Polk (1845-49). County Seat: *Mena*.

Pope County. Created November 2, 1829, from Crawford County, it was named in honor of John Pope while serving as the third governor of Arkansas Territory (1829-35). County Seat: *Russellville*.

Prairie County. Created November 25, 1846, from Pulaski County, it was named for the Grand Prairie *(Carlisle)*. County

Seats: *Des Arc, DeValls Bluff.*

Pulaski County. Created on December 15, 1818, from Arkansas County while still a part of Missouri Territory, it was named for Count Casimir Pulaski, a Polish nobleman and expatriate killed fighting in the American Revolution. County Seat: *Little Rock.*

Randolph County. Created on October 29, 1835, from Lawrence County, it was named in honor of John Randolph, a noted orator and American statesman from Virginia. County Seat: *Pocahontas.*

St. Francis County. Created on October 13, 1827, from Phillips County, and named for the St. Francis River, which bisects the county north-south. County Seat: *Forrest City.*

Saline County. Created November 2, 1835, from Pulaski County, it was named for the Saline River, which mostly bisects the county north-south. County Seat: *Benton.*

Scott County. Created November 5, 1833, from Crawford and Pope Counties, it was named for Andrew Scott, a member of the first Arkansas Territorial Supreme Court *(Russellville, Scotia).* County Seat: *Waldron.*

Searcy County. Created December 13, 1838, from Marion County, it was named for Richard Searcy, a pioneer and Territorial Supreme Court judge (see Marion County, ABOVE). County Seat: *Marshall.*

Sebastian County. Created January 6, 1851, from Crawford, Scott and Polk Counties, it was named for Wm. K. Sebastian, prominent state politician and U.S. senator when the county was formed. County Seats: *Fort Smith, Greenwood.*

Sevier County. Created October 17, 1828, from Hempstead and Miller Counties, it was named for Ambrose H. Sevier, influential Territorial and state politician as well as Arkansas' first U.S senator (1836-48). County Seat: *De Queen.*

Sharp County. Created on July 18, 1868, from Lawrence County, it was named for Ephariam Sharp, an early settler of that area and a member of the state legislature when the county was formed. County Seat: *Ash Flat.*

Stone County. Created on April 21, 1873, from Izard, Van Buren, Independence and Searcy Counties, it was named for the geography of the area. County Seat: *Mountain View.*

Union County. Created on November 2, 1829, from Clark and Hempstead Counties, it was named for the Federal Union. County Seat: *El Dorado.*

Van Buren County. Created on November 11, 1833, from Conway, Izard and Independence Counties, it was named in honor of then Vice-President Martin Van Buren (under President Andrew Jackson), who later became president (1837-41). County Seat: *Clinton.*

Washington County. Created on October 17, 1828, from Crawford and Lovely Counties, it was named for America's first and most honored president (1789-97), George Washington. County Seat: *Fayetteville.*

White County. Created October 23, 1835, from Independence, Jackson and Pulaski Counties, it was named either for the White River, which forms its eastern boundary line, or for Hugh Lawson White, a U.S. senator from Tennessee who, at that time, had close personal and political ties with President

Andrew Jackson. County Seat: *Searcy.*

Woodruff County. Created on November 26, 1862, from Jackson and St. Francis Counties, it was named in honor of Wm. E. Woodruff, the founder and publisher of Arkansas' first newspaper (today the oldest west of the Mississippi River), The Arkansas Gazette. County Seat: *Augusta.*

Yell County. Created on December 5, 1840, from Pope and Scott Counties, it was named for Archibald Yell *(Yellville, Washington),* Arkansas' first U.S. congressman and its second governor (1840-44). Yell died fighting (1847) in the Mexican-American War. County Seats: *Danville, Dardanelle.*

CROSSETT
POP. 6,706   ALT. 164   MAP P-2

Built by the Crossett Lumber Company in 1902 for the families of the men logging 920 square miles of Southern pine, its company/town manager, "Cap" Gates, had the houses painted (both inside and out) "Crossett" gray. Today, Georgia-Pacific's wood-product mills, among the world's largest, employ 3,000 and manage 500,000 acres of pine. Home of Forest Echoes Vocational Technical School.

City Park. The park features a log cabin, a zoo, picnic shelters and a 51-acre fishing pond surrounded by a 3.5-mile jogging/nature *trail.* US 82, S on T-133. WIGGINS CABIN: National Historic Register, c.1830. Relocated with cypress logs intact from *Bayou Bartholomew,* this box-notched log cabin was authentically restored. A mix of local soils for the handmade bricks were fired (using green hickory) for six days. Furnished. KONG CROSSLAND ZOO: Mostly a small animal zoo, it has, among others: monkeys, raccoons, peacocks, alligators and bears.

Levi Wilcoxon Memorial Forest. Natural Heritage Area. Not only pines, but other trees and plants are identified within a 15-acre forest divided into three distinct types of timberland: Virgin Forests (pines of 150 to 250-years-old), Second [growth] Forests (seedlings to 70-years-old) and Third Forests (new types of seedlings producing usable timber in less than 40 years). *Trails.* US 82W, near Jct. SR 81. Signs.

Events/Festivals. Fourth of July: Family Fun Day. Bar-B-Q. Baseball. Fireworks. Mid-Aug: Crossett PRCA Rodeo.

CROWLEY'S RIDGE
MAP BEGINS I-5 & ENDS M-4

Named for Benjamin F. Crowley, a veteran of the War of 1812 who later settled at present-day Crowley's Ridge *State Park,* this unusual natural phenomenon, varying in width from a half mile up to 12 miles, has been a landmark and overland trail through the river bottoms since prehistoric times. Stretching in a shallow arc from the corner of northeast Arkansas at *St. Francis* to near mid-state at *Helena,* the Ridge is an erosional remnant, a highland between two valleys formed by the Mississippi River flowing to the west of it and the Ohio to the east *(Bayou Bartholomew)*. Diversion of the Mississippi to its present course may have been caused by a tectonic uplift in southeast Missouri about 18,000 years ago. Loess (deposits varying in consistency from loam and clay to fine sand on top of the ridge) range from nearly zero feet at Jonesboro to about 50 feet near Helena. It was either trapped (wind-formed) by the already existing ridge or accumulated (as silt) during its early stages. Adding to the uniqueness of this formation is its forest vegetation, which is more like hardwood forests found east of the Mississippi River and in the Appalachian Mountains than in Arkansas. (Introduction, *Why There Is An Arkansas*)

CRYSTAL SPRINGS
COMMUNITY   ALT. 814   MAP E-3

A 1930s recreational area, the clear spring comes from the base of Crystal Mountain, a sandstone formation laced with veins of rose and yellow quartz crystal.

Lake Ouachita Vista. A panoramic view of the lake can be enjoyed from from this overlook or from a U.S. Forest Service fire tower. *(Lakes)*. US 270, 6 m. W; 4 m. N on FR 50.

Womble-Silver Road. On this noteworthy 18-mile stretch of gravel road are the Crystal Mountain Scenic Area (100-acre stand of virgin pine and hardwood), a fire tower offering long views of the Ouachitas and the largest white pine in Arkansas (Crystal Campground, Ouachita *National Forest*). SR 8, 19 m. E to Norman, appx.1 m. N on SR 27 to FS 177 E.

DANVILLE
POP. 1,698   ALT. 387   MAP D-3

The only Arkansas city known to be named for a riverboat, its site was chosen in 1841 as a central location on the Petit Jean *River* as county seat of newly (1840) created Yell County. The Danville continued to work the river during the 1840s.

Events/Festivals. HAVANA, AR. (SR 10, 8 m. W): Early June: Mount Magazine Run (14K) up *Mount Magazine* (Alt. 2,753 feet).

Yell County Courthouse. Seventies Modern, 1975. *Dual County Seat (Dardanelle)*. Features: Arkansas' only courtroom entered from an outside door and brass footrails (made in Italy) for the judge's bench and jury box. *(County Profiles)*

DARDANELLE
POP. 3,621   ALT. 325   MAP C-3

This 300-foot rocky peak jutting into the *Arkansas River* has always been a clear landmark but the name for it and the town are shrouded in history. Some choices are: Dardonnie (of Indian origin, said to mean to sleep with one eye open; whether it refers to an Indian sentinel on top of the rock or the personification of its shape is unclear), Dardenne (the original 1798 Spanish land-grantee) and Dardanelles (for the straits in the

Mediterranean Sea, which the Rock supposedly resembles). The town began as a Cherokee trading post in 1819 and was platted in 1847 by J.H. Bearley, who also laid out *Dover*. County seat in 1875.

Dardanelle Rock. Natural Heritage Area. Sandstone, eroded and partially barren. A 20-minute hike will bring a sure-footed climber to the top and to a spectacular view of *Mt. Nebo, Petit Jean Mountain, Russellville* and the *Arkansas River*. Halfway down the Rock, the 41-ton city water tank is a wonder itself. Somehow put on top in the 1890s, it was moved to its present position in 1939. Courthouse, W to the end of N. Front St.

Council Oaks. In 1820, under the shade of these two oak trees, the Cherokee Nation agreed by treaty to cede all lands south of the Arkansas River. Eight years later the Cherokee relinquished all claims in northern Arkansas, relocating to the present state of Oklahoma *(Trail of Tears)*. Courthouse, W on N. Front St. to Hickory.

Trees Of Distinction. Among the 22 varieties of state and national champions, magnolias over 100 years old line Front and Second as well as other streets. Maps: chamber of commerce, SR 7, 5 blks. S of courthouse.

Arkansas River Visitor Center and Lock & Dam. *(Russellville)* Recreation: *Lake* Dardanelle.

Events/Festivals. Mid-May/June: Mount Nebo Chicken Fry. Family-Oriented. 10K Run. Music. Entertainment.

Yell County Courthouse. Classical Revival, 1914. *Dual County Seat (Danville)*. Features: an ornate cupola and four large columns. Grounds: a six-foot marble statue of a Confederate soldier and historical markers. SR 7, at the river. *(County Profiles)*

National Historic Register. Kimball House (1871), 713 N. Front St. Steamboat House (1889), 601 N. Front.

DE QUEEN
POP. 4,594   ALT. 405   MAP F-1

Names (Calamity, Hurrah City and De Queen) tell the story of a town finally built by the Kansas City Southern Railway (Texarkana & Ft. Smith *Railroad)* with the help of Holland's Queen Wilhelmina and a Dutch investor, John A. DeGeoijen *(Mena)*. Incorporated in 1897, it was supposedly named after DeGeoijen (said to be pronounced De Wheen; later "Americanized" to De Queen). However, the city's newspaper, the De Queen Bee, which was also established in 1897, makes this supposition suspect. Incidentally, according to the De Queen Bee, there is a space in the town's name, De Queen, but in keeping with the the name's uncertain origins, the newspaper also notes that city limit signs spell it with and without the space. Home of Cossatot Vocational Technical School. Possible *De Soto* Route.

Crossroads. US 70 (East Coast-Phoenix) and US 71 (Canada-Gulf of Mexico) cross at downtown.

Ultima Thule. The name is from Latin, loosely translated as "the end of the world." This ghost town (1833-1900) on the Fort Towson *Road* was the last stop before Choctaw Territory. Two yellow houses mark the old townsite. US 70W at the border.

Salt Slough/Little River Lick. *(Arkadelphia,* Hemphill Salt Mines) Now called Salt Lake, it provided salt for the Caddoes, and then for settlers before and during the Civil War ($4 a bushel). Historically a valuable commodity, salt is the origin of the word salary. US 70, 4 m. W.

Sevier County Courthouse. Neo -Classical Revival, 1932. Grounds: a WW II howitzer and several huge pin oak trees. *(County Profiles)*

National Historic Register. Hayes Hardware Store, built c.1900, 214 De Queen.

DE SOTO, HERNANDO
MAP POSSIBLE EXPLORATION

Conflicting theories present probable routes taken by De Soto. The first (•) has been supported since the 1930s and is based on historical evidence and three journals kept by members of the expedition. The second (••) applies the journals and former historical findings to recent archaeological evidence. No consensus has been reached, although each agrees that the king of Spain ordered De Soto to explore the interior of "Florida," and that he eventually crossed the Mississippi River in 1541. In both versions he was searching for gold. All town references are approximate. (•) Probably setting foot on Arkansas soil at Sunflower Landing (20 miles south of *Helena),* he first trav-

eled north to the mouth of the St. Francis River, doubled back to the *Arkansas River* near Arkansas Post *(National Park),* following it to *Little Rock* and then cross-country through *Hot Springs* to *Caddo Gap,* where he was turned back by the Caddoes who forced him down the Caddo and Ouachita Rivers to a winter camp at either *Camden* or *Calion.* Leaving Arkansas in 1542, De Soto died in Louisiana and was buried in the Mississippi River. (••) Unlike the preceding in every respect, De Soto spent two winters in Arkansas and died in Arkansas. Landing near Horseshoe *Lake* (SR 147, S of *West Memphis),* the expedition moved NW near *Greasy Corner* to *Parkin,* then east to the Mississippi River near the Crittenden-Mississippi County line and back to Parkin. From there it went NW via *Newport* to *Batesville,* turning south past *Searcy, Conway* and *Morrilton* to Galla Rock (near *Atkins)* where it crossed the Arkansas River to Bluffton on the Fourche La Fave River, moving SE to the Caddo River and then east thru *Benton* to winter at Redfield (US 65, 20 m. S of Little Rock). In 1542 De Soto moved to Arkansas Post *(National Parks)* and then south to McArthur (SR 1, 5 m. N of *McGehee),* where he died May 21, 1542. The expedition, attempting to return overland to New Spain, cut west across the state between *Malvern* and *Arkadelphia* and then through *Murfreesboro* and *De Queen* to drop down into Oklahoma and Texas, possibly to the Trinity River, only to backtrack to Arkansas Post, wintering somewhere between *Lake View* and Deerfield (SR 44/85, 32 m. S of Lake View). In June of 1543, the remnant of the expedition departed Arkansas down the Mississippi River.

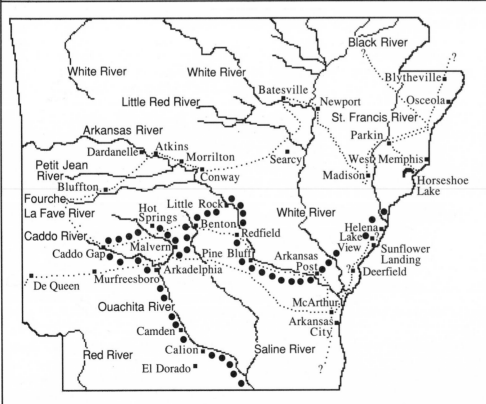

De Soto Expedition

The map shows two proposed routes that De Soto may have taken during his search for gold in Arkansas. These generalized routes are based on journals kept by three of his men and on archaeological evidence.

• Expedition arrives in 1541 at Sunflower Landing, spends one winter and leaves via the Ouachita River in 1542.

•• Expedition arrives in 1541 near Horseshoe Lake, spends two winters and leaves via the Mississippi River in 1543.

NOTE:
All towns listed are present-day

DERMOTT
POP. 4,731   ALT. 140   MAP O-3

First settled in 1832 by Yale University graduate Dr. Charles McDermott, whose large plantation and house also served as a stopover on the route from Gaines Landing *(Halley)* to points west on the Fort Towson *Road*. Much of McDermott's time and fortune were spent designing flying machines in an era without any means of powering them; however, he was granted a patent for one in 1872. Bartholomew, a c.1838 post office, was eventually replaced by Bend (a few miles west) in 1875, which was renamed Dermott in 1877. The arrival of the St. Louis, Iron Mountain & Southern *(Railroad)* in 1887 created a prosperous crossroads town. Incorporated 1890.

Arkansas Lobster. Shipped as far away as China, Finland, Saudi Arabia and Peru, the crawfish or crawdad or even crayfish is said to taste "something like a shrimp; maybe on the lobster side." Dermott has proclaimed itself "Home of" and sponsors a festival each May.

Wallace Lake. The Arkansas Game and Fish Commission stocks this 300-acre lake with bluegill, crappie, bass and catfish. Fishing Only. US 165, S 5 m.

DES ARC
POP. 2,001   ALT. 198   MAP L-2

One of the older *river* ports in the state (settled c.1810), it was laid out in two separate plats by two owners (1846-49). The crooked bayou just north has been carried on maps as Bayou des Arc since the 1820s. The population jumped from about 100 in 1850 to over 2,000 by 1860 when White River steamers took out 13,000 bales of cotton (a bale weighed appx. 500 lbs.). Besides shipping downstream, it was also a receiving point for north- and west-bound freight and passengers *(Cabot)* as well as a stop on the *Butterfield Overland Mail*. County seat since 1875.

Prairie County Museum. The museum features a general store, kitchen and parlor furnished from 19th century prairie life as well as displays of clothing, dolls, toys and other items from the same era. Sharing the grounds: a 150-year-old wagon and a replica of a dogtrot log cabin. SR 38 & 11.

Dr. Charles McDermott was granted a patent for a flying machine in 1872

Ginko Tree. Reportedly the largest one in Arkansas is across from the high school on Main St. In Town.

Lake Des Arc. Adjacent to Des Arc Bayou, this 350-acre lake has bass, crappie, bream and catfish, and is a favorite local weekend camping spot. Boat ramp at SW end but bank fishing is also popular. No commercial facilities. SR 11, 4 m. N.

Prairie County Courthouse. Italianate with a complex mixture of Classicism and Medievalism, 1913. National Historic Register. *Dual County Seat (DeValls Bluff).* Set on the west bank of the White River, it has an elaborate clock tower that strikes the hour. Inside is a large collection of confiscated drug paraphernalia, including pipes ranging from carved ivory to glass telephone pole insulators. Main St. *(County Profiles)*

National Historic Register. Bedford Brown Bethel House (1912), 2nd & Curron. Bethel House, 2nd & Erwin. Frith-Plunkett House (1858), 8th & Main.

DEVALLS BLUFF
POP. 738   ALT. 187   MAP L-2

Settled in the 1840s, this town has had a series of confused names, beginning with its founder's, a Frenchman, DuVall, whose initials have been recorded in histories as C.S., O.S. and C.C. The town was mislabeled as Lake Bluff on maps in the 1850s and 1860s, then listed as DuValls Bluff in the 1860s and 1870s. Although the name DuValls Bluff has never been "officially" changed, tradition claims that when the Memphis & Little Rock *Railroad* was completed from Little Rock to here in 1861, it spelled the town's name DeVall's Bluff and it is recorded as such in State Incorporation Act #58 of 1867. (Incidentally, DuVall is a common name; Maj. E.W. DuVall in 1828 was Pope County's last Indian agent.) When first occupied during the *Civil War* as a Federal supply depot, there were only one store and a house at this White *River* landing. The area then swelled to a reported 35,000 (soldiers, refugees and carpetbaggers), making it at that time the most populated site in Arkansas. Selected county seat twice: 1868-1875 *(Des Arc)*, 1885-present.

Prairie County Courthouse. Neo-Classic, 1939. *Dual County Seat (Des Arc).* This two-story brick building has ornate pressed-tin ceilings and foot-wide wooden baseboards. The cornerstone is from its 1910 predecessor. Grounds: an oak with an 11-foot circumference. *(County Profiles)*

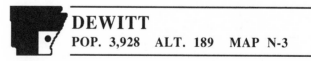

DEWITT
POP. 3,928   ALT. 189   MAP N-3

An Indian village until 1816, the location was selected as county seat in 1852 and platted in 1854. Its name was literally picked out of a hat. The site selection commissioners and surveyor Adam McCool drew slips of paper. The winner, McCool, was an admirer of DeWitt Clinton (sponsor of the Erie Canal and a New York politician). The last name was already an Arkansas post office, so the first was used. Home of Rice Belt Vocational Technical School.

Arkansas County Courthouse. Moderne, 1932. *Dual County Seat (Stuttgart).* Succeeding *Arkansas Post* as county seat, it now has the oldest civil records in the state. Some dating from 1796 show land titles written in French, Spanish and English; however, most of the oldest were taken to Cuba before Spain ceded (again) the Louisiana Territory to France in

1800. *(County Profiles)*
National Historic Register. Halliburton House (1850), 300 W. Halliburton.

DOVER
POP. 948   ALT. 447   MAP C-3

Already a settlement by 1829, the name of this historic cross-*roads* town is obscured by legends. The original plat reads in part: "Laid off into lots by Commissioners Steven Rye and R.W. Jamison with R.S. Witt, the surveyor, in October, A.D. 1843. Plotted by J.H. Brearly [also Brearley], Droughtsman and Typographical Surveyor, etc." Both Rye and Brearly are said to have named Dover for their hometowns: Tennessee and Delaware, respectively. Both also are said to have named it for Dover, England. Selected county seat in 1841, it was, ironically, the site of the first meeting (1853) of the Little Rock & Ft. Smith *Railroad,* which eventually caused Dover's decline by establishing *Russellville* in 1873 (next county seat, 1887). Incorporated 1870.
Salt Pot. The pot, which measures six feet in diameter, was reportedly used by Cherokees to evaporate spring water when making salt. Town Square. Sign.
Old Lake Graveyard. This pioneer cemetery is tucked away in a secluded part of town, and has headstones of the founding families. Signs at town square.
The Record Cave. An historic marker locates the cave where the Pope County records were hidden during the *Civil War*. These records (now stored at the county courthouse in Russellville) date from the original 1829 county seat, Norristown *(Russellville)*. SR 7, 3 m. N.

DUAL COUNTY SEATS
MAP ALL QUARTERS

Of Arkansas' 75 counties, 10 have dual county seats *(County Profiles)*. Historically, the need for two county seats was a geographical necessity. While a courthouse location might have been central, access was restricted by inadequate roads and by bridgeless and unpredictable rivers. Today, these geographical encumbrances are no longer a factor, and most counties have consolidated their county seats *(Ash Flat),* although a few still maintain the tradition by popular vote in spite of the extra expense for maintaining two county governments. For example, *Berryville's* and *Eureka Springs'* county seats are separated by less than 15 miles, making them the closest county seats of the same county in Arkansas. Below are listed the 10 counties with their dual county seats in parentheses: Arkansas *(Stuttgart and DeWitt),* Carroll *(Berryville and Eureka Springs),* Clay *(Corning and Piggott),* Craighead *(Jonesboro and Lake City),* Franklin *(Charleston and Ozark),* Logan *(Booneville and Paris),* Mississippi *(Blytheville and Osceola),* Prairie *(Des Arc and DeValls Bluff),* Sebastian *(Greenwood and Fort Smith)* and Yell *(Danville and Dardanelle).*

DUMAS
POP. 6,091   ALT. 166   MAP O-2

The town wasn't named for the French novelist, nor was it named for the popular 1920s ragtime tune, "Ding Dong Daddy From Dumas," which was inspired by its baseball team and adopted as the city's anthem. W.B. Dumas bought the land for $1.25 an acre in 1851. He built a general store and a cotton gin but the site wasn't incorporated until 1904.
Desha County Museum. Replicas of a mercantile store, bank, doctor's office, school room and post office recreate "the old days" of Dumas. Also displayed: a replica of Eli Whitney's cotton gin, a collection of Sunbeam mixers from the local plant, a log house (c.1850) and collections of other historical items like clothing, toys and books. In town, SR 54.
Events/Festivals. Late July: Ding Dong Days. Music. Bands. Games. Car Show. Early Nov: Annual Delta Arts & Crafts Fair. GOULD, AR. (US 65, 7 m. N): Mid-Aug: Annual Gould Turtle Derby. Turtle Races. Bands. Bar-B-Q. Bingo.
National Historic Register. Merchants & Farmers Bank, Waterman & Main.

DYESS
POP. 446   ALT. 228   MAP K-5

Founded in 1934 as an agricultural cooperative project *(Resettlement Administration),* it was named for W.R. Dyess (first *WPA* administrator in Arkansas). These 16,000 acres of overflow land were divided into 500 individually operated farms of 20 to 40 acres on which small houses with a garden and barn were built, using a five-year lease/40-year mortgage arrangement. Social and business services (from a hospital and school to gins and repair shops) were collectively owned and operated by the community. Today, no longer a cooperative, the remaining farmers have 200- to 300-acre tracts and financial arrangements with the FHA. Nearly 100 of the original houses and the administration building are still intact.

EL DORADO
POP. 25,270   ALT. 286   MAP H-4

El Dorado (locally, L Doe-RAY-doe) is the only major town in Arkansas that cannot trace its beginnings to an historic road, a railroad or a river *(Calion)*. In 1829 Union County included the five counties surrounding it today. As these counties were carved out, the county seats shifted to more central locations*(Camden, Warren)*. When county seat Union Courthouse *(Calion,* Champagnolle Landing) was deemed inconveniently located, El Dorado (more of a location than a town) was selected in 1844. A colorful local story claims the town was founded by Matthew F. Rainey where his wagon broke down. Partly true, he did arrive from New Orleans by wagon in 1843 with a small stock of mercantile supplies and preemption papers (like a homestead deed) for 160 acres, which he donated in December of 1843 for a townsite and proposed county seat. Maj. J.R. Hampton *(Hampton),* a commissioner, suggested the name El Dorado, which literally translates from Spanish as "the gilded one" but whose commonly accepted meaning is a mythical South American city (or country) thought to be fabulously wealthy by 16th century Spanish explorers. By using nearby El Dorado Landing *(Calion)* as a port, it grew into a lumber and *railroad* town (first the Camden & Alexander, then the Little Rock Southern) of 4,202 by 1910 that boomed to 20,000 a few weeks after the Busey oil well blew on January 10, 1921, fulfilling the legend of its name. Home of Charles Portis, author of <u>True Grit</u>, Southern Arkansas University at El Dorado and Oil Belt Vocational Technical School. "Oil Capital of Arkansas."

South Arkansas Arts Center. Along with American oils and watercolors, it also has a rare collection of Japanese woodblock prints. 110 E. 5th. US 167B, E on E. 5th.

Busey Oil Well. The site of the first oil well in Arkansas is just west of Jct. US 82B & US 82. Marker.

Moro Bay Ferry. *(Ferry Boats)* 19 m. E, SR 15 at the Ouachita River.

Union County Courthouse. Neo-Classical Revival, 1928. National Historic Register. Made of Bastesville marble, it is the only courthouse in Arkansas that fronts on a shopping mall. The interior, introduced by a two-story foyer with 12 Corinthian columns, is ornate and overwhelming. Grounds: A marble statue of a Confederate soldier is supported by four upright marble cannons. US 167B at SR 15. *(County Profiles)*

National Historic Register. There are many sites, including the Matthew Rainey House (c.1852), 510 N. Jackson St., which offers tours. Maps: chamber of commerce, 201 N. Jackson, 1 blk. E of the courthouse.

EUREKA SPRINGS
POP. 1,989   ALT. 1,461   MAP A-2

Built on the sides of two mountains, overlooking a downtown (National Historic Register) of cut-stone and brick buildings, this well-preserved Victorian town has San Francisco-style grades and, according to <u>Ripley's Believe-It-Or-Not</u>, 238 streets with no direct intersections. By whom and how is still disputed but on July 4, 1879, this campsite of "health seekers" was named Eureka Springs, presumably for the translation from Greek of "eureka" as "I've found it" (see Basin Springs, BELOW). One year later the new town's population was estimated at 5,000 and by the turn of the century Eureka had become one of the largest cities in Arkansas because of 63 "curative" springs, the promotional abilities of Powell Clayton (gov. 1868-71) and the Eureka Springs Railway (Missouri & North Arkansas *Railroad).* Once a fashionable health resort, the town faded away during the Depression, leaving miles of Victorian houses and buildings intact. Today the boom is back, this time based on spectacular scenery, period architecture and entertainment of all kinds. Platted before motorized vehicles,

Eureka Springs is still primarily a "walking town." Shortcuts (stairs and paths) crisscross downtown. The chamber of commerce has excellent literature and maps, and provides parking for tourists intending to use the trolley system, which, incidentally, ranks Eureka as the smallest city in America with this kind of public transportation. US 62, 2 blks. W of Jct. US 62B/SR 23N.

The Great Passion Play. Billed as "The World's No.1 Outdoor Drama," it depicts Christ's last week on Earth. Exotic animals, elaborate costumes and Middle Eastern architecture add authenticity and spectacle to this nationally famous attraction. Nearly 200 townspeople (men, women and children) hold second jobs as actors, creating a living Bible set in natural scenery among six buildings that are replicas of street scenes in Jerusalem. Among other attractions on the same grounds: The Bible Museum (7,000 rare Bibles written in 625 different languages), The New Holy Land (a partially completed replica, including "The River Jordan") and the Christ of the Ozarks (a seven-story cement statue of Jesus Christ). US 62E or SR 23N. Signs.

Eureka Springs was accidentally founded by Dr. Jackson's Eye Water

---

Eureka Springs & North Arkansas Railway. During the Eureka Springs Railway's *(Missouri & North Arkansas Railroad)* first full year (1883), over 23,500 passengers rode "The Road to Health," an 18.5-mile line from Seligman, Mo., to Eureka. The little train changed names many times, merging with larger companies that eventually laid track all the way to *Helena*. Today's train doesn't go that far but it still goes in high style. Full-scale and standard gauge, the rolling stock (original and restored, including a dining car) is pulled by three different types of locomotives: the Baldwin No.1 and the Alco No.201 (both built in 1906) and the Shay, 1918. The Baldwin No.1 is one of the oldest Cabbage Heads still running in the U.S. Departs from the original and restored cut-stone station (authentic inside and out). SR 23N. City Limits.

Springs. "The town water built" is said to have 63 springs within a mile's radius of downtown and over 1,200 in the western district of Carroll County. Some of the town's springs are listed below. Each offers shade, a place to rest and natural charm. BASIN SPRING: The town began here (see History, ABOVE). Dr. Alvah Jackson, after searching twenty years for legendary Indian Healing Springs, found it by accident on a hunting trip from *Oil Trough* in 1854. He spent more than twenty unsuccessful years selling his discovery as Dr. Jackson's Eye Water until "curing" Judge L.B. Saunders *(Berryville,* Saunders' Museum), who then brought national attention to the "healing" waters. Spring St., adjacent to the Basin Park Hotel. SWEET SPRING: The angular and curving rock work, some two stories high, is an excellent example of the Irish stonemason's craft. The town (according to <u>Ripley's</u>) has more cut-stone retaining walls than any other place in the world (supposedly over 54 miles). Spring St., opposite the post office. HARDING SPRING: Flows from the base of a sheer limestone cliff known as Lovers' Leap, which gives a broad view of downtown. N of the Palace Bathhouse. CRESCENT SPRING: Its water was hauled by wagon for the Crescent Hotel's everyday needs. Now enclosed in stone and surrounded by an ornate Victorian gazebo. Spring St., N of Carnegie Library. GROTTO SPRING: The picturesque cave and mountainside setting gave this spring its name. 2 blks. Spring St., W of The Rosalie. ONYX SPRING: First called Laundry Spring because of its popularity as a place to wash clothes, then renamed for the onyx found in it. Steele St., 1 blk. N of Hatchet Hall. CARRY A. NATION SPRING: Ms. Nation blasted it out of solid rock, forming a "natural icebox" that keeps a constant temperature. The spring and cave supplied water and cold storage for the residents of Steele St., at Hatchet Hall. LITTLE EUREKA SPRING: Supposedly won second place for purity in the 1904 World's Fair at St. Louis. Steele St., 1 blk. S of Hatchet Hall. MAGNETIC SPRING: Believed to be radioactive; locals claim the water can magnetize a knife blade. N. Main, 2 blocks up Magnetic Rd. Many more springs (54) should be noted but listing them and finding them present problems (the most elusive and romantic, Bell Spring, rings like a bell in Magnetic Hollow).

Blue Spring Attraction. Called "the largest spring in NW Arkansas," it was used for powering various mills from 1845 until the last one was torn down in the 1940s. Today a landscaped tourist attraction, Blue Spring has a three-screen theater presenting the story of Eureka Springs from wagons and tents to limestone buildings. The Indian story, in petroglyph, is carved on the rock bluffs. US 62, 5.5 m. W.

Magnetic Spring is supposedly radioactive, and its water can magnetize a knife blade

Thorncrown Chapel. Time magazine: "It is one of the most popular and widely publicized of new American buildings." Narrow, 48 feet high, it comes as close as any building to being ALL glass. The architect, E. Fay Jones, said the design idea hinged on not using anything too big for two men to carry along a narrow hillside path. Set high on an Ozark mountainside, Thorncrown Chapel is a true wonder. US 62, .7 m. W. Signs.

St. Elizabeth's Chapel. (1907). Ripley's listed it as the only church in the world entered through its bell tower. Richard Kerens, part owner of the Crescent Hotel and ambassador to Austria, built the chapel as a memorial to his mother, reportedly placing it at the last spot he ever saw her alive. US 62B, below the Crescent Hotel.

Crescent Hotel. This five-story, cut-stone structure was built in 1884-86 as a first-class, fire-proof hotel on 27 acres of grounds with bridle paths and walks. Always short of money, the hotel was rented twice: once to the St. Louis & San Francisco *(Railroad)* from 1902-07 and then to the Crescent Col-

lege (for young women) in the off-seasons of 1908-33. In 1936 it was sold to "Dr." Norman Baker, who had just finished serving time in a Texas prison for fraud. A flashy dresser (purple and bullet-proof vests), his specialty was miracle cures for cancer, although he did transplant goat glands for those wanting "renewed sexual vigor." The Crescent, vacant after 1938, reopened in 1946 (and has remained open) as a Victorian hotel offering lofty views of the Ozarks and extensive gardens. US 62B. Signs.

According to Ripley's, the seven-story Basin Park Hotel has seven ground floor entrances

Basin Park Hotel. Begun in 1898, this cut-stone hotel rose one floor a year, ending in 1905 with a ballroom overlooking downtown. Featured in Ripley's, the seven-story structure has a ground floor entrance on each of its seven levels. Downtown.

Palace Bathhouse. Cut stone (1901), capped by a silver-painted dome, the hotel's original outdoor advertisement is the only neon sign remaining in downtown and has an ironical shape, considering the nature of the building's business. On Spring St., N of the post office.

Onyx Cave. This old-fashioned attraction was one of the first to use radio-guided tours. The program includes scientific information as well as an onyx elephant, friendly dragon and witch's fireplace. The souvenir shop displays blind cave fish in an aquarium. US 62, 3.5 m. E. Signs.

Gay Nineties Button & Doll Museum. The Button Museum, "the only one like it in North America," features over 10,000 buttons, which range from a 300-year-old Habitat to handpainted porcelains from the French Revolution and Goofies from the Depression. At Onyx Cave (ABOVE).

Pivot Rock & Natural Bridge. Noted in Ripley's, Pivot Rock is about 15 feet tall, 30 feet in circumference at the top and 16 inches at its base. The temptation to try to push it over is irresistible. US 62W to Pivot Rock Rd. Signs.

Hatchet Hall. Carry A. Nation (women's suffrage and ax-wielding temperance advocate) named the house herself, living there from 1909 until her death following a hellfire-and-brimstone temperance lecture at Basin Circle Park in 1911. The house is furnished true to the period and displays memorabilia of her life. Incidentally, she and Dale Carnegie are buried in the same cemetery at Peculiar, Mo. N. Main to Flint. Signs.

Quigley's Castle. Built in the 1940s by an Ozark woman and her family. The materials include petrified wood, fossils, toy marbles, crystals, the prehistoric imprint of a deer's hoof and other collectables. The interior is just as personalized and unusual. SR 23, 4.5 m. S.

The Castle and Museum. Overlooking the White River Valley, this modern castle (early 1900s) with its "point-rock" construction could be the only one of its kind. One end or "point" of each triangular rock juts out, overlapping and shading the one below it, which together supposedly creates a natural air-conditioning effect. The castle and museum both offer tours emphasizing the daily life and technology of the early 1900s. Other buildings (a gas station, blacksmith shop and country store) are from the same period. US 62, 5.5 m. W.

Miracle Mansion. Brochures claim: "Neighbors Refer To It As 'The Flying Saucer.' " Designed by the original director of the Great Passion Play as his residence, the present owners have dedicated it as a shrine to early Christian martyrs and have added a display, The Wonderful World of Miniatures, which features "the world's oldest bug collection" as well as the presidents & first ladies in miniature. Bus Groups. Weddings. US 62, 3.2 m. E.

Eureka Springs Historical Museum. Housed in a three-story stone building (Second Empire, 1889) with a mansard roof of custom-made tin are home furnishings, photographs and documents of early settlers as well as 1880s souvenirs, toys, dolls and replicas of a pioneer parlor and kitchen. Downtown, 95 S. Main.

Miles Musical Museum. It claims to have one of the "largest and most interesting and unusual collections of musical instruments in the world." Besides the Nickle Grabbers, Hurdy Gurdy, singing bird boxes and calliopes, there are button pictures, an animated miniature circus, "Musical Chapel and Court Yards" as well as shrunken heads, mummy beads, blow guns and a lot more in 12,000 square feet of museum. Tours. US 62W, city limits.

Evening Shade's name is due to the Arkansas custom of calling afternoon "evening"

Hammond Museum of Bells. Thirty display cases (representing over 30 years of collecting) group the bells according to type, including: portrait bells, table and tea bells made of silver and porcelain, cow bells, china bells and one-of-a-kind cloisonnés. The oldest, a Luristan bronze bell (800 B.C.), is matched only by a 500-year-old Chinese gong that anyone can gong with the whim. Spring St., opposite the post office.

Iron Bridges. Once the only two bridges across the Osage and Kings Rivers *(Float Streams)* in Carroll County, these plank-bottom, iron-truss structures are still safe and offer a romantic ride through Ozark farmland. US 62, 1.5 m. E to Rocky Top sign, turn S then stay left. Rejoins US 62 in 4 m.

Hog Scald Hollow/Creek. Confederate soldiers, while camped in this rugged Ozark valley, devised a way to skin hogs easily by diverting a creek, trapping water in the natural "kettles" (wide, shallow pits in the limestone bed) and dropping in heated rocks. The creek and the hollow kept the name, Hog Scald. SR 23., 5.2 m. S, turn E on blacktop; then stay left for 2.2 m. The scalds and creek end at Auger Falls, a good place to find crinoid fossils. Beyond the falls, the left branch leads upstream to a steeper group of scalds and falls, the former site of Durham Mill *(Grist Mill)*. Walk: one-hour round trip.

Events/Festivals. Late Mar: Victorian Classic Foot Race (10K & 2 miles). Early Apr: Annual Fiddle Contest & Spring Music Festival; also the Spring Tour of Homes. Mid-May:

Annual Sidewalk Arts & Crafts Fair. Late Oct: Annual Fall Art Fair. Paintings. Jewelry. Crafts. Late Oct: Annual Original Ozark Folk Festival & Arts & Craft Show. Music. Dancing. Late Nov-Dec: Christmas in Lights (Passion Play set decorated with 12,000 lights. Live Nativity Scene. Crafts. Early Dec: Candlelight Tour of Homes.

Carroll County Courthouse. Italian Renaissance Revival, 1908. *Dual County Seat (Berryville).* This three-story cut-stone building is an excellent example of its style. The structure and large courtroom are particularly well-preserved and maintained. S. Main. *(County Profiles)*

National Historic Register. The entire downtown is in the Register. Tour Homes. Maps: chamber of commerce, US 62, 2 blks. W of Jct. US 62B/SR 23N.

EVENING SHADE
POP. 397   ALT. 458   MAP J-2

The town's architecture offers Arkansas history at a glance. Captain J.W. Thompson built a mill *(Grist Mill)* in 1817, grinding corn for settlers and Cherokees. Together with J.W. Shaver, he established a post office in 1848, naming the site for its cool afternoon shade *(Arkansawyers* called any time past noon "evening"). A cotton gin, card mill and steam sawmill followed. Its location and the prominence of *Batesville* caused a steady decline beginning in the early 1900s and ending with the loss of the 99-year-old county seat (since 1868) to *Ash Flat* in 1967.

Plum Spring House. (1906-1941). The townsite was first known as Plum Spring (1817-47). The structure burned; the ornately housed, year-round spring dried up. Recently remodeled (except for the bandstand), the spring flows today. Bring a jug. Main St.

Thompson Mill. Now derelict, its clapboard broken, the mill stands on Piney Creek just east of US 167 on SR 56.

National Historic Register. There are many sites, mostly between High & Main Streets, including J.W. Shaver's house (1854) on the NW corner of Main & Cammack.

FAYETTEVILLE
POP. 36,608   ALT. 1,334   MAP A-1

First called Washington Court House (as late as 1828), the name was changed in 1829 because another *Washington* already existed. Reportedly named after Fayetteville, Tennessee, it is said that two members of the name-selection committee were from there. The town's history has revolved around colleges. In 1836, one week before Fayetteville became one of Arkansas' oldest incorporated cities *(Little Rock, Helena)*, the Fayetteville Female Seminary was established. The seminary was followed in 1852 by Arkansas College (first to issue collegiate degrees in the state), which was destroyed during the *Civil War* when both sides took turns occupying and burning the town. Home of the University of Arkansas and Arkansas' first (1859) telegraph (Fayetteville-St. Louis).

University of Arkansas. With a promise to the state of $100,000 from Washington County and $30,000 from the city, Arkansas Industrial University was established in 1871, changing its name to the present one in 1899. The legislature did not exclude women students, making it (despite popular disapproval) coeducational. Of the nine graduates in 1876, four were women. The enrollment today at Fayetteville is about 14,000 with a statewide total of over 30,000. The nickname, Razorbacks, originated in 1909 when Coach Hugo Bezdek reportedly referred to his football team as "a wild band of razorback hogs." Downtown, SR 471, W on Dickson.

Old Main. National Historic Register, 1873. Its two mansard towers are a landmark for miles. The four-story brick building's foundation was built from stones hauled 70 miles by oxen and wagons. On campus, Arkansas Ave.

Town Square. A blend of different architectural periods, it is still the center of town life. On Saturdays there is a farmer's market centered around the Old Post Office (National Historic Register, 1909), which occupies the site of three former courthouses (1837-1904). SR 471, W at the courthouse.

University Museum. A fully accredited museum divided into four major categories, its "something for everyone" includes pottery (500 B.C.), eggs (hummingbird to elephant bird), American Indians (prehistoric to historic), kites (plain to elaborate dragons) as well as special events covering art (primitive to professional), science (dinosaurs to wildflowers), baskets, fossils, quilts, clothing, photos and more on a rotating basis. Next to the student union (Maple, S on Garland).

Headquarters House Museum. National Historic Register, 1853. Used by both Federals and Confederates as a command post, preserved in its original condition, the house has excellent examples of period furnishings, including a Boston rocker (c.1840), walnut table (c.1820), rosewood pianoforte (1816), writing desk (c.1845) and cannonball bed (c.1820). Downtown, off SR 471, 118 E. Dickson.

Confederate Cemetery. Beneath orderly rows of maples, a two-story monument of a Confederate soldier watches over hundreds of unmarked headstones. Four stone cannons at the base, if shot, would equally divide the four sections: Arkansas, Louisiana, Missouri and Texas. Erected in 1897. SR 471 at the courthouse, 3 blks. E on Rock St.

Old Washington County Jail. Romanesque, 1896. National Historic Register. The crenelated corner towers give the building a first-glance appearance of a medieval castle, which might have been a happy thought for the sheriff and his family who occupied the main floor. Next to the courthouse.

Spiritual Message Barn. In the spirit of SEE ROCK CITY painted on barns across America, this one has advertisements for the soul. E side US 71/62 just S of Jct. SR 112.

Butterfield Overland Mail. Fayetteville was an important stop on the mail route. The company built a hotel on grounds now occupied by the courthouse. Owner John Butterfield, who bought a 360-acre farm near today's western edge of town, is said to have regarded the countryside as "the most healthful and beautiful along the route."

Fayetteville Lake. Situated in the city, it provides fishing (including bluegill, catfish, crappie and bass) as well as picnic facilities and hiking trails. US 471 at N city limits. Signs.

Events/Festivals. Late Apr: Hogeye Marathon (26 miles). Early Oct: Autumnfest. Arts & Crafts. Farmer's Market. Music. Triathlon.

Washington County Courthouse. Romanesque Revival, 1904. National Historic Register. Rare, unusual and beautiful are used to describe this four-story, beveled limestone courthouse. Rare because of its three separate courtrooms, unusual because the circuit court is in the eaves of this building, and beautiful because of the interior appointments, it is even more extraordinary because of the octagonal corner towers and square bell tower. Downtown, SR 471. *(County Profiles)*

National Historic Register. Nearly 20 sites are listed, including the Magnolia Company Filling Station (1925) at 429 W. LaFayette. Maps: chamber of commerce, 123 W. Mountain, south side of the square.

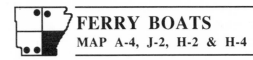

FERRY BOATS
MAP A-4, J-2, H-2 & H-4

There are four free state ferry boats in Arkansas. They operate every day year-round. No private ones remain.

Spring Bank. Red River & SR 160. 5:30 a.m.-9:30 p.m. 15 minutes round trip. Six-car capacity. Map: H-2.

Guion. White River & SR 38. 6:30 a.m.-6:30 p.m. 15 minutes round trip. Six-car capacity. Map: J-2.

Moro Bay. Ouachita River & SR 15. 5:00 a.m.-10:00 p.m. 15 minutes round trip. Six-car capacity. Map: H-4.

Peel. Bull Shoals *Lake* & SR 125. Daylight hours. 45 minutes round trip. Six-car capacity. Map: A-4.

FIFTY-SIX
POP. 157   ALT. 870   MAP J-1

This community submitted the name Newcomb for its new 1918 post office, but Washington, D.C., rejected the suggestion (no reason known) and named it for its school district's number (56).

Blanchard Springs Caverns. First opened in 1963 by the U.S. Forest Service, these caverns offer what has been called "one of the best hiking *trails* in Arkansas." Of the two trails, Dripstone (.7 miles, open year-round) is the less strenuous (handicap accessible) and features smooth pavement with incline ramps. It is said to have every type of calcite formation found in a limestone cave. Discovery Trail (1.2 miles, summer only) begins with an elevator descent of 476 feet. Over 600 stairsteps lead past an underground stream, one of the world's largest flowstones and around geological deposits that "are unique and spectacular." Both trails are dramatically lighted and are provided with a guide who explains the peculiarities as well as the biological and geological processes of the caverns. The Visitors' Center has an audio-visual program and special exhibits that explain the story of Blanchard Springs Caverns. Recreation: Ozark *National Forest*. SR 14, 1 m. E; FR 1110, 3 m. N. Signs.

Barkshed Natural Area. Natural Heritage Area. Called "one of the most outstanding botanical areas in the Ozarks" with "one of the most outstanding localities for spring wildflowers in the state," it is characterized by an excellent mix of cedar, hardwood and pine. Caves, sinkholes, springs and underground streams. SR 14, 7 m. W; FR 1112, 3 m. N.

FIGURE FIVE
COMMUNITY   ALT. 800   MAP C-1

The origin of this name has two versions and one hybrid, all of which revolve around James G. Stevenson and most of which is now buried in legend. Two facts are certain: Stevenson did settle in a nearby community, Bond Special, in the late 1830s, and a post office (c.1904) was established as Figure Five. The legends: (1) Stevenson carried a chain for surveyors marking the road from Fayetteville to Fort Smith in 1832-33 *(Roads)*. He liked the area, blazed a 5 on a large oak *(Witness Tree)* and wrote his family, giving directions. (2) Stevenson, driving cattle north from Van Buren, camped here. Guessing the distance traveled as five miles, he cut a 5 in an oak as information for future travelers. (3) Squire Stevenson, who had surveyed the western part of the county and liked this area, came with his family in 1837. From near Cane Hill he blazed numbers 1-5 at each night's campsite as a guide for those following with livestock. NOTE: It has been said that communities Figure One, Two, Three and Four were also established, as witnessed by Figure Four, which later became Lindsey (post office) c.1909. SR 59, S 10 m.

FLOOD OF 1927
MAP ALL QUARTERS

From January to April heavy and constant rains soaked 31 states with a total of 250 cubic miles of water. Nearly half of Arkansas lay underwater. A Louisiana switchboard operator claimed that a porpoise swam into her office. In Pine Bluff 500 people marooned on a bridge sang "Shall We Gather by the River." All railroads and most bridges, roads and communication lines were unusable. Steamboats, skimming over row crops, rescued the stranded. As a result of this disaster, congressional legislation was eventually passed (1928-1936), establishing full federal responsibility for dams, levees, flood walls and other local protective measures.

FORDYCE
POP. 5,175   ALT. 250   MAP G-4

The townsite was sold by former slave Henry Atkinson to A.S. Holderness for $118 in 1881. Bought in 1882 by the Southern Improvement Company, it was platted that year on the tracks of the Texas & St. Louis *Railroad* before completion of the line in 1883, and named for Samuel W. Fordyce, who was the railroad's surveyor and later president of its successor, the St. Louis Southwestern Railway. Incorporated 1885. Barely in Dallas County, the town was made seat of justice in 1906 and is Arkansas' only county seat (other than *dual county seats*) to have been moved from a central location (Princeton, BELOW). Home of the world's first Southern pine plywood plant.

Princeton. Laid out in 1844 as the county seat for planned Dallas County (1845) and incorporated in 1854, it was a thriving town until bypassed to the north by the St. Louis, Iron Mountain & Southern Railway at *Malvern* and to the south by the Texas & St. Louis at Fordyce. SR 8, 17 m. N to SR 9; 2 m. N.

Coach Paul "Bear" Bryant. The birthplace of this famous University of Alabama football coach is commemorated with a marker. A white frame house now occupies the original home site. SR 8, appx. 11 m. E, just E of Jct. SR 97.

Johnny Cash. Born about five miles north of Kingsland, Ar., in 1932. Kingsland has built a monument to the country singer that features two large black guitars flanked by red stars on a white background. US 79, 9 m. N to Kingsland, E on SR 189 (First Street) to the city park.

Tri-County Lake. This 280-acre lake is stocked by the Game and Fish Commission with bluegill, catfish, crappie and bass. Picnic and camping facilities available.

Events/Festivals. Late Apr: Annual Fordyce on the Cotton Belt Festival. Car Show. Train Rides. Tours. Crafts. 5K Run.

Dallas County Courthouse. Palladian Georgian Revival, 1911. National Historic Register. Features: two-story columns and a four-face clock that strikes the hour in an ornate cupola. Downtown, 3rd & Oak. *(County Profiles)*

National Historic Register. There are over 15 listings on the Register. Maps: chamber of commerce, downtown, SR 274, W 1 blk. on 3rd. PRINCETON, AR. (SR 8, 19 m. N): Culbertson Kiln (1858), just E of town. Princeton Methodist Church, SR 9.

FOREMAN
POP. 1,377   ALT. 405   MAP G-1

This hybrid town began as a post office, Willow Springs, in 1845 but was listed on maps as Rocky Comfort Academy, around which grew a "thriving community" by 1850. Although selected as the first county seat of Little River County in 1868, it lost that position and, consequently, much of its population to Richmond in 1880. Arrival of the Arkansas & Choctaw *Railroad* (St. Louis & San Francisco) one mile north of Rocky Comfort in 1895 threatened to be the final blow, but in 1900 a post office named for Texarkana politician Ben Foreman was set on the railroad tracks and the former community of Rocky Comfort joined it, becoming county seat again (as Foreman), 1902-05.

Laynesport. Nothing much but history remains of this jumping-off place located at the corner of Indian Territory and Mexico. Platted by land owner Benjamin Layne in 1839 (post office, 1845), it was the last American town south of *Paraclifta* on the Texas Road. Other *roads* and towns grew more important; it declined after 1860. No buildings remain. SR 108, appx. 6 m. S. Inquire at Matteson Farms Headquarters.

Western Boundary Marker. Surveyed three times in 52 years (1825-1877, *Boundary Lines),* this cast-iron post dated 1877 and marked 119 (miles from Fort Smith) is one of the few remaining originals (Queen Wilhelmina *State Park).* The first survey was marked with wooden stakes and *witness trees;* the second with oak posts set in mounds and witness trees. Near Matteson Farm Headquarters, SR 108, appx. 6 m. S.

FORREST CITY
POP. 13,803   ALT. 214   MAP L-4

The town began on the western slope of *Crowley's Ridge* in 1867 near the former county seat of Mount Vernon *(Madison)* as a construction camp of the Memphis & Little Rock *Railroad.* Laid out in 1869, it was named for Confederate General Nathan Bedford Forrest (the camp had been called Forrest's Town), honoring him as the contractor who finished the railroad. Incorporated in 1871, it became county seat in 1874. Home of East Arkansas Community College and Crowley's Ridge Vocational Technical School.

C. Hamilton Moses Steam Electric Station. This gas- and oil-fueled power plant is capable of generating 144 megawatts, or enough electricity to light a 144-million-watt light bulb. US 70, 2.5 m. E of SR 261.

Events/Festivals. Early Oct: Harvest Fest. Hot Air Balloon Races. Chili Cook-Off. Sidewalk Sales.

St. Francis County Courthouse. Sixties Modern, 1972. Although built in the seventies, its architecture reflects the sixties. In keeping with some older traditions are the 14-foot ceilings and a clock tower. *(County Profiles)*

National Historic Register. Mann House, 422 Forrest.

FORT SMITH
POP. 71,384   ALT. 463   MAP C-1

In 1817, on orders from Secretary of War Joel R. Poinsett, General Thomas A. Smith detailed Major William Bradford to establish a fort (first Fort Smith at Belle Point) to keep peace between the Osage and the newly arriving Cherokee, and to prevent squatters from settling in Indian Territory. The city of Fort Smith, founded by John Rogers in 1838, was doubled in size by outfitters supplying '49ers headed to the California gold fields. The economy grew from a transportation hub of the *Arkansas River,* pioneer crossroads *(Roads)* and the St. Louis & San Francisco and Little Rock & Ft. Smith *(Railroads)* to an established manufacturing city with the lure of cheap fuels from Sebastian County coal mines *(Greenwood)*

and natural gas reserves. Second largest city in Arkansas. Home of WW II General Wm. O. Darby of "Darby's Rangers" and Westark Community College. Maps: chamber of commerce, downtown at 613 Garrison Ave. (US 64).

Belle Point (Coke Hill). This wedge of land between the Poteau and Arkansas Rivers known as Belle Point since the 18th century became Choctaw property (1825) until "a final adjustment" to the *boundary line* (1909) included the land in Arkansas. Although "always under the jurisdiction of the federal government," Belle Point was actually a no-man's-land of "indigents, outlaws and dope peddlers" that from the mid-1920s to the 1950s was a shantytown referred to as Coke Hill because of the "widespread peddling of cocaine in the area." In 1959 preliminary test excavations uncovered foundation remnants of the first Fort Smith (1817-1824). The city of Fort Smith filed a quit claim deed for the property, which then became a National Historical Site in 1961.

Fort Smith National Historic Site. National Historic Register. The National Park encapsulates Fort Smith's military and frontier days, beginning with the site of the first fort in 1817 and ending with the "hanging judge," Isaac C. Parker. FIRST FORT SMITH: (See History, ABOVE) Abandoned 1824. Foundation Remnants. SECOND FORT SMITH: A steady stream (1828-1840) of the Five Civilized Tribes *(Trail of Tears)* through Fort Smith so alarmed settlers they petitioned for protection. Completed too late (1845) for a need that never materialized, the structure was converted into a supply depot. Partially Restored. BARRACKS-COURTHOUSE-JAIL (1846): Used first for barracks during the Mexican-American War of 1846-48 (General, and later President, Zachary Taylor drilled troops here) and then the Civil War (both sides). Later, in 1871, it served as a federal court room and a jail known as "Hell on the Border," and finally (1887-1917) was converted into a federal prison. It is best remembered for Judge Parker, who presided over 13,000 criminal cases from 1875-1896. Of the 344 capital offense convictions, 79 "stood on nothin', a-lookin' up a rope." During his court jurisdiction 65 U.S. marshalls (known as "The Men Who Rode for Parker") were killed in the line of duty. Remodeled but intact. GALLOWS: Originally designed for six hangings at once, it was enlarged for 12. Replica. AMERICAN FLAG: A 100-foot flagpole flies a 20-by-36-foot American flag (37 stars), the largest of its kind *(Fouke)* in Arkansas. INITIAL POINT MARKER: An 1858 monument commemorates the 1825 *boundary line* dividing the Territory of Arkansas and the Choctaw Nation. For 65 years no settlers were allowed past this line. Downtown, Garrison Ave. (US 64), S on 3rd. For more information: Park Ranger, Box 1460, Fort Smith, 72902.

Belle Grove. National Historic District. The quiet side of Fort Smith's history, these 30 square blocks feature 19th century homes, some of which offer tours. Bounded by 5th and 8th from North "C" to North "H." Downtown, off Garrison Ave. (US 64).

Free Ferry Road. Still lined with turn-of-the-century homes, this street once ended east of the city at the Arkansas River ferry. Midtown, off Rogers Ave. (SR 22).

Patent Model Museum/John Rogers House. The house (c.1840), a smaller version of the second fort's barracks, is believed to have been built by city founder John Rogers, the sutler at First Fort Smith in 1822, who bought the site when abandoned, selling part of it later for Second Fort Smith. The museum displays working scale models of 85 proposed inventions (1836-1870s) that range from refrigerators, rotary engines, wagons and ships to printing presses and toys. Prearranged Tours. 400 N. 8th, Belle Grove.

Fort Smith Art Center. This pink brick house (Second Empire) is a work of art itself. The contents vary according to special exhibits. A permanent collection displays oils and watercolors, sculpture and photography as well as arts and crafts. 423 N. 6th, Belle Grove.

Old Fort Museum. The Atkinson-Williams Warehouse, National Historic Register (1906), houses artifacts pertaining to the fort's history along with a 500-gal. American La France Steam Fire Pump dated 1917, a Darby's Ranger exhibit and a working old-fashioned (1890-1940) drugstore with pharmacy and soda fountain. Next to the National Park, 320 Rogers Ave.

Carlton's Historical Museum. The Carltons have collected antiques for over 40 years. Included are: 76 irons (some weighing nearly 30 pounds), at least a hundred can openers, a National bicycle (1880s) and Old Faithful (a high-speed, 1904 washer). 405 Garrison Ave. (US 64).

St. Anne's Convent. French Renaissance Chateau, 1906. Said to be the only one of its architectural style surviving in Arkansas. W of N.14th on Rogers Ave. (SR 22).

Knoble Brewery. National Historic Register, 1851. One of many German immigrants arriving in Fort Smith (1840s), Joseph Knoble of Wittenberg built this three-story stone building to brew and store beer. Off Garrison Ave. (US 64) at N. 3rd. and "E."

The Legend of Boggy Creek, made into a popular movie, was based on events in Fouke

---

Ben Green Regional Park. The 800-acre city park features an Olympic-sized swimming pool, tennis courts, an 18-hole golf course, hiking trails, bridle paths and picnic pavilions. SR 255 next to Fort Chaffee.

U.S. National Cemetery. Veterans of all wars, including Confederates, are buried here along with Judge Isaac C. Parker (1896). Off Garrison Ave. (US 64), S. 6th at Garland.

Butterfield Overland Mail. A division and distribution point for the *Butterfield Overland Mail;* extra coaches and 50 - 100 mules and horses were kept on hand. The route entered Fort Smith at present-day Second Street.

Lock & Dam #13. Forming part of the 445-mile McClellan-Kerr *Arkansas River* Navigation System (from near Tulsa, Ok., to the Mississippi River), this system and the Ozark-Jeta Taylor Lock & Dam at *Ozark* join to form Ozark *Lake*. Locks at either end of the lake work in stair-step fashion, raising or lowering the water inside the lock to match the level where

river traffic is entering or exiting. SR 59 at the Arkansas River. Recreation: Ozark *Lake.*

Events/Festivals. Early May: Belle Fort Smith Tour of Historic Restorations. Mid-May: Old Fort River Festival. Includes a musical drama about Judge Parker. Late May: Old Fort Days Rodeo. Late Sept: Arkansas-Oklahoma State Fair.

Sebastian County Courthouse. Moderne (some Deco influence), 1937. *Dual County Seat (Greenwood).* On the grounds is a marker noting that Fort Smith in 1913 had more 50-year-old paved streets than any other city in the nation. Also: A three-story Confederate statue originally intended for the U.S. National Cemetery but excluded because the inscription, "Lest We Forget," would not be omitted now stands with its back turned to the cemetery. S. 6th off Garrison (US 64), S of Rogers. *(County Profiles)*

National Historic Register. There are many sites listed in the Register. Maps: chamber of commerce, downtown, 613 Garrison Ave. (US 64).

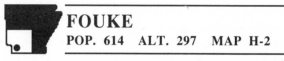

FOUKE
POP. 614   ALT. 297   MAP H-2

Pronounced FOW-ke, it began as a sawmill town on the Texas & Pacific *(Railroad,* St. Louis Southwestern) in the late 1880s and was platted in 1911. Along with problems about which state or nation its county belonged to (Miller County, *Boundary Lines),* this area since 1856 has been plagued by Big Foot.

The Legend of Boggy Creek. This popular movie was based on the May 2, 1971, experience of a resident who, after being treated for scratches and shock, told the sheriff that "a large, hairy creature...about six feet tall" had twice in one night attacked him, once kicking down his back door and once grabbing him from behind in the darkness. Other sightings were reported in 1973 at the junction US 71 and SR 134 on Boggy Creek.

American Flag. Initially begun as a high school project, later adopted as a community effort, this 30-by-60-foot American flag flies from a 125-foot pole. Visible for miles, the flag is believed to be the largest of its kind in Arkansas *(Fort Smith,* National Historic Site). US 71S, Red Cut Rd. to the high school.

Spring Bank Ferry. *(Ferry Boats)* US 71, 10 m. S, SR 160/Red River.

FULTON
POP. 326   ALT. 276   MAP G-2

Before the first deed was recorded here by John Dorlac or Dulac in 1808, the area was known by both Indians and 17th century explorers as a Red *River* crossing, and later the site became a jumping-off place to the Great Southwest from the Southwest Trail *(Roads).* While the Arkansas Gazette in 1819 advertised town lots for sale in "a town named Fulton," none were sold, and no evidence remains of the origin of the proposed town's

name, although it could have been named for Robt. Fulton, inventor of the steamboat. Incidentally, the advertisement was a promotion sponsored by Stephen F. Austin, who subsequently changed his mind about the strategic location of Fulton on the Southwest Trail and chose *Little Rock* instead. Dredging of the Red River *(Great Raft)* prompted interest in the site again, this time as a steamboat landing, and another ad for town lots was placed in the Arkansas Gazette (1835), which, along with the establishment of a post office in 1836, marks the real beginnings of Fulton. Despite being an important steamboat landing by 1850 (first to arrive was The Enterprise in 1831) and the site of the arrival of the Cairo & Fulton *Railroad* in 1874, its prosperity waned while newly founded *Texarkana* (18 miles southwest) continued to grow as the terminus for the Cairo & Fulton and Texas & Pacific *(Railroads,* St. Louis Southwestern).

Fulton Union Church. This 1870s white clapboard church schedules Presbyterian, Baptist, Christian and Methodist services on a rotating basis. In Town.

Levees. It was said that in the 1930s residents would walk calmly around while the Red River whizzed 30 feet over their heads behind the levee walls. Before levees and other Corps of Engineers projects such as dredging, the Red River alternated stagnating *(Great Raft)* and roaring miles beyond its banks. Downtown.

GARLAND
POP. 660   ALT. 246   MAP H-2

Before Corps of Engineers flood control projects *(Fulton, Levees)*, this town on the Red *River* supposedly held the title, Most Washed-Away City in Arkansas. Its founder (settled c.1833) was the father of Augustus H. Garland, who during Reconstruction *(Civil War)* won the U.S. Supreme Court case that allowed Southern lawyers to once again practice law in federal courts (incidentally, all Arkansas Confederate veterans were denied voting rights from 1868-74) and who served as governor (1874-77), U.S. senator and U.S. attorney general under President Grover Cleveland (making Garland the first *Arkansawyer* to hold a cabinet position).

GILBERT
POP. 43   ALT. 995   MAP B-4

Founded c.1901, local tradition claims the community was named for John Gilbert (president of the Missouri & North Arkansas *Railroad* at that time). This lumber town lived by the railroad until the tracks were pulled up in 1949. Located on the Buffalo River *(Float Streams),* today the community outfits camping and float trips.

Mays-Baker General Store. National Historic Register, c.1901. It retains the mercantile flavor of another era. Along with general merchandise and a "pigeon-hole" post office is memorabilia from the early 1900s.

GRADY
POP. 597   ALT. 180   MAP N-2

First settled by J.S. Hall in the late 1840s and called Hall's Station, the establishment of a post office in 1881 by merchant/land owner J.P. Williams resulted in changing the name to Williamsburg until it was renamed for the last time in 1898 after a telegraph operator named Grady. Incorporated 1907.

Grady Public Library. Housed in an original yellow-and-brown railroad depot are the original waiting benches, a "sand bucket" fire extinguisher, old photographs and other items of local history. SR 11E, Downtown. Signs.

Grady Churches. At either end of town on US 65, and three blocks east of downtown on SR 11, are good examples of turn-of-the-century church architecture: two with clapboard and bell towers, one with brick and stained glass.

GRAVETTE
POP. 1,218   ALT. 1,227   MAP A-1

Around 1894, E.T. Gravett moved his newly (c.1892) purchased Chalk Valley Distillery a mile east of Nebo to be on the tracks of two *railroads,* the Kansas City Southern and the St. Louis & San Francisco. The Nebo post office followed, changing its name to conform with the railroad station's traditional spelling of the name Gravette. Mr. Gravett had changed his upon leaving Kentucky because of an argument with his family. Although the town spelled its name Gravette, its founder's bank remained spelled Gravett. Incorporated 1899.

Old Spanish Treasure Cave. An old-fashioned attraction, this one offers a tour through the romance and legend of a mining tunnel where "an old Spaniard" buried his "treasure." Also on the property is a one-story log house said to be over 150 years old, a hand-dug well and nature *trail.* Picnics. SR 59, just S of town.

GREASY CORNER
COMMUNITY   ALT. 203   MAP L-4

In 1919 Bunge "Mac" McCollum built a combination general store-restaurant-gas station at the crossroads of what was then the main highway to Memphis. He called it Mac's Corner. By popular demand, possibly as a comment on the restaurant, it was changed to Greasy Corner. Possible *De Soto* Route.

GREAT RAFT
MAP G-1+2 & H-2

French explorers of the Ohio and Mississippi *Rivers* during the 17th century encountered dangerous snags in the form of log jams and stumps that are said to have been called "chicots" (supposedly "teeth of the river," *Lake Village)* but it was 19th century American surveyors of the Red River who found this particular prehistoric relic, a 140-mile series of natural rafts (logs, stumps and debris) so tightly packed it could be crossed on horseback, and enlarging at a rate of a mile per year and eroding sporadically. Efforts like Capt. Henry Shreve's, beginning in 1833 (four snag boats and 150 men for five years), eventually cleared the river, enabling transportation on the upper Red River and the beginnings of flood control for the farms and towns along it *(Garland)*.

GREEN FOREST
POP. 1,609   ALT. 1,400   MAP A-3

Settled in 1855 and called Scott's Prairie for the surrounding countryside, the town was incorporated in 1895, renaming itself for the specific location. Home of Helen Gurley Brown, publisher of Cosmopolitan.

Banta, Home of Apples. In 1942 the only patented apple in Arkansas, the Quindell, was first seen growing here as a natural hybrid of an Old-Fashioned Winesap and a Red Delicious. Mr. Banta also has an exceptional collection of working Victor Talking Machines, Columbia Gramophones and Edison Phonographs that are demonstrated on request. By the way, the name of the dog listening to the Victor Talking Machine is Nipper. US 62, 5 m. E.

The Antique Doll Museum. High-quality dolls like Bru, Jumeau, Handwerck, Knester, SFBJ and Köpplesdorf are displayed in a series of scale-model rooms carefully arranged with period and replica furnishings. The oldest doll is c.1855, and the largest wears a child's size 6. Some of the props include a Heisly cobalt beer stein, a Steiff Teddy Bear and Rookwood pottery. US 62, 3 m. E.

GREENWOOD
POP. 3,317   ALT. 518   MAP C-1

In 1851 the town was platted as county seat and named for Judge Alfred B. Greenwood of Bentonville, who 10 years later, as a former Commissioner of Indian Affairs, was in charge of recruiting Choctaws and Cherokees for the Confederacy (Battle of Pea Ridge, *National Parks*). From 1861 until 1874 Greenwood and Fort Smith alternated lawsuits with compromises over which would be county seat until finally establishing two separate ones *(Dual County Seats)*. Called the "Coal Capital of Arkansas," the town (1930s) was the chief coal-shipping point for Sebastian County, where in 1937-38 a half-million tons were dug by 1,600 miners *(Hartford)*.

Old Jail Museum. Two previous jails were burned by escaping prisoners. This two-story structure (1892) was built with cut stone. The museum has a large collection of local artifacts. Town Square.

Coleman Observatory. *(Hartford)*

Roadcut. Natural Heritage Area. About 310 million years old, set in vertical beds, this cut in Devil's Backbone Ridge

exposes three major formations (from N to S, oldest last): McAlester, Hartshorne and Atoka. A bed of coal is exposed in the McAlester Formation. US 71, 1 m. S of SR 10.

Sebastian County Courthouse. Sixties Modern, 1969. *Dual County Seat (Fort Smith)*. This courthouse was built on the ruins of its predecessor, which, along with much of the county, was destroyed by a tornado in 1968. Downtown. *(County Profiles)*

GRIST MILL
MAP ALL QUARTERS

Before flour and meal came packaged, the local grist mill served the community, using first water, then steam and finally diesel and electricity to power huge stone wheels for custom grinding grains such as wheat, corn and rye. In 1860 there were 97 of them in Arkansas (second only to lumber in manufactured products). Early "homemade" mills used shafts and pulleys hewn from seasoned hickory with burrs (millstones) cut 12-15 inches wide and over three feet in circumference. Belts for the drive shaft were often made from tanned cowhide. These first mills replaced the primitive but effective "sweep and mortar" that were fashioned by digging a mortar in a stump to grind grain into husks, grits and meal with a spring-pole pestle much the same as a pharmacist or chef would crush ingredients. As centers of gossip and tall tales, grist mills preceded the general store.

GUION
POP. 177   ALT. 313   MAP J-2

Dr. O.T. Watkins established a large plantation and a post office, Wild Haws, c.1853, at present-day LaCrosse (appx. 8 m. NE of *Melbourne*). A steamboat landing on the White *River (Float Streams)* for his plantation was also known as Wild Haws. Although post offices like Yancy and Lewis were established near here in the 1890s, it wasn't until the White River Railway Company *(Mount Olive)* arrived in 1902 that a town was founded. It is believed to have been named for a railroad official.

Silica Sand Mine. First established as a surface operation (c.1915-18), the mines (140-150 feet deep) began in 1925 using small mine cars and mules. The St. Peter sandstone is 97% pure silica, and is used in making glass containers, windshields and windowpanes. Visible from road. No Tours. Signs.

Free Ferry Boat. *(Ferry Boats)* Guion Ferry, W of town, SR 58 at the White River.

GURDON
POP. 2,707   ALT. 210   MAP G-3

Said to have been surveyed beside the roadbed of the Cairo & Fulton *Railroad* c.1874, the town was incorporated in 1880.

Local tradition agrees that the town is named for a railroad official but offers two versions: Gurdon Cunningham, or a Mr. (first name unknown) Gordon whose name was misspelled when applying for a post office.

International Order of Hoo-Hoo/Museum. Said to be the oldest industrial fraternal organization in the world, it is a worldwide forest products association that was founded here in 1892 by six conventioneers stranded by a delayed train. Bolling Arthur Johnson, a lumber trade journalist, conceived the idea, embellishing it with humor. Hoo-Hoo describes "the alarming tuft of hair that grew on the top of the otherwise bald head" of the soon-to-be first Snark of the Universe (president). A black cat, whose tail curls into the number 9, is used to symbolize "Concatenated," a Hoo-Hoo word for "linked together, as in chain or series." Members meet each year at nine past nine on the ninth day of the ninth month. Museum & Hoo-Hoo Monument: SR 53 (Main), E of RR tracks.

The Gurdon Light. "Suddenly the glowing vision appeared before them and began to move across their path." This familar legend relates that just outside Gurdon a train wreck decapitated a crewman whose spirit, lantern in hand, still haunts the track in search of his head. Fox fire? Errant headlights? Walk the tracks and find out. N of town, between US 67 & SR 53.

Reader Railroad. *(Prescott)*

HALLEY
COMMUNITY   ALT. 145   MAP O-3

Cemeteries are a reliable source for town history. A few minutes of detective work can tell an interesting story.

Halley Cemetery/Old Bowie Cemetery. Inside a broken wrought-iron fence a marker states that John Bowie (older brother of Jim, *Washington*) is buried with no headstone. He lived here near Bowie's Station with his family. Two county townships, one in Desha, the other in Chicot, were named for him. He died in 1859. Incidentally, John Bowie was the focus of the so-called Bowie Land Frauds (1829) whereby Spanish land grants were forged and the claims presented for Arkansas titles. Nearby, another grave with a wrought-iron fence in good repair belongs to Judge Charles H. Halley,1853-1913, whose half-brother H.H. Halley is namesake of the town (Eunice, BELOW). N of Jct. SR 35/159 on SR 159.

Levee Road. *(Arkansas City)* Access: Jct. SR 35/159, E on SR 208.

Gaines Landing. Major Wm. Gaines laid a road across his plantation (c.1833) on the Mississippi *River*, charging a toll. The landing was an important port until c.1880 and a pioneer overland *road* through South Arkansas via present-day *Dermott* and *Monticello,* connecting with Ft. Towson, Ok. Vanished. Due E of Halley.

Eunice. The Mississippi, Ouachita and Red River *Railroad* (Arkansas' first railroad, incorporated July 12, 1852) set its eastern terminus here. Before the Civil War a short line was completed to nearby Collins via Dermott with a stop called Bowie Station (John Bowie had bought two miles of land

across its planned path). The terminus was moved to *Arkansas City* when Eunice caved into the river c.1879. The Bowie stop was moved a mile north near town namesake Hilary H. Halley's home. Near Jct. SR 208 and the Levee Road (ABOVE). No Remnants.

HAMBURG
POP. 3,408   ALT. 167   MAP P-2

Selected as "the site of justice" (no name) for newly created Ashley County in 1849, its name appears without explanation on court records of 1850. Tradition claims the origin is associated with deer "hams" (either unusually large or tasty) that so impressed the site selection commissioners in 1849 that they later named the town accordingly. A lame confirmation is that the area was well known for its abundant game. Recently Hamburg has begun sponsoring an annual deerhorn-blowing contest. Incorporated 1854.

Ashley County Museum. A two-story Colonial House (National Historic Register, 1918) displays local history: Indian artifacts, Civil War photographs and household items. The carriage house contains 13 original carriages and buggies (c.1860-1890s). 300 N. Cherry. Signs.

Largest Pine Tree in Arkansas. Reportedly the largest of its species. US 82, 4 m. S. Marker.

Bayou Bartholomew. *(Bayou Bartholomew)* 16 m. E.

Levi Wilcoxon Memorial Forest. *(Crossett)* Natural Heritage Area. 7 m. S of town, US 82 near Jct. SR 81. Signs.

Ashley County Courthouse. Sixties Modern, 1969. It was the first courthouse in Arkansas with a round courtroom. Town Square. *(County Profiles)*

National Historic Register. The Watson-Sawyer House (1870), 503 E. Parker. PORTLAND, AR. (US 165 & SR 278): Dean House and Pugh House, US 165. PARKDALE, AR. (US 165 & SR 8): Williams House, at the corner of SR 8 & SR 209.

HAMPTON
POP. 1,627   ALT. 203   MAP G-4

A recycled town, it was founded in 1851 as the county seat of newly created Calhoun County, lost its economic base during the *Civil War,* then recovered and reincorporated in 1871 as a lumber town on a later spur of the St. Louis Southwestern and Chicago, Rock Island & Pacific *Railroad.* Reportedly named for J.R. Hampton *(El Dorado),* who was an early settler and politician (acting governor in 1851).

Log Houses. Along SR 274 between Tinsman and Fordyce are a number of log houses, some of which are still occupied. SR 274, 10 m. N.

Calhoun County Courthouse. Renaissance Revival, 1909. Features: a clock tower, 18-foot pressed-tin ceilings and the only set of courtroom spectator risers remaining in the state. Downtown. *(County Profiles)*

National Historic Register. Dunn House, 1909. In the front yard is a magnolia tree that was planted c.1865 by Col. L.L. Moss at the grave of his first wife. SR 4, 2 m. W, just W of Little Bay Rd.

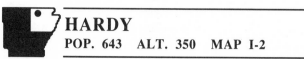

HARDY
POP. 643   ALT. 350   MAP I-2

This construction camp for the Kansas City, Ft. Scott & Gulf *Railroad* received its mail c/o James A. Hardy, Jr. (the subcontractor). When a post office name for a newly created water stop and freight dock community was needed in 1883, the logical choice was to continue using Hardy. Selected county seat 1891-1967 *(Ash Flat)*. Located on the Spring *River (Float Streams)*, the town has been a popular resort since the 1930s. Today native stone buildings line the street, reflecting a nostalgic tourist atmosphere.

Grist Mill. Beside a failed "planned community" stands an abandoned 1959 replica of a *grist mill* whose aura, regardless of age, is historic. US 63, 10 m. E.

HARRISBURG
POP. 1,921   ALT. 287   MAP K-4

Situated on the western slope of *Crowley's Ridge*, settled in 1827 by three Harris brothers from Alabama *(Marianna)* and laid out as a county seat in 1856 (replacing the first one, Bolivar, 1838), the town was incorporated one year after the arrival (1882) of the St. Louis, Iron Mountain & Southern *(Railroad)*.

Buffalo Trail/Missouri-Helena Postal Road. Collectively known as the Missouri-Helena Postal *Road*, its use and destination reflect some of the other names: Chalk Bluff, Military, Wittsburg-Helena and Buffalo (supposedly named for the buffalo that once roamed the area). A portion can be driven along *Crowley's Ridge* from Harrisburg or Jonesboro through *Wittsburg* to Forrest City. SR 14, E to SR 163S, Jct. US 63W; SR 284S to Jct. I-40. Incidentally, other portions can be found along the Ridge by using county maps but vehicles with good traction and ground clearance are necessary. Maps: (State Geological Commission, *Little Rock)*.

Harris Cemetery. The founding family's cemetery (1827) has old and ornate markers. Courthouse, East St. (turns gravel) 1 m. S.

Events/Festivals. Early May: Harrisburg-Lake Poinsett Festival. Held at Downtown Harrisburg & Lake Poinsett *State Park*. Fishing Rodeo. Chili Cook-Off. Crawfish-Eating Contest. Parade

Poinsett County Courthouse. Georgian Revival, 1918. An impressive domed cupola with four clocks is set on a red tile roof. Other features: tall sandstone columns, marble wainscoting and eight gilded plaster eagles. Downtown, East St. *(County Profiles)*

National Historic Register. The Modern News Building, (1888), 216 N. Main.

HARRISON
POP. 9,567   ALT. 1,061   MAP A-3

The town began in 1870 near the 1836 Crooked Creek Post Office and pioneer *road* of today's US 62E *(Yellville)*, SR 206W-SR 68W (Carrollton-Fayetteville Road) and a wagon road to Springfield, Mo. *(Bellefonte)*. Surveyor M.L. Harrison laid out the town while visiting in 1870. In lieu of payment, the town was named for him. Incorporated 1876. The chamber of commerce (US 62, E of SR 7) has maps, railroad memorabilia and a 1950s caboose. Home of North Arkansas Community College and Twin Lakes Vocational Technical School.

Mountain Meadows Massacre. In 1857 a California-bound wagon train formed at present-day Harrison was later attacked near Cedar City, Utah, by Mormons and Indians. Circumstances in 1857: (1) Mormons, occupying what has been called a desert kingdom in Utah, "Deseret," historically had been persecuted by contemporaries, most violently by those in Missouri. (2) Parley Pratt, one of 12 original Mormon apostles, had been murdered by *Arkansawyers* in *Mountainburg*. (3) The federal government was threatening to abolish the church doctrine of polygamy by armed force if necessary. (4) An Arkansas wagon train appeared in Utah, joined by a rowdy group of self-described "Missouri Wildcats" who continually "baited" Mormons along the wagon train's route. Although motivation and official church participation has never been established, in September of 1857 Mormons (said to be disguised as Indians) and Indians attacked the wagon train. After a three-day siege, Mormon John D. Lee, posing as a mediator, claimed he could control the Indians if the wagon train surrendered their weapons and provisions. Once unarmed and away from the wagon train, a reported 118 men, women and children were murdered. Fifteen of the youngest children were spared because "they wouldn't remember enough to be dangerous." Placed in Mormon homes, these children were later found by U.S. marshals and returned to their next of kin *(Leslie)*. Lee was eventually executed for the crime. A granite marker on the courthouse grounds in Harrison lists the victims.

Town Square. One of five cities selected for the Main Street Arkansas preservation program, Harrison has an historic square that is a mixture of modern businesses and old-fashioned architecture. US 65B.

Mystic Caverns. "Two entirely different completely separate caverns" opened in 1982 offer 30-minute guided tours to the eight-story Crystal Dome and the 35-foot Pipe Organ. SR 7, 7 m. S.

The Washington Monument. In 1836 Bellar & Harp Brothers quarried marble for Arkansas' contribution to this national monument, although the reported 2,000-pound block was not shipped until 1849. SR 7, 10 m. S. Marker.

SR 206. Originally (c.1836), the portion of this state highway from *Harrison* to Batavia continued to *Carrollton* as a part of a major *road* system in North Arkansas. Today, older homes and barns reflect its past. Incidentally, SR 206 makes a nice shortcut between US 62 & 65. US 7, S of Town Square.

Events/Festivals. DIAMOND CITY, AR. (SR 7, 22 m. N): Annual Fourth of July Fireworks Program.

Boone County Courthouse. Georgian, 1909. National Historic Register. Features: a wide shaded lawn and interior of local marble, iron and multicolored tile. US 65B, downtown. (*County Profiles*)

National Historic Register. Boone County Jail (1914), US 65B, Central & Willow.

 HARTFORD
POP. 613   ALT. 639   MAP D-1

Founded in 1858 as Sugar Loaf at the base of the mountain of the same name, it changed names in 1869 "for a very deserving widow," Hart, whose property was near a regularly used ford of West Creek. The arrival of the Choctaw & Memphis *Railroad* (Chicago, Rock Island & Pacific) c.1898 flip-flopped towns and names: The community of Gwyne (two miles east) became Hartford and the former one changed to West Hartford.

Coal Dust Pyramids. In the surrounding area are large coal dust pyramids testifying to South Sebastian County's claim as "Coal Capital of Arkansas" (*Greenwood*).

Coleman Observatory. Reportedly the largest of its kind in Arkansas, this facility features a 12-foot tall, 3,000-pound telescope with a 29-inch mirror that, according to its sponsors (Arkansas-Oklahoma Astronomical Society), can bring into very clear focus galaxies up to five billion light years away. Situated at 1,700 feet on Sugarloaf Mountain, plans for the one-acre site include camping, a picnic area and restrooms. SR 45, 7 m. N, SR 252 W. Signs.

 **HAZEN**
POP. 1,636   ALT. 229   MAP L-2

In 1854 Dr. W.C. Hazen brought his family and slaves here from Covington, Ky. The prairie grass (*Carlisle*) was so tall that deer, provided with thick cover right up to the edge of the homestead, could not be kept out of the vegetable garden. The town was surveyed and laid out on his property beside the Memphis & Little Rock *Railroad* in 1873.

Grand Prairie Remnant. Natural Heritage Area (US 70 between *Carlisle* and *DeValls Bluff*). A bird sanctuary, wildflowers and native trees are planned for Hazen's half-mile strip. Visitor's Center, Hazen.

 **HEBER SPRINGS**
POP. 4,930   ALT. 354   MAP K-1

John T. Jones and associates bought Sugar Loaf Springs for $1,500 in 1837, made no improvements and sold the land to Max Frauenthal in 1881 for $10,000. Based on test results of the springs' "medicinal" properties that were obtained by Dr. Heber Jones, son of John T., Frauenthal organized the Sugar

Loaf Springs Company with the intention of creating a spa. The town of Sugar Loaf was incorporated in 1882 at the same time that a post office, Heber, was established. Confusion in mail service and the town's prominent reputation as a spa (1909) brought about the consolidation of the two names in 1910: Heber Springs. Despite the "curative" powers of seven springs and the arrival of the Missouri & North Arkansas *Railroad* in 1908, a general decline in the belief in mineral water ended the town's prosperity by the late 1920s. A different belief in a different kind of water (completion of Greers Ferry *Lake* in 1962) helped revitalize the community.

Spring Park. Housed in modern concrete sheds on this 10-acre park are the old spa's seven medicinal springs whose mineral agents (black, white and red sulphur, iron, arsenic, magnesia and "eye") remain at various, but individually constant, temperatures (54.5°- 61.7°F). Tested by the state health department. Bring a jug. Downtown.

WPA Mural. Actually the mural was financed by the Treasury Department under a fine arts competition program but today most people mistakenly refer to all Depression-era projects as *WPA*. During the 1930s not only farming (*Resettlement Administration*) and construction projects like bridges were sponsored by the federal government but also writing projects (American Guide Series) and art like this 4-by-10-foot mural painted by Louis Freund, representing the pioneer spirit of Arkansas. The mural, one of the last of its kind in the state, is an excellent example of the "heroic style" of painting, which in this instance features a farmer, his wife holding a child, a team of oxen and a log cabin. Downtown, 102 E. Main.

Winkley Swinging Bridge. National Historic Register, 1912. Said to have been designed by the same engineers who built the Golden Gate Bridge, this 550-foot suspension bridge is the only one remaining of three such structures once used to cross the Little Red *River (Float Streams)*. Foot traffic only. SR 110 at Little Red River.

Greers Ferry Lake Visitors Center. Arkansas' first (1983) Corps of Engineers Visitor Center is landscaped with zoysia grass, earthen berms and Bar Harbor Juniper. The redwood and native stone building (6,100-sq.-ft.) is designed for active and passive solar heating and cooling. Guides explain these features as well as conduct special programs with topics like folk music and bald eagles. Along with static displays of geological history and electrical generation, a 30-minute slide show presents the area's history from prehistoric to the present. Recreation and camping: Greers Ferry *Lake*. SR 25, 3 m. N of Heber Springs.

Greers Ferry Lake Dam and Powerhouse. A 45-minute tour gives a close look at the structures and how they work. Recreation and camping: Greers Ferry *Lake*. SR 25, 3 m. N of Heber Springs.

Greers Ferry National Fish Hatchery. Established in 1965, this hatchery produces about 150,000 pounds of trout for northern Arkansas and contiguous states. The water supply comes from 100 feet below the lake surface (44° - 48°F) at a rate of 15,000 gal/min. Small Aquarium. Tours. SR 25, 5 m. N of Heber Springs.

Sugar Loaf Mountain/Trail. *(Clinton)* Shuttle service or boat rental is available at local marinas (25 miles by water) or northern Greers Ferry *Lake* marinas (SR 25, W to SR 16W to E on SR 92).

Hiram Bluffs & Canyon. Across from Hiram Church is an overlook of the "Tiny Grand Canyon." SR 110, 10 m. E.

Events/Festivals. Early Aug: Annual Greers Ferry Lake Water Festival. Arts & Crafts. Auto Show. Hot Air Balloons. Early Oct: Annual Ozark Frontier Trail Festival and Craft Show. City-Wide. Music & Dancing.

Cleburne County Courthouse. Palladian Revival, 1914. National Historic Register. Created February 20, 1883, it is Arkansas' youngest county. Features tall white columns and a large octagonal cupola. Downtown.*(County Profiles)*

HELENA
POP. 9,598   ALT. 189-274   MAP M-4

Situated on the Mississippi *River* at the southern end of *Crowley's Ridge,* Helena was born of two disasters: the *New Madrid Earthquake* (1811-12) and the War of 1812. In each case the federal government offered Louisiana Purchase *(State Parks)* land as reimbursement. It is said that this area was first occupied by Wm. Patterson *(Marianna),* Wm. Strong *(St. Francis, Old)* and Sylvanus Phillips, who settled below the mouth of the St. Francis *River* in the early 1800s, most likely in or near a settlement called St. Francis (vanished). By 1820 Phillips had bought huge tracts of land *(Clarendon),* reselling them and establishing the county *(County Profiles)* named for him. In 1820, along with two other land speculators, Wm. Russell *(Little Rock)* and Nicholas Rightor, Phillips laid out the townsite that was named for his daughter and later made county seat (1830). The second oldest (1833) incorporated city in Arkansas, it and *Little Rock* (1831) were the only two incorporated by the Territorial Legislature. Always a riverboat and cotton town, Helena is a compact composite of Delta life. Home of seven Confederate generals (including Hindman of *Prairie Grove* and Cleburne of Lookout Mountain, Tn.), Conway Twitty, Bishop John Murray Allin (bishop of the Episcopal Church), Phillips County Community College and the National River Academy, where U.S. river pilots receive their training. One of five Main Street Arkansas preservation programs, Helena is an architectural tour town. The chamber of commerce, 111 Hickory Drive (1 blk. off US 49B), and the Arkansas Tourist Information Center, US 49 Bypass W of the bridge, offer excellent maps and visitor guides.

West Helena. Established in 1909 for an expanding industrial base that could not find room in Helena.

Historic Homes. Over 34 houses and buildings are listed in a city guide, including a stucco house believed built in the late 1700s/early 1800s, a lavishly constructed Edwardian mansion and Estavan Hall (1820s), which has a riverfront setting with a terraced lawn and sweeping view. Eighteen are on the National Historic Register. Maps: chamber of commerce and tourist information center. (See History, ABOVE)

Phillips County Museum and Library. National Historic Register. Thought to be the oldest library building (1891) in the state. The museum, one of the few built in Arkansas as a museum, was connected to the library in 1929. The exhibits include: Falconetto (1458-1534) and Boccaccino (1467-1525) paintings, the Stephenson Indian Collection, trophies from the Spanish-American War and items belonging to town founder Sylvanus Phillips and his family.

Confederate Cemetery. Overlooking the Mississippi, a 37-foot monument with a life-size Confederate soldier sculpted from Italian marble was dedicated in 1892 to veterans from East Arkansas and to those who defended Helena *(Civil War).* A magnolia-lined drive leads the way. N of courthouse to Walker to 1801 Holly St. Signs.

Battery D. National Historic Register. It has the only remaining trenches and fortifications of the five main forts used in the Battle of Helena *(Civil War).* US 49B, W on Arkansas to Prairie to 119 Military Rd. Other batteries: maps, chamber of commerce.

American Legion Hut. National Historic Register, 1922. Built after the fashion of WWI doughboy huts in France, it is said that later models across the country were patterned after this one. US 49B, E on Porter, 2 blks.

Old Abner Store. National Historic Register, 1872. Now owned by the Historic Preservation Foundation, it was built by a Swiss immigrant using some of the wood from his flat-bottomed boat. Off US 49B, N to 820 Columbia.

Gravity Hill. This hill can be disorienting for motorists. It gives the impression that the road is climbing when actually it is descending. US 49 to Sulphur Springs Rd. Inquire Locally.

Robert E. Ritchie Steam Electric Station. Red-and-white-striped, the 500-foot chimney can be seen for miles. Gas- or oil-fired boilers produce steam that turns a single shaft turbine generator that was (1961) the largest in the world. Unit Two operates at steam pressures in excess of 3,600 psi, creating temperatures greater than 1,000°F (wood ignites in air at 451°F). SR 20, 4 m. S.

Events/Festivals. Early Apr: Springfest. Music. Activities. Family-Oriented. Downtown. Early May: Historic Helena Tour of Homes. ELAINE, AR. (SR 44, 23 M. S): Early Dec: South Phillips County Christmas Festival. Arts & Crafts. Entertainment. Parade.

Phillips County Courthouse. Classical Revival, 1914. National Historic Register. Renovated in 1984. Features: two-story fluted Corinthian columns on three sides, interior marble stairway and decorative plaster. US 49B, E on Porter, 1 blk. N on Cherry. *(County Profiles)*

National Historic Register. Eighteen structures are on the National Historic Register. (See Historic Homes, ABOVE)

HICKORY FLAT
COMMUNITY   ALT. 665   MAP K-2

Called Davenport, a post office 1890-1932, today's town name reflects the surrounding countryside. From the bluffs south of

the community there is a sweeping view of the Little Red River valley, encompassing *Pangburn,* Center Hill and *Searcy.*
Little Red. The Southwest Trail *(Roads)* crossed the Little Red River *(Float Streams)* just south of this community at Hilger's Ferry (1830s). The Philadelphia Baptist Church, said to be the oldest in the county, was at the site of today's cemetery in Little Red. SR 305, 4.2 m. S at Jct. SR 157.

HIX'S FERRY/PITMAN
GHOST TOWN   ALT. 280   MAP I-4

Said to be the first ferry crossing in Arkansas, it was established on the Current *River (Float Streams)* at the Southwest Trail *(Roads)* c.1800 by Wm. Hix, who sold it c.1806 to Payton Pitman. A reported 2,500 Cherokee wagons passed by it on the *Trail of Tears.* The town of Pitman (settled as Currenton c.1820) was platted here in 1853, gaining a population of 700 by 1860. Temporarily serving as Confederate headquarters (General Hardy) for northeast Arkansas, it was destroyed during the *Civil War.* Randolph and Clay County line at the Missouri border. SR 166, 4 m. N to Supply (directions from Supply can be confusing; inquire locally).
Mt. Pleasant Cemetery. All that remained of Pitman was the 50-60 headstones in this cemetery until the 1970s when a Baptist preacher used all but two for the foundation of his new house. Some Civil War rifle pits can be found about 100 yds. east of here.
Southwest Trail. *(Roads)* Parts of it can be seen across the river in Missouri.

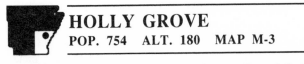

HOLLY GROVE
POP. 754   ALT. 180   MAP M-3

Established on the tracks of the Arkansas Central Railway *(Railroads)* near a group of holly thickets c.1872, incorporated in 1876, it became an important depot between Helena and Clarendon.
The Holly Grove Historic District. National Historic Register. Downtown.
Macedonia Cemetery. Still in use, the markers date from 1861. Inquire Locally.

HOPE
POP. 10,290   ALT. 354   MAP G-2

Surveyed by the Cairo & Fulton *Railroad* c.1853, platted and named for a railroad director's daughter (Hope Loughborough) in 1873, the town was incorporated in 1875. Four years later it began a 60-year political struggle with nearby *Washington* for the county seat, which Hope finally won in 1939. Home of Red River Vocational Technical School, and Bill Clinton, the youngest Arkansas governor (elected 1978 at age 32). Maps: chamber of commerce, 3rd (US 67) & S. Main.

World Champion Watermelons. For over 60 years, with infrequent exceptions, Hope has grown the largest watermelons in the world. The first, a 136-pounder, was sent to President Calvin Coolidge in 1925. The Middlebook family's 195-pound melon held the world's record for 44 years (1935-1979). Since 1979, weights of 200, then 200-plus, have been the standard.
Events/Festivals. Mid-Aug: Hope Watermelon Festival. Crafts. Car Show. Street Dance. 5K Run. Games & Contests.
Hempstead County Courthouse. Moderne, 1939. Replacing two courthouses built in Washington (1836 and 1874), this structure is shaded by some of the largest live oaks in the state as well as many large pines (a few, eight feet in circumference). S. Hervey (SR 4) & 5th. *(County Profiles)*
National Historic Register. Carrigan House (c.1895), 704 W. Ave. B. Foster House, 303 N. Hervey. McRae House, 1113 E. 3rd. K.G. McRae House (1903), 3rd & Edgewood. St. Mark's Episcopal Church (1904), 3rd & Elm.

HOT SPRINGS
POP. 35,781   ALT. 1,450   MAP E-3

Although *De Soto* was probably the first (1541) to record impressions of "The Valley of Vapors," archaeological evidence points to human habitation for 10,000 years. The first "official" report, a survey one year after the Louisiana Purchase *(State Parks)* of 1803, stirred national interest in protecting the hot springs from commercial development, culminating in the nation's first federal reservation in 1832. However, the precedent (later to evolve into the National Park Service) was too late. Prior claims and already existing "bathhouses" (1830) resulted in suits and counter-suits that were not settled until 1876 by the U.S Supreme Court. The arrival (1875) of the "Diamond Jo" narrow-gauge railroad *(Malvern),* settlement of the claims (1876) and separation of the reservation from the city (1877) set development in motion. Today bathhouses, as well as other private businesses in the park (paralleling agreements of 1877), operate as concessions subject to federal inspection and regulations. Home of the Confederate capital of Arkansas (May-July 1862, *Washington),* Quapaw Vocational Technical School, Garland County Community College, Alan Ladd and Bill Clinton (Arkansas' youngest governor, elected 1978 at age 32). The chamber of commerce has excellent maps and literature. Off Central (SR 7) at Convention & Malvern.
The Hot Springs. Naturally sterile, the water was used by NASA to hold moon rocks while searching for signs of life. Beginning a 4,000-year cycle, rainwater percolates deep into the earth, comes in contact with highly heated rock and returns to the surface at 143°F. The combined flow of the 47 hot springs averages 850,000 gallons a day.
Tufa/Algae. Tufa, the insoluble rock around the springs, is calcium and silica salts precipitated by the hot water and "assisted" by algae. One of these algae is found at only four other sites in the world.
Hot Springs National Park. Established 1921 (History, ABOVE). The Visitor Center offers an orientation slide show,

exhibits and tours that include a thermal spring and rock display, the story of the first explorers, a self-guided Thermal and Nature Tour along the Promenade and Bathhouse Row, a visit to Indian Spring at Quapaw Bathhouse and a bathhouse tour. Central & Reserve.

The Fordyce Bathhouse, the most lavish on Bathhouse Row, is the park visitors' center

Bathhouse Row. National Historic Register. Hot Springs Creek, collecting the thermal water as runoff, was first a focal point for the early group of crude canvas and lumber structures, and then later for the grand 20th century bathhouses, most of which were built after the state's worst fire (50 blocks) in 1913. The creek was roofed in 1877 and covered by today's Central Ave. Along this street, scented by large magnolias, are the remaining spas. Only Buckstaff Bathhouse still provides traditional baths. The other bathhouses, retaining their essential character, are now leased for a variety of adaptive uses. Incidentally, plans are being made for a multi-million dollar restoration project of Bathhouse Row, which include additional spas and other recreational facilities. From N to S: SUPERIOR: Classical Revival, 1915. Simple interior (but with the usual generous use of tile and marble). Closed 1983. HALE: Classical Revival, 1915; remodeled as Spanish Revival, 1939. Simple Interior. Closed 1978. MAURICE: Spanish and Classical Revival, 1911. The men's bath hall has a large cobblestone fireplace and wood carvings. Closed 1974. FORDYCE: Spanish Renaissance Revival, 1915. Its library, music room, parlors for men and women, bowling lanes, gymnasium, roof garden, marble (Italian, pink and Vermont) and skylights — including an 8,000-piece dome representing Neptune's daughter, mermaids and fish — make it the most lavish on Bathhouse Row. Closed 1962. Now a part of the park visitors' center. QUAPAW: Spanish Revival, 1921. Its outstanding feature is an exterior dome with insets of colored tile and a decorative cupola. Closed 1984. OZARK: Spanish Revival, 1922. Modest. Closed 1977. BUCKSTAFF: Classical Revival, 1911. White tile floors with floor to ceiling Colorado marble, the bathhouse still offers a full service of bathing equipment (22 porcelain tubs) and massage. Open. LAMAR: Spanish/Classical Revival, 1922. Although simply furnished, it has a gymnasium and murals in the lobby. Closed 1985. Bathhouse Row is owned by the National Park Service. Central Ave. (SR 7), N of US 70/270.

Thermal Water Bathing. Historically taken for therapeutic purposes, the baths are provided in hotels as well as in the park. A traditional bath consists of assignment of bathing attendant according to gender (sheets are worn between bathing procedures), soaking in an oversized tub (100°F) for 20 minutes, scrubbing with a mitt (optional), steam cabinet (2-5 minutes), sitz tub (108°F) for 10 minutes, hot pack for 20 minutes, warm shower for two minutes, massage for 20 minutes (optional), cooling and dressing (30 minutes). Also of-

fered are whirlpools, recreational pools (hot tubs and saunas) and exercise equipment. Hydrotherapy by prescription only. Swimsuits rented for coed baths.

Hot Springs Mountain Tower. Offers an orientation to town from a bird's-eye view. N of Bathhouse Row, E on Fountain to Hot Springs Mtn. Dr.

Oaklawn Thoroughbred Race Track. Opened in 1905 as the Oaklawn Jockey Club, it had the first glass-enclosed, steam-heated grandstand in America. Today it is rated among the top five tracks, drawing over a million in attendance during the season (Feb. - Apr.) and offering, prior to the Kentucky Derby, the nation's richest race for three-year-olds ($500,000). N of Jct. SR 7 & 88.

Wildwood House. Queen Anne, 1884. National Historic Register. Beginning at the 300-pound front door, the interior is unusual. It was designed with indoor plumbing, built-in closets and kitchen cabinets, extra large rooms with seven different native woods, intercoms and air-conditioning. Original Furnishings. Tours. N of Bathhouse Row, SR 7 at Glen.

Architecture. Notable architectural styles ranging from antebellum to Russian are in an area behind the courthouse and along the adjoining streets of Ouachita, Hawthorne, Quapaw, Fern, Prospect and Orange.

Army-Navy Hospital. This 1933 complex replaced the original 1880s structure built on 25 acres for veterans of the *Civil War*. Today it is the Hot Springs Rehabilitation Center, providing therapy for the mentally and physically handicapped. Behind Bathhouse Row, Reserve St.

Spencers Corner. The corner of Central Ave. and Bridge (a street only 60 feet long) was the infamous brothel/gambling section of Hot Springs. Ironically, Ripley's Believe-It-Or-Not listed Bridge St. as "The World's Busiest Street For Its Size." S of Bathhouse Row.

Oaklawn Race Track had the first steam-heated, glass-enclosed grandstand in the U.S.

The Fine Arts Center. Along with a Little Theater Group and works by the Southern Artists Association are paintings, drawings, photos, prints and sculpture. Old Roller Rink. Off SR 7, 815 Whittington.

Mid-America Museum. State-owned, the only "hands-on museum" in Arkansas encourages visitors to experiment with the principles of energy, matter and life. Through a series of exhibits it is possible to "see" how vision can upset equilibrium, create magnets, bend-break-bounce light, walk into a camera to see how it perceives the world, fly (but not in) a hot air balloon, try to crush air to feel how "solid" it is or whip up a do-it-yourself tornado. The museum also has what's said to be the largest outdoor freshwater aquarium in the country. W on US 270, N on SR 227, then N on Mid-America Blvd.

Medical Arts Building. Gothic, 1929. National Historic Register. Count the floors (16). For 31 years it was the tallest building in Arkansas. As of 1987, the 40-story TCBY Tower in Little Rock is the tallest. 236 Central at Fountain.

Mountain Valley Spring. First bottled in 1883, this popular water flows (54,000 gal/day at 65°F) from the largest cold water spring in the area, and is reportedly always in the Senate cloak room and on official trips of Air Force One. Attractively Landscaped. Tours and Tastings. SR 7, 12 m. N.

Arkansas Alligator Farm. In 1902 H.I. Campbell began what was probably the first exhibit of its kind in America. Over 30 of the alligators are said to range in age from 250-350 years. "Pine Bluff" (named for where it was caught) measures 12.5 feet long, and is claimed to be about 450 years old. Also on display is the "merman" skeleton featured on TV in "That's Incredible" and "Ripley's Believe-It-Or-Not." SR 7, N of Bathhouse Row, end of Whittington Ave.

Wax Museum. "They Seem Alive." Josephine Tussaud's 100-plus wax figures are made from beeswax mixed with a "secret" compound to make the "skin" appear translucent. Human hair and "medical eyes" complete the effect. Costumed and placed in seven themes and 36 settings, the wax impersonators portray kings and cartoon characters, history and heroes, murderers and movie stars. Da Vinci's "Last Supper" is staged with sound and light animation. 250 Central at Bathhouse Row.

I.Q. Zoo. For over 30 years it has presented the likes of Chicky Mantle, a baseball-playing chicken, Bert Backquack and his Barnyard Band and a long line of others: a sharpshooter rabbit, roller-skating macaw, piano-playing cat and on and on. Featured in national newspapers, magazines and network television. 606 Central at Bathhouse Row.

Tiny Town. This miniature mechanized village, which took 35 years to build, has animated figures less than three inches high set in scenes as familiar as a farm, blacksmith shop, Indian village and sawmill. Off SR 7, N of Bathhouse Row, 347 Whittington.

Carpenter Dam. This second hydro-electric station built by AP&L (early 1930s) formed 6,000-acre Lake Hamilton by damming the Ouachita River. Picnic Area. E on US 270; then S 2.5 m. on SR 128 to the access road. Signs.

Lake Hamilton/State Fish Hatchery. Built in 1940 and renovated in 1960, it produces mostly warm water species like bass, sunfish, crappie and catfish, although it does raise rainbow trout in late fall and winter as well as Israeli and Chinese carp. Supplied by lake water at 1,800 gal/min, 30 ponds produce .75-2.5 million specimens annually. Boating, swimming and fishing (catfish, bluegill, crappie, bass, hybrid striper, sunfish, trout and walleye). Picnic Area. SR 7, 12 m. S; SR 290, 3 m. E. Signs.

Events/Festivals. Late Oct: Annual Arkansas Octoberfest. German Foods. Bands. Arts & Crafts.

Garland County Courthouse. Renaissance Revival, 1905. National Historic Register. Located in the National Park, it took an act of Congress to acquire the property for county use. From the domed cupola to the massive arches inside, the workmanship and appointments are first rate. S of Bathhouse Row, at Ouachita & Hawthorne. *(County Profiles)*

National Historic Register. There are 17 structures on the Register. Maps: chamber of commerce.

HUNTSVILLE
POP. 1,394   ALT. 1,453   MAP A-2

First named Huntsville by pioneers from Huntsville, Madison County, Alabama, the name was changed to Sevierville by the new postmaster to honor his favorite politician, A.H. Sevier (Arkansas' first U.S. senator), in 1836 at the same time it was made temporary county seat of Madison County. The original founding families had the name changed back when the town was platted and made permanent county seat in 1839. Mostly destroyed during the *Civil War*, it was incorporated in 1877.

Town Square. Still the center of town life, this late 19th - early 20th century town square has modern businesses housed in buildings of field and quarry stone.

Governors Hill. Both Isaac Murphy, who was elected governor (1864-68) by *Arkansawyers* north of the *Arkansas River* when they repudiated the Confederacy and adopted a "Federal Constitution" *(Civil War)*, and Orval Faubus (longest-serving governor, 1955-1967, *Little Rock* Central) built their homes on this hill overlooking town. Murphy's is gone. Faubus's is occasionally open for tours. Near Jct. SR 23 & 68, E side of town. Signs.

Madison County Courthouse. Renaissance Moderne, 1939. Austere and brick, this building was built one year before the first paved county *road* was laid. *(County Profiles)*

National Historic Register. Old Alabam School (c.1875), Jct. AR 68 & 127.

JASPER
POP. 519   ALT. 850   MAP B-3

Settled, platted and named by its first postmaster (1843), John M. Ross (a Cherokee), in 1842 as the county seat of newly created Newton County. No records exist as to why it is named Jasper. The best guess is that the colorful rocks in the area along with the Biblical reference to Jasper ("precious stone") as a cornerstone of the New Jerusalem were the basis, although Wm. Jasper, a Revolutionary War hero, is also a possibility. Newton County claims to be the only Arkansas county never to have a mile of railroad track. As late as the 1940s residents were heard using Elizabethan expressions like "yon side" (the other side) and "air you agoin" (are you going).

Parker-Hickman Homestead. Oral history records it as one of the oldest (c.1838) homesteads on the Buffalo *River (Float Streams)*. The main structure was built with hand-hewn logs, pegged-loft rafters and N. Carolina dovetailing. Lived in continuously until 1979, it shows signs of remodeling: later additions (1896), a metal roof, sample wallpaper squares and newspaper insulation. The chimney (beveled sawn stone) has never needed repair. Set a quarter mile off the river with log outbuildings, a spring and orchard, it is a striking example of Ozark Mountain life. Incidentally, in 1972, the Buffalo River was designated a national river, making it the first of its kind in America (Buffalo National River, *National Parks)*. Take SR

7 appx. 5 m. N to Koen Experimental Forest sign, W on gravel road (mostly downhill) for appx. 6 m.

Diamond Cave. A true 1930s style attraction, this cave was discovered by "Uncle Sammy and Andy Hudson in 1832" *(Parthenon)*. The descent into the 21-mile cave (said to be among the largest in the country) begins by drawing back a plastic shower curtain. The two miles available for guided tours include formations like Icicle Ceiling, Garden of Eden and Japanese Tea Room. The grounds, a large parklike picnic area, has two 19th century log buildings, one of which was a two-story hotel. SR 327, 4 m. S. Signs.

Alum Cove/Natural Bridge. This spectacular 130-by-20-foot natural rock formation was used by both wagons and log trucks. A one-mile *trail* passes over and under it, showing off other inventive acts of nature like "goat houses" (rock overhangs and caves), rocky creeks and wild magnolias (locally called "cowcumber" trees). SR 7, 16 m. S to SR 16 W .5 m.; FM 1206, 4 m. NW (the skeleton of a large log structure is on FM 1206) or via *Parthenon* .

Events/Festivals. Early May: Newton County Arts and Crafts Show and Sale. Late Oct: (same as previous).

Newton County Courthouse. Folk Classicism, 1939. In 1938 a suspiciously convenient fire destroyed this courthouse's predecessor and all the county's records. The sheriff, suspected of embezzlement, fled. Today's structure was built using cement floors and locally quarried granite walls. Each room is designed as a fireproof vault. Downtown. *(County Profiles)*

JENNY LIND
COMMUNITY   ALT. 525   MAP C-1

A community since 1850 and the site of the first court held in newly formed Sebastian County (1851), it was named for "The Swedish Nightingale," who, having "creating an unprecedented sensation" in 1847 London opera circles, retired in 1849 to tour, including one in America from 1850-52 with P.T. Barnum's circus for a reported $125,000. Not included on some maps, it is just E of US 71, appx. 6 m. S of Fort Smith.

Coleman Observatory. *(Hartford)*

JEROME
POP. 54   ALT. 131   MAP P-3

Formerly Blissville (c.1900), situated on the St. Louis, Iron Mountain & Southern *(Railroad)*, the town was renamed (c.1916) for its principal business, the Jerome Hardware Lumber Company (which was named for the owner's son, Jerome). Well on its way to being a ghost town in the mid-1930s, 3,535 acres were bought by the *Resettlement Administration* for an experimental agricultural program similar to *Dyess*. A few Victorian houses and the original lumber company are still standing along the dirt streets.

Denson Relocation Camp. *(Rohwer)* In the summer of 1942, approximately 120,000 Japanese-Americans (75% of whom had been born in America) were relocated because of WWII (all were suspected of sympathy with Japan). About 8,500 were detained here. From 1944-45 German POWs replaced the Japanese. Some salvaged barracks *(Rohwer)* were later used for local buildings. All that remains now is a towering brick smokestack in a farmer's field. E side of US 165.

JONESBORO
POP. 31,530   ALT. 295   MAP J-4

At the site of Loch Bee Post Office (BELOW), the town was founded in 1859 on the eastern slope of *Crowley's Ridge* and was named for Wm. Jones, who proposed formation of the town's new county (1859), Craighead, despite the county namesake's heated opposition (his home county, Mississippi, stood to lose prime farmland). Incorporated in 1883, the population escalated (300 to 2,000) with the arrival that same year of three *railroads* (Texas & St. Louis, the Kansas City, Ft. Scott & Gulf and the St. Louis, Iron Mountain & Southern). Home of Arkansas State University. Maps: chamber of commerce, 593 S. Madison, US 49/63B, W on Jefferson.

Loch Bee Post Office. Established in 1854 to serve 40 families in a two-mile radius, it was supplanted by Jonesborough (changed to Jonesboro, 1894). This log cabin (c.1852) is thought to be the original Loch Bee (Scottish for Lake Bee) Post Office. On the public library grounds, US 49/63B, W on Oak, S on Madison.

Buffalo Trail. *(Harrisburg)*

Arkansas State University Museum. Begun in 1936, accredited by the American Association of Museums, it has a superior collection ranging from 100-million-year-old fossils to an 1868 covered wagon. Highlights include 18th century samplers, artifacts of Arkansas and Southwest Indians, an 1850 Baccarat crystal candelabrum, an English Victorian dollhouse, nearly 40 species of mounted birds in flight, dolls from around the world (folk art, Indian and collectible) and exhibits from American military history (the Revolutionary War to Vietnam). Between Aggie & Marshall. ASU Campus, US 49B/49.

Islamic Center. Said to be Arkansas' only mosque, the architecture (64' x 64' x 64') is authentic, including the conical tower and its orientation towards Kaaba in Mecca, Saudi Arabia (from Jonesboro north-northeast). Built by private Saudi contributions (appx. $400,000), the mosque serves an estimated 250-300 Muslims. W of ASU, US 49B at Rogers.

Saudi Arabian Customs Training Project. The only one of its kind in America, this program, begun in 1982, provides a two-year computer education program as well as others in English and administration for recently recruited and "in service" customs agents. ASU Campus US 49/49B.

Craighead Forest Park Campground. This city-owned facility has an 80-acre lake, fishing, swimming, boat ramps, off-road cycle area, ball field and modern camping conveniences of hot showers, electrical and water hookups, dump station, picnic sites with grills and 26 campsites. SR 141, 3.5 m. S.

Events/Festivals. TRUMAN, AR. (US 63, 11 m. S):

Early Oct: Wild Duck Festival. Arts & Crafts. Bar-B-Q Cook-Off. 5K Run. Duck-Calling Contest. WEINER, AR. (SR 49, 19 m. S): Early Oct: Annual Arkansas Rice Festival. Rice Cook-Off & Tasting. 10K Run. Tractor Pulls. Music. Dancing. Incidentally, Weiner reportedly has the largest rice farm in the world.

Craighead County Courthouse. Art Deco, 1934. *Dual County Seat (Lake City).* The only truly Art Deco Courthouse in Arkansas. On the grounds are two markers representing "firsts": first monument honoring WW I soldiers and sailors in the South, and a monument to Hattie Caraway, the first elected female U.S. senator (1932 & 38), the first woman to head a Senate committee and first to preside over the U.S. Senate. US 49/63B at Washington. *(County Profiles)*

National Historic Register. Bell House (c.1903), 303 W. Cherry. Frierson House (c.1890), 1112 S. Main. Washington Historic District: between Madison and McClure (US 49/63B, 1 blk. W on Washington).

JUDSONIA
POP. 2,025   ALT. 221   MAP K-2

The claim of having the only name of its kind is fitting for Judsonia's unusual beginnings and self-promotion. Originally called Prospect Bluff in 1840, by 1859 it was a prospering steamboat landing. Untouched by the Federals during the *Civil War,* it was invaded afterward by Northern immigrants responding to promotional literature from Judson University's recruitment program (Adoniram Judson, Baptist Foreign Missionary, *Pangburn).* The Northerners established a subdivision on the north side of town, near the university. Although not a separate town, nor even of community status, in 1874 they maneuvered an "incorporation," renaming both Prospect Bluff and its subdivision Judsonia on the basis that it would better advertise the university. Possible *De Soto* Route.

Grand Army of the Republic (GAR) Monument. Unusual for the South, but logical because Judsonia was settled by Northern immigrants, this Union Civil War monument is surrounded by the graves of Yankee soldiers. Traditionally, Federal casualties were removed from local Southern grave sites and reburied in their hometowns or national cemeteries *(Fort Smith).* Evergreen Cemetery. In Town.

Judsonia-Kensett Bridge. Built across the Little Red *River (Float Streams)* in 1917, this iron bridge is set on a turnstile like its nearby railroad counterpart. Just S of town.

KINGSTON
COMMUNITY   ALT. 1,367   MAP A-2

The name King has caused a lot of confusion in this township. Tradition and historical records, including maps, are at odds. Alabama pioneer Henry King, while exploring the area c.1827 died of appendicitis next to the *river,* and in the township, which later were supposedly named for him. King Johnston

reportedly platted the town in 1853, recording it as Kingston (King John*ston).* However, maps (1840s through the 1870s) carry the town as Kings River. Located on the Fayetteville-Hixs Ferry postal *road,* but never incorporated. Proximity to *Huntsville* has kept it relatively small.

Town Square. Small, old and informal, there are interesting structures on and near it, including Bunch's Grocery (two-story white clapboard c.1880) and the Madison Bank & Trust (National Historic Register, 1911: pressed tin ceiling and siding). Picnic shelters north of town overlook rolling pastures.

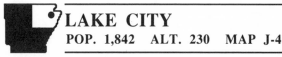

LAKE CITY
POP. 1,842   ALT. 230   MAP J-4

First described in 1848 as a small settlement on the St. Francis *River* known as Old Town, it grew steadily as a steamboat landing and trading post community. In 1878, application for a post office was accepted by Washington, D.C., but as Sunk Lands, not as Old Town (an "Old Town" already existed, *Lake View).* Incidentally, the name was probably selected by Washington because of the *New Madrid Earthquake* that helped shape this region. The two names continued to be used, one for the town and one for the post office, until the residents changed first the name of the town in 1881 and then the post office (1886) to Lake City for a nearby "lake" (no remnants) that was actually a pond or pool of the St. Francis River. Although its first business district was along the St. Francis, selection as a *dual county seat* in 1883 and the arrival of the Jonesboro, Lake City & Eastern *Railroad* in 1897 influenced the literal shifting of the town away from the river to its present "inland" location. Incorporated 1889.

Lake City Bridge. Christened by a "Bridge Queen" with a bottle of beer in 1934, it might be the only drawbridge in the world that has never been raised. Still classified at that time as an inland waterway bridge, it was required to allow river traffic to pass, despite the fact that the St. Francis River, because of extensive flood control projects *(Flood of 1927),* had become unnavigable at this location. SR 18 at St. Francis River.

Craighead County Courthouse. Georgian Revival, 1883. *Dual County Seat (Jonesboro).* It is now the only all wooden courthouse in the state and, although not a requirement of the state statutes, the only county that elects its deputy sheriff and deputy clerk. Downtown. *(County Profiles)*

LAKE DICK
COMMUNITY   ALT. 205   MAP N-2

National Historic Register, c.1935. Encircling the lake c.1935 was an experimental farm cooperative *(Resettlement Administration)* of 80 "modern" houses, syrup and feed mills, a school, retail store, gin and reserved acreage. Unlike *Lakeview, Dyess* and *Plum Bayou,* the land (nearly 4,000 acres), the buildings and the equipment were leased by the cooperative. Members, from farmers to merchants, were paid according to their tasks.

Profits were divided at the end of the year. Government communities structured like this were notable targets for some critics' claims of socialism. No longer listed on some maps, it is directly across the river from *Pine Bluff*, NW of the elbow of SR 88.

LAKE VIEW
POP. 609   ALT. 172   MAP M-4

Over 150 years ago Old Town Lake was an arm of the Mississippi *River* used by boats to supply surrounding plantations near Old Town. The site's name was changed to suit a *WPA* project (BELOW). Possible *De Soto* Route and area of winter headquarters in 1542-43.

Lake View Colony. An experimental agricultural cooperative *(Resettlement Administration)* like its all-white counterpart in *Dyess,* this 1937 project (blacks only) bought 5,600 acres at Old Town Lake to be used as a part-private and part-collective enterprise.

Old Town Lake. One of the many oxbows left by the Mississippi River, this 900-acre lake offers fishing for bluegill, catfish, crappie and bass. Adjacent.

LAKE VILLAGE
POP. 3,088   ALT. 124   MAP P-3

Legend claims that Chicot County, for which this town is county seat, was named for La Salle's 1686 reference to this area as Isle de Chicot (supposedly translated as Island of the Teeth of the River). The "teeth" were cypress knees in Lake Chicot (called Grand Lake, c.1826, and Old River Lake until c.1880), which resembled the snags constantly encountered on *rivers* in that era *(Great Raft)*. Lake Village was laid out in 1856 and made county seat in 1857, the fourth county seat in 34 years: Villemont and Columbia were washed away; Masona was too far from the river for business activity. Lake Village, secluded in a wild swampy wasteland, was popular as a retreat for hunters and the hunted. Today it is still a popular recreational area (Chicot *State Park*).

Lake Chicot. Formerly a horseshoe-shaped false arm of the Mississippi River, today it is the largest natural body of water in Arkansas. (Lake Chicot *State Park*)

Villemont/Point Chicot. A Spanish land grant of Don Carlos Villemont, who died at Arkansas Post *(National Park)* before establishing claim, this 1823 river port was as tough as they came. It served as a mail drop and supply depot for a 60-mile area, and as a port road to Arkansas Post and Little Rock. Later western migration opened a route beginning here through South Arkansas along the Fort Towson *Road*. Washed away in 1847. No Remnants. SR 144 at the river.

Stuarts Island. A stronghold for the infamous John Murrell (1803-44, *Marked Tree),* it was attacked and burned by residents of the county. Near the lake's upper end. No Trace.

Lindbergh Monument. In 1923, four years before his record-setting nonstop New York City to Paris flight, Charles Lindbergh made an emergency landing in a resident's back yard. That night it is said he made aviation history by being the first to fly after dark. (Whether it was actually THE first night flight is arguable, but it was HIS first.) Lakeshore Dr. Private yard, S of the country club, W side. Marker.

Levee Road. *(Arkansas City)* E end of SR 144 or at the Mississippi River Bridge.

Battle of Ditch Bayou. *(Civil War)* Near Ditch Bayou Bridge & US 82, E of town. Marker.

Lake Chicot Pumping Plant. Farmland drainage (silt and pesticides) was ruining the lake's ecosystem; flooding and erosion was destroying farmland. This 74-million-dollar plant, one of the nation's largest *(Marianna,* W.G. Huxtable), uses 12 pumps (10 with nine-foot diameters) to divert water from Lake Chicot to the Mississippi River at a rate of three million gal/min. N of Jct. SR 257/144. Signs.

Chicot County Park. With 90 campsites, it offers water and electrical hookups, heated showers, dump station and boat ramp. US 82, 3.5 m. from foot of Mississippi River Bridge.

Chicot County Courthouse. Fifties Modern, 1956. Possibly the only courtroom in Arkansas with a lake view. A Confederate soldier, high on a pedestal, guards the intersection and lake. Downtown. *(County Profiles)*

National Historical Register. SHIVES, AR. (S end of lake on SR 142): Lakeport Plantation (c.1850), 3 m. S.

LEPANTO
POP. 1,964   ALT. 225   MAP K-4

Settled c.1894, it was laid out on land owned by C.B. Greenwood in 1901 and incorporated in 1909. Named for no known reason in honor of the Battle of Lepanto, 1571 (Christians, in a naval encounter, ended Turkish power on the Mediterranean Sea). One explanation could be that the area was so subject to flooding (Rivervale Tunnel, BELOW; *New Madrid Earthquake)* that the first post office was in a houseboat and the city boardwalk was raised on piers. Neighboring communities referred to the town as Lamp City because of the eccentric habits of the first electric generator operator, who shut down power at will, leaving the town lighted only by oil lamps.

Museum-Lepanto USA. Poinsett County's only museum, it offers "a living model of the Delta's past," using replicas of a country store, doctor's office, blacksmith shop and post office to display items from the Victorian era as well as separate exhibits ranging from fossilized Delta mud to one of the first Maytag washers. Main St. Downtown.

Rivervale Tunnel. Possibly the only place in the world where two rivers cross – one under the other. In an on-going battle with flooding (Flood of 1927) of the St. Francis River *(Marked Tree)* Poinsett County farmers built a tunnel under the bed of the Left Hand Chute (of Little River) for the waters of Buffalo Ditch. SR 135, 5 m. N at Rivervale, Ar.

Events/Festivals. Late Sept: Annual Terrapin Derby. Turtle Races. "Activities."

LESLIE
POP. 501   ALT. 925   MAP B-4

Settled c.1825 on Cove Creek, it was known as Wiley's Cove (post office, 1851). In the late 1880s or early 1900s, the name was changed for either Samuel Leslie (Wiley's Cove's first postmaster) or his brother Jack, who opened the first business, a *grist mill,* c.1880. Incorporated in 1902 as Leslie with the arrival (1903) of the St. Louis & North Arkansas (Missouri & North Arkansas *Railroad).* Stone buildings reflect the early 1900s when the town was surrounded by white oaks, the raw material it used to make barrel staves. Home of Twittie Baker, youngest survivor (seven months old) of the Mountain Meadows Massacre *(Harrison),* who was returned to relatives.

Railroad Depot. The early 20th century cut-limestone depot sits beside vanished tracks of the Missouri & North Arkansas *Railroad.* Just E of US 65 on SR 66 and Cove Creek.

Leslie Grist Mill. Now derelict, this three-story clapboard building serves as a hay barn beside Cove Creek. US 65 to the 1st street N. Inquire Locally.

LEWISVILLE
POP. 1,476   ALT. 237   MAP H-2

The town began with a flip-flop of names and the establishment of the Texas and St. Louis *Railroad.* Originally a few miles north, Lewisville (c.1835, county seat 1840) was named for the euphemism, Lewis's Villa, for Lewis Battle Fort's slave quarters. The present site, first just a depot for the railroad (1883), changed names from Galveston to New Lewisville to today's Lewisville. Old Lewisville, to complete the confusion, has now been misnamed on highway markers as North Lewisville.

LaGrange. Also known as Lafayette Court House as early as c.1827, and located on the Red *River* (eastern boundary for the Caddo at that time), it was county seat until 1840 (Log Jail, BELOW). No Remnants.

Log Jail. Formerly located at La Grange, this c.1828 jail has been relocated and restored. The inside walls still have calendar marks etched by the prisoners. Contains a few historical items. Courthouse Grounds.

Both Little Rock and Arkopolis were used as names of Arkansas Territory's new capital

Old 336. Built in 1909, this mogul-type locomotive operated until 1961, when it was retired and then donated to LaFayette County. SR 29, 6 blks. E on 6th.

Lafayette County Courthouse. Moderne, 1942. On the grounds: a log jail and the only cemetery on a courthouse lawn in Arkansas ("comes with the territory" gains real meaning here). The donated land was previously a cemetery. Tombstone dates begin at 1860. SR 29. Downtown. *(County Profiles)*

National Historic Register. The King-Whatley Building (1902), 2nd & Maple.

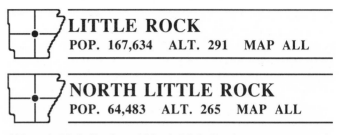

LITTLE ROCK
POP. 167,634   ALT. 291   MAP ALL

NORTH LITTLE ROCK
POP. 64,483   ALT. 265   MAP ALL

Although Little Rock and North Little Rock are separate entities, for the purpose of organization and for the ease of referring to their points of interest, the two cities have been included together in this section.

Early Little Rock History. Established in 1820-21 on a bluff at the intersection of two major transportation systems: the *Arkansas River* and the Southwest Trail *(Roads).* Early explorers noted a large rock prominence on the river's north shore (later to be called "French Rock" by Bernard de la Harp in 1722) that not only marked the approximate 150 river-mile point from Arkansas Post *(National Park)* and the Arkansas River's sweeping bend toward the south but also the transition from alluvial plains to rugged high lands. This "Big Rock" would be the counterpoint for the "Little Rock" (a smaller outcropping just downstream on the south shore) for which the 1820 post office was named. The site was chosen by two rival land speculators (Wm. O'Hara and Wm. Russell) from St. Louis as a likely location for a major city. O'Hara owned *New Madrid Earthquake* (land) Certificates for property here and is said to have been briefly in partnership with Stephen F. Austin *(Fulton, Washington).* Russell held Wm. Lewis's "Preemption Claim" (like a later Homestead Act claim but transferable), which was the first (1812) recorded "deed" of the site. Each claim overlapped the other, with Russell's being "the choicest" riverfront property. O'Hara had the land surveyed in 1820 amid talk that the Territorial Capital was to be moved from Arkansas Post and, with only a permanent population of nine men, petitioned for Little Rock to be selected. While the Territorial Legislature debated (the majority favored *Cadron),* Russell filed suit against O'Hara, claiming trespassing. Meanwhile, O'Hara's group literally moved Russell's Little Rock (except one stubborn building that had to be blown up) to O'Hara's "town," which was now named Arkopolis (although listed on early 1820s maps, Arkopolis was never officially adopted as the capital's name or recognized as a separate entity). Despite this free-for-all, the 1820 State Legislature designated Little Rock as the capital effective 1821 (some members of the legislature had acquired town lots). This boisterous new city (an 1826 law prohibited shooting in the streets on Sunday) grew slowly with the help of mass migration through it to the newly created state of Texas (1836) and the California gold rush of 1849. After the *Civil War* its population boomed from 3,727 in 1860 to 12,000 in 1870, and with the arrival of the Cairo & Fulton *Railroad,* the town more than doubled

(25,874 by 1890). Little Rock was the first (1831) city incorporated in Arkansas, one of two cities *(Helena)* incorporated by the Territorial Legislature and (until captured) the first Confederate State Capital *(Washington, Civil War)*. Home of: Gen. Douglas MacArthur, Brooks Robinson, UALR (University of Arkansas at Little Rock), Philander Smith College, Arkansas Baptist College, the Climber Motor Corporation (Arkansas' only automobile manufacturing company, 1919-24) and, reportedly, the third (1879) telephone exchange established in America. Little Rock Visitors' Center, between US 67/70 and I-30 on Markham at Main (Statehouse Convention Center), should be consulted for a thorough tour of town. (Site listings are combined with North Little Rock's, BELOW.)

Early North Little Rock History. Probably nowhere in Arkansas has any town used so many names so often in such a short period of time. Always a separate city, it was first established in 1838 as DeCantillon by a U.S. Army officer, Richard DeCantillon Collins, at the site of a ferry landing. Briefly reestablished as Huntersville just after the completion of the Memphis & Little Rock *Railroad* in the early 1860s (named for the superintendent of the line, although some say for the hunting in the swamps and bogs), it was primarily used as a troop garrison until renamed Argenta (silver) by the family of Col. Richard Newton in honor of his father's investment in nearby silver mines. Neither the town nor the mines were successful, but the railroad shops of neighboring Barring Cross and its 1873 railroad bridge (also used for other traffic) across the *Arkansas River* marked the area as important. In 1890 Little Rock annexed Argenta as its 8th ward, causing a community north of this new ward to incorporate as North Little Rock in order to block further annexation. Through a 1903 act of the General Assembly and a State Supreme Court decision in 1904, the 8th ward (old Argenta) was annexed by North Little Rock and both renamed Argenta. As a final flip-flop, in 1917 the Argenta City Council voted to change its name to North Little Rock. The old name is no longer heard unless used by old-timers referring to the capital city as South Argenta. Home of Mary Steenburgen, Shorter College, Pulaski Vocational Technical School and Arkansas' largest enclosed shopping center, McCain Mall. Maps: Tourist Information Center, I-40 exit 150. (Site listings are combined with Little Rock's, BELOW.)

Some North Little Rock old-timers still refer to Little Rock as South Argenta

---

The Little Rock. (See Early Little Rock History, ABOVE) The "Little Rock" is marked with a monument and plaque. A pavilion exhibits early history of the area. Riverside Park. Rock & Markham.

The Big Rock. (See Early Little Rock History, ABOVE) A large rock prominence, upstream on the north side, can be seen from Main St. or the I-30 bridge. Used as a quarry, most of it is now defaced.

State Capitol. The second building for state government, it was built 1899-1911 on land appropriated in 1838 for a state penitentiary, and was designed as a scaled-down version (complete with dome) of the nation's capitol. This very impressive structure has a gray limestone exterior and a marble rotunda and staircases. Rotating exhibits are on display. Tours. W end of Capitol Street or I-630 exit 2B, Woodlane. Signs.

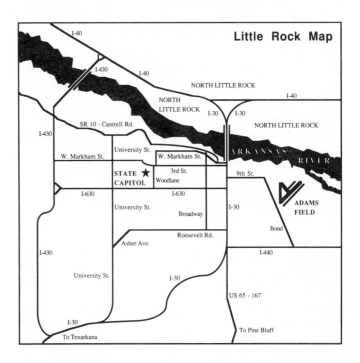

The Old State House. "One of the best examples of Greek Revival architecture in the South," it served as the state capitol from 1836 to 1911. Built of handmade brick (plastered and painted), it now houses a museum with six "period" rooms, legislative chamber and governor's office. Five galleries have changing exhibits. On the grounds are magnolia trees and Lady Baxter, a cannon requisitioned by the Confederacy for defense of the city during the *Civil War*. Ironically, it has never been fired. Markham at Center.

North Little Rock City Hall. Gothic Revival, 1914-15. This building was built in Argenta (interior doorknobs still bear that name). Historic Huntersville's reputation as a bog was underscored when builders, on advice from savvy New Orleans engineers, used cotton bales as a primary foundation to keep the structure from settling. Exterior: cast stone with terra-cotta trim. Interior: Florentine marble and two stained-glass skylights. I-30, Broadway Exit, Main & Broadway.

Arkansas Territorial Restoration. Begun as a restoration project of four houses by the *WPA*, opened in 1941, today's 14 pre-Civil War houses include: THE HINDERLITER HOUSE: (c.1827) Believed to be the meeting place for the last Territorial Legislature in 1835. THE NOLAND HOUSE: Mid-1800s with English boxwood from George Washington's Mt. Vernon, the doors and mantels are hand carved; the grounds have the original well. THE WOODRUFF HOUSE: Wm. E. Woodruff, founder of the Arkansas Gazette (Arkansas Post *Na-*

tional Park), moved his printing office here in 1824. The Washington handpress is restored to working order. THE CONWAY HOUSE: Thought to be the residence of Elias N. Conway, fifth governor (1852-60) and brother of James S. Conway, first governor (1836-40), the frame house is put together with white oak pegs. Guided Tours. Broadway, E on 3rd to Scott.

Mount Holly. "The Westminster Abbey of Arkansas" features "ponderous headstones and tall marble shafts on which are chiseled many of the best known names in Arkansas history." The oldest birth date is 1750 and the first burial, 1843, is the date the four-block area was set aside. Broadway at 12th.

Burns Park. Set beside the *Arkansas River,* and said to be the second largest municipal park in America (1,575 acres), it offers a wide variety of facilities, including a covered bridge and fishing pond, jogging, nature trails, a 27-hole golf course, baseball, basketball, tennis, racketball, archery, a boat ramp, 300 picnic tables and 27 campsites with hookups. North Little Rock. Tourist Information Center/Park, I-40 exit 150.

Murray Park. This modern park offers athletic and recreational facilities: boat ramp, four miles of jogging/cycle trails, a fitness court, playground and soccer field. Restrooms, water, picnic area and pavilions. No Campsites. Camping: *Arkansas River Parks and Campgrounds,* Little Rock-Dardanelle. I-30, exit SR 10W 3 m. to Rebsamen Park Rd.; 3 m. NW following signs to Murray *Lock & Dam.*

Pugh's Mill Park (Old Mill). Authentically designed and landscaped, built in 1933 as a replica of an 1828 mill with "a carefully planned" neglected look, it was later used (1937) for the opening scene in "Gone With The Wind." Along with millstones *(Grist Mills)* dating from 1823, 1828 and 1840 are two mile-marker stones (appx. 1 x 3 ft.) formerly set on a *road* near *Dardanelle* by U.S. Engineer Lt. Jefferson Davis (later president of the Confederacy) as guides for the "Five Civilized Tribes" being transported to Indian Territory *(Trail of Tears).* North Little Rock. I-40, N on US 65/167, W on McClain Blvd; S on North Hills Blvd to Fairway/Lakeshore Dr.

Governor's Mansion. Completed in 1950 on the previous site of the Arkansas School for the Blind. Tours available (advance notice required; usually two weeks). US 67/70, E on 20th; N to 1800 Center.

The Arkansas Arts Center has received worldwide attention for its works-on-paper

---

Arkansas Arts Center. The center has received worldwide attention for its works-on-paper, drawings and its porcelain birds by Edward Marshall Boehm. Along with scheduled special exhibits is a permanent collection of European and American paintings as well as drawings and sculpture from the 16th century to the 20th. MacArthur Park, I-630 & I-30.

Arkansas Museum of Science and History. Built in 1836 as a part of the Little Rock Arsenal, it is the birthplace (1880) of Gen. Douglas MacArthur. Restored in 1940 for its present purpose, the museum provides an audiovisual program ("Arkansas, Its Land and People"), geology, ornithology, Civil War displays, an early pioneer room and special exhibits. MacArthur Park, I-630 & I-30.

Decorative Arts Museum. A separate branch of the Arts Center, housed in Albert Pike's house (built 1839 as Greek Revival; remodeled in 1916 as Colonial Revival), this museum exhibits "creative accomplishments of artists, designers and craftsmen," and features ceramics, glass, textiles, crafts and Oriental works of art. US 67/70, E on 9th, 1 blk N on Rock.

Arkansas Geological Commission. Along with rotating exhibits like Paleozoic rocks, castings of both a dinosaur's foot and the skull of a Cretaceous-age crocodilian are a variety of useful and specialized maps (for sale), including ones for counties, mineral deposits and locations of fossils. 3815 W. Roosevelt, near Jct. with Asher.

Pugh's Mill, built in 1933, was used in the opening scene of "Gone With The Wind"

Boyd Music Center/Musical Museum. Musical instruments collected for over 30 years are displayed and demonstrated. Some of the many are: a "New York Martin" guitar (c.1833-1871), Vivitone's 1924 electric tenor guitar, a Gibson "speakeasy banjo" (hinged for a hidden flask), several all-metal Dobro "Resophonic" guitars (pre-electric efforts to be heard over drums and brass) and hybrids requiring no music lessons that could play melody and chords (built to compete with radio and phonographs). Off University, E to 5702 W.12th.

Mid-America Rosary Museum. Endorsed by Bing Crosby in 1976, this organization collects surplus rosaries to be redistributed throughout the world. On display are over 1,500 "rare, unique and antique rosaries of museum quality" and hundreds of religious articles collected from around the world since 1948. Also exhibited: a relic of both the "True Cross" and the "Blessed Mother's Veil" (documented by the Vatican), a hand-carved wooden statue of Our Lady of Fatima and a miniature replica of Bethlehem with running water, lights, manger and animals. N. Little Rock: Mr. P. Marion Chudy's home at 1603 Marion, I-40 exit Levy to N on Pike, E on 16th St., N on Marion.

War Memorial Park. Adjacent to the city zoo (BELOW), this huge inner city park has playgrounds, picnic areas, tennis courts, an admission-free amusement park, an 18-hole golf course and a swimming pool. Also: 53,000-seat War Memorial Stadium (part-time home of the Arkansas Razorback football team, *Fayetteville)* and 8,000-seat Ray Winder Field (the home of the Arkansas Travelers, a Class AA farm club of the St. Louis Cardinals since 1966 and one of the strongest minor league franchises). I-630 exit 4. Signs.

Little Rock Zoo. "One of the finest zoos in the U.S." Over 500 mammals, birds, reptiles, amphibians and fish are at home in natural exhibits like the Big Cat Display, Gibbon Island, Waterfowl Lake and Giraffe Display. I-630 exit 4. Signs.

Little Rock Central High School. The 1954 U.S. Supreme Court decision (Brown vs. The Board of Education) ordering desegregation of public schools received international attention here when newly elected (1955-67) Governor Orval Faubus *(Huntsville)* overtly defied the court order in 1957 by surrounding the high school with National Guardsmen in order to physically prevent nine black students from entering. I-630 exit 3A, S on Woodrow, E on 16th.

North Little Rock's Sesquicentennial Sundial is said to be the world's largest of its kind

---

UALR (U of A at Little Rock) Planetarium. On a 40-foot hemispherical dome, a Minolta star projector creates a "very realistic" current night sky as well as those of the past and future. Special effects projectors, a large-scale video projector and a laser videodisc player dramatize and explain the beauty and wonder of heavenly phenomena. Most Weekends. I-30, University Ave Exit N to the UALR Natural Science Bldg.

Sesquicentennial Sundial. Said to be the largest horizontal sundial in the world. Bricks or stones from historic structures or communities make up the 40-foot-square "face." A 15-foot wrought-iron gnomon indicates (by casting a shadow) the hour of the day and the day of the year. North Little Rock, Broadway St. near the Arkansas River Bridge.

La Quinta. Legends of gold and silver (Crystal Hills, BELOW; North Little Rock History, ABOVE) were rekindled when La Quinta Motor Inn struck silver ore (800 pounds) in 1982 during foundation excavations. A sample is on display in the lobby. I-630 exit 4, 901 Fair Park Blvd.

Crystal Hill. In 1809 the I-430 or I-40 exit to Crystal Hill would have led to a gold mine. Soft yellowish crystals found on the nearby hills were assayed as pure gold. Shafts were sunk and a smelter built. Too close to the *Arkansas River,* the mines flooded, and today are underneath silt and muddy water. No Remnants.

Bale Chevrolet Building. A fine example of Art Deco, it is best viewed at night when the neon fixtures are lighted. Broadway & 2nd.

Butterfield Overland Mail. Selected at first to be the St. Louis/Memphis converging point for the *Butterfield Overland Mail,* the main line was shifted to *Fort Smith,* leaving Little Rock with only "connecting service" to old Austin *(Cabot)* 25 miles away. Political and financial pressure in 1858 changed the route to include the capital. The Anthony House (bounded by E. Market, Scott, 2nd & Main) served the line.

I-430 Roadcut. Natural Heritage Area. This deep roadcut exposes the Big Rock syncline (beds dipping toward each other rather than away) typical of the eastern Ouachita Mountains. I-430 at SR 10.

Lock & Dam #5, D. D. Terry L&D, Murray L&D. Completed between 1968-69 as a part of the McClellan-Kerr Arkansas *River* Navigation system (from near Tulsa, Ok., to the Mississippi River), these 110-by-600-foot locks can ac-

commodate pleasure boats or barges by raising or lowering the water 18 feet inside the lock, working in stair-step fashion to match the level where river traffic is entering or exiting. For recreation and camping: *Arkansas River Parks and Campgrounds,* Pine Bluff-Little Rock-Morrilton. L&D #5: US 65, 25 m. S to access road; 4.6 m. E. TERRY L&D: From US 71/SR130, 6.1 m. S; access road, 5.7 m. MURRAY L&D: From I-430, SR 10, 8 m. E; access road, 4 m. NW.

Events/Festivals. Early May: Annual Quapaw Quarter Spring Tour of Homes. Early May: Annual Arkansas Territorial Restoration Craft Show & Festival. Continual Entertainment. Memorial Day Weekend: Riverfest. Visual & Performing Arts. Continual Entertainment (Opera, Symphony and Stage). Art Sales. Fireworks. Late Aug: Zoo Days. Arts & Crafts. Music. Elephant Walks. Labor Day Weekend: Summerset. Arts & Crafts. Kid's Carnival. Exotic Foods. Music. Sports Tournaments. Late Sept: Arkansas State Fair & Livestock Show. Late Oct-Nov: Annual Delta Art Exhibition. 7-State Juried Show. Late Nov to Mid-Jan: Annual Toys Designed By Artists Exhibit. National Competition. Early Dec: Annual Christmas Open House (Arkansas Territorial Restoration). 19th Century Holiday Decor. Music. Hot Cider & Gingerbread. MAUMELLE, AR. (I-430 exit, Maumelle): Fourth of July Celebration & Fireworks Spectacular.

Pulaski County Courthouses. This is the only county in the state with two adjacent courthouses. ROMANESQUE REVIVAL, 1887: Trimmed in red stone with a slate roof, it was built using granite from nearby Fourche Mountain. Like its counterpart, the interior has intricate plaster ornamentation. CLASSICAL REVIVAL, 1912: Interior: The central hall has 16 marble columns surrounding a rotunda with an exquisite stained-glass dome. Exterior: Built with Batesville limestone. *(County Profiles)*

National Historic Register. There are over 150 listings. The city has different historic sections like the Quapaw Quarter (roughly an area from lower Broadway east to and around MacArthur Park). Maps, Little Rock Visitors Center.

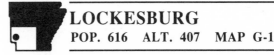

LOCKESBURG
POP. 616   ALT. 407   MAP G-1

Sevier County was divided twice in six years (1867-1873). Although only 10 miles north of the county seat (Paraclifta, BELOW), the Locke brothers (in consensus with county residents) thought a more "central" location was needed, and donated land here in 1869 for a new town and seat of justice.

Paraclifta. Said to have been named for a Choctaw chief, and situated on the Fort Towson *Road,* this first county seat of newly formed Sevier County (1828) lost its position to Lockesburg in 1871. Residents moved to the new county seat, taking their houses and buildings with them. GILLIAM-NORWOOD HOUSE: This large two-story antebellum house with broad porches and square columns is all that remains of Paraclifta. Oral history says newlyweds R.C. Gilliam and Frances I. Russey *(Center Point)* were here by 1849. Restored. Private. SEVIER COUNTY TIME CAPSULE: The vault door supposedly came from the old Mena jail, and the free-standing "Grecian influenced columns" from a building in Texarkana. Dedicated in 1950 as a shrine to Paraclifta, wire recordings, records and mementos were sealed for 25 years. Nearby is a slave cemetery. US 71, 8 m. S to Falls Chapel; CR 19, W to the Cossatot River *(Float Streams)*.

Old Sevier County Jail. The bars are sunk in 12-inch walls built from layered, hand-poured concrete and rock. The door is iron. Behind Lockesburg City Hall.

Caddo Mound. This 20-foot high mound is a good example of the c.1,000 A.D. building techniques of the period. Static displays describe the life and religion of the Caddo as well as the mound's uses. North shore of Millwood *Lake*. US 71, 2 m. S.; SR 317, 18 m. S.

White Cliffs. A landmark in the area, these 150-foot white limestone cliffs were the focus of three different cement companies from the late 19th century to 1925. Two towns (White Cliffs & Folmina) and all three companies went broke. It is said the cement in the basement of the Arkansas Capitol is from these cliffs. Remnants. North shore of Millwood *Lake*. US 71, 2 m. S; SR 317, 18 m. S.

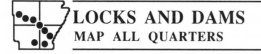

LOCKS AND DAMS
MAP ALL QUARTERS

Built by the U.S. Corps of Engineers for flood control *(Flood of 1927)* and navigation *(Great Raft)*, these engineering feats are open to the public, and provide the area with a variety of recreation and camping *(Arkansas River Parks and Campgrounds)*. The structures on the *Arkansas River* are part of the 445-mile McClellan-Kerr Arkansas River Navigation System (from near Tulsa, Ok., to the Mississippi River), and are designed to accommodate pleasure boats or barges by raising or lowering the water inside the lock, working in stair-step fashion to match the level where river traffic is entering or exiting. Some generate electricity. Below, the locks and dams are listed from south to north (by L&D #) on the Arkansas River. The last two, Calion and Felsenthal, are on the Ouachita River, and are not part of the Arkansas River system. NOTE: There are only 12 locks and dams on Arkansas' portion of the Arkansas River, but Fort Smith's L&D is confusingly numbered 13 because #11 was deleted when Lake Dardanelle and Ozark-Jeta Taylor were enlarged and relocated, eliminating #11's need. Rather than renumber the entire system from Arkansas Post to Tulsa, Ok., the original numbers were retained.

Norrell Lock & Dam. (Arkansas Post *National Park*)
Lock & Dam #2. (Arkansas Post *National Park*)
Locks & Dams #3 & #4. *(Pine Bluff)*
Lock & Dam #5. *(Little Rock)*
David D. Terry Lock & Dam. *(Little Rock)*
Murray Lock & Dam. *(Little Rock)*
Toad Suck Ferry Lock & Dam. *(Conway)*
Lock & Dam #9. *(Morrilton)*
Lake Dardanelle Lock & Dam. *(Lake* Dardanelle)

Ozark-Jeta Taylor Lock & Dam. (Ozark *Lake*)
Lock & Dam #13. *(Fort Smith)*
Calion Lock & Dam. *(Calion)*
Felsenthal Lock & Dam. (Felsenthal *National Wildlife Refuge)*

LONOKE
POP. 4,128   ALT. 239   MAP L-2

The area was first settled by Isaac C. Hicks (Hicks Station, 1.5 m. E, c.1840). Lonoke was laid out in 1867 on the grade of the Memphis & Little Rock *Railroad,* and was named by survey engineers Rumbough and Robinson, who agreed on the spelling and the pronunciation, Lo-NOKE, for the only significant landmark, an exceptionally tall red oak tree (Grand Prairie, *Carlisle).* The landmark was cut down in 1900. Incorporated in 1872, the town (having drained the population away from nearby Brownsville) became county seat and namesake of newly formed (1873) Lonoke County, which makes it the only county seat in Arkansas whose name corresponds with its county's. Home of Joseph T. Robinson, who was elected governor in 1912 while serving in Congress (1902-12), and then in less than six weeks was elected by the Arkansas General Assembly to the U.S. Senate (1913-37).

Brownsville. Begun as the Post Office of Grand Prairie in 1845 on the Memphis-Little Rock *Road,* Brownsville (1851) served as county seat of Prairie County until 1868 *(DeValls Bluff).* Bypassed by the Memphis & Little Rock *Railroad* in 1862, the town eventually lost its population (2,500 c.1861) to Lonoke (people literally moved, taking houses and buildings). By 1889 all that remained was a cemetery (earliest burial 1851) and a few frame houses. Appx. 3 m. N. Inquire Locally.

Rock Island Railroad Depot. National Historic Register, 1912. "The finest depot between Memphis and Little Rock" (marble floors, granite window sills and red tile roof) is being restored. Downtown, US 70.

Joe Hogan State Fish Hatchery. The oldest (1928) warm water hatchery in America, it is also one of the largest in the world. The 200-foot wells pump water at 1,300 gal/min for raising the principal species of catfish, crappie, sunfish and bass, which yield 1-3 million specimens annually. Biologist on duty. Picnic Facilities. SR 31, 1 m. S.

Anderson Minnow Farms. The world's largest of its kind at 6,000 acres, it has 200 miles of levees impounding water for the three species of bait fish: golden shiner, fathead minnow and goldfish. Trucks equipped with liquid oxygen distribute 300 million fish to over 30 states. US 70, 4 m. W.

Eberts Field. Built during WWI (1917), it ranked second among aviation training centers in the U.S. and France with 1,500 personnel, 960 acres and a railroad spur. While it was not unusual to see several hundred planes flying in formation, there was never a fatality. The war ended before the first aviator graduated. SR 89, N of town. Marker.

Events/Festivals. Mid-June: Lonoke's Minnow Madness. Arts & Crafts. Fish Fry. Street Dance.

Lonoke County Courthouse. Renaissance Modern, 1928. National Historic Register. Brass and tile accent the interior. Reportedly, its architectural cue came from the Confederate monument that predates the courthouse by 20 years. Grounds also: *Civil War* cannon. Downtown. *(County Profiles)*

National Historic Register. Trimble House, 518 Center. Walls House, 406 Jefferson. Eagle House, 217 Ash. Wheat House, 600 Center. Boyd House, 220 Park. Shull House, 418 Park.

MADISON
POP. 1,238   ALT. 204   MAP L-4

This early 1800s St. Francis *River* town was made county seat in 1841, losing it for a while to Mount Vernon (1855-57) and then permanently to *Forrest City* in 1874. From 1858 to 1871 it served as a transfer point for a train and riverboat line of the Memphis & Little *Railroad* as well as the *Butterfield Overland Mail.* When passed over as a rail and river depot, it rebounded as a lumber town, incorporating in 1914. It is not known for whom the town was named, although a good guess would be James Madison, who as secretary of state under President Jefferson (1801-09) and as president (1809-17) was instrumental in settling and then removing the Cherokee from this region to the *Arkansas River* Valley *(Trail of Tears)*. Incidentally, Madison died in June of 1836, the month and year of Arkansas' statehood; Madison County in NW Arkansas (created Sept. 30, 1836) was named for him *(Huntsville)*.

MAGAZINE MOUNTAIN
ALT. 2,753   MAP C-2

Natural Heritage Area. The romantic version of the name's origin as a Confederate stronghold for ammunition is put in doubt by the probability that early French hunters saw it as a magasin (barn or storehouse). Said to be the highest vertical point (2,753 feet base to crest) between the Allegheny and Rocky Mountains, it is most definitely the tallest mountain in Arkansas (the lowest elevation in Arkansas is 54 feet, at the Ouachita River near the Louisiana border and Felsenthal *National Wildlife Refuge*). The north side has tall, sheer cliffs; the south side supports rare plants and animals in prairielike openings. A scenic drive to the top leads to picnic facilities and hiking *trails*. Not shown on some maps, it is N of SR 10, appx. 17 m. W of *Booneville*.

MAGNET COVE
COMMUNITY   ALT. 525   MAP E-4

Don't believe a compass around here *(Rison)*. Loadstone (magnetic ore) is even in the road bed of US 270. Beginning in 1834 (Magnet Cove Post Office, c.1835), geologists have studied what is believed to have been a volcano. No spot in the world of the same same size (5.1 square miles) has as many varieties (65) of valuable minerals, including the nation's greatest concentrations of novaculite (whetstones) and vanadium (steel alloy).

MAGNOLIA
POP. 11,909   ALT. 345   MAP H-3

Settled in 1835, chosen for its central location as county seat for newly created Columbia County in 1853, it was named by Miss Elizabeth Harper during dinner with the selection committee at her father's house. Incorporated 1855. A landlocked cotton town of about 600, it built a branch line to the Texas & St. Louis *Railroad* when bypassed in 1882 and grew slowly (c.3,500 in 50 years). Home of Southern Arkansas University.

Events/Festivals. Early Oct: Annual Hospitality House Arts & Crafts Fair.

Columbia County Courthouse. Renaissance Revival, 1905. National Historic Register. Surrounded by huge magnolia trees and St. Augustine grass, its Greek columns, Roman arches and "Southern" porches complement court square, which is said to be a direct copy of the court square in Oxford, Mississippi. Downtown, US 82B. *(County Profiles)*

National Historic Register. Alexander House (1855). Inquire Locally. Columbia County Jail, Jefferson & W. Calhoun. Longino House (1910), 317 W. Main. Turner House, 709 W. Main.

MALVERN
POP. 10,163   ALT. 312   MAP F-4

Like so many other railroad towns, its history is an overnight success story. Laid out in 1873 by the Cairo & Fulton *Railroad,* it was incorporated in 1876 and selected (by 176 votes) as county seat, replacing Rockport (BELOW) in 1878. Reportedly named for Malvern Hills, Va., (some say because of its similar countryside). Home of Ouachita Vocational Technical School. "Brick Capital of the World."

Rockport/Bridges. Originally an Indian crossing at the Ouachita *River (Float Streams)*, this site was later used by the Southwest Trail *(Roads)*. Rockport (now a suburb of Malvern) was first settled c.1832, then selected county seat in 1846. A forerunner of today's bridge has been described as "lattice-type," 300 feet long and completely enclosed. A later structure (built in 1900) still remains as a one-lane, wooden-decked and steel superstructure (National Historic Register). SR 84, downstream of the I-30 bridge. Possible *De Soto* Route.

Hot Spring County Museum. The 1898 Victorian house has antiques and atmosphere, well-tended grounds and gardens, exhibits of local industries (past and present) and Indian artifacts. Kids can put on button-up shoes and bounce on a feather mattress. 2 blks. off Main on 3rd.

The "Diamond Jo" Railroad. Built in 1887 by Chicago capitalist "Diamond Jo" Reynolds, this narrow gauge railroad replaced the slow, often dangerous and always bone-jarring stagecoach ride from Malvern's depot to the popular health spa of *Hot Springs.* No Remnants.

Remmel Dam. An engineering marvel of its day (1926), this dam on the Ouachita River, built as a hydro-electric plant, created Lake Catherine (Lake Catherine *State Park), and was* named for AP&L founder H.C. Couch's daughter. SR 51 or US 270, W to Jones Mill. Signs.

Events/Festivals. Late July: Brickfest. Arts & Crafts. Entertainment. Games. Concessions.

Hot Spring County Courthouse. Moderne, 1936. Made from local brick, the interior features aluminum hardware and colored tile floors. Downtown. *(County Profiles)*

National Historic Register. Clark House, 1324 S. Main. Strauss House, 528 E. Page.

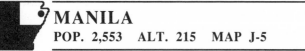

MANILA
POP. 2,553   ALT. 215   MAP J-5

Founded as Big Lake Island in 1852 by Ed Smith. When the Jonesboro, Lake City & Eastern *Railroad* established it as a lumber town in 1901, the name was changed in honor of the U.S. naval victory at Manila Bay, Philippines, during the Spanish-American War, 1898. Downtown streets are named for battleships in the engagement.

Herman Davis Monument. Called by General John J. Pershing "Arkansas' greatest hero" and listed among the general's 100 American heroes of WWI, Private Davis (1888-1923) was cited for saving an entire company single-handedly.

Big Lake National Wildlife Refuge. (Big Lake *National Wildlife Refuge)*

National Historic Register. BUCKEYE, AR. (SR 77, N 6 m.): Zebree Homesteads, NE 2 m.

MARIANNA
POP. 6,220   ALT. 235   MAP M-4

Founded at *Crowley's Ridge* in the 1820s by settlers from Alabama, it is said to have been the original starting point of the Alabama *Road* (now SR 1) to *Harrisburg.* Merchant/planter Col. Walter N. Otey planned to name the town for himself until discovering that his choice for an ideal townsite was owned by Mary Ann Harland, who subsequently donated the property and was appropriately honored. Incorporated in 1870; selected county seat of newly formed (1873) Lee County.

W.G. Huxtable Pumping Plant. One of the largest in the world *(Lake Village),* it regulates a watershed the size of Delaware in a flood control program *(Flood of 1927),* using 10 10-foot diameter pumps that can move 5.4 million gal/min into the Mississippi River when that river begins flooding the St. Francis Basin, or when floodwater is impounded in the basin by the Mississippi or St. Francis River levees. US 79, 4 m. E to SR 121; 10 m. S (or levee road S). Signs.

Marianna-Lee Museum. National Historic Register, 1911.

This two-story red brick building once housed the Elks Club. The second floor has local historical items, Indian artifacts and the original stained-glass windows featuring elks. SR 1B, E to 67 W. Main.

Phillips Bayou. On the Helena-Wittsburg *Road (Harrisburg),* several houses, a store and a cemetery mark this once busy *river* port on the St. Francis near which the infamous John Murrell organization operated *(Marked Tree).* Appx. 8 m. S of Bear Creek *Lake* on the St. Francis River. Some gravel roads. Inquire Locally.

Patterson Marker. Reportedly John Patterson (1790-1886) was "the first white man born on Arkansas soil" (some say west of the Mississippi River). His favorite riddle is on the marker: "I was born in a kingdom [Spain], Raised in an Empire [France], Attained manhood in a Territory [Arkansas], And now am citizen of a state, and have never been 100 miles from where I was born." SR 44, S near Bear Creek *Lake.*

Events/Festivals. Fourth of July Celebration. Crafts. Bar-B-Q. 5K Run. Fireworks.

Lee County Courthouse. Classical Moderne, 1939; remodelled. The 1939 structure remodelled one built in 1889. A 1965 addition replaced the remainder of the original. Grounds: statue of Gen. Robt. E. Lee erected c.1910, and a monument (1986) paid for by private donations listing county veterans who died in WW I & II, Korea and Vietnam SR 1B, E on Main. *(County Profiles)*

National Historic Register. McClintock House, 82 W. Main. McClintock House, 43 Magnolia.

MARION
POP. 2,996   ALT. 225   MAP K-5

Settled in 1803 by Spanish Sergeant Augustine Grande(e) from Ft. Esperanza *(West Memphis)* and known as Grande(e) until 1836, when Matthew Talbot of Hopefield *(West Memphis)* donated 95 lots for its site as county seat. Marion supposedly (disputed) was one of Talbot's names (Marion Tolbert); regardless, he didn't profit from the town and became a resident of the county's newly created (1860) poorhouse in 1861. Incidentally, Marion County *(County Profiles)* was created in 1835 (the year before this town was laid out), and was named for the American Revolutionary War hero, Gen. Francis Marion ("The Swamp Fox").

Greenock. Crittenden County's first seat of justice (1825-1836) and important Mississippi *River* port. Like many early Mississippi River towns, it was washed away. No Remnants.

Lake Grande(e) Also known as Caymen Bayou, Cypress Lake and Marion Lake, it served during highwater as a Mississippi River port as late as 1881. Iron mooring rings still remain. Inquire locally.

Town Square/Military Road. Talbot's original 95 lots comprise the square. The Memphis-Little Rock Military *Road* was (and is) its southern boundary. US 64W or Military Road.

Esperanza Trail. *(West Memphis)*

Crittenden County Courthouse. Neo-Classical Revival,

1910. National Historic Register. Ionic columns and a copper-colored dome now mix with a 1978 addition. Town Square. *(County Profiles)*

National Historic Register. Crittenden County Bank & Trust, Military Road. Dabbs Store (1912), 1320 S. Avalon.

MARKED TREE
POP. 3,201 ALT. 224 MAP K-4

Set at the confluence of the St. Francis and Little *Rivers,* the town began as a camp for the Kansas City, Ft. Scott and Memphis *Railroad* in 1881 (incorporated in 1897) and was named by surveyors for the blazed oak *(Witness Tree)* that marked a ford and portage on the St. Francis. The tree was washed away in the flood of 1890. Home of Delta Vocational Technical School.

The Marked Tree/John Murrell. Two stories revolve around the marked tree. (1) Indians marked the tree to indicate a quarter-mile separation (portage point) of two rivers, saving eight miles of paddling. (2) The infamous outlaw, John Murrell, marked it as an easy ford across the St. Francis to escape the law. Murrell (1803-44), born in a Tennessee tavern and who claimed his mother "learnt me and all her children to steal so soon as we could walk," organized a crime syndicate of nearly 1,000 men held together in a secret society. Taking refuge in remote base camps like Marked Tree, *Marianna* and *Lake Village,* the operation (which included state government officials on both sides of the Mississippi River) specialized in slave-kidnapping (kidnapping, selling and then kidnapping the same slave), piracy, counterfeiting and bank robbery. Captured in Tennessee for horse stealing in 1834, Murrell spent 10 years in prison, dying shortly after his release.

Lock and Dam/Siphons. A major engineering feat, and one of the largest of its kind in the world in 1939, it used three nine-foot-diameter siphons in conjunction with a lock and dam for flood control *(Flood of 1927)* and for maintaining navigation on the St. Francis *River* by drawing water from St. Francis Lake. In principle similar to the Huxtable Pumping Plant *(Marianna),* the siphons swapped water as needed but in this case were "primed" by vacuum pumps. No longer used. Intact. US 63 at the St. Francis.

Singer Forest. Natural Heritage Area. This bottomland forest and overflow swamp is one of the few remaining examples of how this part of Arkansas looked before extensive drainage and associated agricultural projects. Oak Donnick Floodway. Inquire Locally.

MARSHALL
POP. 1,595 ALT. 1,067 MAP B-4

Lebanon, the first (1838) county seat of Searcy, was a few miles west of here at Bear Creek. An 1855 disagreement over the community's location literally divided the town. The faction favoring a move settled (bringing the county seat with

them) at today's townsite, an early 1820s community called Raccoon Springs (36 springs are within a two-mile radius of today's courthouse). A new disagreement, this time over the adopted community's name, was so fiercely contested that the Arkansas General Assemby in 1856 intervened, assigning the name Burrowsville (reportedly John Burrows donated 11 acres for a courthouse site; some say the title was never conveyed). In 1867 the name was changed to Marshall for John Marshall, one of the commissioners who had originally designated Raccoon Springs as county seat. Incorporated 1884.

Downtown. This small court square is reminiscent of another era. The courthouse stands isolated in the center, surrounded by stone and brick buildings.

Searcy County Museum. Housed in the former 1902 county jail (a two-story limestone building with strap-iron bars on the windows), it displays local historical items, old uniforms, Indian artifacts and Jimmy Driftwood albums. Still original and intact, the cells upstairs (the sheriff and his family lived downstairs) offer an intimate look at the confined space, metal bunks and bars of prison life of the early 1900s. US 65, S on Center past the courthouse.

US 65 Roadcut/Overlook. Studied by the Smithsonian Institution, this massive exposure of alternating layers of limestone and shale (300 million years old) demonstrates the uplift forces responsible for building the Ozark Mountains, as well as showing wet-weather waterfalls, droplets of oil and fossils. At the crest of the grade is a spectacular overlook. Picnic Tables. S on US 65 along the W side of the grade.

Searcy County Courthouse. Folk Classicism, 1889. National Historic Register. Built after the third courthouse burned (1886) on the same foundation as the others, this two-story structure is limestone with walls two feet thick. Features: no grounds, black marble wainscoting and pressed metal beneath the roof overhang. Downtown. US 65, S on Center. *(County Profiles)*

MAYFLOWER
POP. 1,381 ALT. 287 MAP D-4

During construction of the Little Rock & Ft. Smith *Railroad* in 1867, a Pullman car, used as headquarters, was stationed on a section of track known as Twenty-Mile Camp (20 miles from Little Rock). When communicating by telegraph, the Pullman car used "Mayflower" (the car's name) as identification. Another story claims the town was named for mayflowers growing beside the track. The *Butterfield Overland Mail* passed by the mouth of Palarm Creek (BELOW) and then just west of here. Incorporated 1928.

Geographic Center of Arkansas. Palarm Creek at SR 365 is about as close as a person can comfortably (or even accurately) get to what is described as the geographic center of Arkansas: "12 miles North of West of Little Rock" *(Benton, Collegeville).* SR 365, appx. 4 m. S.

James Miller Monument. This cement and quartz crystal monument, "I'll Try, Sir," honors the first Territorial governor

(1819-25) who was decorated at the Battle of Lundys Lane (War of 1812) for capturing a British gun emplacement against all odds. His response, "I'll try, sir," when asked if he could do it became a schoolboy's motto and national catchword. Appointed governor by President James Monroe in 1819, Miller proceeded from Pittsburgh, Pa., down the Ohio and Mississippi *Rivers* in a private keelboat outfitted at government expense. With a banner, "I'll Try, Sir," flying in the wind, he was saluted at every port (possibly causing his trip to take 75 days, or 10 miles a day — downstream). Arriving at Little Rock, he disliked the terrain and chose a homesite near today's monument to build his house, trying in vain to relocate the government. SR 365, appx. 4 m. S, at Palarm Creek.

Lollie (Ghost Town). John E. Little bought a small farm here in 1881 and turned it into a 3,100-acre plantation with a barge landing and general store, all of which he named for his wife, Lollie. Only the weather-beaten general store, tucked up next to a levee of the *Arkansas River,* remains. Incidentally, the dirt road leading north to SR 268 (appx. 12 m.) at old Toad Suck *(Conway)* is not only passable during dry weather, it is an excellent example of the Arkansas River Valley's topography: tabletop farmland hemmed in by flat-top mountains.

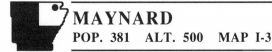

MAYNARD
POP. 381   ALT. 500   MAP I-3

Founded as New Prospect by Confederate Captain John Maynard in 1872 as one of many small communities near and on the Southwest Trail *(Roads),* it changed names when establishing a post office in 1885. Incorporated in 1895, the downtown buildings (1900s) are typical of that era.

Maynard City Jail. Built in the 1930s and possibly one of the smallest in the state, this 6-by-10-foot cement building has a dirt floor and a metal door made from a wagon rim. "When not in use, photographs are allowed." Behind city hall.

Maynard Pioneer Museum and Park. A reconstructed log cabin fenced by split-rails is furnished as a typical pioneer home. An annex displays local artifacts, furniture, toys, farm equipment and locally made (1923) coffins. In town, SR 328.

Events/Festivals. Mid-Sept: Pioneer Day. Parade. Country Music. Pioneer Contests.

MAYSVILLE
COMMUNITY   ALT. 1,029   MAP A-1

Tigret's store (1839) sold whiskey on the Military or Line *Road,* and around it grew a town reportedly larger than nearby *Bentonville* during the 1840s. Records are at odds over the town's name, giving the honor to one or two men whose first names are equally disputed: Martin or John Martin Mays, Runnels or Reynolds Mays. An 1891 fire that destroyed most of its businesses was followed by a worse blow, the junction of the Kansas City Southern and St. Louis & San Francisco *(Railroad)* 10 miles east at *Gravette.*

 # McGEHEE
POP. 5,671   ALT. 149   MAP 0-3

Founded on the tracks of the Little Rock, Mississippi River & Texas *Railroad* in 1878, named for local planter Abner McGehee (Mc-GEE), it wasn't firmly established until the Memphis, Helena & Louisiana Railway (St. Louis, Iron Mountain & Southern) completed its line in 1906. Incorporated 1906. Home of Great Rivers Vocational Technical School. A possible *De Soto* Route; one account claims he died near present-day McArthur; SR 1, 5 m. N.

Wiley McGehee Memorial Park. Wooden walkways thread through an excellent example of a South Arkansas cypress bayou. Two roadside parks. Ducks. Fishing. Picnic Area. Jct. US 65 & SR 1.

Events/Festivals. Mid-June: Annual Railroad Days Festival. Train Tours. Arts & Crafts. Mulligan Stew Cook-Off. Barrel-Racing & Calf Roping.

Desha County Court. McGehee is the only Arkansas town that has a courtroom but not the courthouse — and it is not even a dual county seat *(Arkansas City).*

 # MELBOURNE
POP. 1,619   ALT. 620   MAP J-2

First known as Richardson's Cross Roads and then Mill Creek, its central location at two large springs was selected in 1875 to replace *Mount Olive* as the county seat of Izard County. Melbourne, according to <u>The Oxford Dictionary of English Place Names</u> means mill creek, which is in agreement with local tradition. Home of Ozark Vocational Technical School.

Early Ozark Immigrants. John Lafferty's experiences typify those of early Ozark immigrants. A Revolutionary War veteran, he settled in North Carolina, married, moved to the Cumberland District of Tennessee and then brought his family to Arkansas in 1807, building a log cabin by a creek that still has his name. It is said that bears and buffaloes destroyed his first crops. After fighting at New Orleans with "Andy" Jackson (War of 1812), he came back to Arkansas in 1815.

Lunenburg. A trading post settlement begun about 1820 as Rocky Bayou on the *road* from *Mount Olive* to *Batesville,* its second business was a saloon (a small log building with one wide plank to support barrels). Customers brought their own jugs, and drank outside. The town's new name, reportedly proposed c.1860 at this saloon, was delivered in a heavy German accent: "Name her Lunenburg, by Gott." Although the name was officially adopted (and unofficially called Lunenburg By Gott), maps carried the name Rocky Bayou until the 1880s. The cemetery has about 500 markers. The saloon, a church and a school are still standing. On Rocky Bayou, about 6 m. S. Inquire Locally.

Events/Festivals. Early May: Izard County Pioneer Day. Music. Crafts. Street Dance.

Izard County Courthouse. Moderne, 1940. Built by the

National Youth Administration as the fourth courthouse on the same site (the other three burned), this one is brick and concrete with a limestone veneer. Bicentennial paintings by local art students hang on the second floor. *(County Profiles)*

MENA
POP. 5,154   ALT. 1,143   MAP E-1

Turned down by U.S. investors in 1896, the road-builder for the Kansas City, Pittsburg & Ft. Smith *Railroad* (Kansas City Southern), Arthur Stilwell, had a "hunch" he could raise three million dollars in Holland to finish the proposed line from *Siloam Springs* to Shreveport, La. A young Dutch investor, John DeGeoijen *(De Queen)*, helped raise the funds in Holland. Although it would seem that contemporary Holland's Queen Wilhelmina would be the logical origin of the town's name (sources say her name was shortened after the fashion of railroad names), local tradition insists that the namesake is De-Geoijen's wife (some say mother), Mena. Promoting Mena as a principal townsite on the railroad (the Texarkana & Ft. Smith Railway at that time), Stilwell's publicity campaign of a-mile-of-track-a-day created a tent city of 1,000 in less than 40 days. Home of Rich Mountain Vocational Technical School and Norris Goff (Cove, Ar.: 15 m. S on US 71/59), who portrayed Abner of the popular "Lum 'N Abner" radio-comedy team. NOTE: Both "Lum" *(Alleene)* and "Abner" moved as boys in 1911 to Mena, where they became friends of Dick Huddleston of Walters, Ar. — the model charatcer and town for their radio show *(Pine Ridge)*.

Panther/Dallas. Settled as Panther c.1825, the early county seat of Polk County (created 1851) changed its name to Dallas when incorporated in 1879. Although established on a major crossroads, it lost the county seat after the arrival of the railroad at Mena in 1896. SR 375, 4 m. S.

Jannsen Park. National Historic Register. Four acres donated by Stilwell in 1906 surround an 1851 hand-hewn log cabin (the only structure in the area until 1896) that has been used for nearly everything, including a border-bandit's rendezvous, city hall and a podium for speakers like Carry A. Nation *(Eureka Springs)* and Wm. Jennings Bryan *(Monte Ne)*. Also on the grounds: a sculptured fountain depicting a boy and girl under an umbrella (locally said to be one of three in America), a linden tree from Berlin, Germany, and a bronze cannon from the Revolutionary War. Center of town.

Kansas City Southern Depot. Typical c.1910 railroad architecture, one-story red brick with a red tile roof, today it houses city historical artifacts, a gallery and the chamber of commerce. Downtown.

Queen Wilhelmina State Park. *(State Parks)*

Talimena Scenic Drive. Named for the two towns at either end (Talihina, Ok., and Mena), it provides interpretive signs describing terrain features and historical sites along a 54-mile route across Rich and Winding Star Mountains. The drive itself is famous for its spring wildflowers, fall colors and winter snow. SR 88 & Oklahoma 1. Guidebook: visitor informa-

tion station, SR 88W & city limits.

1877 Boundary Marker. This original octagonal iron post *(Foreman)*, weighing several hundred pounds, marks the 48th mile from Fort Smith on Arkansas' western border as surveyed for the final time *(Boundary Lines)*. As the dividing line between Arkansas and the Choctaw Nation *(Trail of Tears)*, it has "Ark." on the east side and "Choc." on the west. Talimena Scenic Drive, SR 88 at the border.

Forest Ranger Fire Towers. Since helicopters are mostly used now for fire detection, these towers are rarely occupied. For a long look at the Ouachitas: RICH MOUNTAIN LOOKOUT: Just E of Queen Wilhelmina *State Park*, SR 88. FIRE TOWER: Appx. 10 m. SE on SR 235, 1 m. W on CR 56, 1 m. S on FR 56A (unimproved). WOLF PINNACLE: Appx. 9 m. N on US 71, 4 m. E on FR 278 (unimproved, part of Ouachita National Hiking *Trail*).

Events/Festivals. Early Apr: Rich Mountain Classic Run (13K). Late May to Mid-June (two weeks): Lum 'N Abner Days. Arts & Crafts. Nightly Music. 10K Run.

Polk County Courthouse. Deco, 1939. It has brass, aluminum and steel hardware; terrazzo floors. *(County Profiles)*

National Historic Register. Shaver House (1896), 501 12th. Scroggins House (1911), 1215 Port Arthur.

MINERAL SPRINGS
POP. 936   ALT. 325   MAP G-2

Established c.1842 as Saline, it was called Greenville in 1850 (Wesley Green owned the only store) until incorporated as Mineral Springs (1879) in honor of its "curative" mineral water. Despite the general popularity of spring water (bottled commercially in 1907), the town was primarily a cotton center. Later (1914) the downtown business district was moved a half-mile east to the tracks of the newly arrived Memphis, Paris & Gulf *Railroad* (1906).

Old Town. Two of the original buildings remain: a bank and T.J. Dillard's Mercantile. T.J.'s son, Wm. T., became founder and chairman of the board of Dillard Department Stores. SR 355 at the water tower.

Memphis, Paris & Gulf Depot. National Historic Register, 1908. Red shingled roof and bright red wooden siding, it is now owned by the city. Downtown.

MONTICELLO
POP. 8,964   ALT. 298   MAP 0-2

Nearby (appx. a mile south) Independence was settled c.1835. Local tradition claims its name was changed to Rough and Ready (BELOW) when two strangers rode in, climbed down off their horses and shot each other dead. "Old Rough & Ready" is also the nickname of Gen. Zachary Taylor, president 1849-50. Monticello was founded in 1849 as the second county seat of Drew County on the Fort Towson *Road* (Gaines & Main St.) from Gaines Landing *(Halley)*, and was incorporated in 1852 as a cotton trading center. Presumably named for President Jefferson's home. Home of the University of Arkansas at Monticello. Maps: chamber of commerce, 335 E. Gaines (SR 4).

Rough and Ready/Cemetery. The original site of the first Drew County courthouse (1847-49) is today a large parklike area with huge oaks. Marker. The cemetery (E to 1st dirt road, about 200 yds. S) has ornate headstones. The last skirmish of the *Civil War* in Arkansas took place near here on May 24, 1865 (45 days after Gen. Robert E. Lee surrendered). Town square, SR 183, S to Higgins Gro/Gas; E about .5 m.

Drew County Museum. This outstanding example of a county museum has four buildings: two log structures (c.1832 & c.1819), a carriage house/garage with large archives and a two-story main house (National Historic Register, 1906) that was built using individually molded cement blocks to look like stone. Each of the 13 rooms is filled with period furniture and furnishings, representing everyday life down to handkerchiefs and salt shakers. Also included is a fine Indian and mineral collection as well as Civil War artifacts, a gun display and a working Washington #7 press that prints souvenir copies of the original (1861) front page of the local newspaper. 402 S. Main, 2 blks. S of town square.

Turner Neal Museum of Natural History. Although ranging from archaeology to zoology, including a planetarium, the museum mostly specializes in natural history, with collections of moose and mountain goats, an elephant head measuring 11 feet ear-to-ear, a polar bear and fish (tropical and native). UAM Campus.

Historic District. National Historic Register. Said to be one of the wealthiest cities in Arkansas at the turn of the century, its historic district contains about 42 homes representing Victorian, Queen Anne and Colonial architecture. N. Main. Maps: chamber of commerce.

Seven Devils Swamp. Primitive, eerie and romantic, this cypress swamp gives a good idea of what the land was like before being drained for farming. SR 35, 15 m. SE to Timber Access Roads. Signs.

Drew County Courthouse. Deco Classicism, 1932. It is Arkansas' only courtroom with no "bar" separating spectators from court proceedings. Interior: marble stairs, benches and wainscoting. *(County Profiles)*

National Historic Register. Historic District (ABOVE). Hardy House (1908-09), 207 S. Main. Hotchiss House (1895), 509 N. Boyd. Lambert House, 204 W. Jackson. SELMA, AR. (SR 4, 13 m. E, SR 293 2 m. N, near *Bayou Bartholomew*): Selma Methodist Church (1874).

MORRILTON
POP. 7,355   ALT. 347   MAP C-4

The Little Rock & Ft. Smith *Railroad* divided the property of E.H. Morrill and J.M. Moose in 1872. A railroad station built in 1873 – moved twice in 1874 and returned to its original location in 1875 – was named by stationmaster J.W. Boot for E.H. Morrill. A persistent and colorful local legend claims Morrill and Moose flipped a coin for the honor of naming the new town (Mooseville? Mooseton?). The new railroad town soon absorbed nearby Lewisburg, a river port laid out in 1830 on the north bank of the *Arkansas River*. Lewisburg had been incorporated in 1844 and was county seat of Conway County (1831-1850 and again 1873-1884). The older town had also served as a relay station on the Little Rock-Ft. Smith *Road* since 1836 and as a *Butterfield Overland Mail* stop (1858-c.1861). It had an academy in 1838 and by 1874 supported a theater and three newspapers. Morrilton gained the county seat in 1884. Ironically, interstates are now doing to railroad towns what railroads did to riverport towns. Possible *De Soto* Route. Home of Petit Jean Vocational Technical School.

Arkansas' last Civil War skirmish took place near Monticello, 45 days after the war ended

---

Division Street. Divides the historic farms of Morrill and Moose. The former's is to the west, the latter's to the east. Downtown.

Conway County Historical Museum. National Historic Register. Located in the 1915 St. Louis, Iron Mountain & Southern *Railroad* depot (red tile roof, one-story red brick), it exhibits local history of settlers, explorers and Indians as well as 19th and 20th century photos, clothing, jewelry, radios and phonographs. Downtown.

Point Remove/Park. About 1,000 yards east of an historical marker was the NE/SW *boundary line* defining the eastern border of the Cherokee in 1817-1828. A map and short history describe the territory assigned *(Dardanelle* and *Trail of Tears)*. Point Remove (to which in 1817 the Cherokee from Georgia were removed) has been mentioned in 1819 reports using the French root word remous (RE-moo), meaning point or eddy. Whether the name Point Remove resulted from a coincidence or a redundant "Americanization" is uncertain. Across an iron and plank-bottom foot-bridge over Point Remove Creek is a small point of land jutting into the Arkansas River that creates small whirlpools and eddies. Two picnic areas, camping and recreation *(Arkansas River Parks and Campgrounds,* Little Rock-Morrilton). SR 113 (W. Church) to SR 9, near the Arkansas River bridge. Signs.

Cherokee Park. Has the same historical marker as Point Remove Park, and picnic shelters on the river with a view of Lock & Dam #9. SR 113 (W. Church) to SR 9 at the river.

Lock and Dam # 9. Completed in 1969 as a part of the 445-mile McClellan-Kerr *Arkansas River* Navigation System (from near Tulsa, Ok., to the Mississippi River), the 110-by-600-foot lock can accommodate pleasure boats or barges by raising or lowering the water 16 feet inside the lock, working in stair-step fashion to match the level where river traffic is entering or exiting. Recreation: *Arkansas River Parks and Campgrounds,* Little Rock-Morrilton. SR 113 (W. Church) to SR 9 at the river. Signs.

SR 9 Roadcut. Natural Heritage Area. A series of roadcuts exposes colorful sediments in outcroppings of the Atoka Formation. Fossil-bearing regions in the shale are common. SR 9 just S of town.

Winrock International. An autonomous, nonprofit organization established in 1985 with a staff of nearly 120 scientists and technical specialists, it works internationally to improve agricultural productivity and nutrition, and is the legacy of John D. Rockefeller III, who founded the nucleus of the organization in 1953 at the same time that Winthrop Rockefeller (governor 1967-71) moved to Arkansas. Winrock Farms. Self-guided tours. SR 9 S to SR 154, W to Petit Jean *State Park,* right at the "Y" on unmarked blacktop road, 6 m. *(Perryville,* Heifer Project).

Museum of Automobiles/Drugstore. This serious collection of vintage cars, begun by Winthrop Rockefeller, is maintained in mint condition and features in its permanent exhibit (other displays changed annually): one of two surviving 1923 Climbers (Arkansas' only home-built automobile), a 1929 Model A Towncar (rare, open front chauffeur's compartment), Liberace's "solid gold" (23.75-carat gold leaf bumper to bumper) 1931 Cabriolet Cadillac and Rockefeller's two Fleetwood 75s (1951 & 1967). Others range from a 1913 Metz Roadster to a 1982 Talbot Matra Murena. The drugstore (1902) was brought from *Stamps,* Ar., and restored. SR 9 S to SR 154W near Petit Jean *State Park.* Signs.

Overcup Lake. Owned by the Game and Fish Commission, it is stocked with bluegill, crappie, catfish, bass and hybrid striper. Two primitive camping areas. SR 9, 5 m. N.

Events/Festivals. Easter: Annual Great Escape Weekend. Family-Oriented. Outdoor Activities. Easter Egg Hunt. Mid-June: Annual Antique Auto Show & Swap Meet. Awards. Sales. Arts & Crafts.

Conway County Courthouse. Classic Revival, 1929. Exterior: orange brick and cream-colored stone with four round-cut marble columns. *(County Profiles)*

National Historic Register. There are over 10 sites on the Register. Maps: chamber of commerce, US 64, N to 120 N. Division. PLUMMERVILLE, AR. (US 64, 5 m. E or I-40, exit 112): Plummer's Station, (former *Butterfield Overland Mail* stop), Van Buren St., 3 blks. S of RR tracks. Sim's Hotel (1880), Downtown.

MOUNT IDA
POP. 1,023   ALT. 663   MAP E-2

Naming this town was not an easy process. Granville Whittington (secretary of the 1835 meeting that petitioned the U.S Congress for Arkansas statehood), who had emigrated from Boston, Ma., where he reportedly admired that area's Mount Ida, opened a general store in 1837 about one mile north of Montgomery. At his farm (a mile and a half east of Montgomery) in 1842 he established the Mount Ida post office, which in 1848 was moved to Montgomery (county seat since 1845) and renamed for the town. Three months later (January 1849) the post office name was changed back to Mount Ida

(the town remained Montgomery). In 1850 the county court changed the county seat's name from Montgomery to Salem but changed it again four months later to Mount Ida, the same as the post office, and both have remained Mount Ida ever since. Incorporated in 1854. Incidentally, today the site of Whittington's 1837 store (no remnants) is on SR 27N in Mount Ida at the South Fork of the Ouachita *River (Float Streams),* and the 1846 courthouse site is occupied by the present courthouse. The town is now known as the "Quartz Crystal Capital of the World" and was for over 100 years a center of extensive mining.

Quartz Crystal. Taking millions of years to form, these crystals are transparent or translucent six-sided prisms that terminate in six-sided pyramids, and are used for thousands of products ranging from sandpaper to crystal balls. The area has many dig-it-yourself mines and a few "mineral museums."

Events/Festivals. Mid-Oct: Quartz Crystal/Mineral/Native Arts & Crafts Festival. Sales.

Montgomery County Courthouse. Neo-Classic, 1923. National Historic Register. Although called the best example of English Adamesque architecture in the state, structures have been added. Interior features: original pressed-tin ceilings. SR 270, Downtown. *County Profiles).*

MOUNT OLIVE
COMMUNITY   ALT. 341   MAP J-1

One of Arkansas' older settlements (1816), its name was also recorded in Washington, D.C., (but not on maps) as Mt. Vernon. Founded on the White *River (Float Streams)* by Jehoiada Jeffery, it became an important river port/*railroad* town (White River Railway Company, 1902, BELOW) of 1,000 by the turn of the century. Despite a stable economy (a barrel stave company employing 100, the river and the railroad), its isolated location *(Melbourne)* and three wars *(Civil War,* WW I & II) drained its population. Mostly the town was a victim of: "How are you going to keep them down on the farm...." Dropped from some maps, it is appx. 15 m. N of *Mountain View* on SR 9, W at White River access sign.

Mount Olive Cumberland Presbyterian Church. Organized in 1826, today's 1913 church building (white-clapboard with a bell tower) is all that remains (still holding services) of the community's buildings. West and north of it are the railroad tracks, the White River and a few remnants of the businesses that lined both.

CR 1808. This all-weather gravel road leads up the White River to Boswell (known c.1820 as Wideman), whose post office is sandwiched between the railroad track and the river; then to *Calico Rock.* Gives a close-up look at the river valley.

Athens. County seat from 1830-1836, it was named for the Greek city-state in vain hope that it would be the center of culture in North Arkansas. No remnants. Incidentally, John P. Houston, Izard County's first clerk and brother of Sam Houston *(Washington),* is buried here. Marker, Boswell Rd. (CR 1808) near Piney Creek Bridge.

White River Railway Company. Chartered in 1901, it was authorized to build a line from *Batesville* to Carthage, Mo. (239 miles). Like most *railroads,* it has been known by other names. Its brief career ended when sold to the St. Louis, Iron Mountain and Southern in 1903.

MOUNTAIN HOME
POP. 8,066   ALT. 809   MAP A-4

Founded in the early 1850s by Orin L. Dodd, who built a Colonial house and plantation at Rapps Barren (for 1839 settler "Rapp" Talburt in an area barren of trees). Today's name (an 1857 post office) supposedly originated with slaves (shuttled between Dodd's Augusta, Ar., fields and these), who referred to this place as their "mountain home." Made county seat of newly created Baxter (1873); incorporated in 1888.

Events/Festivals. Mid-June: Arts & Crafts Assoc. Fair. Homemade Items. Early Oct: Semi-Annual Arts & Crafts Fair.

Baxter County Courthouse. Moderne, 1939. The lobby contains memorabilia: two large murals of Bull Shoals and Table Rock *Lakes* as well as a commemorative plaque to the U.S.S. Maine (Spanish-American War, sunk 1898) that is made from the ship's metal. *(County Profiles)*

National Historic Register. The Casey House (c.1858), Fairgrounds, off US 62.

MOUNTAIN VIEW
POP. 2,147   ALT. 770   MAP J-1

First established a quarter-mile east of the present courthouse as the designated county seat of newly created Stone County (1873), its 1874 post office name was literally picked from a hat *(DeWitt)* and is presumably for the view of the surrounding mountains. Today's town and its real growth began with the present (1922) courthouse, around which has grown an arts and crafts community as well as a nationally recognized center for traditional Ozark Mountain music. Incorporated 1890. Home of Dick Powell.

Court Square. Looking as dense and heavy as a paperweight, this small town square is built from the same locally quarried stone as the courthouse. Each Saturday night at eight, locals and visitors make their own music. Dance, listen or play along. Bring a lawn chair. Downtown.

Grist Mill. Built in 1914 as a *grist mill,* it was restored in 1983 to again operate as one. 1 blk. W of the square.

Sylamore Swinging Bridge. Washed away in 1982, this 1914 landmark was restored to the last detail, including its original 4,100-pound cables. Open to motor traffic, the 200-foot bridge is 12 feet wide. SR 9, 6 m. N. Sylamore Creek, just W of Jct. SR 5, 9 & 14.

Ozark Folk Center State Park. *(State Parks)*
Blanchard Springs Caverns. *(Fifty-Six)*
Free Ferry. *(Ferry Boats)* Guion Ferry, SR 14, 8 m. E; SR 58, 6 m. N.

Events/Festivals. Mid-Apr: Annual Arkansas Folk Festival; also the Annual Ozark Foothills Craft Guild Show and Sale. Late Oct: Annual Bean Fest and Great Outhouse Race. Folk Music. Tall Tales. Cornbread and Beans. Talent Show. Others: Ozark Folk Center *State Park.*

Stone County Courthouse. Mission Classicism, 1922. National Historic Register. Still the center of town life (Court Square, ABOVE). *(County Profiles)*

MOUNTAINBURG
POP. 595   ALT. 712   MAP B-1

Begun a few miles east as a post office, Narrows (1844), it was a small settlement by 1859 and incorporated as Mountainburg (at the foothills of the Boston Mountains) when the St. Louis & San Francisco *(Railroad)* arrived in 1882. Col. Jacob Yoes *(Chester)* established a mercantile store here as he had at five other towns along the railroad's path.

The Narrows. About six and a half miles east is a ridge as narrow as the road. The land falls off sharply to the north and south, providing a spectacular view. Inquire Locally.

Bloody Sunday. Legend tells the story of a hill country feud brought to church around 1857. A missionary preacher held services, and the two sides held their tongues until it was over. What followed was reported as death and mayhem caused by men using whatever came to hand; women and children wielding kitchen utensils brought for Sunday dinner. No organized religious services were held for 70 years thereafter.

SR 282. Part of an 1870s *road* parallels the railroad through a scenic valley, crisscrossing Frog Bayou on low-water bridges and one iron one. Rejoins US 71 near Deans Market.

Parley Parker Pratt Monument. In 1857 this Mormon leader, a member of The Council of the Twelve and close friend of the Prophet Joseph Smith (founder of The Church of Jesus Christ of Latter Day Saints), was killed while returning to Salt Lake City, Utah, by the husband of the woman he persuaded to join the church – and him (as a plural wife). His murder by an *Arkansawyer* is one explanation (or combination of theories) for the Mountain Meadows Massacre *(Harrison).* At Deans Market, SR 282 (toward *Rudy*) .3 m., .3 m. N on gravel road. Monument, W side, in a field.

Mount Gayler. *(Winslow)*

MULBERRY
POP. 1,444   ALT. 394   MAP C-2

Said to be one of the oldest townsites between the White and Arkansas *Rivers,* it began as a Methodist campgrounds (Mulberry Campgrounds) c.1817 and was one of the few white settlements *(Russellville,* Dwight) allowed to remain through the Cherokee occupation of 1818-1828 *(Trail of Tears).* After 1836 it became a river town, Pleasant Hill, prospering until the arrival of the Little Rock & Ft. Smith *Railroad* in 1876, which helped create Mulberry on its tracks, draining nearby Pleasant

Hill's population. Named for the former campgrounds, which reportedly named the Mulberry *River (Float Streams)* for the mulberry trees growing along it. Incorporated in 1880.

MURFREESBORO
POP. 1,183   ALT. 368   MAP F-2

The post office and temporary county seat, Zebulon (1834), was changed after Murfreesboro was laid out in 1836 by Tennesseans (supposedly for their former hometown). Although peridots (a variety of olivine used as a gem) had been noted by geologists since 1842, nobody paid much attention until 1906, when John M. Huddleston couldn't understand why some of his crops wouldn't grow. The answer: His acreage was over an old "pipe" of a volcano; the two "crystals" sent for assay were diamonds. The only diamond mine in North America, it was unsuccessfully mined commercially by various companies and now is Crater of Diamonds *State Park* (dig-your-own diamonds). Incidentally, Huddleston lived "high" for a while; then died broke in 1936. Possible *De Soto* Route.

Pike County Public Park. Features: two restored log houses, a museum displaying local artifacts, playground, picnic tables and ball field. N edge of town.

KA-DO-HA. The remnants of this prehistoric site discovered in 1964 are open to the public. An "audio museum" and artifacts feature the life and the construction techniques of these mound builders. In a designated area, visitors may conduct their own "dig." SR 27, 2 m. S. Signs.

Pike County Courthouse. Deco, 1932. Oval steps lead to an oval foyer from which oval wooden stairs curve up to the courtroom. Features: original beaded board wainscoting and glass chandeliers. Downtown. *(County Profiles)*

NASHVILLE
POP. 4,554   ALT. 373   MAP G-2

Settled by a Baptist preacher in 1835. Tradition claims the name of the area was Hell's Valley (because of spring flooding, not hellfire and brimstone preaching) until changed officially to Mine Creek in 1848. Michael Womack (Bedford County, Tn.) had enough nostalgia and political influence to have it changed again (1856) to Nashville, after the capital of Tennessee. County seat in 1905. Home of Chicken McNuggets™ (Tyson Foods Incorporated, *Springdale*).

Dinosaur Trackway. There were "never any dinosaurs in Arkansas" until Saturday morning, November 7, 1983, when hundreds of footprints were found at an open gypsum mine that exposed sedimentation from a prehistoric shoreline of the Gulf of Mexico (Introduction, *Why There Is an Arkansas*). Plant-eating pleurocoelus (PLURO-SEELUS), relatives of the brontosaurus, left tracks 36 inches wide, with strides nine feet long, indicating a size of 60 feet head to tail. These 110-million-year-old fossils are displayed outside the courthouse.

Howard County Museum. Housed in a Gothic Victorian

Presbyterian church (National Historic Register, 1912), it has rotating exhibits focusing on local history. SR 27 (Main), 1 blk. E on Hempstead.

Howard County Courthouse. Moderne, 1939. Yellow brick accented by a black marble entrance, it is the only one in Arkansas that shares the same lot with a church. Grounds: Dinosaur Trackway (ABOVE). *(County Profiles)*

National Historic Register. First Christian Church, N. Main. Elbert Holt House, Main. Flavius Holt House (c.1877), Kohler. Womack House (1878), located off SR 4 & SR 24 (inquire locally).

NATURAL DAM
COMMUNITY   ALT. 673   MAP B-1

An early community (c.1828) and post office (Natural Dam, 1839) gathered around the natural dam at Mountain Fork Creek just before it enters Lee Creek *(Float Streams)*. Nearby was an historic *road* with several different names: Line Rd. named for the Indian Territory boundary line, Wire Rd. for the telegraph and Military Rd. for the road from Ft. Scott to Ft. Towson via Fort Smith as well as *Civil War* troop transport connecting the *Arkansas River* Valley to southern Missouri. Although an established community with a church, houses and a *grist mill* by the early 1850s, another nearby community built around Col. Henry King's 1876 store and stage stop on today's SR 59 soon outgrew the older one, taking its name when King was appointed postmaster of Natural Dam in 1885.

The Natural Dam. At first glance the rock formation appears man-made, including spillways along its water-polished, level surface. About 200 feet long, eight feet high and one to two feet wide, this ledge of rock did not wear down as fast as the creek bed, leaving visitors today a terrific swimming hole and shaded picnic area. In town. Signs.

NEW MADRID EARTHQUAKE

The worst earthquake in recorded history struck New Madrid, Mo., at 3 a.m., December 16, 1811, with a speculated magnitude of 8[+]. On January 23 and February 7, two others of 7[+] followed. Over the next year there were more than 1,800 quakes, with periodic ones for several years. Eyewitnesses said the land sunk 50 feet in some areas. The Mississippi River, dammed by an uplift, was reportedly seen flowing backward for two days. During the major events, "the earth was in continual agitation, visibly waving as a gentle sea." The effects of these shocks were felt in Washington, D.C. In Arkansas the land sunk 15 to 20 feet in places, destroying the St. Francis River's channel and creating the St. Francis swamps and the Sunken Lands between *Lake City* and *Marked Tree* (Map J-4 to K-4). The federal government instituted its first "Disaster Relief Fund" by issuing New Madrid Certificates, entitling displaced landowners new acreage in the Louisiana Purchase Territory

(State Parks). Bounty Certificates (payment in lieu of cash to veterans of the War of 1812) located in the damaged area were also exchanged for New Madrid Certificates, a practice that reportedly gave rise to speculators manipulating the two types. Both *Little Rock* and *Helena* were partially founded using these kinds of certificates.

NEWPORT
POP. 8,339   ALT. 225   MAP K-3

David Litchfield in 1827 (Litchfield, county seat 1832-39) operated a ferry across from today's townsite. R. Tidwell bought the ferry in 1831. His 1835 license describes the property as across the White *River* from the "Town of Newport." An 1837 Arkansas Gazette advertised Newport town lots for sale at the crossing of the main United States *road*. Although it was on the river and main road, so was nearby Elizabeth, which was voted county seat (1839-52), causing Newport to fade until the Cairo & Fulton *Railroad* established its depot here in 1872, bypassing *Jacksonport*. Finally voted county seat in 1891. The origin of town's only name is unknown. Home of White River Vocational Technical School. Possible *De Soto* Route.

Jackson County Jail. National Historic Register, 1905. One of the few stone buildings of its kind in Newport, it was used until 1979. The fourth floor (torn down) originally contained a gallows. The building provided space for about 12 cells and quarters for the jailer and his family. Restoration plans include a museum. Inquire Locally. Downtown, 503 3rd.

The White River Monster. Although sightings ("long as three or four pickups; gray, peeling skin") have occurred up and down the river, Towhead Island has been the scene of most. In 1973 the Arkansas State Legislature created the White River Monster Sanctuary and Retreat wherein no monster may be molested, killed or trampled. 6 m. S. Inquire Locally.

Lake Newport. Both Remmel Park (in town, SR 14 to Wilkerson) and Lockwood Park (in town, US 67, E of US 69) offer fishing, picnic facilities and playgrounds.

Events/Festivals. Late July: Riverboat Days & State Catfish Cooking Contest. Arts & Crafts. 10K & Fun Run. Boat Races. Fishing Rodeo. Entertainment.

Jackson County Courthouse. Chateauesque Italianate, 1892. National Historic Register. A statue of blindfolded justice stands on top of a seven-story clock tower. At either corner are bays: one round with a conical top; the other square with a pyramid. Downtown, US 67. *(County Profiles)*

National Historic Register. Empie-Van Dyke House (1891), 403 Laurel. First Presbyterian Church, 4th & Main. Gregg House, 412 Pine. Newport Jr. & Sr. High Schools, SR 14 to Wilkerson at Remmel Park.

NORFORK
POP. 399   ALT. 455   MAP I-1

One of the oldest continuously inhabited towns in Arkansas, it was founded early in the 19th century by Jacob Wolf, who established a trading post at the confluence and headwaters for navigation of the Big North Fork and White *Rivers (Float Streams)* at a trail leading up the White River to Branson, Mo. Norfork's county (Izard) was created in 1825 and within fifty years had four seats of justice with six different names. Cartographers were hard pressed to keep up with the changes. Liberty or Izard Court House (1825-1830), which was also known as the Northfork or North Fork, was followed by other county seats: Athens (1830-1836), *Mount Olive*/Mt. Vernon (1836-1875) and *Melbourne* (1875-present). Northfork (North Fork) had a reestablished post office called Devero in 1902 that was officially changed to Norfork in 1911.

Wolf House. National Historic Register, c.1825. As Indian agent, blacksmith, preacher and Territorial Legislator, Jacob Wolf built this two-story dogtrot log house overlooking the North Fork and White Rivers. An excellent example of the period's architecture with a romantic location, it served as Izard County's first courthouse. City-owned. In Town. Tours.

Wolf Cemetery. Beginning in 1823, it has been used by five generations of pioneer families. Inquire at Wolf House.

Shawnee Boundary Line. Originally an Atlantic Coast people allied with the Algonquians *(Arkansawyer),* an estimated 2,000 were removed *(Trail of Tears)* from west of the Mississippi River c.1819 to share land with the Cherokee west of the White River *(Yellville).*

Norfork National Fish Hatchery. One of the world's largest trout hatcheries, it was built in 1957. Eggs and milt are hand-stripped by fishery workers, incubated for about 45 days, hatched, then fed a commercial dry food. After a year the trout are released in Arkansas waters and those of contiguous states. Tours. SR 177, 3 m. N to Salesville, Ar.; SR 177, 1 m. E.

NORTH LITTLE ROCK
(SEE LITTLE ROCK)

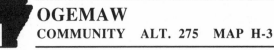

OGEMAW
COMMUNITY   ALT. 275   MAP H-3

First settled in 1859, it was known as Evans when the Texas & St. Louis *Railroad* arrived in 1882. The discontinued post office (1891) was reestablished as Ogemaw (misspelled Ogamaw until 1950) in 1892 by the Johnson Lumber Company's new owner, J.E. Potts, who named it for his former mill site's adjacent county, Ogemaw County, Michigan. Ogemaw is said to be derived from Ogemaw-Ke-Ke-To, who tradition claims was chief speaker of the Chippewa.

Lester and Halton #1 Well Site. National Historic Register, 1920. Drilled by S.A. Hunter on April 14, this is one of the oldest oil wells in Arkansas *(Smackover, El Dorado).* Appx. 1 m. S on the Old Wire Rd. Inquire Locally.

Poindexter General Store. National Historic Register, 1904. Established in 1896 by the present owner's grandfather, it still sells groceries, hardware, feed, dry goods and notions, and has on display memorabilia including old advertising signs and post office boxes. In Town.

OIL TROUGH
POP. 280   ALT. 237   MAP J-2

Nearby Pleasant Island, a thriving White *River (Float Streams)* trading center by 1830 (post office 1832), had trouble with bears until a cosmetic salesman from New Orleans brought news of bear oil (used for everything from softening old shoes to slicking down unruly hair). Tradition claims that so much rendered bear fat (oil) was stored in hollowed-out tree trunks (troughs) that the area became known as Oil Trough Bottoms, which was later shortened in 1849 for the town's new post office (three miles west of Pleasant Island). Although legend claims the troughs were floated downstream to New Orleans, flatboats were probably used. NOTE: The first recorded spelling of the town's area, by Friedrich Gerstaecker in 1838, was Oiltrove. This odd combination of English, as written by a German, has created speculation about its intended meaning in German, which mostly centers around the theory that Gerstaecker was referring to the rich, black soil; not to bear fat.

Hankins Grocery. Turn-of-the-century shotgun architecture, clapboard with a low front porch, its inside walls are wooden, its floor "center-match." A photograph shows former President Jimmy Carter standing on the porch, shaking hands with the owner. In Town.

Hulsey Bend Schoolhouse. Literally a one-room little red schoolhouse (1915), it is set on a lawn in the countryside with an American flag and outdoor water pump. Inside, there is a cloak room, potbelly stove, desks, pictures of presidents, an organ, plank floors and beaded-board ceiling. The room appears to have been momentarily deserted for recess. SR 14, appx. 2 m. E to gravel road across from crop duster hangar; 1 m. N.

Independence Steam Electric Station. The 1,000-foot tower is flanked by two cooling units that make it appear to be nuclear, but it is not. Each week an average of 10 110-car trains bring Wyoming low-sulphur coal to be crushed, pulverized and blown into boilers for combustion, producing 1,678 megawatts or enough electricity to light over 16.5 million 100-watt light bulbs. Tours by appointment (minimum age: junior high school). SR 14, 1 m. E to SR 122, 4 m. N; SR 69 E to plant.

OKAY
COMMUNITY   ALT. 300   MAP G-2

Founded by the Ideal Cement Company to make OK (Oklahoma) brand cement, its motto could have been Ideal's Best Is All Right in Okay but the boomtown created October 2, 1929, when the first kiln was fired, has fizzled. Dropped from some maps, it is on the east side of Millwood *Lake,* on a county road just N of Saratoga.

OSCEOLA
POP. 8,881   ALT. 238   MAP J-5

Said to be named for the Indian chief who led his people during the Second Seminole War in Florida (1835), not for the Indian village that originally occupied the townsite. Wm. B. Edrington bartered with the original occupants for the site in 1830, calling the settlement Plum Point until its incorporation in 1838 as Osceola, a refueling (cord wood) stop for Mississippi *River* steamboats. Home of Kemmons Wilson (the founder of Holiday Inn), The People's Insurance Company (Arkansas' first fire insurance company, 1853) and Francis Smith (later married as Dale Evans to Roy Rogers).

Downtown Historic District. Osceola is one of five participants in Main Street Arkansas, a preservation and restoration program. Many 19th century structures. Downtown.

Events/Festivals. Early Dec: Osceola Winter Festival. Entertainment. Caroling. Crafts. Parade.

Mississippi County Courthouse. Classical Revival, 1912. *Dual County Seat.* Built using foot-long brown bricks that are less than two inches thick, it has a flat roof supporting a large, ornate copper dome. Grounds: Ironically, the statue of a Confederate soldier was sculpted from pink Vermont granite. *(County Profiles)*

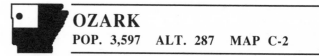

OZARK
POP. 3,597   ALT. 287   MAP C-2

In 1836, while 26 steamboats were trading from Arkansas Post *(National Park)* to Fort Smith, Archibald Yell *(Yellville)* and associates advertised a public auction in the Arkansas Gazette for city lots "at the great North Bend" of the *Arkansas River* (most northern point of the river in the state). County seat by 1837 and incorporated in 1838, the town grew as a river port community until the 1870s, when it became one of the few of its kind to make the transition to a railroad town (Little Rock-Ft. Smith *Railroad,* 1876). The Ozark Mountains appeared on maps long before this settlement was established, and are most likely the inspiration for the town's name. While consensus accepts the French phrase Aux Arcs (Ohs Arcs) as the basis for the "Americanization," Ozark, various explanations for its derivation are offered. Incidentally, aux is plural, meaning "to the" or "in the" (used here as: to the or in the territory of). Possible origins: (1) The Quapaw, like the Osage and Kansa *(Arkansawyer),* were referred to by the French in shortened names (Kans, Os and Arcs). Records of the period reflect hunting or trading aux Kans, aux Os and aux Arcs. NOTE: The Quapaw were, among other names, known as the Bow (arc) Indians. (2) Aux Arcs refers to the many bows (arcs) in either/or both the White and Arkansas Rivers. NOTE: Historically, these rivers formed a series of arcs through the territory of the Quapaw near Arkansas Post *(National Park).* (3) A series of corrupted words beginning with bois (BO-ze) d'arc (the Osage orange tree named by the French and used for making particularly strong bows) ended with the "Americanization," Ozark. NOTE: At one time the White River was free-flowing in tight bows (arcs) through this region, and the mountains here are specifically named the Ozark Mountains. Home of Arkansas Valley Vocational Technical School.

Town Square. Located on a bluff above the Arkansas River, stone buildings are grouped around the courthouse, accurately reflecting their 19th century origins.

Citadel Bible College. National Historic Register. On campus is a unique two-story log house with porches and French doors. The house was built using logs from every state in the union. Nice view of the Arkansas River. SR 64, W to SR 219, S 3 m.

SR 23's Wildflowers. From a mile south of town to seven miles north of I-40 is an ongoing seasonal display of wildflowers like Johnny Jump Ups, Tiger Lily, Prim Rose, Purple Vetch and Yucca.

Citadel Bible College has a house built using logs from every state in the union

---

Reed Mountain Park. This mountain top was bought by former slave Randall Reed from the Fort Smith Railroad Company in 1880. Along with the River Bluff Nature *Trail,* a panoramic overlook has displays showing historical points of interest on the *Arkansas River* along with a bird's-eye view of the town of Ozark and locking procedures at the dam. US 64, 2.5 m. E; 1 m. SW on paved access road. Picnic facilities and recreation: (Ozark *Lake*).

Powerhouse/Lock & Dam. One of two powerhouses in the world with slant-shaft generating units. There are audio-visual displays demonstrating the process, and observation windows to watch the "action." Similar displays show how Ozark-Jeta Taylor Lock & Dam operates in stair-step fashion to match the water level where river traffic is entering or exiting. Recreation and camping: Ozark *Lake,* US 64, 2.5 m. E; 1 m. SW on paved access road.

Franklin County Courthouse. Italianate Moderne, 1904; remodeled in 1944. *Dual County Seat (Charleston).* Although gutted by a fire in 1944, the structure, including a three-story clock tower, was saved. The courtroom has a panoramic view of the river. Downtown. *(County Profiles)*

National Historic Register. Franklin County Jail, 3rd & River St.

PANGBURN
POP. 673   ALT. 335   MAP K-2

First established as Judson *(Judsonia)* in 1858, the name was changed to honor a local doctor, David Pangburn. Supported by cotton and timber until the 1950s, today it benefits from recreation on the Little Red River *(Float Streams).* Home of Rex Humbard.

PARAGOULD
POP. 15,017   ALT. 325   MAP J-4

The only town in the world with this name, it was created in 1882 by Jay Gould's intent to literally cut off the competition by crossing the St. Louis, Iron Mountain & Southern *(Railroad)* at the same point as his competitor's (J.W. Paramore) narrow gauge line, the Texas & St. Louis. Town promoters joined the two rival's names, forming Para-Gould. Gould objected to being last in a hyphen and listed the town as Parmley on his schedules. A compromise resulted in Paragould. While still an uncultivated tract of timber, it was voted county seat in 1883. Home of Crowley's Ridge College.

Engine 303. A reminder of the town's founding, this steam engine is the last one that ran on the "Little Dummy" Line, "The World's Shortest Railroad" *(Augusta),* until abandoned in 1958. Harmond Park (picnic, tennis), US 49B, N of town.

Gainesville. One of the few towns in Arkansas not named for a person, place or thing, it was selected (it "gained") county seat during a competition in 1848 as an uninhabited central location. SR 135, 6 m. N.

King Crowley. Found 10 feet deep in a gravel pit (1921), this four-foot statue with features "part Egyptoid, part Mongoloid" had an inlaid "heart" of copper shaped like a valentine, gold eyeballs and copper earplugs along with items like volcanic pumice and carvings of astronomical symbols, men and animals. Its means of discovery (revealed in a dream) and the declaration of it as a fake by the Smithsonian led to its cheap sale (and disappearance). No remnants, 8 m. S.

Reynolds Park. It has a swimming pool, 30-acre fishing lake and picnic facilities. NW city limits. US 49B, W on Country Club or US 412, N on Reynolds.

Events/Festivals. Early Nov: Harvest Craft Festival.

Greene County Courthouse. Victorian Renaissance Revival, 1888; remodeled 1918. National Historic Register. Its two-foot-thick brick walls are now stucco; its domed clock tower removed in 1973. Grounds: 90-by-90-foot underground bomb shelter (1978), a bronze Statue of Liberty and a replica of the Liberty Bell. *(County Profiles)*

National Historic Register. The Old Bethel Methodist Church (1880). SR 141, W of town.

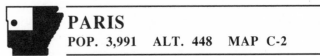

PARIS
POP. 3,991   ALT. 448   MAP C-2

Reportedly settled c.1820 on a pioneer *road* between Little Rock and Fort Smith (also later the *Butterfield Overland Mail* route), it was laid out as a county seat by Jessie D. Waddill and named for Paris, France, in 1874. Incorporated in 1879. Maps: chamber of commerce: SR 309, N of Jct. SR 22.

Logan County Museum/Old Jail. Built in 1886, this red brick building still has strap-iron across the windows and its original cells. On July 15, 1914, Arthur Tillman, convicted of murdering his girlfriend, Amanda Stevens, became the last man to be executed by hanging in Arkansas. Details of the hanging and other local history (coal mining, etc.) are on display. 204 N. Vine. SR 22, W of Jct. SR 309, N on Roseville.

Gill Folk Art Houses. These five houses could have been built by Black Forest elves. They feature native yellow stone, deep grouting, cement railings and supports shaped like logs, turrets and arches as well as cement eagles, log chairs, window sills and lintels. Locations: SR 22 W at Spruce, SR 309S at Grober; SR 22W, dead end of N. Spruce.

Coal Mines. In 1881 George Lumpp opened the first coal mine in Paris, using hand-hewn rails and wheels for the coal cars. During 1937-38 over 400,000 tons were dug by 1,000 union miners. Remnants. Inquire locally.

Magazine Mountain. *(Booneville)*

Cowie Winery. Established in 1967, it offers dinner, "sipping" and fruit wines, including Lavacaberry, which is unique to Cowie Winery. Also unique are painted barrel heads depicting scenes of family and wine history. Tours. Tastings. SR 22, 3 m. W. Signs.

Events/Festivals. Late Aug: The Arkansas Championship Grape Stomp & Wine Fest. Bluegrass Music. Tours & Tastings. Games. Arts & Crafts. Early Oct: Mt. Magazine Frontier Days Celebration. Arts & Crafts. Auto Show. "Old-Timey" Events. Entertainment.

Logan County Courthouse. Palladian Revival, 1908; remodeled in 1958 by R.M. Hardwick during the term of county judge M.B. Hardwick. National Historical Register. *Dual County Seat (Booneville).* This impressive courthouse features columned porticoes on three sides with a one-story octagonal clock tower. SR 22 & SR 309. *(County Profiles)*

 PARKIN
POP. 2,035   ALT. 211   MAP K-4

One of the only cities in Arkansas to invite its namesake to dinner, this town in 1940 asked Wm. Parkin to be guest of honor. He declined, saying he had never given a speech in his life. As a construction engineer for the St. Louis, Iron Mountain & Southern *(Railroad)* in 1887, he was in charge of 20 miles of track (seven of which were bridges, *Augusta)*. The chief engineer told him to build a siding here — "Call it Parkin." Possible *De Soto* Route.

Roberts Museum. Beginning in the mid-1940s, Bob Zirkle began collecting "an item here and there." Today thousands of "items" include farm and household implements, Indian artifacts and a persimmon walking stick listed in Ripley's Believe-It-Or-Not. Housed in a log cabin (c.1861). US 64B, just E of downtown.

Parkin Mound. This main mound (20 found in the area) of the Parkin phase (c.1400-1650 A.D.) is immediately below the confluence of the St. Francis and Tyronza *Rivers*. Undeveloped, it stands nearly 20 feet high on the bank of the river. A "moat" is on the other three sides. Said to have been visited by *De Soto,* who referred to the village as Casqui, it is believed to have been the "capital" of these mound builders' confederation.

US 69, 150 yds. N on gravel road at the E end of the St. Francis River bridge; 30 yds. W at the church to the river.

Events/Festivals. Early Oct: St Francis Riverboat Festival. Arts & Crafts. Bar-B-Q Cook-Off.

 **PARKS**
COMMUNITY   ALT. 668   MAP E-2

Originally White Church, Parks is an area post office today. Established in 1838 by Cy Parks (with only a four-year lapse, 1866-70), it has been in continuous operation since. At 256 square feet, this now modern structure is one of the smallest post offices in the state.

Old Forrester. Once a logging camp and mill site, Weyerhaeuser Corp. has developed it into a recreation area, stocking one of the old mill ponds with fish. Public. SR 28, about 10 m. E. Signs.

Fire Tower. For a long look at the Ouachitas: SR 28, 7 m. E, CR 8200 2 m. N (.5 m. is unimproved).

 **PARTHENON**
COMMUNITY   ALT. 925   MAP B-3

Established by Sam Hudson (Diamond Cave, *Jasper)* c.1840 where Shop Creek enters the Little Buffalo River (Hudson's East Fork then). The post office was named Mt. Parthenon (reportedly by Thos. K. May, "The Bible Man") until changed in 1895. The basis of the name or its change is not known, although it could be for the Parthenon in Greece, or Parthian (local pronunciation approximates the spelling), which was a Biblical settlement at the flank of a mountain.

Shelton Grocery. In business since c.1900, this two-story stone and ornamental tin general store is still serving the community's needs.

Natural Bridge. *(Jasper)* At Shelton Grocery, west at the deadend across a one-way iron bridge and past a log barn will lead down an all-weather gravel road to Alum Cove's natural bridge. Appx. 5 m.

PEA RIDGE
POP. 1,488   ALT. 1,350   MAP A-1

The origin of this town's name has been muddled by conflicting versions and a lack of direct evidence. The settlement's 1850 post office, Pea Ridge, is said to be a modification of the area's original name, Pea Vine Ridge, but it is arguable which name came first or if they were interchangeable (during the Battle of Pea Ridge, BELOW, both were used). One tradition claims the nearby ridge was covered in wild pea vines; another suggests "Pea Ridge" was a former hometown of an early settler. At first it was only a post office community; after 1900 businesses were established. Incorporated 1936.

The Battle of Pea Ridge. (Pea Ridge *National Park)*

Street Names. In keeping with what has been called the most important *Civil War* battle west of the Mississippi, all streets in the town are named for veterans of that bloody conflict. The north-south streets are named for Federal soldiers; east-west for Confederates. Local tradition claims that the selection of east-west for Confederates was because there were more streets laid out in that direction. Incidentally, one east-west street is named for General Stand Waite, a Cherokee, who like the Choctaw fought for the Confederacy. *(Greenwood).*

PERRYVILLE
POP. 1,058   ALT. 310   MAP D-4

It is said that in 1808 Aaron Price grazed cattle about nine miles south of the present town but it wasn't until the 1830s that a settlement began. Made county seat (1841) of newly created Perry County and named for Commodore M.C. Perry in honor of his victories on Lake Erie during the War of 1812 *(County Profiles,* Perry County). It was incorporated in 1878.

Heifer Project International. The Heifer Project International Learning and Livestock Center, a privately financed nonprofit organization, was founded in 1942 to provide livestock and training to low-income farmers in "developing areas" who, in turn, pass on the offspring and newly acquired skills to other needy families. On its 1,200 acres are 1,500 head of cattle, a conference center, lodge and educational hiking *trail.* Guided tours. SR 10, 2 m. S. (Winrock Intern'l, *Morrilton)*

Perry Mountain Roadcut. Natural Heritage Area. Shows an excellent exposure of varieties of sandstone, siltstone and shale of the Atoka Formation as well as some quartz. SR 9, about 2 m. N.

Lake Winona Scenic Area. *(Lake* Winona) Natural Heritage Area. Located in this area and called an opportunity to study "the dynamics of natural ecosystems," 300 acres of short leaf pines (ranging in age from 150-300 years old) were "scattered like jackstraws" by a 1982 tornado. Inquire Locally.

Perry County Courthouse. Georgian Revival, 1888. National Historic Register. Unusual because the restrooms are in an outbuilding (indoor plumbing) and the building, looking more like a house than a public institution, was mostly paid for by individuals, not taxes. Grounds: A pine nearly 13 feet in diameter dwarfs a nearby memorial to local WW II veterans that is 34 feet long. Downtown. *(County Profiles)*

PIGGOTT
POP. 3,762   ALT. 290   MAP I-5

First named Houston in 1882 when F. Knopp put his sawmill on the uncompleted grade of the St. Louis, Arkansas & Texas *Railroad.* A post office two miles northwest, named in honor of Dr. J.A. Piggott, was moved to town in 1883.

Hemingway Studio/Barn. Here Ernest Hemingway wrote much of <u>A Farewell to Arms</u>. Incidentally, the 1933 movie version of the book, starring Gary Cooper and Helen Hayes,

held its world premiere at Piggott. US 62, W on Main, N on 9th, W on Cherry to 10th. Inquire Locally.

Petrified Wood. On the courthouse lawn are examples of petrified wood found in the area. Said to be plentiful, they have been used as tombstones.

Chalk Bluff Park/Battlefield. *(St. Francis)*

Buffalo Trail/Chalk Bluff Road. *(Harrisburg)*

Events/Festivals. Fourth of July Picnic & Homecoming: Parade. Political Speakers. Fireworks. Entertainment.

Clay County Courthouse. Sixties Modern, 1966. *Dual County Seat.* This courthouse and its counterpart in *Corning* were built in the same year by the same architect. Corning's burned; it requested building funds. Piggott tore its down, then requested the same. *(County Profiles)*

National Historic Register. Pfeiffer House & Carriage House (1927-40), 10th & Cherry.

PINE BLUFF
POP. 56,636   ALT. 216   MAP N-2

According to English naturalist Thomas Nutall, in 1819 a small settlement existed at the mouth of Plum Bayou that he recorded as Le Boun's, presumably referring to Joseph Bonne, son of a Frenchman and a Quapaw, who is said to have relocated here after being flooded out of his home at nearby New Gascony that same year. An 1814 deed mentions the area as the Pine Bluff(s), and in 1828 a post office was established across the river as "Pine Bluff Postoffice." According to an 1832 Arkansas Gazette: "Town of Pine Bluff – An election was held...selecting a suitable site for the seat of Justice of that county [Jefferson] which resulted in the favor of the Pine Bluffs...at which point a town has been laid off bearing that name...." Incorporated in 1839. Slow to grow until the 1850s (460 residents), its population then tripled in 10 years with the arrival of steamboats and the beginnings of cotton trading and production, but its real growth (3,203 in 1880 to 9,952 in 1890) began when the tracks for the Texas & St. Louis *Railroad* were completed in 1882 and railroad shops established (1884). Home of Martha Mitchell, U of A at Pine Bluff, Pines Vocational Technical School, WOK (Arkansas' first radio station), the Dollarway (Arkansas' first concrete highway) and Bronco Billy Anderson (Max Aaronson), the first movie-star cowboy. Tour maps and literature: tourist information center, Dexter Harding House, US 65 at Lake Pine Bluff. Signs.

Dexter Harding House. Dismantled, moved and restored, this simple three-room clapboard house (c.1850) serves as the tourist information center and as a good example of the plain but symmetrical architecture of the era. Features: a central fireplace, wooden walls and ceiling, an original map of the 45-block area of "old town" and period furnishings. US 65 at Lake Pine Bluff. Signs.

Sawdust Bridge. In 1850 Dexter Harding (a drummer boy in the War of 1812) traded his Bounty Certificate *(New Madrid Earthquake)* for a 160-acre tract southeast of "old town" (near 11th & State), and set up a lumber mill. Separated from town by a lake, he dumped sawdust across a narrow neck until it formed a bridge. Because the bridge shook for no apparent reason and because of glowing swamp gas and vapor, the lake was said to haunted. No Remnants. Marker, 11th & State.

Steam Locomotive 819. Nearly 100 feet long and weighing about 369 tons, this oil-burning locomotive was originally built here in 1942 at the Cotton Belt Shops. Its type "ruled the rails" for a dozen years until replaced by more efficient diesels. Recommissioned and fully operational. Tours. Information: tourist information center.

The Dollarway, Arkansas' first concrete highway, cost a dollar per linear foot

The Dollarway. National Historic Register. Opened in 1914 as Arkansas' first concrete highway, the 24 miles cost a dollar per linear foot for this nine-foot-wide stretch of road. Farmers complained that the hard surface hurt their horses' feet and wagon rims (the special tax hurt too), but auto enthusiasts (only 5,643 licensed in the state) shipped their cars by rail just for a short ride on the novelty. Replaced (and mostly covered) 18 years later by SR 365. About one mile of the original roadbed remains as a narrow strip of concrete laced through the woods. Remnant: REDFIELD, AR (SR 365, 18 m. N): appx. 3 m. S to access signs (blue street markers), W to 1st gravel intersection, then S (if turned at 1st access) or N (if used 2nd). Incidentally, Redfield is the home of the Mammoth Orange, a drive-in restaurant shaped like an orange. Possible *De Soto Route* and winter headquarters (Jct. SR 365 & 46).

Worker of Kilowatts (WOK) Radio Station. After hearing the first radio station to broadcast on a regular basis (KDAK in Pittsburgh, Pa.), Harvey C. Couch, president of AP&L, decided to build his own for advertising the state of Arkansas (and his company). WOK's first transmission of 1922 was short-lived. In 1923 Couch gave the equipment to Henderson Brown College (now Henderson State University).

Lake Pine Bluff. Right next to downtown is a 500-acre lake said to be "top notch for bass and bream" and also very good for blue gill and redear. Crappie and catfish are also popular. There are nearly two miles of bank fishing. Commercial boat docks rent everything, including boats. Boat Ramp. US 65 & US 79.

Architecture. In an area bounded by Barraque and Second, Oak and State are nine of the 26 noteworthy houses and buildings on the city tour. Over 30 structures are listed on the National Historic Register. US 65 at Lake Pine Bluff, S on State, W on Barraque. Maps: tourist information center.

Civil War's First Shot. In keeping with a state undecided about the *Civil War,* this city has a local legend that the Jefferson (County) Guards, a few days before Ft. Sumter's famous shot, stopped a Federal supply ship on its way to Fort Smith by firing a musket (no cannon available) across the bow.

Trinity Episcopal Church. National Historic Register, 1870. The cornerstone for the oldest Episcopal Church build-

ing in Arkansas was laid in 1866. A good example of Gothic architecture, it features stained-glass windows and an altar of Carrara marble. 3rd & Oak. US 65 at Lake Pine Bluff, S on Pine, W on 3rd.

St. Mary's Catholic Church. Said to the oldest Roman Catholic Church still standing in Arkansas, it was first built c.1834, rebuilt on its present site c.1851, and then remodeled (in brick) in 1927. US 79, 7 m. N, SR 15 appx. 4 m. N to E on St. Mary's county road along Plum Bayou. Signs.

Jefferson County Historical Museum. Located on the first floor of the restored section (1856 and 1980) of the courthouse, it displays local historical items, and has rotating programs ranging from Indian culture to exhibits and demonstrations of 19th and 20th century weaving. Courthouse.

S.E. Arkansas Arts and Science Center. The Center offers varied programs in visual and performing arts (regional to national). The permanent collection features works on paper and canvas, sculpture (Art Deco and Art Nouveau) and c.1900s photography ("Riverboats and Cottonfields"). US 65 at Lake Pine Bluff, S on Pine to jct. Pine & Martin.

Martha Mitchell Home. Reared in this c.1887 Victorian house, later married to U.S. Attorney General John Mitchell (Nixon administration, 1968-74), she described her Arkansas home as having "gingerbread and all that jazz." Open for tours, it features furnishings from the 1920-30s. Elm & 4th. US 65 at Lake Pine Bluff, S on Pine, W on Elm to 4th.

Sarasen's Grave. Among the graves of early settlers is one said to be of a Quapaw chief who died in 1832 at age 97. The inscription is an ageless note of appreciation for his rescuing two settler's children who had been kidnapped by "a wandering band of Chickasaws." Sarasen reportedly was first to be buried here. St. Joseph's Cemetery. US 65 at Lake Pine Bluff, 1 blk. N on Cedar to Pullen.

Arkansas' first radio station, Worker of Kilowatts (WOK), was aired in 1922

Bird Lake. Natural Heritage Area. This oxbow lake is fed during times of high water by *Bayou Bartholomew.* Surrounded by bald cypress and abundant wildlife. Hiking *trails* provide easy access. SR 15, S to city limits. Signs.

Pine Bluff Arsenal. Established in 1941 (present employment 1,400), the arsenal is an Army Industrial Fund installation owned and operated by the government and commanded by an army officer. Its primary mission includes the production of chemical munitions along with their testing, storing, disposal and distribution. Other kinds of testing have involved the effects of marijuana on monkeys. SR 365, N city limits.

Locks & Dams #3 & #4. Completed in 1968 as a part of the 445-mile McClellan-Kerr *Arkansas River* Navigation System (from east of Tulsa, Ok., to the Mississippi River), these 110-by-600-foot locks can accommodate pleasure boats or barges by raising or lowering the water 20 feet inside the lock, working in stair-step fashion to match the level where river traffic is entering or exiting. Recreation: *Arkansas River Parks and Campgrounds,* Arkansas Post-Pine Bluff. L&D #3: US 65, 19 m. S to Grady; SR 11, 3.2 m. to access road. L&D #4: US 65, 3.4 m. S, SR 81, 5.5 m. E.

Events/Festivals. Mid-Sept: Chief Black Dog Crafts Festival. Music. Bar-B-Q Cook-Off. International Food. Crafts. Late Sept: Southeast Arkansas Livestock Show & Rodeo.

Jefferson County Courthouse. Wren Baroque, 1980. It is at once the oldest and newest courthouse in Arkansas. Built in 1840, it was mostly destroyed by fire in 1976. The new section was fitted around the previously restored (1856) center portion and capped with a gold anodized aluminum dome. Barraque & Main. US 65 at Lake Pine Bluff, S on Pine, E on Barraque. *(County Profiles)*

National Historic Register. (Architecture, ABOVE)

PINE RIDGE
COMMUNITY   ALT. 840   MAP E-2

Life does imitate art. Walters, a small farming community founded in the early 1900s, became so entangled in the popularity of "The Lum 'N Abner" radio show that was based on it that in 1936, during an elaborate ceremony at the State Capitol, the town officially changed its name to the fictional setting of the program, Pine Ridge. The actors, Chester "Lum" Lauck and Norris "Abner" Goff *(Mena),* kept in touch with the residents, picking up new material, while the residents listened to the program, hearing what the actors had to say about their town, and all of it began to border on the riddle of Which came first, the chicken or the egg?

Lum 'N Abner Museum. History and memorabilia of the program (seven movies and nearly 25 years on radio from the 1930s-50s) are on display. Incidentally, this "hillbilly humor" show, centered around the owners of a general store (the Jot 'Em Down Store), once received one and a half million letters during one week.

Events/Festivals. Mid-June: Annual Lum 'N Abner Sunday. Movies. Tours.

National Historic Register. The Huddleston Store and McKinzie Store (museum building and a "model" of the radio program's general store). Downtown.

PLUM BAYOU
GHOST TOWN   ALT. 215   MAP M-1

National Historic Register, 1935. Once a plantation operated by prisoners *(Tucker),* this 1930s *Resettlement Administration* project was divided into 30-to-40-acre tracts as an experimental farm cooperative like *Dyess.* Not shown on most maps, just W of Wright.

Plum Bayou Culture. Near here was one of the largest and most complex mound cultures in the lower Mississippi Valley. The people built houses, farmed, fished, hunted and gathered wild plants (Toltec Mounds *State Park).*

POCAHONTAS
POP. 5,995   ALT. 529   MAP I-3

Although local tradition claims the site as a French trading post as early as 1760, recorded history begins when Dr. Ransom Bettis built his house on a bluff (Bettis St. & US 67) overlooking the Black *River.* From c.1815-1835 the settlement was known as Bettis Bluff, a popular layover for traders and rivermen, a relay station on the postal *road* from Harrisonville, Il., to Louisiana and a port for steamers like The Laurel (the first steamboat to ascend the Black River, 1829). Later, arrival (1912) of the St. Louis & San Francisco *(Railroad)* helped continue its prosperity as a center of commerce. Of the possibilities offered for changing its name to Pocahontas when becoming county seat in 1835, the most romantic is that the grandmother of county namesake John Randolph was THE Pocahontas *(Powhatan)* who in 1614 married John Rolfe of Jamestown, Va. Home of the toy, Wonder Horse, Thomas S. Drew, Arkansas' fourth governor (1844-49) and Black River Vocational Technical School.

Columbia. First settled c.1801 and known by its post office Fourche du Mars (a corruption of maux), this temporary 1835 county seat's residents attended a legendary free picnic (food and liquor) sponsored by Bettis and his son-in-law, Thomas Drew *(Biggers),* to determine the permanent location. Full of harmony, the men of Columbia voted for newly named Pocahontas, but the morning after said its name should be pronounced "Poke-it-on-to-us." Columbia was also known as Fourche de Thomas, Lindseyville, Foster and Jarrett. 8 m. NE. Vanished.

Town Square. Grouped around the old courthouse (1872), the buildings reflect the 19th and early 20th century history of the town.

Randolph County Library. National Historic Register, 1872. According to many architects this former courthouse of 1872-1940 is one of the best examples of Victorian Italianate architecture in America. Two stories of narrow arched windows capped by a decorative "lantern" cupola make it the centerpiece of town square. Downtown.

St. Paul's Roman Catholic Church. Built with native stone in 1901 with an ornamental tin roof, it has the feeling of a basilica. The simple interior has a vaulted ceiling, wooden pews and outstanding stained-glass windows. The landscaped grounds has a man-made grotto comprised of an assemblage of rocks, flowers, icons and water that was built in 1932. From town square, W on Broadway to Cedar.

Frisco Railroad Bridge. One of the longest spans of its kind, it was built in 1912 so as to turn, allowing river traffic to pass. Incidentally, Jim Shivley rode the first train across the bridge in 1912 and the last one leaving in 1985. US 62/67, south side of downtown.

Living Farm Museum. Operated by the Good Earth Association, its goal is to maintain, demonstrate and display historical farm equipment, and to teach the skills necessary to run a low-technology, self-sustaining family farm. Downtown, 202 Church Street.

Randolph County Courthouse. Moderne, 1940. Steps 48 feet wide lead up to a white brick building trimmed in black marble and cement. On the grounds are sunken gardens and attractive landscaping. *(County Profiles)*

National Historic Register. Bates House (1905), US 67, W of Broadway.

POTTSVILLE
POP. 564   ALT. 370   MAP C-3

Named for Kirkbride Potts, who, after building a two-story log cabin for his wife and family (c.1835), made the first of three cattle drives (late 1840s) to the California gold fields to raise money for what is now Potts Tavern.

Potts Tavern. National Historic Register. Built 1850-58, it was occupied by a member of the Potts family until 1970. Called one of the best-preserved stagecoach stations on the *Butterfield Overland Mail* route between Memphis and Fort Smith, this two-story antebellum-style home was built from hand-planed wood and bricks fired on the property. It also served as the Galla Creek Post Office. Furnished according to the period. In town, Main & Center.

Hat Collection Museum. Claimed to be one of two such museums in America, this unusual collection, "100 Years in Hats," features ladies' hats, showing changes in style and decoration from 1870 to 1970. Designed by Michael McClean, an *Arkansawyer* who designed and made the inaugural dress for Mrs. Calvin Coolidge, the collection represents over 100 hats. Potts Tavern.

POWHATAN
POP. 49   ALT. 265   MAP I-3

Said to have been named for Powhatan (chief of the powerful Powhatan confederacy of Indian tribes in the Jamestown, Va., area) whose 13-year-old daughter, *Pocahontas,* reportedly saved the life of Capt. John Smith in 1607 by placing her head between his and the executioner's war club. Settled as a ferry landing in 1820, it became an important steamboat port on the Black *River*, dominating the county until the Kansas City, Ft. Scott & Gulf *Railroad* laid track two miles north of it at *Black Rock* in 1883. County seat, 1869-1963.

Powhatan Courthouse State Park. (Powhatan Courthouse *State Park*)

Powhatan Methodist Church. Victorian "Church Architecture," 1874. National Historic Register. Still in use today, it has the original pews and organ. SR 25. In Town.

Lebanon Church/Cemetery. This Presbyterian church is a one-story log building (c.1842/46) built using hand-hewn logs and wooden pegs. Slightly remodeled (a wire is strung for light bulbs; the floor is cement) but the low ceiling supported by huge pine logs gives an authentic feeling. The first interment was a man who left one evening to help a neighbor slaughter hogs. Three dead wolves were found the next day. One had a

knife in it. What parts could be found of the man were brought back for burial. Just S of Eaton, SR 25, 9 m. S.

National Historic Register. Powhatan School House, c.1880. SR 25, 2 blks S of town. Powhatan Courthouse (1888). In Town.

PRESCOTT
POP. 4,103   ALT. 319   MAP G-3

First settled as Moscow (BELOW) on an Indian Trail and the Fort Towson *Road,* its present site was platted on the grade of the Cairo & Fulton *Railroad* in 1873, drawing away the older town's population. All historical sources agree W.H. Prescott is the town's namesake. Which W.H. is still disputed. W.H. of Salem, Ma., was a noted historian and a friend of the railroad's executives. W.H. of Nevada County, Arkansas, was county surveyor during construction of the railroad, and later the presiding county judge when the town was incorporated (1874) and made county seat (1877). Incidentally, the town was one of the first (1899) in Arkansas to operate its own utilities.

Prairie DeAnn. About 30 square miles of this portion of Nevada (knee-VAY-dah) County were known as Prairie DeAnn in the 1860s because it was an oasis of clear, dry land in the midst of dense forests and nearly impassable swamps. In 1864 Federal forces, organizing an attack on *Washington* during the Red River Campaign *(Civil War),* first met concentrated Confederate resistance here. Ironically, Confederate veterans of the battle were so impressed with the area that many returned to build their homes. Remnants: Earthen fortifications appear as shallow, regular holes just W of I-30 between exits 44 & 46 (or N & S of SR 24 just W of Prescott).

Moscow/Moscow Church. Only the white clapboard church and cemetery remain from this trading post town of 1850-1860s. The last day's battle of Prairie DeAnn took place near the church, forcing the Federals to withdraw to *Camden.* US 67, S on E. Main to Cale, then 2 m. S.

Depot Museum. Standard railroad architecture (1912), it houses various displays of *railroad* memorabilia as well as Civil War artifacts, old photos and documents (including those of Gov. Thos. McRae, 1921-25) and "the finest pair of cotton scales in Arkansas," 300 W. First (US 67).

Reader Railroad. Said to be the oldest all-steam, standard gauge railroad operating in North America, this "cabbage head" departs daily on the Possum Trot Line from Reader to the old logging camp of Camp DeWoody. SR 24, 19 m. E to Reader.

Iron Bridge. Still safe to use, it crosses the Little Missouri River in style. N on US 67; W on CR 8 past Grassy Lake. Crossing the river, CR 8 joins SR 51 near Okalona (settled 1854) to *Arkadelphia*.

Nevada County Courthouse. Sixties Modern, 1964. The most recent of five, this one has the old Bank of Prescott's clock on the lawn. *(County Profiles)*

National Historic Register. T.C. McRae, 506 E. Main. The Bemis Flower Shop, 117 E. Second. D. L. McRae, 424 E. Main.

RAILROAD HISTORY
MAP ALL QUARTERS

Should a heated argument develop over which railroad was where under what name, don't take sides. Railroads were usually financed through bonds, then bought, sold, leased, consolidated, returned to and retrieved from receivership, and often renamed in the process (sometimes merely changing the designation from railroad to railway). Frequently, larger companies operated smaller lines under different corporate names. The eventual consolidation in 1917 of the Missouri-Pacific Railroad (formerly the Missouri-Pacific Railway) involved no less than 156 separate company names.

Impetus for early Arkansas railroads originated with men like Roswell Beebe *(Beebe)* and Wm. Woodruff, founder of the Arkansas Gazette (Arkansas Post *National Park),* who during 1845-1854 envisioned a railroad extending from the Mississippi River via Little Rock to the Pacific Ocean. Later (1880s-1900), Arkansas railroads were mostly dominated by financier Jay Gould's manipulation of the Missouri-Pacific Railway and his competition with James W. Paramore's Texas & St. Louis Railroad (commonly known as the Cotton Belt Route; later to become the St. Louis & Southwestern).

The federal government offered six sections (one section equals a square mile or 640 acres) for every mile planned to be built, using the logic that companies could sell the land to raise money and also develop customers for shipping goods. By these means railroads made (and broke) Arkansas towns from the 1870s through the turn of the century.

A poignant footnote to the coming of the railroad was the loss of historic towns. Those by-passed usually faded from the maps, their populations absorbed by the new railroad towns that were customarily named by (and for) the friends, family or officials of the line.

Arkansas Central Railway. Although plans were made in the early 1850s for a line from Helena to Little Rock, finances and the Civil War postponed them. When construction resumed, only 48 miles (Helena-Clarendon) were completed in 1872. Bought by the Arkansas Midland Railroad by 1879, it was later sold in 1910 to the St. Louis, Iron Mountain & Southern Railway (BELOW).

Cairo & Fulton Railroad Company. Both Missouri (1854) and Arkansas (1853) organized a Cairo (KAY-ro) & Fulton Railroad Company for the mutual purpose of laying track from Cairo, Il., to the Texas border near Fulton. Only 25 miles of road were graded before 1859. Both were stymied by the Civil War but the Missouri branch remained financially weak and poorly managed. Eventually bankrupt, the Missouri branch emerged briefly in 1872 as the Cairo, Arkansas & Texas Railroad Company (with investors from the Missouri-Pacific Railway Company) to complete the planned line in 1873. The Arkansas branch completed its line in 1874, the same year a Missouri-Pacific-dominated (and insolvent) railroad, the St. Louis & Iron Mountain, was merged with the Missouri branch (through stock options and consolidation of smaller lines) to form the St. Louis & Iron Mountain Railroad Company. A month later, the Arkansas branch was joined to the new company, and the name was changed again: the St. Louis, Iron Mountain & Southern Railway Company.

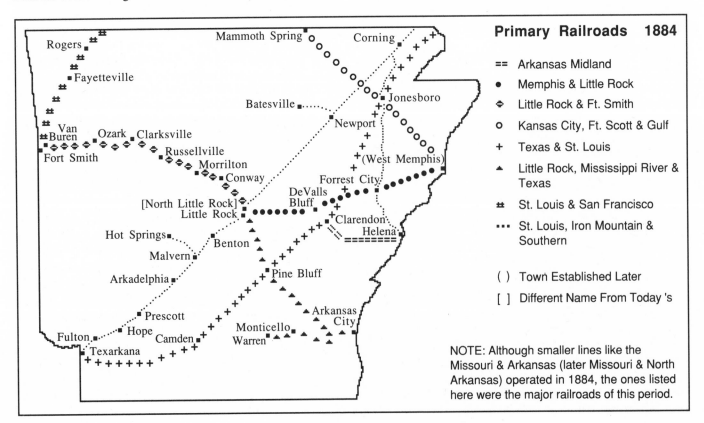

Primary Railroads 1884

==	Arkansas Midland
●	Memphis & Little Rock
⬦	Little Rock & Ft. Smith
o	Kansas City, Ft. Scott & Gulf
+	Texas & St. Louis
▲	Little Rock, Mississippi River & Texas
♯	St. Louis & San Francisco
•••	St. Louis, Iron Mountain & Southern

( ) Town Established Later

[ ] Different Name From Today's

NOTE: Although smaller lines like the Missouri & Arkansas (later Missouri & North Arkansas) operated in 1884, the ones listed here were the major railroads of this period.

Chicago, Rock Island & Pacific Railway. This company's history in Arkansas is one of acquisition, not construction. Beginning in 1904 it bought and leased (999 years) lines as large as the Choctaw, Oklahoma & Gulf (successor of the Memphis & Little Rock) and some as small as the "Diamond Jo" *(Malvern)*.

Kansas City, Fort Scott & Gulf Railroad. (See St. Louis and San Francisco)

Until 1871 a trip on the Memphis & Little Rock involved stage coaches and riverboats

Kansas City Southern Railroad. Incorporated in 1887 as the Kansas City, Nevada & Ft. Smith, it changed names two times: 1893 to Kansas City, Pittsburg & Ft. Smith, and 1901 to Kansas City Southern. Part of the line, the Texarkana & Ft. Smith, laid track in Arkansas between Texarkana and Fort Smith c.1889-97.

Little Rock & Ft. Smith Railroad. Chartered in 1854, it had surveyed and graded road from Little Rock to Morrilton before running out of money in 1860. After the Civil War, construction resumed; tracks were completed in 1874. Sold to the St. Louis, Iron Mountain & Southern in 1906.

Little Rock, Mississippi River & Texas Railway. Formed by the reorganization of the 1868 Little Rock, Pine Bluff & New Orleans Railroad in 1877 and the purchase of the Mississippi, Ouachita & Red River (BELOW) in 1875, it built a road from Little Rock to Arkansas City, and a division from Trippe (southeast of McGehee) to Warren. Foreclosed in 1886 and bought by Jay Gould (Missouri-Pacific, BELOW) who then conveyed the property in 1887 to the St. Louis, Iron Mountain & Southern Railway (BELOW).

Memphis & Little Rock Railroad. The first actual railroad construction (Mississippi, Ouachita & Red River, BELOW) began with this line from Hopefield (West Memphis) to Madison on the St. Francis River in 1858, and from Little Rock to DeValls Bluff in 1860-61. Until 1871, the "train ride" involved: railroad to Madison, stage coach to Clarendon, riverboat to DeValls Bluff, railroad to Argenta (N. Little Rock) and ferryboat to Little Rock. Tracks were completed in 1871. Sold to the Choctaw, Oklahoma & Gulf Railroad in 1902, then consolidated by the Chicago, Rock Island & Pacific Railway in 1904.

Mississippi, Ouachita & Red River Railroad. Although only minimal grading and track was completed, it's said that this was the first Arkansas railroad (incorporated July 12, 1852). Begun in 1854 as a roadbed from Eunice *(Halley)* on the Mississippi River to Fulton on the Red River, an 1856 report stated that the portion to Camden was "under contract and at least two-thirds ready for iron," but a drought wiped out financing. In 1870-71 it secured state bonds but failed again. Bought by the Little Rock, Mississippi River & Texas Railway (ABOVE) in 1875 (and reorganized with the Little Rock, Pine Bluff & New Orleans in 1877), track was laid by the Little Rock, Mississippi River & Texas from Little Rock south to Arkansas City, and then west as a division from near Trippe *(McGehee)* to Warren toward the proposed Fulton terminus, but foreclosure caused its sale in 1886 to Jay Gould (Missouri-Pacific, BELOW), who then conveyed the property to the St. Louis, Iron Mountain & Southern (BELOW) in 1887, which, in a roundabout way, nearly completed the original plan (Mississippi River to Fulton, Ar.).

Missouri & North Arkansas Railroad. Branching from the St. Louis & San Francisco Railway (BELOW) at Seligman, Mo., to Beaver, Ar., as the Missouri & Arkansas Railroad in 1882, it was continued to *Eureka Springs* by Powell Clayton under a new name, the Eureka Springs Railway. By 1901 a main line from Beaver was in Harrison as the St. Louis & North Arkansas Railway, and by 1903 it was completed to Leslie. Hesitating there for financial reorganization until 1907, the line emerged as the Missouri & North Arkansas Railroad, which was completed via Heber Springs, Searcy and Cotton Plant into Helena by 1909.

Missouri-Pacific Railroad (Mo-Pac). Originally organized as the Pacific Railway Company by the Missouri Legislature in 1849, it was financed by bond, never paid its interest and went back to state ownership in 1866. Mismanaged by other companies for 10 years, its property was sold to the Missouri-Pacific Railway Company (created by the legislature for that purpose), which was bought by Jay Gould in 1879. By 1881, Gould was chairman of the board of the Texas & Pacific Railroad Company and had gained control of the St. Louis, Iron Mountain & Southern, which was a loose confederation of common ownerships and leases of smaller lines. In 1909 all subsidiaries of the Missouri-Pacific Railway were consolidated under the one name, with the exception of the St. Louis, Iron Mountain & Southern, which continued to operate under its corporate name until 1917, when both it and the Missouri-Pacific Railway were consolidated to form the Missouri-Pacific Railroad Company.

The Mississippi, Ouachita & Red River claims to be Arkansas' first railroad

St. Louis, Iron Mountain & Southern Railway. It began in 1837 as the St. Louis & Bellevue Mineral Railroad Company, but never got off the ground. Recharted by the Missouri Legislature in 1851 as the St. Louis & Iron Mountain Railroad Company to radiate from St. Louis to adjoining states, it floundered from the start, requiring refinancing (some investors from Missouri-Pacific Railway) and reorganization that eventually changed its name in 1874 to the St. Louis, Iron Mountain & Southern Railway Company (eventually becoming a loose confederation of common ownerships and leases of smaller lines). From its beginning it was, in part, owned by Missouri-Pacific Railway interests that by 1881 had acquired control through an exchange of stock (Missouri-Pacific Railroad, ABOVE). Further exchanges resulted in complete ownership by 1909, although it kept its corporate name until both it and the Missouri Pacific Railway were consolidated as the Missouri Pacific Railroad Company in 1917.

St. Louis & San Francisco Railway (Frisco). The Arkansas Division of the St. Louis & San Francisco arrived in Fayetteville in 1881, completing its line to Fort Smith in 1882, which marked the company's first road into Arkansas. Although plans for branching a line from Fayetteville to Little Rock ended in Pettigrew (appx. 40 miles), it eventually acquired other companies like the Kansas City, Ft. Scott & Gulf (Memphis) by 1901.

St. Louis Southwestern Railway. Also known as the Cotton Belt Route, it was originally organized in 1871 by citizens of Tyler, Tx., as the Tyler Tap to "tap" either the International & Great Northern or the Texas & Pacific. It laid 21.5 miles of narrow gauge (three feet wide as opposed to the standard four feet, eight and a half inches) by 1877, when financial problems caused its sale to a group led by James W. Paramore, who renamed it the Texas & St. Louis Railroad, intending to use it as a feeder to Texarkana's St. Louis, Iron Mountain & Southern, thereby gaining access to St. Louis. Jay Gould's Missouri-Pacific gained control of the St. Louis, Iron Mountain & Southern in 1881, and then revoked Paramore's traffic agreement, attempting to block access to St. Louis or force a sale. Paramore's and the railroad's titles, "The Narrow Gauge King" and "The Yard-Wide Road," began at this point when he decided to run a separate line through Texarkana to St. Louis and on to Cairo, Il., on the Ohio River. Hiring S.W. Fordyce to locate the route, Paramore's aim was to transport mostly cotton, reasoning that the compressed bales could be hauled on smaller (narrow gauge) roads using lighter equipment at half the bond debt. The tracks were laid from Gatesville, Tx., to Birds Point, Mo., by 1883. In 1886 the company reorganized into the St. Louis, Arkansas & Texas because of financial trouble and pressure to link standard gauge roads (it set railroad history by switching gauges in 24 hours, using 1.5 million cross ties in the process). Fordyce became president, holding the receivership; Paramore, although a majority stockholder, dropped out, dying a year later. Still floundering in 1891, it consolidated as the St. Louis Southwestern Railway, arriving in St. Louis in 1903.

Texas (Arkansas) & St. Louis Railroad. See St. Louis & Southwestern Railway.

RAVENDEN SPRINGS
POP. 338   ALT. 500   MAP I-3

Although this area was first settled by John Janes c.1809, tradition attributes Reverend Wm. Bailey (who after suffering chronic stomach ailments, dreamed three times of a curative spring "deep in the earth") with beginning the town in 1880. Known locally as Dream Town, it supported itself as a spa until about 1910. Chemical analysis of the water reportedly shows an excess of oxygen. Raven's Den, a cave on Hall's Creek where ravens were said to roost, gave the town its name.

Hall's Creek. The walls of the creek rise 100 feet in places. Natural formations like Lone Rock (smaller at the base than top), Needle's Eye (a split in a solid cliff) and Devil's Bath Tub (a washout dammed for swimming) make a hike an adventure. SR 90, in town, W across the bridge. Inquire Locally.

Ravenden Spring. The main spring, which was the principal water supply for town (and cured stomach ailments), is enclosed in concrete with a spigot. Bring a jug. Hall's Creek.

Arkansas' First Schoolhouse. According to legend, a sign in an unnamed cave on Hall's Creek claims that Arkansas state school records list it as the first (1820) schoolhouse in Arkansas (Dwight, *Russellville*) and Cable Lindsey as its first teacher. The Lindsey family was among the original settlers (c.1801) of Columbia *(Pocahontas)*. Inquire Locally.

RESETTLEMENT ADMINISTRATION

An offshoot of the Works Project Administration *(WPA)* of President Roosevelt's New Deal *(Heber Springs,* WPA Mural), by 1935 this project comprised over 50 "plantations" in 23 counties. Arkansas was chosen for the new program because at the time it was the most rural and the poorest state in America (in 1931, 28% of the total population needed Red Cross assistance). Some of the larger projects represent a socioeconomic experiment that has been called, then and now, either socialism or American self-help. The idea was to relocate destitute tenant farmers (90% in some counties) to 20-to-40-acre tracts centered around a cooperative-type community (such as a general store, school, bank, gin and hospital). Specifics varied from total collective farming to mixtures of private/collective property *(Dyess, Plum Bayou, Lakeview, Lake Dick)*. Ironically, because of a fierce independence and political conservatism, most farmers viewed these programs only as a way to save money for a new farm. Although unsuccessful as a solution for small farmers' problems, historians point to this experiment as a precedent for some of today's federal farm programs.

RISON
POP. 1,325   ALT. 236   MAP N-1

Settled on the tracks of the Texas & St. Louis *Railroad* in 1882 and named for Wm. R. Rison of Huntsville, Ala. (a close friend of Samuel *Fordyce),* this town was incorporated in 1890, and a year later won a lawsuit with Kingsland *(Fordyce)* over which town would replace Toledo as county seat.

Toledo. Refusing right-of-way to the railroad c.1882 (Jacksonport *State Park),* this 1873 county seat (formerly Pleasant Ridge) first lost the seat of justice in 1890 and then its post office in 1913. No Remnants.

Pioneer Village. This representation of a late 19th century South Arkansas community has all the authentic touches, including two buildings on the National Historic Register (Mt. Olive Methodist Church, 1867, and the county clerk's building, 1902). Other structures like the McMurtrey's Victorian home (1892), a one-room log cabin (c.1900) and blacksmith's shop (c.1900) have been moved to the site intact. Each is furnished according to its use; some with the original furniture and implements. Fairgrounds. Signs.

The Rison Magnetic Anomaly. Don't believe a compass around here *(Magnet Cove)*. The town is located at the center of an estimated 15-by-6-mile iron deposit containing as much as 42% magnetite. The Rison Mineral Co. determined the top at 3,500 feet with no known bottom.

Events/Festivals. Mid-Mar: Annual Pioneer Craft Festival. Early Dec: Country Christmas. Tours of Pioneer Village. Old-Fashioned Supper. Carolling.

Cleveland County Courthouse. Georgian Revival, 1911. National Historic Register. Exterior: ornate clock tower and red tile roof. Interior: 20-foot pressed-tin ceilings and large coal-burning fireplace. Downtown. *(County Profiles)*

RIVERS
MAP ALL QUARTERS

Few states have as many natural highways as Arkansas. Even before the Corps of Engineers' river management projects like locks and dams began in the thirties, 51 of Arkansas' 75 counties had navigable streams, of which 3,500 miles could be used by steamboats, including 1,500 miles on a year-round basis (see map, *Roads).*

These "river roads" were essential for the settlement and commercial development of the state during the 19th century. In the early 1800s explorers and traders used canoes. Interior posts were established to ship trade goods like furs *(Clarksville,* Spadra). Later traders banded together, building flatboats to ship as far south as New Orleans *(Oil Trough)*. Flatboats, stable but slow and at the mercy of the currents, used a big "sweep" (as long as the boat sometimes) for a tiller. At the destination, the boat was usually scrapped for other uses *(Helena,* old Abner Store) and a keelboat, which could be "cordelled" upstream (pulled by ropes, pushed by poles), was bought for the return home. A 2,000-mile round trip took approximately three months.

The first steamboat to ascend the Arkansas River, The Comet docked at Arkansas Post *(National Park)* in 1820. Two years later The Eagle stopped at Little Rock, then continued upriver nearly to Dwight Mission *(Russellville)*. By 1828 Captain Phillip Pennywit, using a lighter ship, The Waverly, established a 30-day schedule between New Orleans and Fort Gibson in present-day Oklahoma, stopping at *Arkansas River* ports. Three years later (1831) he added White River ports as far north as *Batesville*.

Although men like Henry Shreve had cleared snags *(Great Raft)* since 1833, and shallow-draft steamboats that "could run anywhere the ground was a little damp" (three inches empty, 24 inches loaded) were typical by the mid-1850s, disastrous accidents involving fires, boiler explosions and snags were accepted risks that too often proved to be reality. As late as

1872, the Arkansas Gazette newspaper listed 177 steamboats as lost on the river (most were ripped apart by snags). Despite these tragedies, until the 1870s, steamboats shaped the growth of Arkansas *(Ozark)*.

And then the *railroads* came. Ironically, the year that railroads began earnest competition with river traffic (1881), the Corps of Engineers established a Little Rock office for river control in an attempt to keep the rivers clear for traffic. For the next 30 years the railroad and the steamboat competed for Arkansas' transportation business. Towns — some with more pride than good sense — bet their fortunes on the outcome (Jacksonport *State Park).* Others never had a chance to choose (Lewisburg, *Morrilton).* But in the end it was acts of nature and not man that finally determined the winner.

At first, nature was evenhanded. High water washed out rails; low water scuttled navigation. The flood of 1898 damaged both. But at the turn of the century, nature turned against river traffic. The drought of 1901-02 signalled the end of the steamboat. It was followed by two years of slack water and heavy mud capped by the winter of 1904-05, which saw the Arkansas River frozen over at Little Rock. By 1910 steamboats had cancelled their most profitable route, daily service between Little Rock and Memphis. Fares were higher by rail but were considered more efficient.

Today, Arkansas' rivers are held in tight check by *locks and dams;* in their wakes are *lakes* and *float streams.*

ROADS C.1819-1836
MAP ALL QUARTERS

Topographically, Arkansas can be divided into two distinct sections: mountains to the north and west, alluvial plains to the east and south. This topography and the major *rivers* dictated early Indian trails, later roads, *railroads* and today's highways, many of which parallel or overlay each other. Prior to 1819 (Arkansas Territory) these trails were paths, impassable by wagon, but slowly improved by settlers for commerce, and by the federal government for troop movement and later for Indian removal from east of the Mississippi River *(Trail of Tears)*. Other public roads (the majority of the traffic) were a local responsibility whereby "all free male inhabitants between the ages of 16 and 45 years and all slave inhabitants" of the township could be drafted into roadwork.

After roads were cleared to accommodate wagons, what remained were narrow corridors of stumps, mud and water made worse, if possible, by churning hooves and wagon wheels. Also keep in mind that most roads were a collection or series of trails broadened by necessity. Like a magician's handkerchiefs, these trails became roads joining roads, joining roads, and so on. Marked only by blazed trees in thick forests, getting lost was not just possible, it was probable. However, backtracking to the right road, repairing broken wagon wheels and gumbo mud were only a small part of the hazards. Bridges were nonexistent. Fording countless rivers, creeks and bayous presented real danger of drowning, illness from exposure during

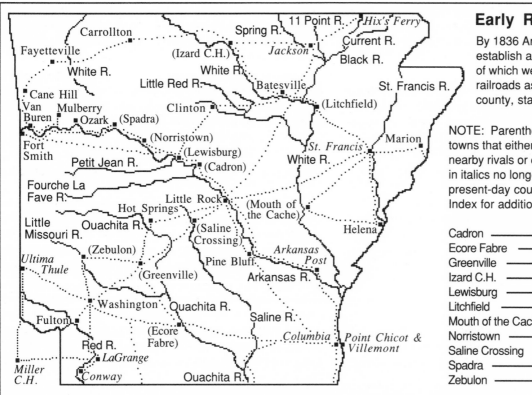

Early Roads & Traces

By 1836 Arkansas had begun to establish a network of roads, some of which were later paralleled by railroads as well as present-day county, state and federal highways.

NOTE: Parentheses ( ) denote historic towns that either were absorbed by later, nearby rivals or changed names. Towns in italics no longer exist, and have no present-day counterpart (refer to the Index for additional information).

Cadron	Conway
Ecore Fabre	Camden
Greenville	Hollywood
Izard C.H.	Norfork
Lewisburg	Morrilton
Litchfield	Newport
Mouth of the Cache	Clarendon
Norristown	Russellville
Saline Crossing	Benton
Spadra	Clarksville
Zebulon	Murfreesboro

cold weather and loss of possessions, including draft animals and the entire wagon. An example of the hardships can be seen on a map of 1836 where a trip down the best established road in Arkansas, the Southwest Trail (BELOW), involved no less than 45 fords.

Throughout Arkansas history, roads and towns have waxed and waned, each born of the other, each greatly affected by changing modes of transportation: horses, wagons, steamboats, railroads, paved highways and, recently, interstates. The following roads were established by the time Arkansas was admitted to the Union in 1836. For the most part, their names identify routes, and for convenience, east-west and north-south have been used to describe directions.

Southwest Trail. This important Indian trail was later used by the Spanish and then by the U.S Army and American settlers. It traveled from St. Louis through *Hix's Ferry* at the Arkansas-Missouri border and then followed the foothills of the Ozarks and Ouachitas to near *Fulton* on the Red River. Here the trail divided. The main fork continued through present-day Texas into the Great Southwest. At first a military road, it was designated a national road in 1835. Today it vaguely approximates (north to south through Arkansas) SR 166, U 67/167 and I-30.

Arkansas Post-Cadron Road. One of the earliest permanent roads, it connected *Arkansas Post* and *Cadron* (near present-day *Conway*) via Crystal Hill *(Little Rock)* before Little Rock was established. Later, c.1826, the road extended as far south as Villemont *(Lake Village)* on the Mississippi River.

Memphis-Little Rock Military Road. Beginning in 1826 appropriations improved an historic trail, opening over-land immigration from the East. The main artery stretched from Memphis to Little Rock with branches fanning out at *St. Francis (Old)*: south to *Helena* along *Crowley's Ridge,* northwest to follow the White River and southwest to *Clarendon.*

Little Rock-Fort Smith Road. A road paralleling the north side of the *Arkansas River* branched shortly after Lewisburg *(Morrilton)* to follow both sides of the river. The southern road loosely paralleled SR 22 west of *Dardanelle,* while the northern one followed the river much like US 64 until past present-day *Clarksville,* where it crisscrossed the river until joining the southern road to Fort Smith.

North Arkansas Road. The main road ran from *Hix's Ferry* to Jackson (Old Davidsonville *State Park),* where it cut west through Izard Court House *(Norfolk)* and *Carrollton* to end in *Fayetteville,* at which point it branched in all directions.

South Arkansas Road. Under various names but generally called the Fort Towson Road (to supply this Indian Territory post in present-day Oklahoma, see map *Trail of Tears),* it began at Villemont/Point Chicot near Columbia *(Lake Village)* to travel through Ecore Fabre *(Camden),* Washington, Paraclifta *(Lockesburg)* and Ultima Thule *(De Queen).*

East Arkansas Road. (See Memphis-Little Rock Military Road, ABOVE)

West Arkansas Road. Connecting Ft. Scott in northern Indian Territory (Kansas) to Ft. Towson in southern Indian Territory (Oklahoma), this military road went south through *Fayetteville, Natural Dam, Van Buren* and *Fort Smith.* Another western road between Fort Smith and *Mulberry* later joined the northern route of the Little Rock-Fort Smith road (ABOVE) via newly established *Ozark* and *Clarksville.*

Other Roads. BATESVILLE-CLINTON-LEWISBURG: Cut diagonally SW across north-central Arkansas. LITTLE ROCK-GREENVILLE:Via *Hot Springs* it joined the Southwest Trail at Greenville, branching southeast to Ecore Fabre *(Camden)* and west to Zebulon *(Murfreesboro),* then south to *Washington.* WASHINGTON ROADS: Roads branched in all directions from this important frontier settlement. Of interest is one south to LaGrange *(Lewisville)* and to Conway, a settlement founded by the first governor of Arkansas (Conway *State Park).* The road then cut due west to Miller Court House (also Millersburg), which was then county seat of Miller County, Arkansas, later a Texas county *(Boundary Lines).* LITTLE ROCK-VILLEMONT/PT. CHICOT: A later road similar to the Cadron-Arkansas Post road (ABOVE) but it ran along the south side of the Arkansas River. FT. TOWNSON BRANCH ROADS: Nearly halfway between *Washington* and *Camden* a road branched south to Natchitoches, La. Another, east of Columbia *(Lake Village),* arced south along the Saline and Ouachita Rivers to Alexandria, La.

Trail of Tears. There was no specific route. *(Trail of Tears)*
Butterfield Overland Mail Route. This famous mail company built no roads. Like the *Trail of Tears,* it used existing roads along with various means of transportation. *(Butterfield Overand Mail)*

ROGERS
POP. 18,086   ALT. 1,386   MAP A-1

In March of 1881 the townsite had one dilapidated cabin near the *Butterfield Overland Mail* route. By May of 1881 it was surveyed, laid out, incorporated and named for Capt. W.C. Rogers, general manager of the St. Louis & San Francisco *(Railroad),* which had bypassed the older town (and county seat of Benton County), *Bentonville* (6 m. NW).

Historic Downtown. One of five participants in the Main Street Arkansas Program, part of a national preservation project for downtown areas, its red brick streets and turn-of-the-century buildings blend with modern businesses.

Daisy International Air Gun Museum. Begun as a promotional idea by the Plymouth Iron Windmill Company of Michigan (each farmer buying a windmill also received a free air rifle), the company soon (1885) changed priorities, becoming the world's largest manufacturer of nonpowder guns and ammunition. The name Daisy originated after general-manager L.C. Hough saw the action of a new model in 1888, and exclaimed, "Boy, that's a daisy." Today's museum has the first Daisy as well as the famous "Red Ryder" and all the other variations. Said to be the world's most complete collection of air guns, it also displays historical counterparts from 1770 to the present, including the type used by Austrians to harass Napoleon's invasion army, and ones designed to look like flintlock rifles and canes. Next to Daisy Manufacturing Headquarters, US 71, just S of SR 12.

Monte Ne. National Historic Register. In 1893 Wm. "Coin" Harvey's book advocating a silver rather than gold monetary standard, Coin's Financial School, set world publishing records (over a million sold). Friend and adviser to the 1896 presidential candidate and silver standard advocate, Wm. Jennings Bryan, he lost his campaign (as did Bryan). Harvey "retired," founding Monte Ne (supposedly Italian and Indian for mountain water) where he built a resort in 1902, featuring the world's largest log hotels (one was 305 feet long, made from 8,000 logs), and a spur railroad whose passengers transferred to flower-covered gondolas waiting in a lagoon. By 1910 the stockholders had pulled out; the resort failed. Ten years later, convinced civilization was doomed, he started constructing a 130-foot pyramid that would contain an explanation for its "death" and most of the world's history. Meanwhile, he created the Liberty Party in 1933 and ran for president, receiving 50,000 votes. "Coin" Harvey died in 1936 before completing the pyramid. Little evidence of Monte Ne remains since flooded by Beaver *Lake* in the mid 1960s but at low water remnants are visible. SR 94, S appx. 2 m. Inquire Locally.

Rogers Historical Museum. A turn-of-the-century brick house furnished c.1900 displays items like quilts and coverlets from every period in American history, as well as special exhibits on a rotating basis. 322 S. 2nd (SR 94).

Lake Atlanta. City-owned, it offers fishing (bluegill, catfish, crappie and bass), picnicking and swimming in a pool adjacent to the lake. US 62; SR 12 appx 1 m. W.

Events/Festivals. Late Oct: Annual Guild Arts & Crafts Fair. Late Oct: Annual Antique Show.

National Historic Register. Applegate Drugstore (1906), 116 S. 1st. Bank of Rogers (1906), 114 S. 1st. Mutual Aid Union Building (1914), 2nd & Poplar. Frisco Depot, 1st & Cherry.

ROHWER
COMMUNITY   ALT. 135   MAP O-3

Local tradition claims that although the area had been farmed since c.1860, no post office was established here until 1901 when "Harding" was first approved and then disallowed by Washington, D.C. (another already existed). A second suggestion, "Sainsville," is said to have been rejected for the same reason. The survey engineer for the soon-to-arrive Memphis, Helena & Louisiana Railway (St. Louis-Iron Mountain & Southern) was given the honor, and the post office, town and station were named Rohwer (ROAR) in 1904. Incorporated 1913. Possible *DeSoto* route (one account claims he died near present-day McArthur, 6 m. S.).

Rohwer Relocation Center. *(Jerome)* National Historic Register, 1942-45. In the summer of 1942 approximately 120,000 Japanese-Americans (75% of whom had been born in America) were relocated because of WWII (all were suspected of sympathy with Japan). About 8,500 were detained here in board-and-batten cabins that were 100-by-20 feet (100 sq. ft. per person) and contained army cots and cookstoves. Communal baths/laundries were designed for 250 persons each. Today, in the middle of a row crop field, is a small grass plot shaded by trees. Overshadowing 24 graves are three large monuments (two shafts about 20 feet tall and a cement scale model of an American tank) that commemorate these detainees and the all-Japanese 100th and 442nd (said to be the most highly decorated units of the war) that fought at places like Salerno, Anzio and Cassino while their families remained at Rohwer. N edge of Rohwer. Signs.

Bayous, Sloughs and the Levee Road. Before the railroad, access to the county seat from Rohwer required fording Boggy Bayou, traveling east to the Mississippi River, and then south, following beside the levee. Today, it is possible to approximate that route with the aid of bridges and a drive on top of the world's longest and tallest levee *(Arkansas City).*

ROMANCE
COMMUNITY ALT. 570 MAP K-1

First settled by families from Kentucky whose later discontinued post office (1858-66), Kentucky Valley, was reapplied for in 1884. Washington, D.C., turned down the name this time but accepted the suggestion, Romance, of local school teacher J.J. Walters, who reportedly thought the location was "very romantic." It is possible to get there from Searcy by driving west on Pleasure Street through Joy and Harmony to Rose Bud, or by a rural route from Conway along the rocky road to Romance. Despite the puns, the view from any road to Romance is very scenic.

Little Clifty Creek. Bring a picnic lunch. This old-fashioned swimming hole has an idyllic setting near a waterfall. Inquire at the post office.

National Historic Register. ROSE BUD, AR. (SR 5, 8 m. N): The Darden-Gifford House (1887), N of town off SR 5. Inquire locally.

RUDY
POP. 79 ALT. 502 MAP C-1

First known as Kenton, the area was settled in 1830. Property was first recorded in 1835. Plans for the townsite, platted by the St. Louis & San Francisco *(Railroad)* in 1882, were filed by Geo. S. Rudy, who was also the first postmaster (1883).

Frog Bayou. Listed on maps as early as 1826, it flows under a one-lane iron bridge and past a short row of turn-of-the-century buildings where it forms a swimming hole that has a knotted rope-swing. SR 282. In Town.

Parley Parker Pratt Monument. *(Mountainburg)*

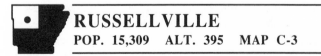

RUSSELLVILLE
POP. 15,309 ALT. 395 MAP C-3

Older, more prosperous towns in the immediate area *(Dover, Dwight, Norristown and Scotia, BELOW)* faded away when the Little Rock & Ft. Smith *Railroad* completed track through this 1840s settlement in 1873. Although named for British Dr. T.J. Russell, who had lived at the townsite since 1835, the town's best known personality is Jeff Davis, 1862-1913, (U.S. senator and three times governor, 1901-07), who claimed "I am a hard shell Baptist by religion; believe in foot-washing, saving your seed potatoes, and paying your honest debts." Incorporated in 1870; county seat in 1887. Home of Arkansas Tech University and headquarters for POM (Park-O-Meter), manufacturer of the world's first parking meter. Maps: chamber of commerce, 1019 W. Main (I-40, SR 7 S, W on Main).

Dwight. Historically, this area has been important because of the easy ford at the *Arkansas River* and the east-west trail along the north side of it (later the Memphis-Fort Smith *Road*). In 1813 Maj. Wm. Lovely (Lovely's Purchase, *Boundary Lines),* a veteran of the Revolutionary War and agent for the Cherokee for 15 years, arrived at the Illinois River about a mile from where it joins the Arkansas, which at that time was approximately the center of a recent Cherokee settlement *(Madison).* Lovely died in 1817, shortly before the establishment of *Fort Smith.* Dwight's Mission was founded here by Rev. Cephas Washburn in 1820, who upon passing through Little Rock supposedly delivered the town's first sermon. Requested by the Cherokee *(Trail of Tears),* the state's first school *(Ravenden Springs)* was established here in 1820. The first steamboat (The Eagle) to reach Little Rock in 1822 proceeded upstream to supply Dwight, which reportedly was the first Protestant mission west of the Mississippi River in an era when it was said: "If you hear something coming through the canebreak, you may know it is either a bear or a preacher, and both of them will be hungry." Sequoya (the only person to solely invent a written language) is said to have completed work on the Cherokee alphabet here and at Galla Rock *(Atkins).* The 86 characters were so simple the language could be mastered in a few days. Today's evergreen sequoia is named for him. No Remnants. Marker, US 64 at *Lake* Dardanelle.

Norristown. Founded by Samuel Norris in 1829, it was the county seat (1834-41) and later the last stop for the *Butterfield Overland Mail* before crossing the Arkansas River. Here it is said Edward Washburn (the son of Cephas, Dwight, ABOVE) c.1858 painted "The Arkansas Traveller" (a squatter sitting on a keg and playing a fiddle while being watched by a gentleman on horseback), which is, if there is one, the state's trademark *(County Profiles,* Faulkner). Norristown is now a suburb of Russellville on a ridge near the river. No Remnants.

Scotia. This 1830 post office, located west of Dwight on the Memphis-Fort Smith *Road* at the Arkansas River, was established at the farm of Andrew Scott (namesake of Scott County), who was appointed in 1819 by President Monroe as one of three superior court judges for Arkansas Territory. Scott's residence was made county seat of Pope County in 1830. This post office community was carried on maps for about 40 years. A nearby railroad station, Georgetown, took its place on the map, but was not at the same location. No Remnants.

Bona Dea Trails & Sanctuary. This outstanding Corps of Engineers' park consists of 186 acres of wetlands and low woods, and includes nearly six miles of walking/jogging *trails.*

Two of the four trails provide a physical fitness "parcourse" whose 18 stations range from chin-up bars to balance beams. The walking/jogging distances are measured; the parcourse is explained in detail. Along the trails can be seen over 200 species of birds (loons to mockingbirds), animals like the coyote and white-tailed deer, turtles and frogs, flowering dogwood and pawpaw as well as vines and shrubs (button bush to soapberry). SR 326 at *Lake* Dardanelle (appx. .3 m. S of I-40 & SR 7). Signs.

Arkansas River Visitor Center/Lock & Dam. Called "Renaissance of a River," exhibits and audio-visual presentations in this $700,000 center trace the history and development of the *Arkansas River* Valley from the Indian culture to the present. Other attractions: overlook of the river, lake, lock and dam (*Lake* Dardanelle) and old Post *Road* Park. Recreation: *Lake* Dardanelle. SR 7; W 2.2 m. on SR 7 spur to the river.

Arkansas River Valley Arts Center. Local and regional art exhibits like the Arkansas Wildlife Federation Art Exhibition are presented on a rotating basis along with community performing arts like theater and band performances. US 64, 1 blk. N at "B" and Knoxville.

Completed in 1891, "the world's longest pontoon bridge" had a span of 2,343 feet

---

Pontoon Bridge. "The longest pontoon bridge in the world" was built on the *Arkansas River* in 1889-91, and not replaced until 1929. Teddy Roosevelt (president, 1901-09) walked across it in 1912. The 2,343-foot wooden structure (load limit of 9,000 pounds) was floated on 72 boats, using 11 spans with six boats under each span and a "draw-span" of nine boats. Its 12-foot width had a few 16-foot passing lanes. The five cement "pyramids" used to anchor it are still visible on the downstream side of today's bridge. SR 7 at the Arkansas River.

Arkansas Tech Geological Museum. Since 1963 this museum has exhibited interesting geological material such as rocks and minerals as well as fossils and Indian artifacts. S of I-40 at SR 7 & 124.

Arkansas Nuclear One (ANO). Acting much like a car radiator (except it holds four million gallons of water) and certainly the most visible structure at ANO, the concrete cooling tower (447 feet high, 396 feet wide at its base) cost 13 million dollars (a small sum when compared to the 12.3 million labor-hours it took to build the entire plant). The primary nuclear systems (not a part of the cooling tower) are housed in cylindrical structures 200 feet tall and 120 feet in diameter with walls varying from three to nine feet thick, and were built to withstand a tornado, flood or earthquake. Total output is rated at 1,694 megawatts or enough power to light 16,940,000 100-watt light bulbs. Tours: Advance notice of four to six weeks required (or luck might shorten the requirement); check during the summer with Lake Dardanelle *State Park* Information. For a close-up look without notice, use the visitors' parking lot at the intake canal (good fishing). Incidentally, the "smoke" fre-

quently seen coming from the cooling tower is steam. US 64, 6 m. W; S on CR 333 to ANO.

Russellville Depot. Standard railroad architecture with a breezeway; still a working depot. Jct. US 64 & SR 7.

Events/Festivals. Fourth of July: River Valley Jubilee. Auto Exhibit. Entertainment. Fireworks. Early Nov: Annual Arkansas Valley Craft Fair & Sale.

Pope County Courthouse. Mission Deco, 1932. Because the county records were hidden during the Civil War *(Dover)*, they are continuous from 1829. Features: extensive marble in the interior. Jct. US 64 & SR 7. *(County Profiles)*

National Historic Register. White House (1908), 1412 W. Main. Wilson House (1902), 214 E. 5th.

ST. CHARLES
POP. 199 ALT. 188 MAP M-3

Hernando *De Soto* supposedly crossed the White *River* here in 1541, and a fur trader named Peturis or Pedturis built a cabin on his Spanish land grant here in 1797, but it wasn't until Charles W. Belknap bought the land grant in 1839 that any settlement began. First a steamboat port called Belknap Bluff, it was platted c.1851 by Belknap, who then changed the name to St. Charles, which is said to be for the original Spanish ownership by King Charles V. Incorporated in 1880.

The Mound City. Sunk during the Battle of St. Charles *(Civil War)* by what some historians call "the single most destructive shot of the War Between the States," this Federal ironclad (gunboat) was hit by a Confederate round from a "32-pounder" that tore through the steam drum. Of the 175 officers and seamen, only 23 survived. Marker. SR 1 at the river.

Striplin Woods. Natural Heritage Area. The high canopy of overcup oak, water hickory, willow oak and honey locust (some exceeding two feet in diameter) gives an idea of what the virgin hardwood forests of East Arkansas looked like. Just S off SR 1 on a gravel road along the west bank of the river.

ST. FRANCIS
POP. 266 ALT. 297 MAP I-5

Laid out by the St. Louis, Arkansas & Texas *Railroad* in 1882, it picked up the bypassed population and post office of Chalk Bluff, naming itself St. Francis after the *river*.

Chalk Bluff Crossing & Town. The St. Francis River breaks through *Crowley's Ridge* from west to east here, forming the eastern Arkansas-Missouri border *(Boundary Line)*. A prehistoric trail and later pioneer *road* crossed at this point, continuing down the Ridge via Jonesboro and Wittsburg to Helena. Abraham Seitz established the first ferry (discontinued in 1903) c.1840, and a town grew at the site that was named for the bluff's white clay that resembles chalk. Vanished. Once near Chalk Bluff Park.

Chalk Bluff Park. Natural Heritage Area. National Historic Register. Dedicated in 1982 to both the chalk bluff landmark for early travelers and the site of a *Civil War* battle in 1863. Nearly a mile of asphalt *trails* winds through an oak-hickory forest on top of Crowley's Ridge; another leads down to the St. Francis River, where the ravines are characterized by pawpaw and Christmas fern. Historic Markers. Observation Platform. Picnic Area. 6 m. N. Inquire Locally. Signs.

Chalk Bluff Road. Also called Buffalo Trail and Military Road *(Harrisburg),* it connected with the Wittsburg-Helena and the Memphis-Little Rock *Road.*

ST. FRANCIS (OLD)
GHOST TOWN   ALT. 400   MAP L-4

Only history remains of this *Crowley's Ridge* town on the dividing point of the Memphis-Ft. Smith *Road.* Established in 1820 by Wm. Strong *(Helena)* whose son, Erastus B., was Arkansas' first West Point Academy graduate (class of 1844). Although known as Strong's Point, the post office was named St. Francis. Strong (a tavern owner, sheriff and government contractor) influenced the poor choice of the road's placement (wetlands) through his property at a ferry crossing on the St. Francis *River.* His unsavory reputation (hinted to be associated with John Murrell, *Marked Tree)* and unaccountable deaths of travelers at his inn eventually forced him to move to Memphis, Tn., c.1848, the same year *Wittsburg* was established. Inquire at Village Creek *State Park.*

ST. JOE
COMMUNITY   ALT. 794   MAP B-4

Established c.1860. Strictly a guess, it might have taken the nickname of St. Joseph, Mo. (est. 1826), legendary jumping-off place for the West and eastern terminus (1860) of the famous Pony Express. First located about a mile and a half west of today's site, it was relocated when the St. Louis & North Arkansas (Missouri & North Arkansas *Railroad)* arrived in 1903. Originally laid out on a north-south street with permanent buildings, but closure of the railroad here in 1946 (and subsequent blacktopping of US 65) caused the town to turn, facing the highway.

ST. PAUL
POP. 198   ALT. 1,485   MAP B-2

Set near the headwaters of the White and Kings *Rivers (Float Streams),* "Old" St. Paul was founded by J.C. Sumner c.1837 and was also known as Old Skully due to its reputation for fist and "skull" fights. "New" St. Paul's site, owned by J.P. Salyer, boomed overnight in 1887 with the arrival of the St. Louis & San Francisco *(Railroad)* that was intended to terminate in Little Rock, but Pettigrew (11 m. E on SR 16) turned out to be the extent of the line. Local tradition claims the town was so new that everything had to be shipped in from

"outside." Laid out in lots in 1887, today's SR 23 makes a dogleg on the north side of the former town square between the 1930s depot and the c.1887 Methodist-Episcopal church. Origin of its name is not known, although St. Paul (died c. 67 A.D.), author of several of the Epistles, is a likely choice. Incorporated 1891.

Capt. Smith Cemetery. Representative of community cemeteries, this one has an outhouse labelled "women" and a chain link fence. Orderly headstones underneath shade trees range from polished marble to white rocks. Still used today, the land (like the church in nearby Witter) was donated c.1872 by Capt. Smith. It is reached by fording Slow Tom Creek and following a gravel road (appx. .7 m.) past a stone house to a fence. Drop the wire; drive across the pasture. Incidentally, the creek makes a nice picnic site. The ford (a wide bed of flat limestone) forms an ideal swimming hole. SR 23, appx. 12 m. N; just N of Slow Tom Creek. Sign.

Kings River Falls. Natural Heritage Area. A large grindstone once used in a *grist mill* can be found downstream from the 10-foot falls. This area is characterized by a mixed pine-hardwood forest with steep slopes, bluff shelters, white rock walls and dense vegetation, including azaleas, wood iris, trillium and blueberries. An abandoned road serves as a trail beside the river. Along the trail, creeks cascade over steep slopes. Inquire Locally.

SALEM
POP. 1,424   ALT. 664   MAP I-2

There is no recorded origin for this "Salem" although a county history book suggests that there was a town dog by that name. The townsite, at the base of Pilot Hill, was selected county seat of newly created (1842) Fulton County in 1843. Maps until the 1880s alternated carrying it as Salem and Pilot Hill. Reportedly, "Salem" was adopted officially in 1872. The name is most commonly identified with the Biblical reference to a separate kingdom near Jerusalem (Genesis 14).

Morris' Tombstone. A 1964 Salem Headlight reports that when descendants of town founder Wm. P. Morris asked that a tombstone be placed at his grave, the county court made the purchase and did as requested. The lawyer whose front yard contained the historic grave (and suddenly the marker) was not amused. Since then the tombstone has been in a closet at the courthouse, but plans are to make a memorial on the courthouse grounds.

Events/Festivals. Late May: Salem Country Music Association Band, Fiddler & Jig Dance Contest. Late June: Annual String Band & Fiddle Contest.

Fulton County Courthouse. French Empire (Truncated), 1892. In 1973 the third floor (a masonic lodge) was torn off; the hip roof replaced with a flat one. The handmade bricks are painted red. Downtown. *(County Profiles)*

National Historic Register. GEPP, AR. (US 62, 17 m. W): County Line School and Lodge (c.1879), 7 m. NW to the Baxter-Fulton Co. Line; near state line. Inquire Locally.

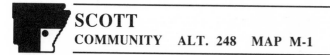

SCOTT
COMMUNITY   ALT. 248   MAP M-1

Although first appearing on tax records in 1836, Major Wm. Scott is said to have settled here during "Territorial Days." This "gin and farming" community first used the *Arkansas River* for transportation, and then switched (and moved closer) to the arriving (1888) St. Louis, Arkansas & Texas *Railroad* (St. Louis Southwestern Railway), which designated the site Scott's Crossing.

Plantation Agriculture Museum. This one-story brick building (1912) formerly served as a general store, post office and depot. The museum is still under development by the state although farm machinery and implements are now on display as well as other items like a folk art "Do-Funny" machine and a wire bull made by a blind man. SR 161 at the tracks.

All Souls Interdenominational Church. National Historic Register, 1906. Built for all religions of the community, each sect takes turns presenting Sunday services with the unifying understanding that they all accept the Apostles Creed. The Cottage Gothic architecture is as pristine as the grounds. Old US 30.

Old US 30. Making a dogleg to the west, reconnecting to US 165 before I-430, this narrow cement highway from another era passes All Souls Church, an old plantation house and a dogtrot cabin while crossing farmland beside a tree-lined bayou. Jct. of US 165 & SR 161.

Indian Mounds. (Toltec Mounds *State Park*)

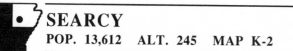

SEARCY
POP. 13,612   ALT. 245   MAP K-2

A bear-hunting area known as White Sulphur Springs in the 1820s, its "therapeutic" waters were described in the Arkansas Gazette as early as 1834, establishing it as a mid-19th century health spa until the springs dried up when the city drilled its water well. In 1837 the town was made county seat of White County and named Searcy (1837 post office, Frankfort; 1838, Searcy), although both White Sulphur Springs and Searcy appeared on maps in the 1840s. Named in honor of Richard Searcy, a Territorial Supreme Court judge. Home of Harding University and Foothills Vocational Technical School.

Spring Park. The town's original spring flowed from here. Picnic Tables. Jct. US 67B/SR 36.

Downtown. Some buildings predate the Civil War but most, like the First Methodist Church (1871), were built in the late 1800s and early 1900s.

Georgetown. Said to have been settled and farmed by the Francure brothers from 1745-1820, it was also recorded by travelers in 1808 as a colony of blacks, presumably escaped slaves, and was known as Negro Hill. The Missouri & North Arkansas *Railroad* crossed the White River here. SR 36, 16 m. E (dead end).

Southwest Trail and Mt. Pisgah. This historic *road* is identified by Mt. Pisgah (709 feet), which can be seen from Searcy (to the NW, appx.10 miles). At the base of this mountain is the cemetery of the Magness family, who settled the area c.1816. SR 16, 9 m. N; SR 310, 2 m. W to Letona; SR 320, 1 m. S. NOTE: Paved and gravel portions of SR 305 between Floyd (SR 31) and Little Red (near Jct. SR 305/124) approximate the Southwest Trail.

West Point. Established in 1852 as the most northern year-round steamboat port on the Little Red River *(Float Streams)*, it declined after being bypassed by the Cairo & Fulton *Railroad,* which created nearby Kensett c.1873. Although shelled by Federal gunboats during the *Civil War,* several 19th century structures still remain intact.

The House That Dimes Built. In 1936 Ripley's Believe-It-Or-Not featured Mady Armstrong's "Searcy Dime House." Said to have been inspired by a church hymn, "Little Things Grow to Big Things," Armstrong began in 1926 to insist on payment in silver for her "odd jobs," saving 90% of the dimes. Ten years later, in the middle of the Great Depression, with 16,000 dimes, she built a small house. Now used for storage. 504 E. Vine. Inquire Locally.

White County Courthouse. Classical Revival, 1871; addition, 1912. National Historic Register. Said to be the oldest functional courthouse in Arkansas, it has an elaborate clock tower whose 1855 bell, which resembles the Liberty Bell, is struck on the hour. Interior: streaked marble wainscoting and iron columns supporting the courtroom roof. Court Square, downtown. *(County Profiles)*

National Historic Register. Black House (1874), 300 E. Race. Deener House, 310 E. Center. Lightle House, 605 Race. Smyrna Church (1854), SR 36, 7 m. W.

SHERIDAN
POP. 3,042   ALT. 237   MAP F-4

Representative of Arkansas' divided *Civil War* loyalties, this town and county were created from the existing counties of Hot Spring, Jefferson and Saline during Reconstruction by Federal sympathizers. To affirm allegiance to the Union (possibly to assure success in forming the county), the 1868 petition to Governor Powell Clayton *(Eureka Springs)* stipulated the county's name as Grant for Ulysses S. Grant and the town's as Sheridan for the Federal general, Phillip Sheridan. Established 1869. Incorporated in 1887.

Grant County Museum. Called "the best small historical museum in the region," it features Indian artifacts, relics from the nearby Battle of Jenkins Ferry *(Civil War)*, log structures, a "Fireman's Display" (including Sheridan's first fire truck) and remnants of early water-powered mills *(Grist Mills)*. 409 W. Center (US 270W).

Architecture. Bradley-Rushing Building (c.1912, restored), Oak & Center. Butler House (c.1912-15, original), Oak & High. CROSS ROADS, AR. (US 167, 6 m. S): Cross Roads School (pre-1900, two-story frame), in town. Rhodes House (c.1850, two-story log house), SR 167, 4 m. S.

Tull Bridge. An "iron through truss" structure built c.1913-16 over the Saline River (*Float Streams*). SR 35, 18 m. NW to Tull, Ar.

White Rock. Formed by deposits of a prehistoric lake bottom and quarry operations. US 167, 6 m. S; W at Cross Roads on CR 8, S on CR 9.

Lee's Ferry. This pioneer crossing on the Saline River has an early 1900s iron bridge in the river. US 167 to SR 35 S to Grapevine (16 m.); W on CR 8, S on CR 9 to the river.

Grant County Civil Defense Park. Not designed as a place to picnic during a nuclear attack as the name might imply, but a community project built in 1975 as a comfortable, tree-shaded rest area. US 167, N of town.

Events/Festivals. Mid-May: Timberfest. Arts & Crafts. Square Dancing. Timber Games. Chili Cook-Off.

Grant County Courthouse. Greek Revival, 1964. This fourth courthouse since 1871 has been recycled from the twice-repaired 1910 version, using the same brick and the original clock, which is set in a 76-foot cupola. The courtroom is entirely modern. Interestingly, there is no witness stand, just a chair. Downtown, US 270. (*County Profiles*)

SILOAM SPRINGS
POP. 7,940   ALT. 1,183   MAP A-1

Settled by Simon Sager in the 1830s, the site (now a suburb of Siloam Springs) was originally Hico, an Indian trading post/post office c.1845, until Siloam City (platted 1880 and named for the healing spring/pool near Jerusalem) drew away Hico's businesses to support a newly created summer resort that offered "healthful" spring water. Incorporated in 1881 as Siloam Springs. The arrival of the Kansas City Southern (*Railroad*) in 1892 helped counteract a dwindling tourist trade. Home of John Brown University.

Historic Downtown. Over 34 interesting historic sites include Queen Anne, Victorian and Colonial architecture. Excellent walking and driving maps: chamber of commerce, N. Broadway & E. University (SR 43, E on University).

Simon Sager Cabin. National Historic Register (c.1830s). This fine example of a pioneer log cabin was built by German immigrant Simon Sager, a cabinetmaker. John Brown University, SR 43, W on University.

Tree Trunk Tombstone. U.S. Marshall Dave Rusk, one of "the men who rode for Parker" (*Fort Smith*, National Historic Site), is buried beneath this unusual marker. SE corner of Oak Hill Cemetery. SR 43, W on University to Holly.

Siloam Springs Museum. A former church displays regional history ranging from the Sager brothers' locally made (1839-1863) furniture like a cherry bedroom suite and pine jelly cupboard to permanent and rotating exhibits of clothing styles and Indian culture. Also featured are replicas of a late 19th century parlor, kitchen and bedroom. 112 N. Maxwell. SR 43, E on University.

National Historic Register. There are numerous sites. (Historic Downtown, ABOVE)

SMACKOVER
POP. 2,453   ALT. 121   MAP H-4

This rags-to-riches oil town has trouble explaining its one-of-a-kind name. Local tradition suggests that the area, "covered by sumac," was called Sumac Covert (SUE-mack CO-veer) by the French, which was then reduced by an *Arkansawyer's* accent to Smackover. However, historical records and maps designating a local creek differ but don't offer an explanation. In 1804 the creek was recorded as Chemin Couvert, in 1844 Suc Obert, in 1857 Smack Overt and in 1884 Smackover. This town of 100 in 1922 was so isolated that a heavy rain could stop travel to nearby *El Dorado*. That same year it boomed to nearly 30,000 with the first gush of oil. Men paid money to sleep on floors or even the ground. Mules were lost in mud holes, fortunes in dry holes and souls in "Barrel Houses" (combination saloon, gambling joint, hotel and brothel).

Arkansas Oil and Brine Museum. The entrance to this project of the Arkansas Museum Services is through a 1930s service station. All exhibits are in working order and include artifacts, tools and vehicles used in the 1920s oil industry. Photographs and videos feature interviews with boom-time residents. Outside are oil rigs of the 1920s-30s made of wood, pipe and angle iron along with demonstrations of how the 1930s "pumping jacks" operated. SR 7 Bypass.

Events/Festivals. Late July (one week): Oil Town Festival. Games. Music. Contests. Crafts.

SNOWBALL
COMMUNITY   ALT. 768   MAP B-4

First settled as a farming community c.1858, the town formed around B.F. Taylor's steam-powered *grist mill* in 1875 (exploded in 1879, killing four men; rebuilt 1880). When naming the new masonic lodge (c.1887) Snow Hall in honor of county sheriff Ben Snow, the town also applied for a post office but (according to local tradition) accidentally ran the handwritten name together (possibly Snowhall). Washington, D.C., took the "h" for a "b" and sent back Snowball. Today: one stone building (1920s).

Richland Creek Skirmishes. In this valley four *Civil War* skirmishes and one scouting action took place, most often during harvest. Today, it is a scenic place to drive through, or stop and picnic. SR 74, appx. 5 m. W at Richland Creek.

Witts Spring. Supposedly settled c.1814, its 1874 post office took the name that was found carved on a rock near the town spring: Witts. SR 377, 11 m. S.

SPRINGDALE
POP. 23,458   ALT. 1,352   MAP A-1

The nucleus of the town formed around a wagon "factory" (1838), a tannery (1840) and Shiloh Primitive Baptist Church (c.1840). A post office, Lynch's Prairie (1859), served Shiloh until the community (located near the Wire *Road* and *Butterfield Overland Mail* route) was destroyed by the *Civil War*. Rebuilt and platted as Shiloh in 1868, the name was changed (for the many springs feeding Spring Creek) in 1872 when the new post office discovered the existence of another Shiloh. Incorporated in 1878, the arrival of the St. Louis & San Francisco *(Railroad)* in 1881 helped to establish the town. Home of Northwest Vocational Technical School and Tyson Foods Inc., which in 1987 rated as the largest producer of chickens and hogs in America as well as the largest singly owned farm in America *(Nashville)*.

Shiloh Museum. This award-winning museum is situated on an entire city block that was donated for a town square, and is known for its Indian artifacts (the Howard Collection features 10,000 relics), history of N.W. Arkansas (50,000 items) and photographs (35,000 images and negatives). The Vaughan-Applegate Collection of photography equipment, called "the largest and finest in the Southwest," shows the evolution of this equipment for over 200 years. Also on the grounds are the Ritter Log Cabin (c.1855), the Steele General Store (c.1870), a doctor's office (c.1880) and the Searcy House (early 1870s). US 471, 6 blks. E on Johnson.

Arts Center of the Ozarks. This multifaceted arts organization features visual arts, crafts, theater and music for all ages. US 471, E on Emma, 2 blks. S on Blair.

Zero Mountain. Probably named for its low temperatures when first excavated in 1955, this dome-shaped mountain is laced with caverns that are artificially cooled (-10°F to +50°F, depending on the product). Nearly 45 million pounds of food can be stored in its 275,000 square feet. The entrance looks like a small railroad tunnel. US 471, near S city limits, W on Johnson Rd. to RR tracks. Signs.

Bluff Cemetery. Established in the mid-19th century, its more ornate stones were designed and sculpted c.1910-40 by local craftsmen. Just N of Shiloh Museum.

Shiloh Memorial Park. Located on a former Indian trail (later a military *road)*, it has picnic tables and historical markers. Just E of Shiloh Museum.

Shiloh Historic District. These 32 acres bounded by Spring Creek, Shiloh, Johnson, Mill and Spring are all on the National Historic Register.

Shiloh Church. National Historic Register, 1870. Called "the best surviving example of community architecture in the state," this two-story clapboard building of simple Greek Revival is Springdale's oldest standing structure. N of Shiloh Museum, Huntsville & Main.

Events/Festivals. Early July: Rodeo of the Ozarks. Late Nov: Annual Arkansas Christmas Fair. Selected Exhibitors.

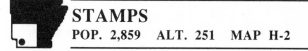

STAMPS
POP. 2,859   ALT. 251   MAP H-2

Stamp collectors from all over the world send mail to be cancelled here. Established by the Texas & St. Louis *Railroad* in

1883, the town was named by the first postmaster (1887) for her father, Hardy James Stamps.

Boxcar Lumber Company. Capable of cutting 350,000 board feet per day, the "largest manufacturer of yellow pine lumber in the world" operated here from 1889 to 1931. A spur railroad built by the company was eventually bought by the Kansas City Southern *(Railroad)*. Only a small brick structure with a bronze commemorative plaque remains. Inquire Locally.

Harvey Couch Steam Electric Station. Gas-fuel powered, it can also burn oil. Named for AP&L founder Harvey Couch, the plant generates 161 megawatts or enough power to light about 1.6 million 100-watt light bulbs. US 82, 2 m. E.

STAR CITY
POP. 2,066   ALT. 300   MAP N-2

Although selected as a site for the county seat in 1871 by a committee charged with finding a location within three miles of the center of newly created Lincoln County, the geography of the choice missed its mark considerably (records indicate the county judge and committee owned land in this area). The proposed town was also named at that time by the committee ("We fully recommend Star City as an appropriate name"), but no reason is now known why. Tradition suggests that the surrounding five hills form the points of a star. While believed to be the only town of this name in America, there is a Star City in the U.S.S.R. that is similar in purpose to Florida's Cape Canaveral. Incorporated 1876.

Rust Cotton Picker. An example of the world's first mechanical cotton picker is by the side of the highway at the Rust Foundation Farm. SR 54, appx. 16 m. N (S of 1st Jct. SR 54/15).

Cane Creek Lake. This 1,700-acre lake, presently administered by the Arkansas Game and Fish Commission, has fishing for bluegill, catfish, crappie and bass. It is also the future site of Cane Creek State Park. SR 11, E 4 m.

Events/Festivals. Early May: Spring Festival. Arts & Crafts. Square Dancing.

Lincoln County Courthouse. Forties Moderne, 1943. Grounds: live oaks, a Confederate statue and five acres of lawn. *(County Profiles)*

STUTTGART
POP. 10,983   ALT. 224   MAP M-2

Like its counterparts on the Grand Prairie *(Carlisle)*, granaries and gins on the horizon appear to be medieval castles. The town, named after Stuttgart, Germany, was established by a colony of German Lutherans who settled the area in 1878, platting the town two years after the arrival of the Texas & St. Louis *Railroad* in 1882.

Stuttgart Agricultural Museum. This award-winning museum is agricultural in the sense that its 10,000 artifacts represent farming life on the Grand Prairie from the 1880s to

1921. Displays begin with Indian culture (including a rare collection of c.1100 A.D. duck effigy pots and bowls), then continue through the years using authentic items from local pioneer families (like a German Bible, bridal trousseau, toys, quilts and rifles). Other exhibits include a restored one-room schoolhouse, scaled-down replicas of period community buildings (like a church, mercantile and jail), a furnished 1880s home and 6,000 square feet of early farm equipment. Also noteworthy are two audio-visual programs: a realistic prairie habitat scene and a simulated duck hunt with a walk-through blind. 921 E. 4th, US 79B or US 165. Signs.

Frozen Ducks. Nov. 30, 1973, in the Duck Capital of the World, hail and an unestimated number of ice-encrusted mallards fell into town.

Konecny Grove. Natural Heritage Area. Of the three major vegetation types on the Grand Prairie, this remnant of "prairie slash [low, swampy area] environment" comprises 22 acres surrounded by a margin of persimmon, green ash and honey locust with a four-acre bog known locally as a former buffalo wallow. The willow flycatcher, which was discovered first in 1822 and painted by J.J. Audubon at Arkansas Post *(National Park)*, can be seen here. SR 11, 7 m. N; 2 m. W on SR 86. 1 m. S of Slovak.

Smoke Hole. *(Carlisle)*

Events/Festivals. Mid-Sept: Annual Grand Prairie Festival of the Arts (all media, sales). Late Nov: World's Championship Duck Calling Contest and Wings Over the Prairie Festival. Duck Gumbo Cook-Off. Carnival. Arts & Crafts.

Arkansas County Courthouse. Early Modern & Greek Revival, 1929. *Dual County Seat (DeWitt)*. Its courtroom has pressed tin ceilings; its grounds a water oak measuring 12.5 feet in diameter. *(County Profiles)*

SUBIACO
POP. 744   ALT. 465   MAP C-2

In 1878 the Little Rock & Ft. Smith *Railroad* (in an effort to populate this part of the *Arkansas River* Valley) donated 740 acres and cash to the Benedictine Order of St. Meinrad Abbey in Indiana to establish a monastery. Both the town's (1909) and the abbey's (1898) names are from a small Italian city near Rome. Incidentally, the Benedictines are the oldest religious order in the Catholic Church (c.535 A.D.).

New Subiaco Abbey. The present monastery was built between 1898 and 1927 from locally quarried sandstone *(Altus, St. Mary's)*. The church, designed like a basilica on the outside, has an Umbrian Romanesque interior featuring Botticino marble from Italy, Alicante marble from Spain, 182 stained-glass windows from Germany, an 18-ton altar of marble and gold leaf and a custom-made Wicks pipe organ (appx. 2,000 pipes) that can produce both classical and romantic music from all periods. The effect is awe-inspiring. While not as self-sufficient as in the 1930s, the 76 monks do most of the handyman work (from plumbing to tailoring), have their own water supply, build furniture, garden and run 400 head of beef cattle

as well as raise hogs, rabbits and bees. In addition, they offer a college preparatory school for boys, and conduct retreats and a summer camp. Lodging at guest cottages, tours of the museum and monastery: by appointment only. In Town.

New Subiaco Abbey Museum. Called a "small Smithsonian," this serious collection was begun in 1906 and is filled with hundreds of New Subiaco and Logan County historical items like a 1673 edition of <u>Don Quixote De La Mancha</u>, late 19th century church vestments (some crocheted, others made with gold thread or needlepoint), a collection of several hundred salt and pepper shakers, rare books, a Keystone projector with 700 glass slides, Indian artifacts, toys, an 1860 grand piano and old postcards (some c.1898).

SULPHUR SPRINGS
POP. 496   ALT. 930   MAP A-1

Established in 1878 as a post office named for the four springs around it, the town (called Round Top for four months) was laid out in 1885 as a resort for "invalids and pleasure seekers," and joined to the Kansas City Southern *(Railroad)* by a spur line. Listed in 1907 by both the KC Southern and the St. Louis & San Francisco Railway as a summer resort, its popularity (as with most spas) waned during the 1930s. The downtown remains turn of the century with its stone buildings.

The Springs and Park. Charming, rustic and old-fashioned best describe this park's tree-shaded grounds, cut-stone water lily pond and four springs. Three original six-foot pumps have separate shelters with labels describing their cures: alkaline (stomach ailments), white sulphur (liver disorders) and black sulphur (malaria). Bring a jug. The fourth spring, Lithia, has a cut-stone dam that forms a very small, clear swimming lake. Adjoining grounds: picnic tables, gazebo, a playground with swings and a basketball/tennis court. In town.

Mini-Museum. Fossils, minerals, gems and Indian artifacts "from 20 states, plus some foreign countries" are displayed: fossilized plants, crinoids, petrified wood, geodes, quartz, gypsum, amethyst, spear points, axes and a pot. Downtown.

Shiloh Farms Products. In Charles Hibler's former resort hotel (1880s, cut stone) the emphasis now is on the bakery that offers fresh breads: sprouted wheat, rye, grain, gluten and soy-sunflower, as well as dried fruits and nuts, granolas, pancake mix and honey. The proprietors, a religious community established in New York during the 1940s, moved here in the 1960s to centralize their national distribution network. Tours. SR 59, in town. Signs.

TEXARKANA
POP. 21,779   ALT. 325   MAP H-2

Legend claims railroad surveyor Col. Gus Knobel named the spot where the Cairo & Fulton and the Texas & Pacific *Railroads* were to meet by combining the names <u>Tex</u>as, <u>Ark</u>ansas and Louis<u>iana</u> (although the Louisiana border was missed by about 30 miles). When each side of the state line was platted by its respective railroad in 1873, the towns used the original site name. The Arkansas side became county seat of reestablished (1874) Miller County *(Boundary Lines)* and incorporated in 1880 (seven years after the Texas side). Lying squarely in two states, divided only by a survey line, the two city governments have had to work out taxation, liquor laws, arrest warrants, marriages and other problems unique to shared but dissimilar state jurisdiction.

U.S. Post Office – Photographers Island. Texarkana, U.S.A. 75501, is the only federal building straddling two states. The border runs directly through the post office, which is built half and half: Arkansas limestone and Texas granite. In front is Photographers Island, where all two-state antics imaginable can be captured for life.

Perot Theater. Neo-Italian Renaissance, 1923. Built by the Saenger Amusement Company, it attracted performers like Will Rogers, Douglas Fairbanks and Orson Wells along with vaudeville, silent movies and the silver screen. Suffering the same loss of appeal as other theaters of its era, the Saenger closed in 1977. Bought by the city, and generously endowed ($800,000) by Ross Perot, its restoration ($1.9 million) included detailed plaster work, gold leaf, a British reproduction of the 1924 carpeting and refurbished original theater seats. Featured today are ballet, symphony and touring Broadway plays. 221 Main St.

Texarkana Historical Society & Museum. Housed in one of the oldest brick buildings in town (1879), it displays Caddo artifacts, railroad memorabilia, pioneer kitchen, turn-of-the-century business office, Victorian parlor and early photographic equipment. 219 State Line Ave.

Free Ferry Boat. *(Ferry Boat)* Spring Bank Ferry. Red River & SR 160.

Events/Festivals. Late May: Strange Family Bluegrass Festival. Late Sept: Texarkana Quadrangle Festival. Music. Square Dance. Collectibles. 5 & 10K Run. Historical Exhibits. Early Oct: 4-States Fair & Rodeo.

Miller County Courthouse. Moderne, 1939. Built on land donated by the railroad, this four-story courthouse has pink marble floors bordered with maroon wainscoting and accented by painted-gold molding. *(County Profiles)*

National Historic Register. There are many sites on the Register. Maps and literature: Arkansas Tourist Information, I-30, Exits 1 or 2. Signs.

THREE CORNERS
ARKANSAS-MISSOURI-OKLAHOMA

Stacked one on top of the other are state line markers erected between 1821 and the 1960s. On top, shaped like a headstone, is the original marker with "Mis. 1821" (Mo. statehood) on the north side and "Ark." (no date; still a territory) on the south. Oklahoma, at the time, was known only as Indian Territory and is not mentioned *(Boundary Lines)*. This stone is said to be the western survey pin *(Witness Tree)* for the Mis-

souri Compromise (1820, excluded slavery from the Louisiana Purchase Territory north of latitude 36°30′). Below it, a marble pedestal (Ozark Culture Club, 1915) identifies all three states along with their dates of admission to the Union (Ar., 1836; Mo., 1821; Ok., 1907). At the bottom is a 10-foot cement circle with three bronze "state lines" (erected by the Lions Club, 1960s). Only Four Corners (Ut., Co., N.M. & Az.) has more converging state lines. Had the Kansas boundary been extended about 35 miles further south, this spot would have shared that distinction. Neglected, these markers are easy to miss. Across from a gas station/grocery store on SR 43.

TONTITOWN
POP. 615   ALT. 1,311   MAP A-1

Italian immigrants sharecropping in the Lake Chicot area *(Lake Village)* wrote home complaining of their treatment. In 1897 a priest (Pietro Bandini) was sent to investigate the reports of half-starved and malaria-ridden people. After confirming the reports, he relocated the sharecroppers, selecting today's townsite (1898) because it reminded him of Italian hill country. Bandini named the new community in honor of Henri de Tonti, founder of Arkansas' first settlement, Arkansas Post *(National Park)*. Incidentally, De Tonti changed his original Italian name of Tonti to Tonty, and has been sited in references as Henry de Tonty.

Wineries. Tontitown was the first community in Northwest Arkansas to grow grapes as a cash crop. Several small businesses still sell wine. Signs. US 68. Near Town.

Boccie Court. Little known or played in America, except in Italian communities, boccie is similar to lawn bowling in that balls are rolled down an alley (usually dirt, 60 x 10 feet) at a smaller ball. The closest ball of each team is counted as a point; 12 points win. This is reportedly the only public court in Arkansas. US 68. City Park.

Events/Festivals. Mid Aug: Tontitown Grape Festival. Music. Spaghetti. Arts & Crafts. Carnival.

TRAIL OF TEARS
ARKANSAS INDIAN HISTORY

Early in the 19th century when settlers began immigrating in large numbers to the present-day central and southern states, they found well-established populations of Native Americans. Many of these tribes, especially the so-called Five Civilized Tribes of the southern regions (Cherokee, Choctaw, Chickasaw, Creek and Seminole) were not living the stereotypical lives presented by Hollywood, nor were they the nomadic people found later in the Great Plains. Southern Indians were farmers who raised crops and livestock, built roads and mills, and educated their children in missionary schools. Some had even formed representative-style governments patterned after the U.S. Constitution.

Until the election of Andrew Jackson (president, 1829-37),

there was no organized national policy regarding the relocation of Native Americans, who were crowded off their land by an ever-expanding white culture. Jackson, a veteran of the Creek and Seminole wars, effected The Indian Removal Act of 1830. This bitterly fought act of Congress authorized the federal government to exchange lands with any tribe "residing within the limits of the states or otherwise." Formerly unable to remove these relatively well-educated people by reciprocating land agreements or guile, the government now had the legal means, but not the comprehension of the magnitude of responsibility and administration required.

The relocation process, which mostly involved the Five Civilized Tribes, was a vast undertaking spanning millions of square miles and involving countless displaced families. Moving large numbers of unwilling people required complicated logistics, wagons, boats, mules, horses and armed military escorts. It has no tidy history or specific route. For nearly 10 years it maintained what has been called a seemingly endless stream of humanity through Arkansas, which was the "funnel" through which these people were poured into their appointed lands in Indian Territory. Thousands died of hunger, depression and hardship. Each group followed *roads,* trails and *rivers* that were suited to their originating locations and intended destinations in Indian Territory. The forced removal of these Indian nations is what encompassed an uncharted Trail of Tears.

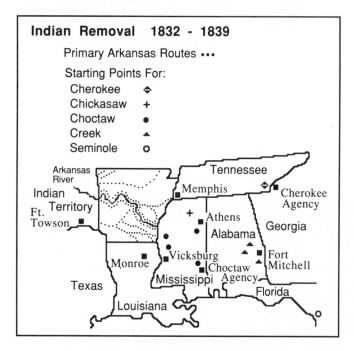

Indian Removal   1832 - 1839

Primary Arkansas Routes •••

Starting Points For:

Cherokee   ⇔
Chickasaw   +
Choctaw   •
Creek   ▲
Seminole   ○

Paleo Indian Period (9,500-8,500 B.C.). Assuming that immigration across the prehistoric "land bridge" between Siberia and Alaska began c.12,000 B.C., arrival in Arkansas could have been as early as 9,500 B.C. Little evidence remains of these people other than fluted projectile points that were used in darts and spears for hunting large, now mostly extinct, animals. Map: Introduction, *Why There Is an Arkansas.*

Archaic Indian Period (8,500-1000 B.C.). People from the Paleo Indian Period, adjusting to a warmer climate and evolving new technology, lived a hunter-gatherer life along the White, Red and Ouachita Rivers in the south, in bluff shelters (overhangs, not caves) in the Ozarks and Ouachita Mountains and beside rivers and lakes of Northeast Arkansas. Evidence indicates they wove baskets and cloth, made simple tools such as axes and adzes, and adopted a new hunting device, the atlatl, which was a spear launched by a separate but parallel stick, giving the thrust a slingshot effect. Though they buried their dead, no ceremony appears to have been attached. Map: Introduction, *Why There Is an Arkansas.*

"Woodland" Indian Period (1000 B.C.-700 A.D.). During this period geographical and cultural divisions evolved among the original inhabitants. The mountainous portions of the state continued life mostly in the same pattern, while in the southern and eastern areas there appeared larger, more complex societies marked by agriculture, pottery making and special treatment of the dead. Burial mounds (literally mounds of earth used strictly for burial and becoming increasingly larger over the years) included nonutilitarian objects indicating a basic idea of religion.

"Mississippian" Indian Period (700-1700 A.D.). While the mountainous portions of the state continued to support a static society, a marked increase in cultural growth divided the lowlands into two distinct groups of mound builders: those north of the Arkansas River and those south. The best evidence of the cultural differences is indicated by their pottery. Northern potters used mussel shells for temper or grog to prevent shrinking and cracking while drying; southern potters used dry clay and sand. Also, northern pots were colored (red and white), incised (decorated while still wet) and often had animal and human shapes included, while in the south, the pots were engraved (decorated when dry) and lacked color and effigies. Both group's mounds were large flat-topped pyramids that served as political and religious centers as opposed to the previous use for burial only. Buildings on top (probably constructed of interwoven cane or branches covered with clay) were periodically razed and rebuilt, causing the mounds to rise higher and giving today's excavations the look of a layered cake. Advancement toward the Historic Period (BELOW) included the bow and arrow c.700 A.D., a primary base of agriculture (mostly corn, beans and squash), ceremonial burials and fortifications using moats and log palisades. Sites at *Wilson,* Millwood *Lake* and Toltec Mounds *State Parks* display these cultures; *Parkin* and *Blytheville* have unrestored mounds. Map: Introduction, *Why There Is an Arkansas.*

Historic Indian Period (1700-1835 A.D.). Although *DeSoto's* 16th century records recount almost constant contact with villages, 130 years later in 1673 Marquette and Joliet (Arkansas Post *National Park)* encountered only a few scattered villages along the Mississippi River *(Blytheville).* After 1700 the principal groups occupying Arkansas were the Quapaw around the mouth of the Arkansas River and the Caddo, who were concentrated at the big bend of the Red River and in the southwest portion of the state. The Osage, while claiming hunting rights in the mountains north of the Arkansas River, maintained permanent villages in south and central Missouri.

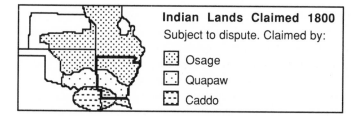

Indian Lands Claimed 1800
Subject to dispute. Claimed by:

⬚ Osage
⬚ Quapaw
⬚ Caddo

QUAPAW: Responsible for naming Arkansas *(Arkansawyer)* and noted for their "hospitality to strangers," they most likely developed from already existing cultures in the lower Mississippi River Valley (Chickasawba Mound, *Blytheville*). These farmers lived in multi-family thatched "Quonset" huts with bark walls and fireplaces. Called "the tallest and best shaped savages on the continent," they wore tanned skins as well as woven grass and cloth, and often painted their bodies with several colored designs. Assigned treaty lands near *Pine Bluff* in 1818, they ceded the property in 1825 and joined the Caddo on the Red River. In 1833 with an estimated population of only 500, the Quapaw were transferred to Indian Territory (present-day Oklahoma). OSAGE: These farmers from southern and central Missouri have been characterized as preferring hunting and war, and on occasion "defended" their hunting territory in northern Arkansas by attacking Quapaw villages near the mouth of the Arkansas River and pursuing the Caddo as far south as Louisiana. The men dressed in breechcloth, leggings and moccasins; women in skirts and dresses of skins. Multi-family houses were rectangular shapes built from saplings covered with brush, mats or hides. Despite an 1808 treaty with the U.S. that relocated them in Indian Territory (present-day Oklahoma), they continued hunting in northern Arkansas, engaging in constant warfare with newly arriving Cherokee. As a result, *Ft. Smith* was established in 1817; however, permanent peace between the two tribes was not arranged until 1831. CADDO: Although in Arkansas they were concentrated in the southwest, the nation lived in a region formed by the borders of present-day Arkansas, Louisiana, Texas and Oklahoma. As expert farmers, they often double-cropped and stored reserves that supported craftsmen and political/religious leaders. Multi-family houses shaped like conical beehives were thatched with grass. Like their agriculture, construction was a community project. Also expert tanners, men's clothing was mostly deerskin but women wore woven grass or cloth skirts. Although they were called "naturally well-featured," their extensive tattooing and body paint shocked the first Europeans. An 18th century population estimated at 8,000 shrunk to about 1,500 by 1800. The Caddo sold all of their Arkansas lands to the U.S. in 1835, leaving for Texas, as the last Indian nation to own property in the state. Later they were relocated in Indian Territory (present-day Oklahoma).

Later Arrivals (Late 18th - Early 19th Century). CHEROKEE: The Cherokee population (estimated at 20,000 in the 16th century) was second only to the Navajo of the Great Southwest. "Civilized," they lived in houses, invented an alphabet (Dwight, *Russellville),* became Christians, raised cash crops and owned African slaves. Pressured by constantly

increasing white settlements in Tennessee, Alabama and Georgia, some began arriving voluntarily in Arkansas as early as the late 18th century, growing into a settlement of about 2,000 along the St. Francis River Valley by 1816 *(Madison).* A treaty in 1817 swapped this acreage of the Arkansas Cherokee (as distinguished from those who remained east of the Mississippi River) for an area roughly defined by Batesville, Harrison, Ft. Smith and Morrilton. At their request a Presbyterian school, Dwight Mission *(Russellville),* was established in 1820. After ceding their lands south of the Arkansas River (Council Oaks, *Dardanelle)* in 1820, the Cherokee relinquished all assigned Arkansas territory eight years later, accepting lands in northwest Indian Territory (present-day Oklahoma). The eastern Cherokee joined them after the Indian Removal Act of 1830 (ABOVE). CHOCTAW: Although assigned "exchanged lands" in southwest Arkansas in 1817, they never inhabited the state in significant numbers, and in 1825 signed another treaty that established part of the present-day *boundary line* between their land in present-day Oklahoma and Arkansas.

OTHERS: Indian nations that passed through Arkansas (often making sparse settlements): the Chickasaw, Seminole, Creek, Delaware and Shawnee *(Yellville).*

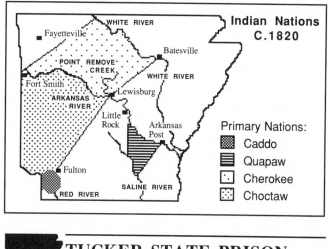

Indian Nations C.1820

Primary Nations:
⬚ Caddo
⬚ Quapaw
⬚ Cherokee
⬚ Choctaw

TUCKER STATE PRISON
MAP M-2

Established in 1916 shortly after the prisoner leasing system was abolished. *(Varner, Coal Hill)*

TULIP
COMMUNITY   ALT. 481   MAP F-4

Although first settled in 1838, legend claims a French hunter, Tulipe, used this site c.1804 on an Indian trail as a cache, a hiding place for goods (most likely too cumbersome for fast travel). A nearby 1848 post office (Brownsville, two miles north) changed its name to Smithville and then to Tulip (either for the hunter or the area's bayou). By 1851 the community included the Tulip Female Collegiate Seminary, the Arkansas Military Institute and the state's first monthly magazine, The

Tulip. By 1860 the cash crop was cotton, the town's legend as "The Athens of Arkansas" was established and its residents were referred to as "The Lords of Arkansas." Miles from a railroad or river, never incorporated, it was mostly a collection of communities sharing the same high ideals and post office.

Tulip Cemetery. National Historic Register. Final resting place for early settlers and "many of Arkansas' celebrities." Off AR 9. Signs.

National Historic Register. The Welch Pottery Works (1851), S of town. CARTHAGE, AR. (SR 9S to SR 48E, 6m.): Bank of Carthage, SR 229. PRINCETON (*Fordyce*), AR. (SR 9, 8m. S): Culbertson Kiln (1858), just E of town. Princeton Methodist Church, SR 9.

UMPIRE
COMMUNITY   ALT. 839   MAP F-2

At first only a meeting point between the Cossatot and Saline *Rivers (Float Streams)*, it was named (c.1880) at the same time the growing settlement needed a name for its new post office, and two rival community schools learned the new game of baseball.

Cossatot River Natural Area. These 4,230 acres (also included in a proposed state park) follow 15 miles of the Cossatot River *(Float Streams)* between SR 246 and SR 4. The area, called "wild and scenic," includes Cossatot Falls, rugged canyons and a swift mountain stream as well as rare plants and animals like the leopard darter and twistflower. Limited Facilities: camping, a primitive *trail* above the river and a small visitor center. Incidentally, the view from SR 4 bridge is said to be reminiscent of the "Great West." SR 4, appx. 7 m. W.

VAN BUREN
POP. 12,020   ALT. 438   MAP C-1

Reportedly settled as early as 1818 across the river from *Fort Smith*. The steamboat Robert Thompson is said to have docked here in 1822. Thomas Phillips bought an 1828 claim and established Phillips Landing on the *Arkansas River* in 1830, changing the name in 1836 to honor presidential candidate Martin Van Buren (president, 1837-41) and offering town lots for sale. Incorporated in 1842, it boomed as an outfitter for the California gold rush (49ers) and later expansion westward. Arrival of the *Butterfield Overland Mail* and then both the Little Rock & Ft. Smith and the St. Louis & San Francisco *(Railroads)* helped continue its prosperity. Home of Bob Burns (BELOW). Architectural tour maps: excellent self-guided tours, chamber of commerce, Frisco Depot (1902), US 59 at E. Main.

Historic District. National Historic Register. Used in the TV mini-series "The Blue and the Gray" as both Gettysburg and Vicksburg, it has over 70 restored buildings dating mostly from the 1870s. The *Butterfield Overland Mail* came through Van Buren – down Signal Hill and through Main St. to the ferry at the Arkansas River for Fort Smith.

Mystery Grave - Fairview Cemetery. This grave (now missing the footstone) is marked by a headstone with a joined double XX. Said to have been here before the first white settler, it is not mentioned in Indian oral histories. Local legends vary, some claiming the remains to be one of *De Soto's* men or a Viking explorer (some historians suggest 11th century Vikings ascended the *Arkansas River* as far as Tulsa; contested physical evidence supports them). Fairview Cemetery (1846) was laid out around this mysterious grave, and has ornate and simple stones for pioneers, soldiers and Arkansas' notables like steamboat master Phillip Pennywit *(River)*. In Town. SR 59 (Fayetteville Rd.) at WM Penn (N of SR 162).

Historical Murals. In the heroic style of the *WPA*, Van Buren High School art students (1981-85) painted the history (prehistoric-1970s) of the town on a 12-by-1,200-foot wall. Main at the river.

Albert Pike Schoolhouse (c.1820). In 1833 Albert Pike taught school here for $3 a month after returning to Van Buren from Santa Fe with "his fortunes at a low ebb." Pike, best known for his voluminous Masonic writings, is usually described as explorer, poet, teacher and soldier. Not only did he fight in the Mexican-American War (1846-48), he also led a brigade of Cherokee for the Confederacy at the battle of Pea Ridge *(National Park)*. Courthouse Lawn.

Radio and movie comedian Bob Burns is responsible for naming the WWII bazooka

---

Bob Burns Home and Crawford County Museum. National Historic Register, 1885. Burns' childhood residence houses local historical artifacts. A radio and movie comedian (humor much the same as "Lum 'N Abner," *Pine Ridge*), he focused national attention on his hometown (1930s-early 40s) and was the originator of a musical instrument, the "bazooka," for which the later WWII weapon was named. 9th & Jefferson (US 59, N on Jefferson).

Mt. Olive Methodist Church. National Historic Register, 1889. Said to be the oldest black church west of the Mississippi River. Knox & Lafayette. US 59, W on Knox.

Events/Festivals. Early May: Old Timer's Day. Arts & Crafts. Period Costumes. Carnival. Antique Show. Early Sept: Annual Lake Lou Emma Arts & Crafts Fair. Early Oct: Fall Festival. Arts & Crafts. Entertainment. Costumes.

Crawford County Courthouse. Italian Villa (Hudson River Bracketed Style), 1878. Called the oldest active county courthouse west of the Mississippi River *(Searcy,* courthouse), the original (1841) 22-inch-thick walls were used in the present building. Inside, a Seth Thomas 1878 tower clock is displayed. On the grounds, sharing the same place where the *Butterfield Overland Mail* passed by and where Mexican War and Confederate volunteers drilled, are the Albert Pike Schoolhouse, an 1840s sundial and reportedly the "first monument built in America" honoring the first three servicemen to die in

WWI. *(County Profiles)*
National Historic Register. Numerous listings (Historic District, ABOVE). Maps: chamber of commerce, Frisco Depot (1902), US 59 at E. Main.

VARNER
COMMUNITY   ALT. 181   MAP N-2

Settled c.1844 by the Varner, Rice and Douglas families, it was named for W.F. Varner and his daughter Medora Varner Rice. Establishment of the post office coincided with the arrival of the Little Rock, Pine Bluff & New Orleans *Railroad* (St. Louis, Iron Mountain & Southern) in 1871. Although incorporated in 1907, today the original town is gone, leaving only memories of its 1885 race track and legends of its racy and high-rolling reputation.
Cummins Prison Farm. Since 1902 it has been a part of the Arkansas penal system, which from 1849-1893 "leased" convicts to commercial companies and individuals. A sit-down strike at *Coal Hill* in 1886 helped to modify the system and by 1916 the practice was officially abolished. The Cummins and Maple Grove Plantations (appx. 10,000 acres) were bought to build this new penal system, using prisoners to farm for the state. Arkansas' largest prison escape (36 convicts) took place here in 1940.
Henry M. Stanley. Stanley of "Dr. Livingstone, I presume?" and the man known as "the discoverer of the African Congo" grew up in South Arkansas. Born John Rowlands of a poor Welsh family, he escaped from an English workhouse, worked his way to New Orleans as a cabin boy and was adopted by his namesake. In 1860, Stanley began work as a clerk in the store of Louis Altschul at Cypress Bend near Cummins until joining first the Confederates, and then the Federals.

WABBASEKA
POP. 428   ALT. 198   MAP M-2

This small farming town, established c.1890 on the tracks of the St. Louis Southwestern Railway *(Railroad),* is supposedly named for an Indian princess, but which tribe and why is unknown. Home of author Eldridge Cleaver.
Taylor Woodlands. Natural Heritage Area. Representative of the lowland forest that once dominated the Delta; the wetter parts are characterized by bald cypress, black willow and ash. Inquire Locally.

WALDO
POP. 1,685   ALT. 350   MAP H-3

First settled after the Mexican War (1846-48) three and a half miles north of its present site as Lamartine (after the French poet/statesman), in 1883 C.H. Pace moved the Lamartine post office to the newly constructed Texas & St. Louis *Railroad,*

hoping to establish a regular station. Laid out in 1883, it was reportedly named for Col. J. Waldo, V.P. of the Texas division of the railroad.
Frog Level/Ferguson & Morgan Store. National Historic Register, 1852. Frog Level was designated temporary county seat of newly formed Columbia County. The 1853 proceedings were held at this store on the Frazier plantation. Restored. 6 m. SW. Inquire Locally.
National Historic Register. The Bank of Waldo, Locust & Main.

WALDRON
POP. 2,642   ALT. 648   MAP D-1

The town's early history began in confusion because of two brothers, a post office and competition for the county seat of Scott County. Additionally, the present town of Winfield is not located where its historic counterpart was founded. In 1838, Wm. Featherston established Poteau Valley Post Office at the present site of Waldron. His brother, Ed Featherston, was also a land speculator with hopes of building a town. In 1843 the county seat was moved from Cauthron (not present-day Cauthron but a site possibly near today's community of Ione, SW of *Booneville)* to a more central location, Ed's farm, which was called Winfield and was located one and a half miles northeast of Wm.'s post office. Poteau Valley P.O. was also moved to Winfield in 1843 but Wm. donated 10 acres for a county seat location in 1845 and back the post office came (1846) along with the courthouse, and all of it was renamed for the town's surveyor, John P. Waldron. Incorporated 1875.
Blythe's Museum. Gary F. Blythe says he has over 8,000 Indian artifacts, 800 photographs of early Scott County and about 150 firearms "flint to new" along with coins, stamps and "anything old I happen to pick up." US 71B, 1 m. S of Jct. US 71 Bypass.
Events/Festivals. Mid-May: Scott County Rodeo.
Scott County Courthouse. Deco, 1934. Inside is a handmade, 16-inch wooden drum from which wooden disks are still drawn to determine jury duty. Downtown. *(County Profiles)*
National Historic Register. Forrester House (c.1870-86), 115 Danville.

WALNUT HILL
COMMUNITY   ALT. 248   MAP H-2

Settled as a large plantation on the Shreveport-Washington *Road* in 1823 by Arkansas' first governor (1836-40), James Sevier Conway, it was reportedly named for the large walnut groves in the area. Conway, who surveyed Arkansas' western *boundary line* near here, lived at Walnut Hill after serving as governor until his death from pneumonia on March 3, 1855. Incidentally, the Conways were a dominant political force (by marriages and alliances) from early territorial days until 1860. Three of the seven brothers held high offices: Henry W. (Territorial delegate to Congress, 1823-27), James S. (ABOVE) and Elias N. Conway (governor, 1852-60).

Conway. This town was laid out in the 1830s at the Red *River* and on a *road* joining one from Washington that cut into Old Miller County *(Boundary Lines)*, a few miles northwest of Walnut Hill Plantation. Its sole owner and promoter, James S. Conway, offered lots for sale in 1840. The town was carried on maps for 40 years, then faded away.

Conway Cemetery State Park. *(State Parks)*

Free Ferry Boat. *(Ferry Boats)* Spring Bank Ferry. SR 160, 13 m. W.

WALNUT RIDGE
POP. 4,152   ALT. 270   MAP J-3

Laid out by the chief engineer of the Cairo & Fulton *Railroad* in 1873 on land owned by Col. C. M. Ponder, whose nearby post office already carried the name (presumably for the walnut trees in the area). Incorporated in 1880. Home of Southern Baptist College.

Hoxie. Named for a railroad official and laid out in 1883 on the Kansas City, Ft. Scott & Gulf *Railroad* when the tracks crossed just SE of Walnut Ridge. Incorporated in 1888. The two towns share the same backyards.

Lawrence County Courthouse. Sixties Modern, 1965. From 1889 until consolidated in 1963, Walnut Ridge was a *dual county seat (Powhatan, County Profiles)*.

National Historic Register. CLOVER BEND, AR. (US 67, 8 m. S; SR 228, 5 m. W): Clover Bend High School and Alice French House (1895). In Town.

WAR EAGLE
COMMUNITY   ALT. 1,157   MAP A-2

The 1830s settlement on War Eagle Creek, several miles south of War Eagle Mill (BELOW), was a community post office beside an historic North Arkansas *road*. The name appeared and disappeared from postal records and maps until c.1880 when it was listed at today's mill site. The creek's name reportedly existed before the first settlers arrived, and is based on a familiar romantic legend: War Eagle (son of a Cherokee chief) killed a white trapper who kidnapped his bride-to-be. War Eagle died at this creek as a result of the struggle. His unnamed bride died of sorrow. A less romantic possibility for the name: an Osage, Hurachis the War Eagle, who signed treaties with the federal government during the 1820s. The community, not shown on most maps, is just off SR 12, appx. 6.4 m. N of Best.

War Eagle Mill. Sylvanus Blackburn's first (1832) sawmill and *grist mill* was washed away by a flood in 1838. The second was burned by Confederates. Rebuilt in 1873, it operated until 1924. Today's is a working, water-powered replica of the 1873 mill located on the original site and is said to be the only "undershot" water wheel west of the Mississippi River. "Stone buhr ground" cornmeal, whole wheat flour, cereals, rye, grits

and mixes are sold. Fishing. Swimming. Picnicking. Off SR 12. Signs.

War Eagle Cavern. Advertised as beginning with a "spectacular entrance," a quarter-mile guided tour (appx. 40 min.) wends along a clear stream through this level cavern of high ceilings and "abundant fossil outcroppings." CR 98N; SR 12, appx. 2 m. E. Signs.

Events/Festivals. Early May: Back-in-the-Hills Antique Show & Heritage Crafts Fair. Late Oct: Annual Ozarks Arts & Crafts Fair.

WARREN
POP. 7,646   ALT. 205   MAP O-1

Selected as a site for the permanent county seat (1843) of newly created Bradley County (1840), it grew slowly as a cotton and lumber town (1890 census, 600), using first the Saline *River* and then the Little Rock, Mississippi River & Texas *(Railroad)*. Prior to the establishment of the town, I.M. Pennington (namesake of the township) lived south of the site and Hugh Bradley (namesake of the county) lived north. Both men were very influential and both have been mentioned in naming the town for "a colored body servant," Warren, who is the only slave for whom an Arkansas town has been named. Incorporated in 1851; commerce still revolves around town square.

Warren Prairie is said to be reminiscent of the Serengeti Plain in East Africa

---

Warren Prairie. Natural Heritage Area. This strange-looking place (said to be reminiscent of the Serengeti Plain in East Africa) is not thoroughly understood, but it has been suggested that the area could be the bed of a former alkali lake, or a playa like those in the western states. It supports unusual vegetation such as palmettos, plant species of extremely limited distribution and others that occur nowhere else in Arkansas. SR 4, 5 m. E; SR 8 to end of pavement.

Ozment Bluff. There isn't much left of this early 19th century steamboat landing on the Saline *River (Float Streams)* except some pilings, a log cabin (White Hall Rd.) and a do-it-yourself picnic area. SR 4, 5 m. E; SR 8, S to access sign.

Southern Bluff/Bradley County Park. Natural Heritage Area. Actually a north-facing bluff, it was created by Franklin Creek (a clear stream), which now divides it from a low flood plain. During the spring, dogwoods, azaleas, wild violets and native orchids bloom ("an outstanding assemblage of plants"). A footpath leads to the 280-foot bluff. Small Lake. Picnic Areas. SR 376, appx. 2.5 m. N; sign at a gravel road to Bradley County Park.

Bradley County Courthouse. Neo-Italianate, 1903. National Historic Register. A different color brick accents the quoins and a four-story clock tower (in an ornate cupola). In the main hall are county artifacts, including Confederate cur-

rency. Jct. SR 4 & 15. *(County Profiles)*
National Historic Register. Warren & Ouachita Valley Railway Station (1909), 325 W. Cedar. County Clerk's Office (1890), E of Courthouse. Bailey House (c.1898), 302 Chestnut. Ederington House, 326 Main.

WASHINGTON
POP. 265   ALT. 374   MAP G-2

Selected as the site for Hempstead County seat in 1824 and named (presumably) for President George Washington in 1825, it was reportedly laid out in 1826 (first recorded plat, 1835) and then built on legends, romance and the crossroads of two important pioneer routes *(Roads,* the Southwest Trail and the Ft. Towson Road). Ironically referred to as the birthplace of the Republic of Texas, it is said that Sam Houston plotted the Texas Revolution at a Washington tavern, recruiting men like Davy Crockett and Jim Bowie. Stephen F. Austin's *(Fulton, Little Rock)* last residence before leaving for Texas was here. Supposedly in 1835-36 James Black (a Washington blacksmith) forged the famous bowie knife (some sources claim that Jim Bowie's brother Rezin P. invented it). During the Mexican War (1846-48) the town was a rendezvous for volunteers from Kentucky, Tennessee and Arkansas (10 companies were formed as a regiment under Archibald Yell, Arkansas' second governor, 1840-44, *Yellville).* Reaching its peak as the Confederate capital of Arkansas (1863-65), it was bypassed by the Cairo & Fulton *Railroad* in 1873, after which it slowly lost its population and, 66 years later, the county seat to *Hope.*
Old Washington Historic State Park. *(State Parks)*
Events/Festivals. (Old Washington Historic *State Park)*
National Historic Register. Excellent examples of antebellum architecture. Maps: state park vistors' center. Historic District. Confederate Capitol (c.1836), Main St. Grandison D. Royston House (c.1830), Alexander St.

WEST FORK
POP. 1,526   ALT. 1,340   MAP B-1

Settled in 1828 by Eli Boyd. An 1848 post office was named for the west fork of the White River *(Float Streams),* but no town sprung up until the establishment of a water-and-steam-powered *grist mill* (1875-76) and the arrival of the St. Louis & San Francisco *(Railroad)* in 1881. Incorporated 1885.
Grist Mill Site. Although the structure is no longer there, the pond and dam have a nice setting against rock bluffs. At the bridge on SR 156.

WEST MEMPHIS
POP. 28,138   ALT. 215   MAP L-5

This area was first settled by Benjamin Foy (or Fooy), who was authorized (c.1794) by the Spanish governor of Louisiana,

Gayoso, to be an agent for the Chickasaw. Gayoso, pressured by America to remove a fort from Chickasaw Bluffs (Memphis, Tn.) c.1797, established Ft. Esperanza on the west bank of the Mississippi River as a "toll booth" that collected tribute for use of the river. Foy settled just north of the fort where his community continued to grow, becoming Hopefield (reportedly a loose translation of esperanza) and later the terminus of both the Memphis-Little Rock *Road* and *Railroad*. Although carried on maps into the 20th century, Hopefield was first destroyed during the Civil War and then was decimated by yellow fever in 1878. Despite the road, the railroad and its strategic location across from Memphis, Hopefield was overshadowed by *Marion* until well after the turn of the century. The present city began on stilts *(Flood of 1927)* as a railroad station in 1875 and is a combination of logging communities like Bragg Mill, Hulbert and Boltz Cooperage Mill (incorporated, 1927). The name West Memphis (platted in 1884) is said to have been selected because of the premium prices paid for "Memphis" lumber.
Southland Greyhound Park. Southland, one of the major dog-racing tracks in America, reportedly has the largest average daily pari-mutuel handle of its kind in the world. Open April-November on 140 acres, it has seating (air-conditioned or outdoors) for 10,000 and a standing capacity of about 22,000 as well as wide-screen TV and more than 272 closed-circuit monitors. Restaurants. Concessions. Jct. I-40 & I-55.
Esperanza Trail. This 10.5-mile hiking *trail* circles Dacus Lake (a bend of the Mississippi River until the mid-1920s), winding between the west bank of the river and the levee, affording an excellent opportunity to see the Delta's unique terrain and how the levee system *(Flood of 1927)* stabilized the floodplain of the river. The trail passes remnants of a roundhouse and turn-around yard (Memphis-Little Rock *Railroad)* as well as historical areas like the site of Hopefield (ABOVE), Indian mounds and the Memphis-Little Rock *Road*. I-55 east city limits, N to Mound City. Signs.
National Historic Register. Dabbs Store (1912), 1320 S. Avalon.

WILSON
POP. 1,115   ALT. 340   MAP K-5

Robert E. Lee Wilson built a sawmill on the washed-away townsite of Midway at the Mississippi *River* in 1880, creating a new city named for himself in 1899. Wilson has been called an excellent example of business paternalism in that the man and the town shared the profits from one of the world's largest cotton plantations (appx. 64,000 acres). Orphaned at 15, he began with 160 acres that he traded for 2,100 acres of swamp and timber, and then began (1880s-1900s) a cycle of cutting timber, draining the land and planting cotton as well as investing in sawmills, banks, companies (like lumber, grocery, cotton) and a *railroad* (Jonesboro, Lake City & Eastern).
Tudor Architecture. Very unusual for an Arkansas farming town (or for any town), this one has carried a Tudor architectural theme throughout, including a church, cafe, post office,

bank and gas station.
Hampson Museum State Park. *(State Parks)*

WINSLOW
POP. 326   ALT. 1,729   MAP B-1

Reportedly the highest incorporated city in Arkansas, and the highest point (from base to crest) reached by railroad between the Allegheny and Rocky Mountains in 1881, it was also the point at which southbound stagecoaches in the Boston Mountains changed horses for the often hair-raising descent to Van Buren, causing one contemporary traveler to comment: "I can assure you, we were by no means sorry when that Herculean feat was accomplished" (US 71, BELOW). Founded as a post office, Summit Home, in 1876, it changed names to honor E.F. Winslow, president of the St. Louis & San Francisco *(Railroad)* when it arrived in 1881. Home of the first woman mayor in America (Maud Duncan, 1925), who was also editor of The Winslow American newspaper and one of Arkansas' first women pharmacists.

US 71. The 15 miles of switchbacks and broad views between Winslow and *Mountainburg* are not only beautiful and lined with old-fashioned roadside attractions but they are also very dangerous. In a three-year period, 16 people were killed in traffic accidents. Be Careful.

Frisco Tunnel. An engineering feat when built in 1882 at 1,729 feet, it is claimed that this 1,700-foot railroad tunnel (dimensions, 18-by-9 feet, enlarged in 1968) is the highest on the "Frisco Line" (St. Louis & San Francisco). Presumably, the altitude was measured from base to height. Inquire Locally.

Ozone. Laboratory tests conducted by the railroad determined the air here had "a higher ratio of ozone than found anywhere in the world," except the Tennessee Cumberland Mountains.

Mount Gayler. At and near what is called "The Top of the Boston Mountains," there is a collection of nostalgic tourist sites, including a display of Indian artifacts (a skull with an arrowhead in it) and a stuffed horse (only its head now), a 1944 fieldstone church containing the Virgin of the Smile statue, and spectacular panoramas from observation platforms.

Events/Festivals. Late June: Annual Ozarks Native Arts & Crafts Fair. Demonstrations. Entertainment.

WITNESS TREE
MAP ALL QUARTERS

A term rarely used anymore, or even listed in reference books, it applies to a surveyor's mark blazed into a tree to designate the physical point that corresponds to the survey coordinates. In a wilderness like Arkansas, trees were the handiest and most visible means of noting division points like state boundaries *(Louisiana Purchase)*, townships and private property lines. Other means such as stone *(Three Corners)* and wooden or iron poles *(Foreman)* were also used. Often earth was just piled in mounds, and in them were buried glass or rock or even cinders.

NOTE: Some archaeologists speculate that the pyramids of Egypt, in the absence of trees and other natural landmarks, were (among other purposes) also used as geodetic markers.

WITTSBURG
GHOST TOWN   ALT. 400   MAP L-4

Local tradition claims the site as a 1739 French fort, Bienville, built during their second war with the Chickasaw. Established on a Spanish land grant, platted in 1848 at the same time *St. Francis (Old)* acquired an unsavory reputation, it was ideally located where *Crowley's Ridge,* the headwaters for navigation of the St. Francis *River* and the Memphis-Little Rock *Road* met. Possibly named for the pioneer Witt family of Crittenden County, it was county seat (1868-84) but began fading away after bypassed by the St. Louis, Iron Mountain & Southern *(Railroad)* in 1883 *(Wynne)*. One grocery store and several houses remain. Inquire at Village Creek *State Park*.
Village Creek State Park. (Village Creek *State Park*)

WPA 1939-1942
WORKS PROJECTS ADMINISTRATION

Originally called Works Progress Administration when created by President F.D. Roosevelt's New Deal in 1935. The name was changed to Works Projects Administration in 1939, when consolidated with the Public Works Administration, the Public Buildings Administration and the U.S. Housing Authority as a part of Roosevelt's Reorganization Plan of 1939. The idea behind WPA programs, as well as others like the Civilian Conservation Corps (C.C.C.) and *Resettlement Administration,* was to provide billions of dollars for employment and relief during the Great Depression through work-oriented and quasi-welfare agencies. The WPA was liquidated in 1942, after the United States entered WWII. Today, many Depression-era projects are mistakenly called WPA when actually they were financed by other agencies *(Heber Springs,* WPA Mural).

WYNNE
POP. 7,805   ALT. 235   MAP K-4

Probably the only Arkansas town laid out at the junction of the same *railroad* (the St. Louis, Iron Mountain & Southern Railway, 1883, crossed itself east-west, north-south), the town was reportedly named for J.W. Wynne, a prosperous merchant residing in nearby *Forrest City*. Incorporated in 1888, it became county seat in 1889 after the seat of justice passed from *Wittsburg* to Vanndale (BELOW).

Vanndale. County seat for five years (1884-89), the original two-story courthouse now stands derelict just east of the railroad tracks. In town, SR 1, 10 m. N.

Cross County Historical Museum. The one-room museum is packed with local pioneer and Indian artifacts. Along with the census from 1830 to 1900 and 76 microfilm rolls of archives, it has a four-point buck deer (stuffed), a prehistoric mastodon tooth the size of a foot and nearly 50 pots from the mound builder period of the 1700s *(Parkin)*. Courthouse.

Events/Festivals. Mid-June: Wynne Funfest. Games. Bar-B-Q Contest. Arts & Crafts.

Cross County Courthouse. Sixties Modern, 1969. It is the only one in Arkansas housing an historical museum and whose court room is arranged so that the jury sit with their backs to the spectators. Downtown, SR 1. *(County Profiles)*

YELLVILLE
POP. 1,044   ALT. 683   MAP A-4

First settled by the Shawnee *(Norfork)* c.1819 who built split-cedar cabins. Whites took up the settlement (cabins and fields) known as Shawneetown when the Indian nations were removed c.1828 *(Trail of Tears),* changing the name in 1836 upon applying for a post office. Named for Archibald Yell, who was a Territorial judge, Arkansas' first U.S. congressman and second governor (1840-44). Platted in 1845. Incidentally, legend says the old Seminole War veteran offered $50 for the honor of the town's name when campaigning here in 1844 for a second term in Congress. He was elected, but resigned to fight in the Mexican War *(Washington),* where he died in action.

Rush Ghost Town. Occupied by Bluff Dwellers *(Trail of Tears)* from 8,000 B.C. to 500 A.D., its historical period began with the Sunshine Mine (the most famous zinc mine in the Arkansas field). A 12,750-pound ore sample was sent to the Chicago Columbian Exposition in 1893. Although settled prior to the Civil War, discovery of zinc in the early 1880s created a mining town that periodically boomed and faded for 25 years, reaching its height in 1914 as a town of 2,000 built by the demand for zinc during WWI. Derelict structures (1880-1945) like a general store, blacksmith shop and livery still remain as well as mine tunnels, roadbeds and retaining walls. South along Rush Creek to the Buffalo *River (Float Streams).* SR 14, appx. 11 m. S (appx. 1 m. S of Caney); E on gravel road for appx. 4 m. Access Sign.

Free Ferry Boat. *(Ferry Boats)* Peel Ferry. SR 15N to SR 125N, 27 m. N.

Events/Festivals. Early Oct: Annual Wild Turkey Calling Contest & Turkey Trot Festival. Arts & Crafts. Music.

Marion County Courthouse. Folk Classicism, 1943. Because of the rugged cut stone and windowless first floor, this small courthouse has the feeling of a medieval castle. Front offices have five-sided walls formed by the angles of a "flying buttress." Other features: marble floors and wainscoting. Town Square. *(County Profiles)*

National Historic Register. Cowdry House (1902), 1 Valley. Layton Building (1906), 1110 Mill.

ARKANSAS CAMPGROUNDS

Grouping all public campgrounds under a single heading would be confusing. Arkansas has two separate and distinct mountain ranges, three multi-million-acre national forests, 600,000 acres of lakes and 9,000 miles of streams and rivers. Over 200 public-owned campgrounds are available with nearly 6,700 individual family campsites. Some campsites can be reserved; most are on a first-come, first-served basis. Generally, U.S. Corps of Engineers sites are water-oriented and have boat-launching ramps, drinking water and modern restrooms. National forests provide campsites divided by green belts, are developed around a geographic attraction with hiking *trails* and have primitive restroom facilities. State parks are scattered throughout Arkansas with a wide range of attractions and offer modern camping conveniences including hot water showers. Of the five national parks services in Arkansas only two of them

(Hot Springs and Buffalo National River) provide campsites. Other state and federal properties, like wildlife management areas and national wildlife refuges as well as Game and Fish Commission lakes, provide a variety of recreational and camping opportunities. Municipal parks are listed under their respective towns: Beaver, Jonesboro, Lake Village and Little Rock. For a detailed description of and directions to public parks and campgrounds, refer to these separate headings, which are also *italicized* in the text and listed in the Index and Table of Contents: Arkansas River Parks and Campgrounds, Lakes, National Forests, National Parks, National Wildlife Refuges, State Parks and Wildlife Management Areas. NOTE: Although numerous private campgrounds provide campsites in these same areas, only those sponsored by the city, state or federal government are listed in this guide.

ARKANSAS RIVER PARKS AND CAMPGROUNDS

Generally U.S. Corps of Engineers sites have drinking water, boat-launching ramps, picnic facilities and restrooms. Listed below in east to west geographic sections are parks and campgrounds along the *Arkansas River* between Arkansas Post *National Park* and *Fort Smith*. WARNING: Swimming or even wading in the Arkansas River is extremely dangerous because of strong currents, undertows, unstable and crumbling banks, suctions, whirlpools and sinkholes. Keep a close watch on children. Always wear a flotation device when boating.

ARKANSAS POST-PINE BLUFF
MAP N-2+3

Water level and traffic along this stretch of the river are controlled by Norrell Lock & Dam and L&D #2 near Arkansas Post *National Park* and by L&D #3 and #4 near *Grady* and *Pine Bluff* respectively. Fishing offers bass, bream, crappie and catfish. Hunters can expect duck, deer, wild turkey and small game. Commercial docks provide boat and motor rentals as well as supplies. Corps of Engineers, Bx. 7835, Pine Bluff, 71611. Directions to the following campsites are from the capitalized town: ARKANSAS POST, MAP N-3: Moore Bayou. 4 Campsites. Boat ramp, water & restrooms. SR 169, 2 m. W. ARKANSAS POST, MAP N-3: Notrebes Bend. 28 Campsites. Boat ramp, water, restrooms & hookups. 7 m. W of Canal Roadway Bridge, adjacent to Dam #2. ARKANSAS POST, MAP N-3: Wild Goose Bayou. No Campsites. Boat ramp, water & restrooms. E on paved road to Lock & Dam #1. GILLETT, MAP N-3: Big Bayou Metro. No Campsites. Boat Ramp. US 165, 2 m. S; SR 144, 4 m. W. GILLETT, MAP N-3: Pendleton. 31 Campsites. Boat ramp, water, restrooms & group pavilion. US 165, 10 m. S to Pendleton; 1 m. N on paved access road. GILLETT, MAP N-3: Morgan Point. No

Campsites. Boat Ramp. SR 1 to Pendleton; 1 m. N on gravel road. GRADY, MAP N-2: Huff Island. 4 Campsites. Water & restrooms. SR 11 E to paved road; 7.5 m. E. NADY (Not on some maps; near Lock #2), MAP N-3: Merrisach. 57 Campsites. Boat ramp, water, restrooms, group pavilion, playground, electrical hookups, dump station & amphitheater. .5 m. W of Lock #2 on paved road. NOBLE LAKE, MAP N-2: Trulock. 15 Campsites. Boat ramp, water, restrooms, group pavilion & playground. US 65, 4 m. N on paved road. PINE BLUFF, MAP N-2: St. Marie. No Campsites. Boat ramp, water, restrooms & group pavilion. US 79, 4 m. NE to paved access road. Signs. ROB ROY (Not on some maps; near Lock #4), MAP N-2: Sheppard Island. No Campsites. Boat ramp, water & restrooms. 3.5 m. SW, adjacent to Lock & Dam #4. RYDEL, MAP N-2: Little Bayou Metro. No Campsites. Boat Ramp. 2 m. S on paved road. TAMO, MAP N-2: Rising Star. 25 Campsites. Boat ramp, water, restrooms, group pavilion, playground & electrical hookups. US 65, 5 m. N. Signs.

PINE BLUFF-LITTLE ROCK
MAP M-1

Water level and traffic along this stretch of the river are controlled by Lock & Dam #5 near Jefferson and David D. Terry L&D near *Little Rock*. Fishing offers bass, bream, crappie and catfish. Hunters can expect duck, geese, dove and quail in the surrounding rice country. Commercial docks provide boat and motor rentals as well as supplies. Corps of Engineers, Bx 7835, Pine Bluff, 71611. Directions to the following campsites are from the capitalized town: JEFFERSON, MAP M-1: Dam Site. No Campsites. Water, restrooms & group pavilion. SR 365, 4.5 m. E; adjacent to Lock & Dam #5. LITTLE ROCK, MAP M-1: David D. Terry West. No Campsites. Boat ramp, water & restrooms. US 165, 6 m. SE, adjacent to Lock & Dam #6. REDFIELD, MAP M-1: Tar Camp. 56 Campsites. Boat ramp, water, restrooms, playground, group pavilion, electrical hookups, dump station & showers. SR 365, 2 m. N; 6 m. E on paved road. SCOTT, MAP M-1: Willow Beach. 21 Campsites. Fishing area for the handicapped, water, restrooms, boat ramp, group pavilion, playground, electrical hookups & dump station. US 165, appx. 2.5 m. to paved access road. Signs. WRIGHTSVILLE, MAP M-1: Wrightsville. No Campsites. Boat Ramp. SR 386, 1 m. N to gravel road; 4 m. S then 1.5 m. E.

LITTLE ROCK-DARDANELLE
MAP D-4 & C-3+4

Water level and traffic along this stretch of the river are controlled by Murray L&D at *Little Rock,* Toad Suck Ferry L&D near *Conway* and Lock & Dam #9 near *Morrilton.* Fishing offers all species native to Arkansas, including bass, crappie, bream and catfish. Situated on the eastern edge of the Ouachita and Ozark Mountains, the area has quail, ducks, geese, wild turkey, deer and small game. Commercial docks provide boat and motor rentals as well as supplies. Lake Manager, Toad Suck Ferry, Rt. 5, Bx. 140, Conway, 72032. Directions to the following campsites are from the capitalized town: ATKINS, MAP C-3: Sweeden Island. 28 Campsites. Boat ramp, water, restrooms, electrical hookups, dump station & group pavilion. SR 105, 8 m. S. BIGELOW, MAP D-4: Bigelow. 8 Campsites. Boat ramp, water, restrooms & group pavilion. 2 m. E on paved road. CENTERVILLE, MAP C-3: Pontoon. No Campsites. Boat ramp, water, restroom and access to Petit Jean River. SR 154, 6 m. E. CONWAY, MAP D-4: Cadron Settlement Park. No Campsites. Day use only. Boat ramp, water, restrooms, nature trail, picnic sites, group pavilion. US 64, 6 m. W; SR 319, 1.5 S. CONWAY, MAP D-4: Old Ferry

Landing. No Campsites. Boat ramp, picnic sites, restroom, water and group pavilion. CONWAY, MAP D-4: Palarm. No Campsites. Day use only. Boat ramp, water, restrooms & picnic sites. SR 365, 12 m. S. CONWAY, MAP D-4: Toad Suck Ferry. 32 Campsites. Boat ramp, water, restrooms, showers, playground, electrical hookups, dump station & group pavilion. Exit 129, 6 m. W on SR 286. HOUSTON, MAP D-4: Cypress Creek. 9 Campsites. Boat ramp, water, restrooms & picnic sites. SR 113, 2 m. N. LITTLE ROCK, MAP D-4: Cooks Landing. No Campsites. Day use only. Boat ramp, water, vault toilet, fishing pier, picnic sites & group pavilion. I-430 & Crystal Hill Rd. Jct. Signs. LITTLE ROCK, MAP D-4: LaHarpe View. No Campsites. Picnic sites, water, restroom and fishing walk. South side of dam. LITTLE ROCK, MAP D-4: Murray Overlook. No Campsites. Picnic sites, water and restroom. South side of dam. LITTLE ROCK, MAP D-4: Maumelle. 44 Campsites. Boat ramp, water, restrooms, showers, dump station, playground, electrical hookups & pavilion. SR 10 W to old Penal Farm Road; 3 m. N. MORRILTON, MAP C-4: Cherokee. 26 Campsites. Boat ramp, water, restrooms, showers, dump station, playground, electrical hookups, picnic sites & group pavilion. SR 9, S to the river. Signs. MORRILTON, MAP C-4: Point Remove. 21 Campsites. Boat ramp, restrooms, showers & group pavilion. SR 9, S to SR 113. Signs. MORRILTON, MAP C-4: Sequoya. 14 Campsites. Boat ramp, water, restrooms, showers, playground, dump station, picnic sites & pavilion. SR 9, 4 m. S to Lock & Dam #9 access road, 1.6 m. W.

DARDANELLE-FORT SMITH
MAP C-1+2+3

The parks and campsites between Dardanelle and *Fort Smith* are listed individually under *Lake* Dardanelle and Ozark *Lake,* or can be found by name in the Index.

FLOAT STREAMS

Like Arkansas' legendary steamboats, canoes can run anywhere the ground is a little damp. Outfitters/shuttle services will provide information, transportation, canoes and equipment. Arkansas Parks and Tourism (One Capitol Mall, Little Rock, 72201) has more detailed information. The following streams (listed clockwise from NW, NE, SE and SW) are some of the more prominent ones offering scenic adventures for a few hours or a few days. Terms like beginner and intermediate are experience levels for normal floating conditions. Water conditions vary according to terrain, seasons and, most important, weather and hydroelectric generation (dams release millions of gallons of water, which can change a peaceful stream into a wide, swift-flowing river). Inquiring locally is not just advisable, it is critical. Always bring a change of clothes, and at all times wear a flotation device. Although the vast majority of streams are not life threatening, they do require some basic water skills and a lot of common sense. Some recommendations are: (1) Avoid a stream during flooding. (2) Walk the canoe through or around rapids if uncertain about conditions. (3) Wear shoes (tennis shoes are ideal). (4) If capsized, hang onto the canoe (it floats) and remain on the upstream side to avoid downstream obstacles. (5) Keep gear waterproof and as low as possible in the center of the canoe. (6) Carry spare paddles (one per person). (7) Camp at least four feet above water level.

UPPER WHITE RIVER
MAP A-2 & B-2

An excellent fishing and floating stream, it begins in Boston (near *St. Paul*) and is eventually impounded in several lakes in Arkansas and Missouri before exiting at Bull Shoals *Lake*. From Boston to east of Fayetteville the river changes constantly and is susceptible to flooding. Usually shaded by over-

hanging trees, the bank varies from a few feet to 30-foot bluffs with pastures and dense forests. Length: 31 miles. Access: SR 16 runs parallel to the river. No Services. Intermediate. (White River, BELOW)

 KINGS RIVER
MAP A-2 & B-2

Best floated April-June, the river has some of the finest gravel bars in NW Arkansas. From Boston (near *St. Paul*) to the Arkansas-Missouri border it flows through dense forests under overhanging bluffs. During the summer the river can usually be floated above US 62. The upper reaches can be extremely dangerous where the shoals are narrow and swift. From SR 221 at Trigger Gap near *Eureka Springs* to the US 62 bridge is the most popular stretch (12 miles). Length: 77 miles. Access: gravel roads, highways. Guide. Shuttle Services. Intermediate.

 BUFFALO RIVER
MAP A-3+4 & B-3+4

America's first national river (1972) is owned and maintained by the *National Park* Service. Beginning in the Boston Mountains near *St. Paul* and ending at the White River, the Buffalo is one of the few remaining river systems in Mid-America unobstructed by dams. It offers spectacular beauty highlighted by towering colorful bluffs, waterfalls, steep rock outcroppings and dense hardwood forests. The swimming, hiking, fishing and camping are outstanding. UPPER BUFFALO: The average drop of the river is 10 feet per mile. From *Ponca* to Pruitt there are steep drops, hairpin turns and swift chutes. Boulders choke the river in its upper reaches. Floatable during the summer only after a heavy rain (spring and fall best). Length: 68 miles. Access: low water bridges, state and county roads, canoe services. Numerous guides and shuttle services. Experienced. LOWER BUFFALO: A much more peaceful float stream, it drops three feet per mile and can be enjoyed all year. Length: 71 miles. Access: US 65, state and county roads; also Pruitt, *Gilbert,* Buffalo Point *(National Park)* and Rush *(Yellville).* Guides. Shuttle Services. Beginner.

MULBERRY RIVER
MAP B-2 & C-2

Considered to be the state's finest white-water float stream, it rises in the Boston Mountains and flows through the Ozarks to empty into the Arkansas River south of *Mulberry.* Falling 13 feet per mile, the river rushes past massive boulders, hairpin turns, choppy chutes and willow jungles. Bluffs, rocky canyons and dense forest line its course. Seasons: October-June between SR 103 and US 64; July-October between SR 23 and US 64. CAUTION: Avoid camping on gravel bars and islands; the river can rise several feet in a short period. Length: 55 miles. Access: numerous. Occasional shuttle service at Turner Bend (SR 23 bridge, *Cass).* Expert.

BIG PINEY CREEK
MAP C-3

Picturesque but dangerous for the inexperienced, this white-water float stream needs a gauge-reading from the U.S Corps of Engineers in Little Rock. WARNING: Long Pool below two feet is unnavigable; above three is unsafe. Beginning above Long Pool Campground in the Ozark *National Forest,* it cuts through deep canyons, narrow valleys and boulder-strewn rapids past high bluffs and dense forests. Best floated during spring and fall. Length: 67 miles. No Services. Most canoeists use Long Pool for a base camp and then float sections (SR 7, 2 m. W on FR 1801; N on FR 1804 appx. 2 m.). ABOVE LONG POOL: Hurricane Creek to Jack Phillips Ford, appx. 3 hrs. Jack Phillips Ford to Long Pool, 6-8 hrs. BELOW LONG POOL: Long Pool to SR 164, appx. 3 hrs. CAUTION: Inexperienced canoeists should not float Big Piney above Long Pool. Expert.

WHITE RIVER
MAP BEGINS A-4 & ENDS N-3

Claimed to be one of the finest year-round fishing and float streams in Arkansas, it flows from *Bull Shoals* to the Mississippi River near Arkansas Post *(National Park).* The first 100 miles from Fairview (south of Bull Shoals) to Batesville offers the best floating and is characterized by bends, riffles, shoals and pools surrounded by forests, rock overhangs and hillsides. Excellent trout fishing. After Batesville, it becomes

mostly a "flatland" river. CAUTION: Bull Shoals Dam periodically releases water, causing the river to become extremely wide and swift. Inquire Locally. Access: public launch ramps, boat docks, gravel roads and paved highways. Guides. Shuttle Services. Beginner. (Upper White River, ABOVE)

STRAWBERRY RIVER
MAP I-2 & J-3

Sometimes isolated, always at a constant current, it begins near Viola (west of Wiseman on SR 354) and empties into the Black River below Shirley-Rainey Brake *Wildlife Management Area.* The 110-mile stretch from Viola to the Black River is easily traveled except near Poughkeepsie during the summer. Between Poughkeepsie and Jessup is prime smallmouth bass fishing. Dense foliage, pasture, gravel bars and sand beaches. Access: gravel roads, state highways. No Services. Beginner.

SPRING RIVER
MAP I-2+3

Fed by Mammoth Spring *(State Park)* on the Arkansas-Missouri border (36 million gallons a day), this cold water stream flows into the Black River at *Black Rock.* The upper portion (23 miles) between Mammoth and Hardy offers good year-round floating with occasional stair-step shoals, excellent trout fishing and scenic banks lined with hardwood forests. Limited access and guide/shuttle service except in the Hardy or Mammoth Springs areas. Intermediate.

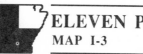

ELEVEN POINT RIVER
MAP I-3

Kept high enough for year-round floating by 11 principal tributaries, it flows from the Arkansas-Missouri border to the Spring River at *Black Rock.* Dense foliage and wildflowers, steep sand and gravel banks characterize the river. CAUTION: Rock dams can come up unexpectedly. Length: 40 miles. Access: five bridges along its course and guide/shuttle service at Dalton. Beginner.

LITTLE RED RIVER
MAP J-1 & K-1+2

From the base of Greers Ferry Dam near *Heber Springs,* it flows through the deep foothills and spectacular scenery of the eastern Ozarks, merging with the White River (ABOVE) at Hurricane Lake *Wildlife Management Area.* Best floated from the dam (excellent trout fishing) to Ramsey Public Access east of *Pangburn,* this usually peaceful year-round stream is controlled by water released for electrical generation and can become swift and dangerous in spots. Check with the Corps of

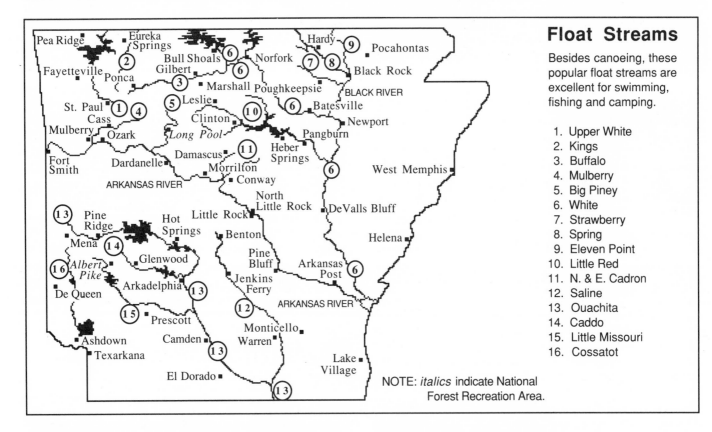

Float Streams

Besides canoeing, these popular float streams are excellent for swimming, fishing and camping.

1. Upper White
2. Kings
3. Buffalo
4. Mulberry
5. Big Piney
6. White
7. Strawberry
8. Spring
9. Eleven Point
10. Little Red
11. N. & E. Cadron
12. Saline
13. Ouachita
14. Caddo
15. Little Missouri
16. Cossatot

NOTE: *italics* indicate National Forest Recreation Area.

Engineers at Greers Ferry. Length: 29 miles. Access: boat docks and public launch ramps. Guides. Shuttle Services. Beginner (unless generating). MIDDLE FORK: Above Greers Ferry *Lake* between *Leslie* and Shirley, this 30-mile stretch is characterized by a sharp fall with a series of rapids. Very swift after a heavy rain. Intermediate. SOUTH FORK: Above Greers Ferry *Lake* between Scotland and *Clinton,* it has 13 miles of outstanding smallmouth bass fishing. Scenic. Beginner.

 CADRON CREEK
MAP K-1 & L-1

In a southwest arc from the Faulkner-Van Buren County line (E of Damascus on US 65 N) to the Arkansas River, it flows by tall bluffs, rock outcroppings and dense forests, passing through quiet pools, swift rapids and sharp bends. Dangerous after a heavy rain. Low during the summer. Length: 39 miles. Access: gravel roads, paved highways and bridges. No Services. Intermediate.

OTHER NORTH STREAMS
MAP NW QUARTER

LEE CREEK: Devil's Den *State Park* (Map B-1) to *Ft. Smith* (through Oklahoma). It can be extremely dangerous. Spring Only. ILLINOIS RIVER: near Farmington (Map A-1) to near *Siloam Springs.* WAR EAGLE CREEK: Old Alabam (Map A-2) to *War Eagle.* Spring Only. CROOKED CREEK: Platt

(Map A-4) to *Yellville.* Spring Only.

 SALINE RIVER
MAP E-4, F-4, G-5 & H-5

The only free-flowing stream in the Ouachita Basin rises as three forks (North, Alum and Middle) in the eastern foothills of the Ouachita Mountains (between *Lake Ouachita* and *Lake Winona*) to flow south as one river from NW of *Benton,* joining the Ouachita River (BELOW) at Felsenthal *National Wildlife Refuge.* Except for the upper reaches, which generally run shallow, it is a year-round float stream with excellent smallmouth bass fishing (Benton to Jenkins Ferry State Park is most popular) and mostly "flatland" scenery that is isolated with tree-lined banks. Length: 204 miles. Access: gravel roads, highways and public launch ramps. No Services. Beginner (intermediate in upper reaches).

 **OUACHITA RIVER**
MAP BEGINS E-1 & ENDS H-5

Rising north of *Mena,* it flows east through the Ouachita Mountains to be checked by several dams and then continues south as a "flatland" river from *Malvern* to Louisiana. The 45-mile section between *Pine Ridge* and *Lake* Ouachita begins as a narrow stream of rapids that widens into deep pools, offering excellent smallmouth bass fishing. Best floated during spring and fall, the river winds past towering bluffs and dense forests.

Access: SR 88; located in the Ouachita *National Forest;* well-marked landing sites are provided by the park service. Flatboats and shuttle services: Pencil Bluff (12 m. E of Pine Ridge). Length: 45 miles. Beginner.

 ## CADDO RIVER
MAP E-2 & F-2+3

An unpredictable mountain stream, it should be investigated before floated. Usually floated during spring from Norman to west of Glenwood (6 m. run), Glenwood to near DeGray *Lake* (8 m. run) at other times. Access: along the highway. Shuttle Services. Beginner.

 ## LITTLE MISSOURI RIVER
MAP E-2, F-2+3 & G-3

Rugged and remote, this springtime float stream has spectacular scenery, complex rapids, a willow jungle and occasionally four-foot standing waves that can swamp open canoes. Most popular section: from Albert Pike Recreation Area (Ouachita *National Forest*) to the US 70 bridge near *Lake* Greeson. WARNING: During high water this stream can be dangerous. Inquire Locally. Length: 20 miles. Expert from Albert Pike Recreation Area to SR 84 bridge; intermediate from SR 84 bridge to US 70 bridge.

 ## COSSATOT RIVER
MAP E-1, G-1 & F-1

Beginning near *Mena* and joining the Little River near Millwood *Lake,* its course is checked by Gillham *Lake,* which also divides white water from calm. Length: 87 miles. Winter and early spring. Inquire Locally. ABOVE GILLHAM LAKE: Falling rapidly, it cuts through a narrow gorge characterized by jagged rocks, cascading waterfalls, long rapids and quiet pools. Scenic mountain vistas (Cossatot River Natural Area, *Umpire),* dense pine forests and excellent smallmouth bass fishing. The Duckett Ford area is best for kayaks. Length: appx. 22 miles. Access: numerous. No Services. WARNING: Only well-equipped, experienced canoeists should float the upper Cossatot. BELOW GILLHAM LAKE: The river gradually loses its mountain identity, becoming a peaceful stream winding through the flatlands. Length: appx. 22 miles. Access: numerous. No Services. Intermediate.

 ## OTHER SOUTH STREAMS
MAP F-2 & G-2

Dropping steeply from Dierks *Lake* to Millwood *Lake,* the Lower Saline River provides short stretches of floating with white water during certain times. Inquire Locally. WARNING: The upper reaches are seasonally unpredictable. Expert.

LAKES

Arkansas' 600,000 acres of lakes range from mountain settings to swamps, and from impounded rivers to spring-fed reservoirs. The White River National Wildlife Refuge alone has over 169 small lakes; the Corps of Engineers administers 16 large projects totaling nearly 4,000 miles of shoreline. These agencies along with state parks, the U.S. Forest Service, the Arkansas Game and Fish Commission and municipalities administer most of these recreational facilities. Some large lakes in Arkansas are private. Make certain the lake is public before entering and be sure to have the appropriate license. Take time to find out what restrictions, if any, apply to recreation. Keep a close watch on children. Never swim alone. Below are listed the most notable of Arkansas' public lakes that are 300 acres and larger. NOTE: All lakes are listed alphabetically without the use of "lake" in the name. The smaller black states are locaters for lakes described elsewhere. Abbreviations used in the subject headings: M (Miles), NF (National Forest), NWR (National Wildlife Refuge), SP (State Park), R (River) and WMA (Wildlife Management Area).

ASHBAUGH
SEE DAVE DONALDSON-BLACK R. WMA

ATKINS
SEE ATKINS

ATLANTA
SEE ROGERS

AUSTELL
SEE VILLAGE CREEK SP

BAILEY
SEE PETIT JEAN SP

BEAR CREEK
SEE ST. FRANCIS NF, MARIANNA

BEAVER
SHORE 449 M.   ALT. 1,130   MAP A-2

This newest Arkansas Corps of Engineers' lake was completed in 1966 for the purpose of flood control, hydroelectric power and recreation. Created by damming the White *River (Float Streams)* in an Ozark Mountain valley, the lake is surrounded by rock bluffs and outcroppings as well as rugged terrain and thick forests. Paved roads lead to nine parks and *campgrounds* and seven boat docks that provide access to fishing, hunting, boating, swimming, camping, picnicking, spelunking, water skiing, hiking and scuba diving. (WARNING: The water is cold, turbulent & extremely deep.) Scattered around the lake, designed for easy walking, are seven nature *trails* offering panoramic views, rock bluffs and shelters, wildflowers, shrubs, mixed hardwoods, an old homesite, benches for rest stops and restrooms. Trails vary in length from five hours to 20 minutes and have interpretive markers. Fishing includes a wide variety: bass (white, large & smallmouth), crappie, bream, channel catfish, northern pike and walleye. Game in season is generally deer, wild turkey, quail, rabbit and squirrel. Resident Engineer, P.O. Drawer H, Rogers, 72756. Directions to the following parks and *campgrounds* are from the capitalized town. EUREKA SPRINGS: Dam Site has 56 campsites with electrical hookups, water, restrooms, boat ramps, dump station, showers, swimming & overlook. US 62, 9 m. W; SR 187, 2.5 m. to dam. EUREKA SPRINGS: Starkey has 32 campsites with electrical hookups, water, restrooms, playground, boat dock & ramp. US 62, 4 m. W; SR 187, 7 m. to paved access road. GATEWAY: Indian Creek has 39 campsites with boat ramp, water, restrooms & swimming. US 62, 1.5 m. E; 5 m. S on gravel access road. GARFIELD: Lost Bridge has 80 campsites with electrical hookups, water, restrooms, boat dock & ramp, swimming, youth group camp area & playground. SR 127, 5 m. SE. ROGERS: Horseshoe Bend has 115 campsites with electrical hookups, water, restrooms, showers, boat dock & ramp, swimming & playground. SR 94, 8 m. E. ROGERS: Prairie Creek has 108 campsites with electrical hookups, water, restrooms, showers, boat dock & ramp, trailer & marine dump stations, swimming & playground. SR 12, 3.3 m. E; 1 m. on access road. ROGERS: Rocky Branch has 50 campsites with electrical hookups, water, restrooms, showers, trailer & marine dump stations, swimming & playground. SR 12, 11 m. E; SR 303, 4.5 m. NW to paved access road. SPRINGDALE: Hickory Creek has 38 campsites with electrical hookups, water, restroom, showers, boat dock & ramp, swimming, playground, trailer & marine dump stations. US 71, 4 m. N, SR 264, 7 m. E. SPRINGDALE: War Eagle has 22 campsites with electrical hookups, water, restrooms, boat dock & ramp, swimming & dump station. SR 68, 10 m. E; 3 m. N on paved access road.

BEAVER FORK
SEE CONWAY

BENNETT
SEE WOOLLY HOLLOW SP

BIG
SEE BIG LAKE NWR

BIRD
SEE PINE BLUFF

BLUE MOUNTAIN
SHORE 50 M.   ALT. 387   MAP D-2

Spread out 2,400 feet below *Magazine Mountain*, this lake was created by damming the Petit Jean River in 1947 for the primary purpose of flood control but it also provides recreation and five parks and *campgrounds*. Deer, rabbits and squirrels are hunted in season. Fishing: largemouth, spotted and white bass as well as bream and crappie. A good area for hiking *(trails)*, there are over 300 species of birds, colorful rocks and a variety of minerals. Swimming, scuba diving and boating are also popular. Park Manager, Waveland, 72867. Directions to the following parks and *campgrounds* are from the capitalized town. BLUE MOUNTAIN: Ashley Creek has 8 campsites with boat ramp, water, restrooms, dump station & group pavilion (7 tent-only campsites). 1.5 m. S on gravel access road. SUGAR GROVE: Hise Hill has 8 campsites with boat ramp, water, restrooms & group pavilion (6 tent-only campsites). SR 217, 2 m. E. WAVELAND: Lick Creek has 5 campsites with boat ramp, water, restrooms & group pavilion (3 tent-only campsites). SR 309, 5m. S. WAVELAND:

Outlet Area has 27 campsites with water, restrooms, dump station & overlook pavilion. SR 309, appx. 3 m. S; below dam on Petit Jean River. WAVELAND: Waveland Park has 49 campsites with electrical hookups, boat ramp, restrooms, water, dump station & group pavilion. SR 309, 1 m. S; 1 m. paved access road.

BREWER
SEE CONWAY

BULL SHOALS
SHORE 740 M.   ALT. 708   MAP A-3+4

Created by damming the White River *(Float Streams)*, it was dedicated in 1952 by President Harry S. Truman for flood control, hydroelectric power and recreation. Located in the center of the Ozarks, this fifth largest concrete dam in America is ringed with rugged terrain, rocky bluffs, unusual rock formations, forests and cedar glades. Nationally known as the home of "lunker bass" (up to 12 pounds), the lake also has crappie, channel catfish, bream and walleye as well as brown and rainbow trout in the White River below the dam. Commercial docks have boats, motors and guides for hire. For hunters there are deer, rabbit and squirrel along with duck, quail and wild turkey. Other popular recreation includes swimming, water skiing, hiking, and scuba. (WARNING: The water is deep, cold & turbulent.) Of the 21 state and federal parks and *campgrounds* in the area (Bull Shoals Lake *State Park)*, the Corps of Engineers administers 10. Resident Engineer, Bx. 369, Mountain Home, 72653. Directions to the following parks and *campgrounds* are from the capitalized town. BULL SHOALS: Bull Shoals has 12 campsites with electrical hookups, boat ramp & dock, water, restrooms & marine dump station. SR 178, just W of town. BULL SHOALS: Dam Site has 35 campsites with electrical hookups, restrooms, boat ramp, water, dump station, playground, basketball court & swimming beach. 1 m. SW at the dam. BULL SHOALS: Point Return has 22 campsites with boat ramp, restrooms, water, dump stations, change shelter, swimming beach & group pavilion. NE of town on paved access road. LAKEVIEW: Lakeview has 97 campsites with electrical hookups, boat ramp & dock, water, showers, restroom, dump station, group pavilion, playground and swimming beach. SR 178, N of town. LEAD HILL: Lead Hill has 78 campsites with electrical hookups, boat ramp & dock, water, restrooms, trailer & marine dump stations, heated fishing dock, restaurant, swimming beach, change shelter, group pavilion & playground. SR 7, 4 m. N. LEAD HILL: Tucker Hollow has 30 campsites with electrical hookups, boat ramp & dock, water, restrooms, trailer & marine dump stations, change shelter, swimming beach & playground. SR 14, 7 m. N; SR 281, 3 m. N. OAKLAND: Oakland offers 35 campsites with electrical hookups, boat ramp & dock, water, restrooms, trailer dump station, change shelters, swimming beach, restaurant, group pavilion & playground. SR 202, 4 m. W. OAKLAND: Ozark Isle has 106 campsites with boat ramps, water, restrooms, showers, group camp area, swimming beach, change shelter, group pavilion, playground & boat dock nearby. SR 202, appx. 4.5 m. W. PEEL: Highway 125 has 38 campsites with electrical hookups, boat ramp & dock, water, restrooms, trailer & marine dump stations, group pavilion, swimming beach & playground. SR 125, 5 m. N. PROTEM, MISSOURI: Buck Creek (in Arkansas) has electrical hookups, boat ramp & dock, water, restrooms, dump station, change shelter, swimming beach, showers, group pavilion & playground. SR 125, 5.5 m. S.

CALION
SEE CALION

CANE CREEK
SEE STAR CITY

CATHERINE
SEE LAKE CATHERINE SP

CHARLES
SEE LAKE CHARLES SP

CHICOT
SEE LAKE CHICOT SP

CONWAY
SEE CAMP ROBINSON WMA

COVE
SEE OZARK NF, PARIS

COX CREEK
ACRES 350   ALT. 220   MAP F-4

Stocked by the Arkansas Game and Fish Commission, the lake offers bluegill, catfish, crappie and bass. Camping and swimming areas provided. Signs, SR 46 at Leola.

CRAIGHEAD FOREST
SEE JONESBORO

DARDANELLE
SHORE 315 M.   ALT. 338   MAP C-3

Completed in 1969 as a part of the 445-mile McClellan-Kerr *Arkansas River* Navigational System (from near Tulsa, Ok., to the Mississippi River), the lake was created by two dams (Ozark Lake) on the Arkansas River. Locks at either end work in stair-step fashion, raising or lowering the water inside the lock to match the level where river traffic is entering or exiting. An explanation and opportunity to watch the procedure is available at the Arkansas River Visitor Center *(Russellville)*. Only two miles wide at its maximum and 50 miles long, it is

one of the most accessible in the state. Fishing includes largemouth and white bass, catfish, bream and crappie. Nearby Ozark and Ouachita *National Forests* offer hunters deer, turkey and wild boar as well as providing hikers excellent *trails*. Along the length of the lake are 12 parks and *campgrounds*, all of which have water and restrooms. Resident Engineer, Bx. 1078, Russellville, 72801. Directions to the following parks and *campgrounds* are from the capitalized town. CLARKSVILLE: Spadra has 30 campsites with electrical hookups, boat ramp & dock, water, restroom, showers & group pavilion. SR 103, 2 m. S to Jamestown; 1 m. S on access road. DARDANELLE: Riverview has 17 campsites with overlook, water & restrooms. N .7 m. on paved road to dam. DELAWARE: Delaware has 13 campsites with boat ramp, water, restrooms, overlook & group pavilion. SR 22, .3 m E; SR 393, 2.5 m. N. DUBLIN: Dublin has no campsites. Boat ramp, water & restrooms. SR 197, 3.5 m. E. HARTMAN: Horsehead has 10 campsites with boat ramp, water, restrooms & group pavilion. US 64, 1 m. E; SR 194, 2 m. E; 1.7 m. S on access road. KNOXVILLE: Cabin Creek has 9 campsites with boat ramp, water, restrooms & group pavilions. 1.5 m. W on paved access road. NEW BLAINE: Shoal Bay has 54 campsites with electrical hookups, boat ramp & dock, trailer & marine dumping stations, restrooms, group pavilion, amphitheater and Bridge Rock Nature *Trail*. PARIS: O'Kane has no campsites. Boat ramp, water, restrooms & group pavilion. SR 309, 6 m. N. PINEY: Flat Rock has 15 campsites with boat ramp, water, restrooms and group pavilions. US 65, .7 m. E; SR 359, .5 m. N; .7 m. W on access road. PINEY: Piney Bay (north of river) has 39 campsites with electrical hookups, water, restrooms, dump station, amphitheater & group pavilion. US 64, .7 m. E; SR 359, 4 m. N. RUSSELLVILLE: Old Post Road Park has 16 campsites, with boat ramp, water, restrooms, dump station, tennis court, basketball court, playground, baseball field, soccer-football field, group pavilions, Information Center & Arkansas River Visitor Center. SR 7, appx. 2 m. N of river, W on SR 7 spur for 1.3 m. SCRANTON: Cane Creek has 14 campsites with boat ramp, water, restrooms & group pavilion. SR 197, 3.5 m. N; 2 m. N on paved road.

DE QUEEN
SHORE 32 M.   ALT. 437   MAP F-1

Located on the Rolling Fork River, the dam was completed in 1977 for flood control, water supply, recreation, and fish and wildlife conservation. Rugged ridges bordering the lake are heavily forested with hardwoods and pine that typify the Tri-Lakes area (Dierks & Gillham *Lakes*). The Corps of Engineers provide seven parks and *campgrounds* for boating, skiing, scuba diving, picnicking, hiking, fishing and hunting. Fishing offers bass (largemouth, smallmouth, spotted, black & white), crappie (black & white), catfish (channel & flathead), walleye and various species of sunfish. The nearby hunting includes quail, dove, turkey, squirrel, rabbit and deer. Park Manager,

Tri-Lakes, Rt. 1, Bx. 358C, De Queen, 71832. Directions to the following parks and *campgrounds* are from the capitalized town. DE QUEEN: Glen Canyon has no campsites. Picnic sites & restrooms. US 71, 3 m. N; 4 m. on gravel access road. DE QUEEN: Oak Grove has 36 campsites with electrical hookups, boat ramp, water, restrooms, showers, dump station, playground, swimming beach & amphitheater. US 71, 3 m. N; 5 m. W on gravel access road. DE QUEEN: Oak Grove Landing (day use only) has no campsites. Boat ramp, swimming beach, restrooms & fishing berm. US 71, 3 m. N; 5 m. W on gravel access road; .5 m. on county road (signs). DE QUEEN: Pine Ridge has 45 campsites with boat ramp, water, restrooms, showers, dump station & amphitheater. US 71, 3 m. N; 5 m. W on gravel access; 2 m. N on county road. DE QUEEN: Story Creek has no campsites. Boat ramp, water, group pavilion, restrooms, swimming beach & 6 picnic sites. US 71, 3 m. N, 2 m. W on gravel access road; 1 m. N on county road. GILLHAM: Bellah Mine has 20 campsites with boat ramp, water, restroom & 4 picnic sites. US 71, 2 m. S; 5 m. W on Bellah Mine Rd. GILLHAM: Rolling Fork Landing has no campsites. Boat ramp, water, restrooms, group pavilion, swimming beach & 6 picnic sites. US 71, 2 m. S; 4 m. W on Bellah Mine Rd.

DEGRAY
SHORE 207 M.   ALT. 408   MAP F-3

Completed in 1972 for hydroelectric power and recreation, the lake was created by using nearly seven million cubic yards of compacted earth-fill to dam the Caddo River just a few miles above the Ouachita River *(Float Streams)*. In addition to the 1,000-acre DeGray *State Park,* the Corps of Engineers' area provides 16 parks and *campgrounds,* including 200 acres of remote camping, boating, swimming, hiking *trails* and fishing for several species of bass (also "hybrid fighting" bass), crappie and catfish (channel, blue & flathead). Resource Manager, No. 30 I.P. Circle, Arkadelphia, 71932. Directions to the following parks and *campgrounds* are from the capitalized town. ALPINE: Alpine Ridge has 49 campsites with electrical hookups, boat ramp, water, trailer dump station, heated showers, 4 picnic sites & day-use area. SR 8, 10 m. E. ALPINE: Brushy Creek has 55 campsites with boat ramp, 4 picnic sites & restrooms. SR 8, 7.5 m. E. ALPINE: Ozan Point has 50 campsites with boat ramp, restrooms, water, 4 picnic sites & day-use area. SR 8, 12 m. E. AMITY: Amity Landing has no campsites. Boat ramp, water, restrooms & 6 sheltered picnic sites. SR 84, 5 m. E; SR 364, 3 m. S. AMITY: Cox Creek has 53 campsites with boat ramp, restrooms & 5 picnic sites. SR 84, 5 m. N; SR 346, 4 m. S. ARKADELPHIA: Caddo Drive has 72 campsites with electrical hookups, boat ramp, restrooms, heated showers, playground, swimming beach, dump station, day-use pavilion & 30 picnic sites. SR 7, 15 m. N to Ore's One Stop; 3 m. W on gravel access road. ARKADELPHIA: Edgewood has 51 campsites with electrical hookups, heated showers, restrooms, water & dump station.

SR 7, 15 m. N to Ore's One Stop; 4 m. W on gravel access road. ARKADELPHIA: Lakeview has no campsites. Water, chemical toilet, 32 picnic sites & day-use pavilion. SR 7, 8 m. N. BISMARK: Arlie Moore has 87 campsites with electrical hookups, boat ramp, restrooms, dump station, heated showers, playground, pavilion, swimming beaches, 20 picnic sites & day-use area. SR 7, 4 m. S to Oak Bower Community; 2 m. W on paved access road. CADDO VALLEY: Iron Mountain has 69 campsites with restrooms, electrical hookups, water, boat ramp, dump station, heated showers, 25 picnic sites, playground & day-use area. CADDO VALLEY: Lower Lake has no campsites. Boat ramp, water, restrooms, 7

It took seven million cubic yards of dirt to dam the Caddo River for DeGray Lake

sheltered picnic sites & group pavilion. SR 7, 1 m. N; SR 390, 2 m. W. CADDO VALLEY: Spillway has no campsites. Boat ramp, restroom, water & 27 picnic sites. SR 7, 3.3 m. N; W to the dam. LAMBERT: Lenox Marcus has 200 acres of remote camping, boat ramp, water, restrooms & 30 picnic sites. SR 84, 3 m. S. LAMBERT: Oak Bower is for group use only and has 8 cabins, kitchen/dining hall, restroom, showers, playground & electricity. Reservation Only. POINT CEDAR: Point Cedar has 62 campsites with boat ramp, water, restrooms, 9 picnic sites & day-use area. 2 m. S on paved access road. POINT CEDAR: Shouse Ford has 100 campsites with electrical hookups, boat ramp, water, restrooms, dump station, heated showers, playground, 25 picnic sites, swimming beach & day-use area. 2 m. S on paved access road.

# DES ARC
SEE DES ARC

DIERKS
SHORE 33 M.   ALT. 526   MAP F-1

Completed in 1975 on the Saline River *(Float Streams),* the dam is used for flood control, water supply, recreation, and fish and wild life conservation. Like the other Tri-Lakes area environment (De Queen & Gillham *Lakes)* the lake is ringed with rugged ridges, hardwoods and pine. The Corps of Engineers provides three parks and *campgrounds* for boating, skiing, swimming, fishing and hunting. Most of the lake fish are found in the downstream area and include: bass (smallmouth, largemouth & spotted), crappie, catfish (channel & flathead), walleye and sunfish. Hunting offers deer, quail, dove, waterfowl, rabbit and squirrel. Park Manager, Tri-Lakes, Rt.1, Bx. 358C, De Queen, 71832. Directions to the following parks and *campgrounds* are from the capitalized town. DIERKS: Blue Ridge has 22 campsites with boat ramp, restrooms & swimming beach. US 70, 3 m. N; SR 4, 4 m. N; 3 m. W on gravel road. DIERKS: Horseshoe Bend has 11 campsites with swimming beach, restrooms, pavilion & change house. US 70, 2 m. W; 4 m. NW on paved road. DIERKS: Jefferson Ridge has 84 campsites with water, boat ramp, pavilion, electrical hookups, showers & swimming beach. US 70, 2 m. W; 7 m. NW on paved road.

DUNN
SEE VILLAGE CREEK SP

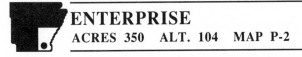
ENTERPRISE
ACRES 350   ALT. 104   MAP P-2

The lake is stocked by the Arkansas Game and Fish Commission with bluegill, catfish, crappie and bass. Skiing Allowed. US 165 at Wilmont.

ERLING
SEE LAFAYETTE COUNTY WMA

FAYETTEVILLE
SEE FAYETTEVILLE

FELSENTHAL
SEE FELSENTHAL NWR

FORT SMITH
SEE LAKE FORT SMITH SP

FRIERSON
SEE LAKE FRIERSON SP

GILLHAM
SHORE 32 M.   ALT. 502   MAP F-1

A part of the Tri-Lakes area (De Queen & Dierks *Lakes*), the dam was built on the Cossatot River *(Float Streams)* for flood control, water supply, and fish and game conservation. Although recreation was included as an incidental, the lake now offers fishing, hunting, boating, skiing, swimming and four parks and *campgrounds*. Most of the lake fish are found in the downstream area and include: bass (smallmouth, largemouth, white & spotted), crappie, catfish (channel & flathead), walleye and sunfish. Hunting offers deer, quail, dove, waterfowl, rabbit and squirrel. Park Manager, Tri-Lakes, Rt.1, Bx. 358C, De Queen, 71832. Directions to the following parks and *campgrounds* are from the capitalized town. GILLHAM: Coon Creek offers 21 campsites with boat ramp, water, restrooms, swimming beach & playground. 6 miles NE via county road. GILLHAM: Cossatot Point has no campsites. Restrooms, picnic sites & boat ramps. 6 m. NE via county road. GILLHAM: Cossatot Reefs has 30 campsites with water, electrical hookups, restrooms & showers. 6 m. NE via county road. GILLHAM: Little Coon Creek has no campsites. Boat ramp. 6 m. NE via county road; appx. 3 m. N on paved/gravel road.

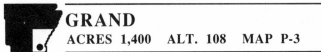
GRAND
ACRES 1,400   ALT. 108   MAP P-3

This oxbow lake, formerly a part of the Mississippi River, offers fishing for bluegill, catfish, crappie, bass and sunfish. SR 8, 4 m. E of Eudora.

GREENLEE
SEE BRINKLEY

GREERS FERRY
SHORE 276 M.   ALT. 461   MAP K-1

Dedicated by President John F. Kennedy in 1963, this dam on the Little Red River *(Float Streams)* was created for flood control, hydroelectric power and recreation. Located in the eastern foothills of the Ozarks, set in the shadow of both Round and Sugar Loaf Mountains, the lake provides 15 parks and *campgrounds* for boating, swimming, water skiing, hiking (Mossy Bluff, Sugar Loaf & Buckeye *Trails),* picnicking and scuba. (WARNING: The water is extremely deep, cold & turbulent.) Every game fish native to Arkansas is stocked, including walleye, bream, channel catfish, bass (largemouth & white) and rainbow trout (also below the dam). Commercial boat docks rent boats and motors. The area around the lake offers hunters deer, quail, duck, geese, squirrel, rabbit and wild turkey. For other attractions (the Visitor Center, National Fish Hatchery, Dam and Powerhouse Tour) see *Heber Springs.* Resident Engineer, Bx. 310, Heber Springs, 72543. Directions to the following parks and *campgrounds* are from the capitalized town. BROWNSVILLE: Cherokee has 33 campsites with boat ramp, water, restrooms & swimming beaches. 4.5 m. S on paved access road. CHOCTAW: Choctaw has 146 campsites with electrical hookups, boat dock and ramps, water, restrooms, swimming beach, dump station, group pavilion & playground. SR 33, 3.7 m. E. CLINTON: South Fork has 13 campsites with water & restrooms. SR 16, 2 m. E; 7 m. SE on gravel access road. GREERS FERRY: Devil's Fork has 55

Greers Ferry Lake was dedicated by President John F. Kennedy in 1963

---

campsites with boat ramp, water, restrooms, dump station, swimming beach, playground & pavilion. SR 16, .5 m. N. GREERS FERRY: Narrows has 60 campsites with electrical hookups, boat dock & ramp, water, restrooms, dump station & 2 pavilions. SR 16, 2.5 m. SW. GREERS FERRY: Sugar Loaf has 95 campsites with electrical hookups, boat dock & ramp, water, restrooms, dump station, swimming beach, playground & pavilion. SR 92, 6 m. W; SR 337, 1.5 m. W. GREERS FERRY: Mill Creek has 39 campsites with boat ramp, water, restrooms, swimming beach & group pavilion.

SR 92, appx. 5 m. SW; 3 m. N on gravel access. GREERS FERRY: Shiloh has 116 campsites with water, electrical hookups, trailer & marine dump stations, water, restrooms, playground, boat dock & ramp. SR 110, 3.5 m. SE. HEBER SPRINGS: Dam Site has 269 campsites with electrical hookups, boat dock & ramp, water, restrooms, trailer & marine dump stations, swimming beach, cold showers, playground, amphitheater and pavilion (200 capacity/by reservation only). SR 25, 3 m. N. HEBER SPRINGS: Heber Springs has 142 campsites with boat dock & ramp, water, electrical hookups, restrooms, trailer & marine dump stations, playground, cold showers, swimming beaches & pavilion. SR 110, 2 m. W; .5 m. N on paved access road. HEBER SPRINGS: John F. Kennedy has 50 campsites with electrical hookups, water, restrooms, dump station, warm showers and boat ramp. PEARSON: Cove Creek has 65 campsites with boat ramp, water, restrooms, swimming beach & group pavilion. SR 16, 3 m. NW; .3 m. NE on paved access road. SHIRLEY: Van Buren has 65 campsites with boat dock & ramps, water, restrooms, trailer & marine dump stations, swimming beach & pavilion. SR 16, 2 m. S; SR 330, 5 m. S. TUMBLING SHOALS: Old Highway 25 has 100 campsites with water, restrooms, boat ramps, electrical hookups, dump station, swimming beach, group camp area & group pavilions. SR 25; 3 m. W.

GREESON
SHORE 70 M.   ALT. 504   MAP F-2

In the southernmost part of the Ouachita Mountains, on the Little Missouri River *(Float Streams),* a dam was built (1950) for flood control, hydroelectric power, wildlife conservation and recreation. Around the lake are rock outcroppings and ridges, dense pine forests, islands, long peninsulas and crystal-clear water that provide opportunities for hiking, boating, swimming, scuba, fishing, and hunting. Nearby Daisy *State Park* offers the Cinnabar Mine Trail and the Bear Creek Cycle Trails (O.R.V. trail). Below the dam are rainbow trout; above are bass (largemouth, smallmouth, spotted & white), bluegill, crappie (black & white) and catfish (channel & flathead). Hunters find rabbit, squirrel, quail, wild turkey, deer, mallards, teal and wood duck. The Corps of Engineers provides 12 parks and *campgrounds.* Resource Manager, Lake Greeson, Murfreesboro, 71958. Directions to the following parks and *campgrounds* are from the capitalized town. DAISY: Self Creek has 119 campsites with boat rental, dock & ramp, showers, restrooms, water, 75 picnic sites & swimming beach. US 70, 1 m. W. KIRBY: Bear Creek has 36 campsites with boat ramp, water, restrooms, 18 picnic sites & Bear Creek Cycle Trail. SR 27, .5 m. S; 1.7 m. W on access road. KIRBY: Cowhide Cove has 77 campsites with water & electrical hookups, boat ramp, restrooms, showers, dump station, 3 picnic sites, hiking & O.R.V. trails. SR 27, 6 m. S; 2 m. W on access road. KIRBY: Kirby Landing has 152 campsites with electrical hookups, boat dock & ramp, water, showers,

restrooms, dump station, 20 picnic sites, swimming beach bathhouse, hiking & Bear Creek Cycle Trail. US 70, 2.5 m. W; 1.3 m. S on access road. KIRBY: Laurel Creek has 34 campsites with boat ramp, water, restroom, 5 picnic sites, hiking & Bear Creek Cycle Trail. SR 27, 5.3 m. S; 4 m. W on gravel access road. MURFREESBORO: Buckhorn has 30 campsites with water, restrooms & 3 picnic sites. SR 19, 6 m. N; 3 m. NW from dam; 2 m. E on gravel access road. MURFREESBORO: Narrows Dam Site has 58 campsites with electrical hookups, boat rental, dock & ramp, dump station, restrooms, water, showers, 34 picnic sites, swimming area & hiking *trails.* SR 19, 6 m. N. MURFREESBORO: Parker Creek has 49 campsites with boat ramp, restrooms, water, 13 picnic sites & hiking *trails.* SR 19, 6 m. N; 6 m. NW from dam on gravel road. MURFREESBORO: Pikeville has 18 campsites with water, restrooms, 4 picnic sites & hiking *trails.* SR 19, 6 m. N; 2 m. NW from dam, 2 m. E on gravel access road. NEWHOPE: Highway 70 Landing has no campsites. Boat dock & ramp, water & 3 picnic sites. US 70, 4 m. E. NEWHOPE: Star of the West has 46 campsites with water, restrooms & 4 picnic sites. US 70, appx 3 m. E.

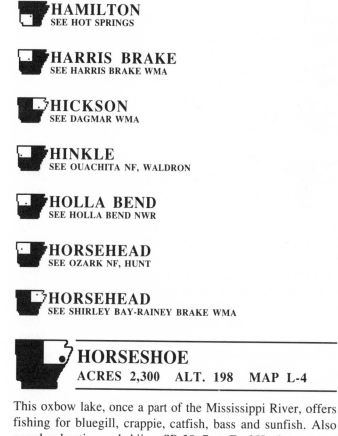

HAMILTON
SEE HOT SPRINGS

HARRIS BRAKE
SEE HARRIS BRAKE WMA

HICKSON
SEE DAGMAR WMA

HINKLE
SEE OUACHITA NF, WALDRON

HOLLA BEND
SEE HOLLA BEND NWR

HORSEHEAD
SEE OZARK NF, HUNT

HORSEHEAD
SEE SHIRLEY BAY-RAINEY BRAKE WMA

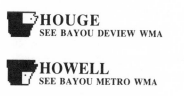

HORSESHOE
ACRES 2,300   ALT. 198   MAP L-4

This oxbow lake, once a part of the Mississippi River, offers fishing for bluegill, crappie, catfish, bass and sunfish. Also popular: boating and skiing. SR 38, 7 m. E of Hughes.

HOUGE
SEE BAYOU DEVIEW WMA

HOWELL
SEE BAYOU METRO WMA

 **HUBBLE**
SEE DAVE DONALDSON-BLACK R WMA

 **HURRICANE**
SEE HENRY GRAY WMA

 **LODGE**
SEE FELSENTHAL NWR

 **LONG**
SEE FELSENTHAL NWR

 **LUDWIG**
SEE OZARK NF, OZONE

 **LUTHER**
SEE FELSENTHAL NWR

 **MALLARD**
SEE BIG LAKE WMA

MAUMELLE
SEE PINNACLE MOUNTAIN SP

MERCER BAYOU
SEE SULPHUR RIVER WMA

 # MILLWOOD
SHORE 65 M.   ALT. 259   MAP G-1+2

Built on the Little *River* just upstream from its confluence with the Red River, this dam was dedicated in 1966 for flood control, water supply, recreation and conservation. In addition to other facilities at Millwood *State Park,* the lake offers boating, swimming, skiing, fishing and hunting. Known as "the hottest bass (largemouth, spotted, white & striped) fishing lake in the nation" it also stocks bluegill, sunfish, buffalo, drum and catfish (channel & flathead). "During the fall, mallard is king" but deer, quail, squirrel, dove and rabbit are available during their seasons. The nearby Cossatot, Rolling Fork and Lower Saline Rivers have some of the "whitest" white water canoeing in the state *(Float Streams).* Situated in a valley with sharply rising hills, the area is dotted with marshes and dense hardwood forest. Of special interest are Caddo Mound (a good example of a prehistoric Indian mound) and White Cliffs (150-foot limestone cliffs formerly used for making cement), which are at the end of SR 317 on the north side. See *Lockesburg* for details. NOTE: Peak season here is during the early spring and fall, when national fishing organizations hold tournaments. The Corps of Engineers provides 11 parks and *campgrounds.* Resident Engineer, Rt. 1, Bx. 37A, Ashdown, 71822. Directions to the following parks and *campgrounds* are from the capitalized town. BROWNSTOWN: White Cliffs has 18 campsites with boat ramp, water, restrooms & archaeological sites (ABOVE). SR 317, 4 m. S. OKAY: Okay Landing has

no campsites. Boat Ramp. Day Use Only. 1 m. N on paved access road. PARALOMA: Paraloma Landing has 75 campsites with electrical hookups, boat ramp, restrooms, water, dump station, playground & amphitheater. 1.5 m. S on paved access road. SARATOGA: Beards Bluff has 33 campsites with water & electrical hookups, restrooms, boat ramp, swimming beach, amphitheater & playground. SR 32, 3 m. S. SARATOGA: Beards Lake has 5 campsites with boat ramp, water, restrooms & playground. SR 32, 4.2 m. S. SARATOGA: River Run East has 13 campsites with boat ramp, water & restrooms. SR 32, 5.8 m. S; below dam. SARATOGA: River Run West has 4 campsites with boat ramp, restrooms & water. SR 32, 6 m. S; below dam. SARATOGA: Saratoga Landing has 38 campsites with boat ramp, water & restrooms. SR 32, 1 m. S; 1 m. W on paved access road. TOLLETTE: Cottonshed Landing has 50 campsites with electrical hookups, boat ramp, water, restrooms, dump station, playground & amphitheater. SR 332, 4 m. W to Schaal; 2 m. S on paved access road. WILTON: Ashleys Camp has no campsites. Restroom. US 71, 2.5 m. N to N of bridge; 2 m. S on 1st road. WILTON: Wilton Landing has no campsites. Boat ramp. US 71, 2.5 m. N; S of bridge.

 **MORO BAY**
SEE MORO BAY SP

 # NIMROD
SHORE 77 M.   ALT. 345   MAP D-3

Built in 1942 on the Fourche LaFave *River* for flood control and recreation, the lake is known for water skiing, hunting and crappie fishing (other fish include bass, channel catfish and bream). For hunters there are duck, geese, quail, wild turkey, deer and rabbits. Situated between the Ouachita and Ozark Mountains, the lake is lined with pine and hardwood, and offers boating, swimming, picnicking and six Corps of Engineers' parks and *campgrounds.* Resident Engineer, Plainview, 72857. Directions to the following campsites/parks and *campgrounds* are from the capitalized town. FOURCHE JUNCTION: Carden Point has 9 campsites with restrooms, boat ramp & water. SR 60, 2.3 m. W. FOURCHE JUNCTION: County Line has 17 campsites with water, electrical hookups, restrooms, dump station & swimming beach. SR 60, 1.7 m. W; S on access road. FOURCHE JUNCTION: Quarry Cove has 31 campsites with electrical hookups, boat ramp, water, restrooms, dump station, swimming beach & pavilion. SR 60, .5 m. W; S on access road. FOURCHE JUNCTION: River Road has 12 campsites with boat ramp, water, electrical hookups, restrooms, dump station, pavilion & playground. SR 7, S of town, below dam. PLAINVIEW: Carter Cove has 16 campsites with boat ramp, water, dump station, restrooms, pavilion & swimming beach. SR 60, 3 m. E; 1 m. S on access road. PLAINVIEW: Sunlight Bay has 29 campsites with electrical hookups, boat ramp, water, restrooms, dump station & pavilion. SR 60, 1.5 m. E; 2.3 m. SW on access road.

NORFORK
SHORE 380 M.   ALT. 550   MAP I-1

Situated in the Ozark Mountains, the dam was completed in 1944 on the North Fork River for flood control, hydroelectric power and recreation. Said to have a "worldwide reputation for lunker bass" (largemouth up to 12 pounds), the lake also has nearly every member of the walleye, crappie, bream and catfish family as well as brown and rainbow trout below the dam. Commercial docks have boats, motors and guides for hire. Hunters can expect deer, squirrel, rabbit, duck, geese, dove and quail. Scattered along the shoreline in dense hardwood forests are 20 Corps of Engineers' parks and *campgrounds* offering hiking, boating, picnicking, water skiing, swimming and scuba. (WARNING: The water is deep, cold & turbulent.) Of special interest is one of the world's largest trout hatcheries *(Norfork)*. Resident Engineer, Bx. 369, Mountain Home, 72653. Directions to the following parks and *campgrounds* are from the capitalized town. GAMALIEL: Bidwell Point has 48 campsites with electrical hookups, water, restrooms, dump station, swimming beach, change shelter & group pavilion. SR 101, 5.5 m. S. GAMALIEL: Gamaliel has 28 campsites with electrical hookups, boat ramp, boat & motor rental, water, restrooms, swimming beach & pavilion. SR 101, .5 m. S to paved access road. GAMALIEL: Howard Cove has 12 campsites with water, electrical hookups, restrooms, boat & motor rental. SR 101, 5 m. S; E on access road. GAMALIEL: Red Bank has 12 campsites with restrooms, boat ramp & water. SR 101, 1 m. S; 1 m. W on gravel access road. GEPP: Hand Cove has no campsites. Boat ramp, water & restrooms. US 62, 2.5 m. W; Hand Road (paved access), 9 m. SW. GEPP: Woods Point has 11 campsites with boat ramp, water, restrooms & dump station. US 62, 2.5 m. W; Hand Road (paved access), appx. 4 m. SW to paved/gravel access; appx. 3 m. S on gravel access. HENDERSON: Henderson has 38 campsites with electrical hookups, water, restrooms, boat ramp, dump station, swimming beach & group pavilion. US 62 at bridge. JORDAN: Jordan has 38 campsites with electri-

---

Lake Ouachita's Geo-Float Trip claims "the most unique geologic features in the world"

---

cal hookups, boat dock, water, restrooms, swimming beach, change shelter & group pavilion. 3 m. N on paved access road. MOUNTAIN HOME: Buzzard Roost has no campsites. Boat ramp, water & restrooms. US 63, 3 m. E; 4 m. on paved access road. MOUNTAIN HOME: Cranfield has 74 campsites with dump station, electrical hookups, swimming beach, change shelter, water, restrooms, boat & motor rental, group pavilion & playground. US 62, 5.5 m. E; 2 m. N on paved access road. MOUNTAIN HOME: Panther Bay has 28 campsites with boat ramp & dock, swimming beach, restrooms, water, trailer & marine dump stations. US 62, 10 m. E.

MOUNTAIN HOME: Pigeon has 5 campsites with boat dock & ramps, restrooms & marine dump station. SR 201, 6.5 m. N; E on paved access road. MOUNTAIN HOME: Robinson Point has 102 campsites with electrical hookups, restrooms, water, dump station, swimming beach, change shelter, showers & group pavilion. US 62, 9 m. E; 2.5 m. S on paved access road. MOUNTAIN HOME: Tracy has 7 campsites with boat dock, water & restrooms. SR 5, 6.5 m. S, SR 341, 3m. E. SALESVILLE: George's Cove has 12 campsites with boat ramp, water, restrooms, swimming beach & dump station. SR 5, 5 m. N; SR 342, 2.5 m. E. SALESVILLE: Quarry Cove & Dam Site have 59 campsites with swimming beach, change shelter & group pavilion, electrical hookups, boat dock, water, restrooms, trailer & marine dump stations. SR 177, 2 m. E.

OLD DAVIDSONVILLE
SEE OLD DAVIDSONVILLE SP

OLD TOWN
SEE LAKE VIEW

OUACHITA
SHORE 690 M.   ALT. 578   MAP E-2+3

Completed in 1953 for flood control, hydroelectric power, navigation and recreation, the dam is situated on the Ouachita River *(Float Streams)*. The lake is surrounded by dense pine forests and private timberland in the midst of the Ouachita Mountains. While stocking the usual bass, bream, crappie and catfish, it also offers rainbow trout, northern pike and ocean stripers. A special attraction is a Geo-Float Trip where "the most unique geologic features in the world" are displayed along a 16-mile "boat trail" (appx. 1.5 hours) that is clearly marked by bright yellow buoys. Bent, twisted and deformed by geological forces 250-300 million years ago, 12 formations like Whirlpool Rock, Submarine Slide and Mini-Caves are explained in a booklet of stops along the "trail." Self-guided. B.Y.O.B. (Bring Your Own Boat). The Corps of Engineers provides 13 parks and *campgrounds* for boating, swimming, scuba, skiing, fishing and hiking *(trails)*. An additional full-service marina and other campsites are available at Lake Ouachita *State Park*. Resource Manager, Bx. 4, Mountain Pine, 71956. Directions to the following parks and *campgrounds* are from the capitalized town. AVANT: Buckville has 30 campsites with boat ramp, water & pit toilets. 3.6 m. S on gravel access road. AVANT: Avant Primitive Area. No Facilities. 3.2 m. W on gravel access road. BEAR: Brady Mountain has 70 campsites with boat ramp, water, showers, restrooms, dump station, swimming beach, hiking trail, restaurant, marina, store, group picnic pavilion, lodge & 18 tent-only campsites. 4.5 m. N on paved access road. BEAR: Spillway Area has no campsites. Boat ramp, water, restrooms, swimming beach, restaurant, marina, 28 picnic sites & group picnic pavilion. 4.2 m. NE on gravel access road. BLUE SPRINGS: Lena Landing has 34 campsites with boat ramp, water, restrooms, restaurant, marina & 12 picnic sites. CRYSTAL SPRINGS: Crystal Springs has 65 campsites with boat ramp, water, showers, restrooms, dump station, 18 picnic sites, 2 group picnic pavilions, day-use swimming beach with change house & playground, restaurant, marina, store & 26 tent-only campsites. 2.9 m. N on paved access road. CRYSTAL SPRINGS: Joplin has 66 campsites with boat ramp, water, restrooms, showers, dump station, 10 picnic sites, swimming beach, restaurant, marina & nearby motel. SR 270, 8.1 m. W; 2.4 m. N on paved access road. CRYSTAL SPRINGS: Tompkins Bend has 134 campsites with boat ramp, water, restrooms, showers, dump station, amphitheater, 14 tent-only campsites, restaurant, marina & nearby cabins. SR 270, 9.1 m. W; 2.4 m. N on paved access road. EBONE POINT WILDERNESS AREA: Reached by water only. Group camp/reservation only. MOUNTAIN PINE: Stephens Park/Avery has 9 campsites with water & electrical hookups, restrooms, pavilion, 25 picnic sites & boat ramp. 1 m. W on paved access road. MOUNT IDA: Denby Point has 122 campsites with boat ramp, water, showers, restrooms, dump station, 9 picnic sites, amphitheater, hiking trail, restaurant, marina, 2 group camping areas (6- & 7-site reservations accepted), 9 tent-only campsites, swimming beach & nearby lodge. US 270, 8 m. E; 1 m. N on paved access road. MOUNT IDA: Little Fir has 145 campsites with boat ramp, water, electrical hookups, restrooms, marina & dump station. SR 188, 13.7 m. NE. MOUNT IDA: Twin Creek has 70 campsites with boat ramp, water, restrooms & 15 picnic sites. US 270, 8 m. E; 1 m. N on gravel access road. STORY: Iron Forks has 5 campsites, boat ramp, water & pit toilet. SR 298, 8.3 m. E; 1.3 m. S on gravel access road. WASHITA: Highway 27 has 115 campsites with boat ramp, water, restrooms, electrical hookups, swimming beach, restaurant, 22 picnic sites, marina & trailer dump station. SR 27, 2.5 m. S.

OVERCUP
SEE MORRILTON

OZARK
SHORE 293 M.   ALT. 370   MAP C-1+2

Completed in 1969 for hydroelectric power and navigation, Lock & Dam #13 at Fort Smith and this lock & dam (Ozark-Jeta Tayor) join with Dardanelle Lake to form part of the 445-mile McClellan-Kerr *Arkansas River* Navigation System (from near Tulsa, Ok., to the Mississippi River). Locks at either end work in stair-step fashion, raising or lowering the water inside the lock to match the level where river traffic is entering or exiting. An explanation and opportunity to watch the procedure is available at Ozark-Jeta Taylor Powerhouse *(Ozark)*. Said to have the best sauger fishing in the nation, the area also has all game fish native to Arkansas, including catfish, crappie, bream, white and largemouth bass as well as the added species of striped sea bass and walleyed pike. Public land along the shoreline offers hunters deer, quail, squirrel, rabbit, dove,

wild turkey, duck and geese. Situated in the Arkansas River Valley between the contrasts of open farm land, steep river bluffs and flat-topped mountains of the Ouachitas and Ozarks, 12 Corps of Engineers' parks and *campgrounds* provide picnicking, boating, swimming and hiking. Lake Manager, Rt. 1, Bx, 267X, Ozark, 72949. Directions to the following parks and *campgrounds* are from the capitalized town. CECIL: Citadel Bluff has 36 campsites with boat ramp, restrooms, water & group pavilion. SR 41, 1.2 m. N. CECIL: River Ridge has 24 campsites, boat ramp, water & restroom. SR 96, 12 m. W; 1.5 m. N on county road. FORT SMITH: Fort Smith has no campsites. Boat ramp, water, restrooms & group pavilion. US 64, S of the river; SR 59, .3 m. W. FORT SMITH: Springhill has 77 campsites with electrical hookups, boat ramp, water & restrooms. SR 59, S of river. KIBLER: Clear Creek has 41 campsites with electrical hookups, boat ramp, water, restrooms, dump station, showers & pavilion. SR 162, 3.6 m. E; N on paved access road. LAVACA: Vache Grasse has 29 campsites with boat ramp, water & restrooms. SR 255, 2.4 m. W; N 1.2 m. on county road. MULBERRY: Bluff Hole has no campsites. Water, restrooms, group pavilion & picnic sites. Day Use Only. US 64, 1 m. E. MULBERRY: Vine Prairie has 54 campsites with boat ramp, restrooms, water & dump station. SR 215, 1.7 m. S. OZARK: Reed Mountain *(Ozark)* has no campsites. Boat ramp, restrooms, water, picnic sites, overlook, hiking trail, playground & pavilion. Day Use Only. US 64, 2.5 m. E; 1 m. SW on paved access road. OZARK: White Oak has 7 campsites with boat ramp, water & restrooms. US 64, 7 m. W; 1.7 m. S on county road. VAN BUREN: Lee Creek has 14 campsites with boat ramp, water, restrooms, dump station, showers & pavilion. US 64, N of river; W on Main Street, S to levee; W to the park. WEBB CITY: Aux Arc has 29 campsites with electrical hookups, water, restrooms, boat ramp & pavilion. SR 23, .8 m. E.

PINE BLUFF
SEE PINE BLUFF

POINSETT
SEE LAKE POINSETT SP

RAYMOND
SEE MORO BAY SP

REYNOLDS
SEE PARAGOULD

ROOSEVELT
SEE PETIT JEAN SP

SHADY
SEE OUACHITA NF, ATHENS

SHEPHERD SPRINGS
SEE LAKE FORT SMITH SP

 **SHIRLEY BAY**
SEE SHIRLEY BAY-RAINEY BRAKE WMA

SHORES
SEE OZARK NF, MULBERRY

SPRING
SEE OZARK NF, BELLEVILLE

STORM CREEK
SEE ST. FRANCIS NF, WEST HELENA

 # SUGARLOAF
ACRES 334   ALT. 520   MAP D-1

The lake is stocked by the Arkansas Game and Fish Commission: bluegill, crappie, catfish and bass. Designated Camping Areas. SR 252, 5 m. W of Midland.

SYLVIA
SEE OUACHITA NF, WILLIAMS JCT.

 # TABLE ROCK
SHORE 745 M.   ALT. 915   MAP A-3

Completed in 1958 on the White *River (Float Streams)* for flood control, hydroelectric power and recreation, this lake is mostly located in Missouri. The small portion of the 745-mile shoreline that dips into Arkansas offers the same recreational opportunities, fishing and hunting as the other White River lakes of Bull Shoals and Beaver. Resident Engineer, Branson, Mo., 65616. Directions to the following park and *campground* are from OMAHA, AR. (Map A-3): Cricket Creek has 39 campsites with electrical hookups, boat ramp, restrooms, water, swimming beach, showers, trailer & marine dump station, boat & motor rental. US 62, 5 m. N; SR14, 4 m. W.

 **TRI-COUNTY**
SEE FORDYCE

 **WALCOTT**
SEE CROWLEY'S RIDGE SP

 **WALLACE**
SEE DERMOTT

 WAPANOCCA
SEE WAPANOCCA NWR

 **WEDDINGTON**
SEE OZARK NF, FAYETTEVILLE

 WHITE OAK
SEE WHITE OAK SP

WHITE RIVER
SEE WHITE RIVER NWR

 # WILHELMINA
ACRES 300   ALT. 1,125   MAP E-1

The lake is stocked by the Arkansas Game and Fish Commission with bluegill, catfish, crappie and bass. Primitive camping and picnic facilities available. SR 8 at Rocky. Signs.

WINONA
SHORE 25 M.   ALT. 542   MAP E-3

This *WPA* dam on the Alum Fork of the Saline River *(Float Streams)* was completed in 1938 as a municipal waterworks project for Little Rock, replacing drinking water from the *Arkansas River*. A 35-mile-long pipe, 39 inches in diameter, delivers a million gallons of "high quality, soft, pure water" per day. Only boating (10 hp limit), fishing, picnicking and camping are permitted. These activities are restricted to "use areas," which are clearly marked along the shoreline. Prohibited: swimming, bathing, wading, skin/scuba diving and any craft with toilet, cooking or sleeping facilities. Appx. 9 m. NW of Paron. Signs.

NATIONAL FORESTS

Arkansas' three national forests contain over three million acres and are mostly situated in ruggedly beautiful mountain terrain. Campgrounds have been located at scenic points and are designed to blend with the environment. The campsites are divided by green belts that have been developed around a geographical attraction. Generally they offer hiking *trails* and primitive restroom facilities. Also listed here by a separate heading are 12 remote national forest regions (wilderness areas) that are barred to motorized vehicles, and have no developed campgrounds. These 150,000 acres of Arkansas backcountry can be reached only by canoe, horseback or foot.

OUACHITA
MAP NW & SW QUARTERS

Set aside for the public in 1907 by President Theodore Roosevelt, these 1,663,300 acres offer recreational opportunities like hiking, fishing, boating, bird watching, horseback riding, hunting, fishing and photography as well as other activities such as berry and mushroom collecting. Incidentally, the word Ouachita was first used in the early 18th century by French explorers who referred to a tribe ("apparently Caddoan") found along the Black River in northeast Louisiana as the Ouachita, meaning Black River (Indians). Forest Supervisor, USFS Bx. 1270, Hot Springs, 71902. Directions to the following campsites are from the capitalized town: ATHENS, MAP F-2: Bard Springs. 17 Campsites. Central restrooms & water. Attractions: swimming, hiking, fishing & hunting. SR 246, 2 m. W; FR 38, 8 m. ATHENS, MAP F-2: Shady Lake. 97 Campsites. Central restrooms, showers & water. Attractions: 25-acre lake, swimming beach, boat dock (no motors), fishing, hiking, interpretive *trail* about trees & outdoor theater programs. SR 256, 2 m. N; FR 38, 5 m. N. BOONEVILLE,

MAP C-2: Jack Creek. 5 Campsites. Chemical toilets & water. Attractions: natural pool in creek, swimming, fishing, hiking & hunting. SR 23, 3 m. S; SR 116, 1 m. E; gravel road, 4 m. S. BOONEVILLE, MAP C-2: Knoppers Ford. 6 Campsites. Chemical toilets & water. Attractions: swimming, natural pool in creek, hiking & hunting. SR 23, 3 m. S; SR 116, 1 m. E; gravel road, 6 m. S. CRYSTAL SPRINGS, MAP E-3: Charlton. 61 Campsites. Central restrooms, showers & water. Attractions: near *Lake* Ouachita, fishing, interpretive *trail* about trees, swimming, mountain streams & outdoor theater nature programs. US 270, 7 m. W. CRYSTAL SPRINGS, MAP E-3: Hickory Nut Mtn. 8 Campsites. Picnic Area. Vault Toilet. Attractions: panoramic view of Lake Ouachita. FR 47, 6 m. N. HOLLIS, MAP D-3: South Fourche. 7 Campsites. Chemical toilets & water. Attractions: hiking & hunting. SR 7, 1 m. S. JESSIEVILLE, MAP E-3: Iron Springs. 13 Campsites. Chemical toilets & water. Attractions: hiking, hunting & *trail* connection to Ouachita National *Trail*. SR 7, 8 m. N. LANGLEY, MAP F-2: Albert Pike. 46 Campsites. Central restrooms, showers & water. Attractions: natural pool in Little Missouri River *(Float Streams)*, canoeing, swimming, fishing, interpretive *trail* explaining Forest Service History, hunting & Little Missouri Falls. FR 25, 7 m. NW. FR 73, 6 m. N. MENA, MAP E-1: Rich Mtn. No Campsites. Picnic Area. Vault toilets & water. Attractions: fire lookout tower, panoramic view of mountains & near connection with Ouachita National *Trail*. SR 88, 10 m. W. MOUNT IDA, MAP E-2: Fulton Branch Float Camp. 7 Campsites. Vault toilets & boat ramp. Attractions: float fishing on the Ouachita River *(Float Streams)*, swimming, hiking & hunting. SR 27, 1 m. N. MOUNT IDA, MAP E-2: Gap Creek. No Campsites. Picnic Area. Chemical toilets & water. Attractions: rest stop. US 270, 10 m. E. MOUNT IDA, MAP E-2: River Bluff Float Camp. 7 Campsites. Vault toilets, water & boat ramp. Attractions: float fishing on Ouachita River *(Float Streams),* swimming, hiking, hunting & trail connection of Womble *Trail* to Ouachita National *Trail.* SR 27, 1 m. N; gravel road, 5 m. N. NORMAN, MAP E-2: Collier Springs. No Campsites. Picnic Area. Vault toilets & water. Attractions: natural setting at a spring. SR 27, 1 m. N; FR 177, 6 m. E. NORMAN, MAP E-2: Crystal. 9 Campsites. Chemical toilets & water. Attractions: swimming, interpretive *trail* about soil formation, scenic drive & hunting. SR 27, 1 m. N; FR 177, 3 m. E. PENCIL BLUFF, MAP E-2: Big Brushy. 11 Campsites. Chemical toilets. Attractions: hiking, fishing & hunting. US 270, 7 m. W. PENCIL BLUFF, MAP E-2: Rocky Shoals Float Camp. 7 Campsites. Vault toilets, water & boat ramp. Attractions: float fishing on the Ouachita River *(Float Streams),* swimming, hiking, hunting & trail connection of Womble *Trail* to Ouachita National *Trail.* US 270, 2 m. E. ROVER, MAP D-3: Fourche Mtn. Picnic Area. 5 Campsites. Vault toilets & water. Attractions: hiking & hunting. SR 27, 5 m. S. SIMS, MAP E-2: Dragover Float Camp. 8 Campsites. Chemical toilet & boat ramp. Attractions: float fishing the Ouachita River *(Float Streams),* swimming, hiking & hunting. SR 88, 4 m. E; gravel road, 2 m. S. WALDRON, MAP D-1: Little Pines. 21 Campsites. Central restrooms, showers & water. Attractions: Lake Hinkle (980-acre), swimming beach, boat launch, hiking & hunting. SR 248, 4 m. W; gravel road, 7 m. W. WILLIAMS JCT, MAP D-4: Lake Sylvia. 19 Campsites. Central restrooms, showers & water. Attractions: 14-acre lake, swimming beach, boating (no motors), fishing, hiking, hunting, outdoor theater programs & interpretive *trail* about trees & wildlife. SR 9, 1 m. N; SR 324, 4 m. W. "Y" CITY, MAP E-1: Mill Creek. 27 Campsites. Central restrooms & water. Attractions: natural pool in creek, swimming, fishing, hiking, hunting and interpretive trail ("Briar Patch"). US 270, 4 m. E.

OZARK
MAP NW & NE QUARTERS

Established in 1908 by President Theodore Roosevelt, these 1.1 million acres are open for camping unless posted otherwise. Developed campsites are also available (BELOW) from which hundreds of miles of *trails* can be explored. Other recreational opportunities are offered like fishing, boating, bird watching, horseback riding, hunting, fishing and photography as well as activities such as berry and mushroom collecting. See the city of *Ozark* for how this unique name originated. Also maintained by the Forest Service is Blanchard Springs Caverns *(Fifty-Six).* Forest Supervisor, Bx. 1008, Russellville, 72801. Directions to the following campsites are from the capitalized town. BELLEVILLE, MAP D-3: Spring Lake. 13 Campsites. Central restrooms, water, boat ramp (10 hp limit), bathhouse & showers. Attractions: 82-acres mountain lake, swimming beach, hiking *trail,* picnic sites & hunting. SR 307, 4 m. N; FR 1602, 3 m. BEN HUR, MAP B-3: Richland Creek. 4 Campsites. Chemical toilets & water. At-

tractions: mountain stream, fishing, swimming, hunting & Richland Creek Wilderness Area (BELOW). SR 16, 2 m. S; gravel road, appx. 8 m. N. CASS, MAP B-2: Gray's Spring. No Campsites. Chemical toilets & water. Attractions: scenic vistas, picnic sites & hunting. SR 23, 1 m. S; FR 1003, 4 m. W. CASS, MAP B-2: Redding. 27 Campsites. Flush toilets, showers & water. Attractions: access to Ozark Highland *Trail,* fishing, hunting and canoeing the Mulberry River (WARNING: white water, expert canoeists only, *Float Streams).* N of Cass, FR 1003, 3 m. E. Signs. CASS, MAP B-2: White Rock Mountain. 8 Campsites. 3 Housekeeping Cabins. Toilets & water. Attractions: mountain scenery, bluffs, panoramic views, cool climate, picnic sites, hiking, access to Ozark Highlands *Trail* & hunting. SR 23, appx. 1.5 m. S; FR 1003, 12 m. W. Signs. DEER, MAP B-3: Alum Cove Natural Bridge. No Campsites. Chemical toilets, water, picnic sites & *trail.* Attractions: Alum Cove & *Jasper,* Ar. SR 16, 1 m. W; FR 1206, 3 m. N. FAYETTEVILLE, MAP A-1: Lake Wedington. 18 Campsites. Central restrooms, dump station, water,

---

The Ouachita and the Ozark National Forests were set aside by Teddy Roosevelt, 1907-08

---

boat ramp (10 hp limit), canoe & paddleboat rentals, bathhouse & showers. Attractions: 102-acre lake, picnic sites, hiking *trail* & swimming. SR 16, 13 m. W. FIFTY-SIX, MAP B-5: Barkshed. 1 Campsite. Chemical toilets. Attractions: mountain stream, picnic sites, pavilion, hiking *trail,* fishing & hunting. SR 14, 7 m. W; FR 1112, 3 m. N. FIFTY-SIX, MAP B-5: Blanchard Springs Rec. Area. 32 Campsites. Central restrooms, water & bathhouse with showers. Attractions: streams, spring (1200 gal/min.), caves, small lake, scenic *trails,* bluffs, float fishing on the White River *(Float Streams)* & Blanchard Springs Caverns featuring tours, slide shows and live programs. SR 14, 1 m. E; FR 1110, 3 m. N. FIFTY-SIX, MAP B-5: Gunner Pool. 32 Campsites. Chemical toilets & water. Attractions: mountain stream, bluffs, small lake, fishing, hiking & hunting. SR 14, 1 m. W; FR 1102, 3 m. N. HAVANA, MAP D-2: Mount Magazine. 16 Campsites. Chemical toilets, water & picnic sites. Attractions: highest point in Arkansas (2,753 feet), cool climate and mountain scenery. At nearby Cove Lake is swimming, fishing, hunting and hiking *trail.* SR 309, 12 m. N. HECTOR, MAP C-3: Bayou Bluff. 7 Campsites. Chemical toilets & water. Attractions: Illinois Bayou, bluffs, fishing, hunting and picnic shelters. SR 27, 6 m. N. HUNT, MAP C-2: Horsehead Lake. 10 Campsites. Central restrooms, water, boat ramp (10 hp limit), bathhouse & showers. Attractions: 98-acre mountain lake, picnic sites & swimming beach. SR 164, 2 m. N; FR 1408, 3 m. W. MULBERRY, MAP C-2: Shores Lake. 22 Campsites. Chemical toilets, water, group pavilion, picnic sites, dressing rooms and boat ramp (10 hp limit). Attractions: 82-acre mountain lake, swimming, fishing, hunting and access to Ozark Highland *Trail.* SR 215, 15

m. N; FR 1501, .5 m. N. OARK, MAP B-2: Wolf Pen. 6 Campsites (tent only). Chemical toilet & water. Attractions: rock bluffs, picnic sites, hunting and canoeing the Mulberry (WARNING: white water, experts only, *Float Streams*). SR 215, 1 m. W; SR 103 1 m. S; FR 1003, 2 m. W. OZONE, MAP B-3: Ozone. 8 Campsites. Chemical toilets & water. Attractions: tall pines, old CCC camp, access to Ozark Highland *Trail*. At nearby Lake Ludwig (10 m. S) is swimming, boating and fishing. SR 21, 2 m. N. PARIS, MAP C-2: Cove Lake. 29 Campsites. Central restrooms, picnic sites, boat ramp, water & showers. Attractions: swimming beach, fishing, hiking, hunting. SR 109, 1 m. S; SR 309, 9 m. E. PELSOR, MAP B-3: Fairview. 11 Campsites. Chemical toilets & water. Attractions: Ozark Highland *Trail* & hunting. SR 7, 1 m. N. PELSOR, MAP B-3: Haw Creek Falls. 8 Campsites. Chemical toilets & water. Attractions: mountain stream, waterfalls, bluffs, access to Ozark Highland *Trail*, fishing, hunting & canoeing Big Piney Creek. (WARNING: Upper portion is extremely dangerous; expert canoeists only, *Float Streams*.) SR 123, 12 m. W. PELSOR, MAP B-3: Rotary Ann. No Campsites. Chemical toilets & picnic sites. Attractions: scenic overlook. SR 7, 3 m. S. PLEASANT VALLEY, MAP C-3: Long Pool. 14 Campsites. Chemical toilets, water, pavilion, picnic sites & changing shelter. Attractions: natural pool in creek, bluffs, fishing, hiking, swimming, hunting and canoeing Big Piney. (WARNING: Upper portion is extremely dangerous, expert canoeists only, *Float Streams*). SR 7, 2 m. N; SR 164, 3 m. W; FR 1801, 3 m. E; FR 1804, 3 m. N.

ST. FRANCIS
MAP SE QUARTER

Previously administered by the Federal Soil Conservation Service, set aside in 1960, these 20,946 acres constitute the smallest national forest in America. The steep hills and valleys are thick with vines and undergrowth, making hiking and hunting difficult. However, Bear Creek Lake and Storm Creek Lake are very popular weekend and vacation spots for fishing, boating, swimming and picnicking. St. Francis Ranger District, Marianna, 72360. Directions to the following campsites are from the capitalized town. MARIANNA, MAP M-4: Bear Creek Lake. 41 Campsites. Toilets, water & boat rental (10 hp limit). Attractions: 625-acre lake on top of *Crowley's Ridge,*

swimming beach, fishing, picnic sites & hiking. SR 44, 7 m. E. HELENA, MAP M-4: Storm Creek Lake. 18 Campsites. Toilets, water, boat ramp (10 hp limit), bathhouse & showers. Attractions: 420-acre lake on top of *Crowley's Ridge;* swimming beach. SR 242, 2 m. N; FR 1900, 3 m. E.

WILDERNESS-OUACHITA
MAP NW & SW QUARTERS

BLUE MOUNTAIN, MAP C-2: Dry Creek Wilderness. 6,300 acres. Forest, streams & sandstone bluffs. Bx. 417, Booneville, 72927. EAGLETON, MAP E-1: Blackfort Mtn. Wilderness. 7,500 acres. Rugged terrain, rock glaciers & a forest of dwarf oaks. Rt. 3, Bx. 220, Mena, 71953. THORNBURG, MAP D-4: Flatside Wilderness. 10,100 acres. Small creeks, views & access to Ouachita National *Trail*. Rt. 2, Bx. 19E, Perryville, 72126. VANDERVOORT, MAP F-1: Caney Creek Wilderness. 14,400 acres. Forest, streams & 12 miles of hiking *trails*. Rt. 3, Bx. 220, Mena, 71953. WALDRON, MAP D-1: Poteau Mtn. Wilderness. 10,800 acres. Forest, streams & rock outcroppings. Bx. 100, Waldron, 72958.

WILDERNESS-OZARK
MAP NW & NE QUARTERS

BEN HUR, MAP B-3: Richland Creek Wilderness. 11,800 acres. Waterfalls, streams, bluffs & rugged terrain. Bx. 427, Jasper, 72641. BIG FLAT, MAP B-4: Leatherwood Wilderness. 16,900 acres. Streams, springs, caves, bluffs & close to Buffalo National River *(Float Streams)*. Hwy. 14 N., Henderson Bldg., Mountain View, 72560. HARRIET, MAP B-4: Lower Buffalo Wilderness. 22,500 acres. Buffalo National River, streams & rugged country. Bx. 1173, Harrison, 72601. HECTOR, MAP C-3: East Fork Wilderness. 10,700 acres. Rugged country, upland swamps & waterfalls. Rt. 1, Bx. 36, Hector, 72843. NAIL, MAP B-3: Upper Buffalo Wilderness. 14,200 acres. Caves, bluffs & headwater of Buffalo National River *(Float Streams)*. Bx. 1173, Harrison, 72601. PELSOR, MAP B-3: Hurricane Creek Wilderness. 15,100 acres. Natural bridge, streams, black bears & access to Ozark Highland *Trail*. Bx. 427, Jasper, 72641. PONCA, MAP B-3: Ponca Wilderness. 10,800 acres. Waterfalls, bluffs, caves, streams & rough terrain. Bx. 1173, Harrison, 72601.

NATIONAL PARKS

Arkansas has the distinction of having the nation's first national reservation (Hot Springs, 1832; national park, 1921) and first national river (Buffalo River, 1972). By an Act of Congress in 1916 the National Park Service was established to "conserve the scenery, the natural and historic objects and the wildlife therein...." Although the name, National Park Service, would seem to imply administration of just parks in America, this agency has assumed responsibility for many different categories of national property, including scenic rivers, historic sites, monuments, battlefields and even the White House. As of 1987 there were 338 properties totaling over 79.5 million acres (54 million of them in Alaska). Of Arkansas' five National Park Service properties (104,795 acres) only *Hot Springs* is a national park. The others are held in trust under different categories.

ARKANSAS POST
NATIONAL MONUMENT   MAP N-3

Although visited by *De Soto* (1541), Marquette and Joliet (1673) and La Salle (1682), this first permanent European settlement in the lower Mississippi River Valley (before New Orleans or Natchez) was established by Henri de Tonti as a French trading post, Poste de Arkansea *(Arkansawyer)* in 1686. Afterward it served as a Spanish fort (1771), a Revolutionary War battleground (1783), the capital of Arkansas Territory (1819) and finally (ending its life) as a Confederate fort (1861) destroyed by Federal troops and later washed away by the *Arkansas River*. It also saw the first issue of the Arkansas Gazette (oldest newspaper west of the Mississippi River, Nov. 20, 1819), and the first *road* into the interior of the West. The full story and some of the physical evidence are available at the Visitor Center. Day Use Only. Park Superintendent, Gillette,

72055. For recreation and camping: *Arkansas River Parks and Campgrounds,* Arkansas Post-Pine Bluff. ARKANSAS POST COUNTY MUSEUM. Established in 1960, it was the first county-supported museum in Arkansas and has quality artifacts dating from the Stone Age to the present, including a fully furnished 1930s playhouse, a 1910 Stoddard-Dayton automobile, the old *DeWitt* gallows, a log cabin, Indian pottery and a collection of buildings representing a homestead of the 1800s. SR 169, near Arkansas Post. NORRELL LOCK & DAM AND LOCK & DAM #2. Completed in 1967 as a part of the 445-mile McClellan-Kerr *Arkansas River* Navigation System (from near Tulsa, Ok., to the Mississippi River), these 110-by-600-foot locks can accommodate pleasure boats or barges by raising or lowering the water 30 feet inside the lock, working in stair-step fashion to match the level where river traffic is entering or exiting. Inquire Locally. For camping and recreation: *Arkansas River Parks and Campgrounds,* Arkansas Post-Pine Bluff.

BUFFALO
NATIONAL RIVER   MAP A-2+3+4

Set aside for public use as America's first national river in 1972, this 148-mile river is lined with towering bluffs, hardwood forests, caves, hiking *trails* and excellent fishing. (Buffalo River, *Float Streams*). Like a national park, the river and adjacent land cannot be used for commercial or private purposes without express permission of the U.S. government. Former private and commercial property was bought by the government. All campgrounds except Lost Valley are adjacent to the Buffalo River. Park Superintendent, Bx. 1173, Harrison, 72602. Directions are from the capitalized town: HARRIET, MAP B-4: Buffalo Point. 107 Campsites. Housekeeping Cabins. Central restrooms, cold water showers, water, picnic sites, 3 pavilions, 20 tent-only sites, 87 RV sites with electric & water, 5 group tent sites. Attractions: mountain scenery, trails, caves, overlooks, river access, swimming, fishing & naturalist programs. SR 14, 7 m. N; SR 268, 3 m. E. HARRIET, MAP B-4: Highway 14 Bridge. No Campsites. Vault Toilet. Attractions: river access, swimming & fishing. SR 14, appx. 6 m. N to bridge. GILBERT, MAP B-4: Gilbert. No Campsites. Vault Toilet. Attractions: river access, swimming, fishing, hiking. In Town. HASTY, MAP B-3: Carver. Open Camping. Vault Toilet. Attractions: river access, swimming & fishing. SR 123, 2.5 m. S to bridge. HASTY, MAP B-3: Hasty. Open Camping. Vault Toilet. Attractions: swimming, bluffs, river access & fishing. SR 123 S appx. 2 m. to W side of river. JASPER, MAP B-3: Erbie. Open Camping. Vault Toilet. Attractions: river access, swimming & fishing. Historic cabin & homestead. SR 7, 4 m. N; 6.5 m. W on dirt road at Koen Experimental Forest sign. JASPER, MAP B-3: Kyles Landing. Open Camping. Vault toilets & water. Attractions: river access, trail for wilderness area hiking (Hemmed-in-Hollow & Indian Creek). WARNING: no RVs or large trailers; road steep, rough & winding. SR 74, 5 m. W; 3 m. N on gravel road. JASPER, MAP B-3: Ozark. Open camping with water, restrooms, picnic sites & pavilion. Attractions: river access, swimming, fishing, bluffs & 5 m. round-trip Ozark-Pruitt Trail. SR 7, 5 m. N; 2 m. down dirt road. Sign. JASPER, MAP B-3: Pruitt. No Campsites. Day use only. Vault toilets, water & information station. Attractions: river access, swimming, fishing, bluffs & 5 m. round-trip Ozark-Pruitt Trail. SR 7, 6.5 m. N to river. MORNING STAR, MAP B-4: Maumee South. Open Camping. Vault Toilet. Attractions: river access. 6 m. N on paved/dirt road. PINDALL, MAP A-3: Mount Hersey. Open Camping. Vault Toilet. Attractions: river access. 6 m. S on dirt road. Inquire Locally. PINDALL, MAP A-3: Woolum. Open Camping. Vault Toilet. Attractions: river access. 8.5 m. W on gravel/paved road. PONCA, MAP B-3: Lost Valley. 15 Campsites. Vault toilets, water & picnic sites. Attractions: 3 m. round-trip trail (Eden Falls & Cobb Cave) & Ponca River access (2 m. E). SR 21, appx. 2 m. S. PONCA, MAP B-3: Steel Creek. Open Camping. Vault toilets, water & nearby ranger station. Attractions: river access, bluffs & trail for wilderness hiking (Hemmed-in-Hollow). SR 74, appx. 2 m. E to sign; 2 m. N down steep/winding gravel road. RALPH, MAP A-4: Maumee North. No Campsites.

Vault Toilets. Attractions: river access. SR 14, 6.2 m. S to Caney; 8 m. E on paved/dirt road. RALPH, MAP A-4: Rush. Open Camping. Vault toilet & water. Attractions: river access, trail for wilderness hiking & the ghost town of Rush (Yellville). SR 14, 6.2 m. S. to sign; 8 m. E on paved/gravel. ST. JOE, MAP B-4: Woolum. Open Camping. Vault Toilet. Attractions: river access. SR 374, 7 m. W. SILVER HILL, MAP B-4: Highway 65 Bridge. No Campsites. Vault Toilet. Attractions: river access, swimming & fishing. US 65N, 1 m.

FORT SMITH
NATIONAL HISTORIC SITE   MAP C-1

Listed with *Fort Smith*. Park Ranger, Box 1460, Fort Smith, 72902.

HOT SPRINGS
NATIONAL PARK   MAP E-3

Listed with *Hot Springs*. Park Superintendent, Bx. 1860, Hot Springs, 71902.

PEA RIDGE
NATIONAL MILITARY PARK MAP A-1

Called Arkansas' most important *Civil War* battle, it was also the strangest: The South attacked from the north using some French-speaking soldiers and over 1,000 Cherokees; the North fought from a defensive position on Southern soil using some troops who spoke German. The 4,301-acre park provides a brochure for a self-guided driving tour of the battlefield, noting the important engagements, historical structures like Elkhorn Tavern, fixed positions like the Little Sugar Creek trenches and an overlook showing 60 percent of the battlefield. Also offered is an 11-mile Boy Scout Trail that leads through the site, indicating points of interest. Static displays and recorded messages explain each stop. The Visitor Center has exhibits of Civil War artifacts such as muskets, cannons and uniforms as well as a 12-minute presentation of events leading up to and the tactics of the Battle of Pea Ridge. Picnic Sites. No Camping. Pea Ridge, 72751.

NATIONAL WILDLIFE REFUGES

Ladies' hat fashions were responsible for beginning the first national wildlife refuge. President Theodore Roosevelt in 1903 signed an executive order protecting egrets, herons and other birds on Florida's Pelican Island whose feather plumes were used in hat designs. Today's system provides food, water, cover and space totaling 90 million acres for approximately 60 endangered species and hundreds of other plant, animal and bird specimens. Administered by the U.S. Fish and Wildlife Service, and set in wilderness environments, these areas also offer spectacular scenery and recreational opportunities that include photography, observation, hiking, boating, restricted hunting and fishing as well as facilities like visitor centers, interpretive trails and drives, observation towers and blinds. NOTE: Altitudes listed below are averages. During hunting seasons, non-hunters should (1) dress in bright colors (day-glo orange hats and vests are ideal), (2) keep a close watch on children, (3) avoid traveling through dense underbrush and (4) be aware that the sound of gunfire is serious; remain alert and in the open.

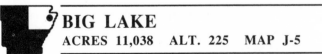

BIG LAKE
ACRES 11,038   ALT. 225   MAP J-5

Established in 1915, it is the oldest federal refuge in Arkansas and one of the oldest inland refuges in America (5,000 acres are designated a national natural landmark). The area contains a variety of outstanding features including virgin timber, one of the last northern remnants of a southern bottomland hardwood and swampland forest, a 10-mile road (Bald Cypress Wildlife Drive), Timm's Point Observation Area (waterfowl, ospreys, wading birds and bald eagles), and the Zebree Archaeological Site, which contains evidence of human occupation since 500 B.C. In addition there is limited hunting for deer, raccoon and squirrel as well as excellent fishing on Big Lake (5,000 acres)

for crappie, bream, catfish and bass by boat and from the bank at the south end of the refuge. Fishing Season: Mar. 1 - Sept. 31. Incidentally, Big Lake has an outstanding array of yellow water lotus, which can reach heights of over four feet during their prime in mid-summer. The pads, some two feet wide, repel water, breaking it into droplets that shine like crystals. Day Use Only. Refuge Manager, Bx 67, Manila, 72442.

FELSENTHAL
ACRES 65,000   ALT. 80   MAP P-1

The newest (1975) of Arkansas' national wildlife refuges is located in an extensive natural depression that was once a lake extending as far south as Monroe, La. Today a vast complex of sloughs, bayous, lakes at the confluence of the Ouachita and Saline Rivers *(Float Streams)* creates a wetland that combines with a bottomland hardwood and pine forest to produce a wide variety of wildlife like feral hogs, bobcat, beaver, mink, river otter and over 200 species of birds, including endangered ones such as the red-cockaded woodpecker, alligator, bald eagle and golden eagle. Hunting by permit is allowed, with the most popular being deer, duck and squirrel. Fishing for largemouth bass, crappie, bream and catfish is said to be excellent. Boat ramps, canoe trails and hiking trails. Designated campsites are available. Incidentally, nearby is the lowest elevation (54 feet) in Arkansas. FELSENTHAL LOCK & DAM: This recently completed (1985) facility is a part of the Ouachita River Basin System to improve navigation and flood control. The 84-by-600-foot lock can accommodate pleasure boats or barges by raising or lowering the water 18 feet inside the lock, working in stair-step fashion to match the level where river traffic is entering or exiting. Signs at Huttig, Ar. Refuge Manager, Bx. 279, Crossett, 71635.

HOLLA BEND
ACRES 6,367   ALT. 350   MAP C-3

Called "Arkansas' most outstanding area for viewing and photographing wildlife," the main attractions are waterfowl and eagles. Although geese and duck make up the majority of migratory birds, great heron and egrets are also present. Of the mammals, most seen are deer, rabbit, bobcat and coyote. An eight-mile all-weather road offers frequent observation points, picnic tables and a photo blind. Said to be one of the state's best archery spots, bow-hunting for deer is permitted annually. Permits are required for dove hunting. The former river channel and three shallow lakes (Long, Lodge & Luther) provide excellent springtime fishing for crappie, bass and bluegill. Day Use Only. Refuge Manager, Bx. 1043, Russellville, 72801.

OVERFLOW
ACRES 6,140   ALT. 100   MAP P-2

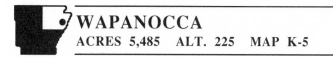

Established in 1980 to conserve the diminishing bottomland hardwood forest of this area, it is also important for wintering migratory waterfowl such as mallard, wood duck, teal, pintail and gadwall. Lower elevations support oak, pecan and sweetgum while the upper regions are dominated by cypress and tupelo. Hunting varies by season and includes waterfowl, quail, deer, rabbit and raccoon as well as beaver, opossum and feral hog. Refuge Manager, Bx. 279, Crossett, 71635.

WAPANOCCA
ACRES 5,485   ALT. 225   MAP K-5

In the late 1800s most of this area was owned by a group of businessmen from Memphis, Tn., who formed the Wapanocca

Hunting Club, which was bought by the U.S. Fish and Wildlife Service in 1961 with revenue collected from duck stamps. Called a "wildlife island in an agricultural sea," this area is one of the few remaining examples of the once vast bottomland-forest-wetland environments of East Arkansas. A 3.5-mile canoe trail leads through a cypress-willow swamp, highlighting huge trees untouched for nearly 100 years. South of the swamp a 10-mile "nature drive" gives a close look at migratory birds that during January and February total an estimated 25,000 Canadian geese and 50,000 ducks. Along with 600-acre Wapanocca Lake, the area's April-September fishing provides catfish, bass and crappie. Hunting season is limited to six-weeks for squirrel and two-weeks for raccoon. Day Use Only. No camping or picnicking is allowed. Refuge Manager, Bx. 279, Turrell, 72384.

WHITE RIVER
ACRES 113,000   ALT. 175   MAP N-3

The largest national wildlife refuge in Arkansas also has the largest remaining tract of bottomland hardwood forest in the state. Dedicated in 1935 as a sanctuary for migratory waterfowl, it is a home for approximately 3,000 Canadian geese and 250,000 ducks during the fall and early winter. Reportedly a bird-watcher's paradise, over 227 species have been identified, including half of the state's endangered species. In the summer large numbers of heron, egret and ibis inhabit the area. Wild turkey are common, and in winter the golden and bald eagle nest here. The refuge is characterized by more than 60 miles of the White River, 169 natural lakes and 125 miles of bayous and sloughs. Fishing is normally best from March to October (restricted during spring floods) and is mainly for bass, crappie, and bream. Hunting is limited to some duck and several managed deer hunts. Designated Camping. Refuge Manager, Bx. 308, DeWitt, 72042.

STATE PARKS

State Parks are scattered throughout Arkansas with a wide range of attractions. Although all have some kind of water recreation on or nearby the premises, Arkansas parks also offer archaeological sites, historical structures, arts and crafts, Civil War battlefields, environmental education and even a diamond mine. The modern camping conveniences include hot showers and electrical hookups for RVs. Along with hike-in primitive sites there are Rent-A-Camp and Rent-A-Backpack concessions that furnish all the necessary equipment except sleeping bags, blankets (etc.) and cooking utensils. The picnic sites generally provide tables, grills and water, and often have nearby restrooms. Special programs usually include supervised hikes, nature talks and demonstrations (from geology and history to plant and animal life) as well as slide shows and films shown in an outdoor amphitheater or pavilion. Some parks are open only seasonally and accept reservations but most are open year-round on a first-come, first-served basis with a 14-day maximum length of stay. NOTE: Altitudes listed below are averages. For information about facilities at each park, refer to the State Park Facility Chart on the opposite page

BEAVER LAKE
ACRES 2,400   ALT. 1,200   MAP A-2

Still being developed, this state park has no facilities, however, the Corps of Engineers (Beaver *Lake)* provides parks and campsites. Adjacent Hobbs Management Area *(Wildlife Management Areas)* is popular with hikers, bird-watchers and photographers, and Beaver *Lake* (appx. 1,100 feet deep), surrounded by rocky cliffs and dense forests, offers hundreds of miles of water recreation, mountain scenery and – according to some – a sense of the Mediterranean Sea in places. Resident Engineer, Drawer H, Rogers, 72756.

BULL SHOALS
ACRES 662   ALT. 708   MAP A-4

The park has 85 campsites and 20 tent sites along the White River *(Float Streams),* which is nationally acclaimed for its brown and rainbow trout. Hiking *trails* give a close look at the streams, rivers and mountain springs of the rugged Arkansas Ozarks, while nearby Bull Shoals *Lake* offers good fishing (lunker and white bass, stripers and crappie) and unlimited water recreation. Commercial boat docks rent boats and motors. *State Park Facilities Chart.* Bull Shoals, 72619.

CONWAY CEMETERY
ACRES 11   ALT. 250   MAP H-2

National Historic Register, grave of Arkansas' first governor, James S. Conway. This park lies on the edge of a row crop field and consists of approximately 40 tombstones from the Conway and Bradley (his wife's) family. Governor Conway's monument (not readily visible due to other ornate markers) is a five-foot vertical white marble pylon at the rear of the cemetery. No Facilities. Not listed on some maps, it is near *Walnut Hill,* Ar.: SR 160, in town, S on CR 9 (appx. .5 m. to entrance); E to cemetery. Signs. Parks and Tourism, 1 Capitol Mall, Little Rock, 72201.

CRATER OF DIAMONDS
ACRES 887   ALT. 370   MAP F-2

Since the first diamond was discovered by John Huddleston in 1906 *(Murfreesboro),* over 70,000 have been found at this 40-

acre eroded volcano "pipe." At the only diamond mine in North America, visitors take home an average of 1,000 diamonds per year, including noted gem-quality ones like the Uncle Sam (40.23 carats), which was cut into an emerald setting of 12 carats, and is valued today at $600,000. Semi-precious gems and minerals like amethyst, agate and jasper can also be found. According to "regulars," finding these gems is as much perse-verance and luck as it is know-how. Free identification and certification are available at the Visitor Center, which also provides special programs like diamond "mining" methods and geology to assist the novice diamond hunter or to inform the curious. A 1.3-mile hiking *trail* leads down to the Little Missouri River *(Float Streams)*. 60 Campsites. *State Park Facilities Chart*. Rt 1, Bx. 364, Murfreesboro, 71958.

LEGEND

- ■ In Park
- ⊞ No Lifeguard
- □ Facilities Nearby

STATE PARKS	Cabins	Motel-Style Units	Restaurant	Snack Bar	Store	Camping	Shower/Restroom	Restroom Only	Coin Laundry	Dump Station	Swimming	Picnic Areas	Playground	Special Programs	Trails	Tennis Courts	Fishing	Marina	Boat Rental	Exhibits	Museum	Pavilions	QUICK FACTS
Bull Shoals	□		□		■	■	■		□	■	⊞	■	■	■	■		■	■	■			■	740-Mile Shoreline
Crater of Diamonds			■		□	■	■		■	■	□	■	■	■	■		□			■			Genuine Diamonds
Crowley's Ridge	■	■		□	□	■	■		□	■	■	■	■	■	■		■		■			■	Rare Vegetation
Daisy	□		□		□	■	■		□	■	⊞	■	■				■	□	□			■	30-Pound Striped Bass
DeGray		■	■	■	■	■	■				⊞	■	■	■	■	■	■	■	■	■		■	State's Only Resort Park
Devil's Den	■		■	■	■	■	■		■	■	■	■	■	■	■		■		■	■	■	■	WPA Project of 1933
Hampson Museum			□	□	□			■	□			■								■	■		Indians 1350-1700 A.D.
Jacksonport			□		□	■	■		□	■	⊞	■		■				□	□	■	■	■	Steamboat Port, C.1833
Jenkins Ferry								■			⊞	■					■					■	Civil War Battle Site
Lake Catherine	■		■		■	■	■		■	■	⊞	■	■	■	■	□	■	■	■	■		■	WPA Project, 1937
Lake Charles				□	■	■		□	■	■	■	■	■		■		□	□	□	□	□	■	Minutes From 5 Rivers
Lake Chicot	■				■	■	■		□	■	■	■	■	■			■		■			■	Ringed By Cypress
Lake Dardanelle	□		□		■	■	■		□	■	⊞	■	■	■	■		■	□	□			■	On The Arkansas River
Lake Fort Smith	■	■	□		□	■	■		□		■	■	■	■	■							■	Inside A National Forest
Lake Frierson			□	■	■			■				■	■	■	■		■						Fisherman's "Hot Spot"
Lake Ouachita	■		■	■	■	■	■		■	■	⊞	■	■	■	■		■	■	■	■		■	975-Mile Shoreline
Lake Poinsett			□		□	■	■		□	■	■	■	■		■		■	□	□			■	On Crowley's Ridge
Logoly		□	□	□		■						■	■	■	■						■	■	Designated Natural Area
Louisiana Purchase														■					■				Headwater Swamp
Mammoth Spring	□		□		□			■		□		■	■				■			■	■	■	9 Million Gallons An Hour
Marks' Mill											■											■	Civil War Battle Site
Millwood	□		□		■	■	■		□	■	⊞	■	■				■	■	■				Famous For Bass Fishing
Moro Bay			□		□	■	■		□	■		■	■		■		■	□	□			■	A Bay, Lake & River
Mount Nebo	■		■	■	■	■	■		□		■	■	■	■	■	■	□			■		■	WPA Project of 1933
Old Davidsonville			■		■	■	■		□	■		■	■		■		■		■	■		■	Historic 1815 Townsite
Old Washington		□		□			■					■		■						■	■		Birthplace of Texas
Ozark Folk Center	■	■	■	■	■	□		□			⊞	■	□	■	■	□	□			■			Ozark Culture 1820-1920
Petit Jean	■	■	■	■	□	■	■		□		■	■	■	■	■		■		■			■	South's Highest Waterfall
Pinnacle Mountain			□	□				■				■	■	■	■		■	□	□	■		■	7 Hiking Trails = 42 Miles
Poison Spring				□								■		■		□			■				Civil War Battle Site
Powhatan Courthouse		□		□	□	■	□	□		□		■		■			□			■	■		Handmade Bricks, 1888
Prairie Grove Battlefield		□	□	□	□		■	□				■	■	■						■	■	■	18,000 Men Fought Here
Queen Wilhelmina		■	■	■	■	■	■		□			■	■	■	■				■				World's Highest Mini R.R.
Toltec Mounds					□		■					■		■						■	■		Indians, 700-950 A.D.
Village Creek	■			■	■	■	■			■	■	■	■	■	■	■						■	Rare Trees/Historic Sites
White Oak Lake			□	■	■	■	■		□	■	⊞	■	■	■	■		■		■			■	For Anglers & Naturalists
Withrow Springs			□	■	□	■	■		□		■	■	■	■	■	■	■		■			■	On A Spring-Fed Creek
Woolly Hollow			■	□	■	■	■		□		■	■	■	■	■		■		■	■		■	WPA Lake & Trails

CROWLEY'S RIDGE
ACRES 271   ALT. 400   MAP J-4

Formerly a campground of the Quapaw and the homestead of Benjamin F. Crowley (veteran of the War of 1812), this 1933 CCC project is located in a forest of hardwood and pine on the western slope of *Crowley's Ridge*. A massive log structure, built by the CCC, houses the main recreational facilities, a dance pavilion and a bathhouse for a spring-fed swimming and canoeing lake (sand beaches). Also on the grounds are a pioneer cemetery and the homesite of Crowley's Ridge namesake Benjamin F. Crowley. A larger lake, 31-acre Walcott, offers fishing for bass, crappie, catfish and bluegill. Two developed *trails* lead through the forest's unique vegetation and geology. Rustic housekeeping cabins and group lodging with dining hall; 18 campsites and tent camping area. Ball Field. *State Park Facilities Chart.* Bx. 97, Walcott 72474.

DAISY
ACRES 272   ALT. 500   MAP F-2

Situated in the rolling hills of the Ouachita Mountains on the north shore of 5,000-acre *Lake* Greeson, this park is surrounded by mountain scenery and large pine-hardwood forests, featuring a 31-mile cycle trail and a .7-mile self-guided hiking *trail* past a former cinnabar mine. Known for its fishing, the lake has 30 lb. lunker striped bass. Nearby Little Missouri River *(Float Streams)* stocks rainbow trout. 97 campsites, 21 tent sites (10 are "hike-in"). *State Park Facilities Chart.* Daisy Rt., Bx. 66, Kirby, 71950.

DEGRAY
ACRES 938   ALT. 408   MAP F-3

Set in the foothills of the Ouachita Mountains and called Arkansas' finest resort state park, it features a 96-room lodge and convention center located on its own island in 13,400-acre DeGray *Lake*. The rooms have color TV and phones; the lodge has a lakeside pool, tennis courts, 200-seat restaurant, fireplace and courtesy dock. An 18-hole (6,900-yard, par 72) USGA-rated golf course also has a putting green, driving range and pro shop. The full-service marina (132 slips) supplies rentals: boats and motors, sailboats, party barges, canoes, tube skis, jet skis and a fully equipped houseboat. For campers at the park there are 113 sites with swimming beaches, boat ramps, playgrounds and picnic areas. Fishing is very good, featuring hybrid fighting bass and northern pike. Three *trails* provide short nature walks. Park programs offer guided hikes, lake cruises, evening slide shows, movies, hayrides and square dances as well as "just for kids" activities like arts and crafts and storytelling. Events include: Late Jan: Eagles, Et Cetera. Field Trips. Lectures. *State Park Facilities Chart.* Rt. 3, Bx. 490, Bismark, 71929.

DEVIL'S DEN
ACRES 2,280   ALT. 1,699   MAP B-1

Set in the Boston Mountains beside Lee Creek, this 1930s CCC project offers spectacular scenery, a picturesque lake, 127 modern and primitive camping sites, equestrian (no horse rentals) camping areas with bridle trails through the Ozark *National Forest,* unique geological formations, wildflower walks and one of the best assortment of hiking *trails* in the state. Devil's Den Lake (eight acres) has bluegill, catfish and bass. Among the many attractions of the park are springs, erosional remnants, wet weather waterfalls, Devil's Den Cave (Devil's Icebox never rises above 60°F), scenic overlooks, steep bluffs and a 100-year-old homesite. Other features: rustic cabins with stone fireplaces, park restaurant and swimming pool. Events include: Early Apr: Annual Wildflower Weekend. Hikes. Programs. Early May: Annual Birdwatch Weekend. Hikes. Programs. *State Park Facilities Chart.* West Fork, 72774.

HAMPSON MUSEUM
ACRES 4   ALT. 237   MAP K-5

National Historic Register. This Nodena Phase Indian site (Chickasawba, *Blytheville)* was located at a meander bend of the Mississippi River during 1350-1700 A.D. and contained a 15-acre palisaded Indian village including two pyramidal ceremonial mounds and a plaza as well as dwellings, other structures and burial grounds. Exhibits at the park explain the culture of these farmers, using items like pottery, tools, weapons and jewelry as well as diet, trade routes and building techniques. Also displayed is a "chunky" field. Called "the little brother of war," chunky was a particularly violent variation of the game lacrosse that used stones and "sliding" sticks. *State Park Facilities Chart.* Wilson, 72395.

JACKSONPORT
ACRES 155   ALT. 225   MAP K-3

"Pride goeth before a fall" is the best explanation for why this town is now a state park and nearby *Newport* is the county seat of Jackson County *(County Profiles)*. Tradition claims this site began as a White *River (Float Streams)* trading area of the late 1700s. Said to have been an established trading post and landing by the 1820s, the town was laid out in 1833 and named Jacksonport, presumably for "Old Hickory," President Andrew Jackson (1829-37). A year-round river port, it was made county seat in 1854. During the *Civil War,* five major generals (both sides) used it as headquarters. In 1872, when the Cairo & Fulton *Railroad* offered to detour to it (by extending tracks to the town in exchange for depot land and a $25,000 bonus), local businessmen refused the barter, saying that no sensible railroad could afford to bypass such an important commercial point anyway. Newport, three miles away, accepted. OLD JACKSON COUNTY COURTHOUSE: National Historic Register, 1869. This two-story building is made from local brick and set on a foundation of Izard County limestone. Architectural features like arched and narrow stilted windows, mansard roof and cupola are worth noting. Downstairs rooms depict local history from prehistory to the early 20th century. Upstairs, the courtroom remains as it was when used for trials and for gala balls. MARY WOODS NO. 2: Said to be the last stern-wheeler to work the White River, this 139-ton ship (built 1931) was patterned after 19th century ones with Victorian styling, twin smokestacks and a nine-foot pilot wheel. On board are riverboat memorabilia and some antique furnishings. OTHER ATTRACTIONS/FACILITIES: Also on the grounds are a carriage house with buckboard, buggy, surrey and sulky as well as 20 campsites with bathhouse, swimming beach and picnic areas by the river. *State Park Facilities Chart.* Bx. 8, Jacksonport, 72075.

JENKINS FERRY
ACRES 40   ALT. 258   MAP F-4

This park and battleground monument beside the Saline River *(Float Streams)* commemorate the Confederate and Federal soldiers who fought here in the spring of 1884 during the Red River Campaign *(Civil War)*. *State Park Facilities Chart.* One Capitol Mall, Little Rock, 72201.

LAKE CATHERINE
ACRES 2,180   ALT. 600   MAP E-3

Arkansas' first major water-power project, Remmel hydroelectric dam, was dedicated here in 1924. The park, initially built by the CCC in 1937, is situated in tall pines and hardwoods of the Ouachita Mountains, and features three hiking *trails* (one begins at a waterfall), good bass fishing (30+ lb. ocean stripers) and a prehistoric novaculite (whetstones) quarry listed on the National Historic Register. A restaurant overlooks *Lake* Catherine. Facilities: 17 housekeeping cabins (five are rustic with stone fireplaces), 70 lakeside campsites, 13 campsites in the woods and 57 tent-only sites. Park programs include party barge tours. Events: Early to Mid-Apr: Wildflower Weekend. Hikes. Programs. *State Park Facilities Chart.* Rt. 19, Bx. 360, Hot Springs, 71913.

LAKE CHARLES
ACRES 140   ALT. 265   MAP J-3

Within minutes of five scenic rivers and situated on a 645-acre lake, this park is best known for swimming and fishing (particularly largemouth bass and catfish but also crappie and bream). Limited to 10-hp motors. A 1.5-mile *trail* leads along the lake shore. Scattered among the trees are 96 campsites. *State Park Facilities Chart.* Star Rt., Powhatan, 72458.

LAKE CHICOT
ACRES 130   ALT. 125   MAP P-3

Once an arm of the Mississippi River, this oxbow lake is Arkansas' largest natural body of water. Ringed with cypress and groves of wild pecans, the bayou-like environment is famous for its bream, crappie, bass and catfish. Other attractions include boat and party barge rentals, over 127 campsites, housekeeping cabins, 25-meter swimming pool and a separate wading pool as well as archery lessons and johnboat tours through cypress swamps. The Visitor Center has four aquariums featuring fish, turtles and two alligators, and sponsors nature exhibits like live snakes and mounted animals such as mink, muskrat and fox. Events include: Late Mar: Annual Spring Arts & Crafts Fair. Early Apr: Annual Celebration of Birds. Programs. Field Trips. Films. Fourth of July: Horseshoe Tournament. Games. Films. Fireworks. *State Park Facilities Chart.* Lake Village, 71653.

LAKE DARDANELLE
ACRES 294   ALT. 340   MAP C-3

Actually three separate parks, each offers access to 34,000-acre *Lake* Dardanelle (formed by the *Arkansas River)* and shares the background views of the Ouachita and Ozark Mountains. Best known for fishing, the lake has crappie, bream, catfish (some 40 lbs.), bass and ocean stripers (some 20 lbs.). RUSSELLVILLE AREA, 234 ACRES: Considered the main park, it has the Visitor Center, 64 campsites, 48 picnic sites, miniature golf, boat dock (commercial), .8-mile hiking *trail,* bicycle rentals and park programs. From Russellville: SR 326, 2 m. W of town. DARDANELLE AREA, 32 ACRES: 19 campsites, 16 picnic sites, bathhouse, boat ramp and dock (commercial). From Dardanelle: SR 22, 3 m. W of town. OUITA AREA, 28 ACRES: 15 campsites, 12 picnic sites, boat ramp and courtesy dock. From Russellville: US 64 at the lake. *State Park Facilities Chart.* Rt. 5, Bx. 358, Russellville, 72801.

LAKE FORT SMITH
ACRES 125   ALT. 850   MAP B-1

Originally built for Fort Smith's recreation in the 1930s, this park has some of the most beautiful scenery in Arkansas. Set in a wooded valley of the Boston Mountains, surrounded by the Ozark *National Forest,* its two lakes offer fishing (crappie, catfish, walleye and bass) but no swimming (city water supply). An Olympic-size pool is provided. The western terminus of the 175-mile Ozark Highlands *Trail* and seven-mile Evan's Loop (waterfalls, box canyons and towering bluffs) provide backpacking and day-hiking. Group lodging (110 persons) as well as housekeeping cabins (fireplaces) may be rented by the day. 12 Campsites. *State Park Facilities Chart.* Bx. 4, Mountainburg, 72946.

LAKE FRIERSON
ACRES 114   ALT. 400   MAP J-4

Located on the western edge of *Crowley's Ridge,* primarily a fishing and picnicking park, it has only seven campsites (but numerous picnic sites) and one nature *trail.* The lake is regularly stocked with bass, bream, catfish and crappie. Boat (no motor) rental. *State Park Facilities Chart.* Rt. 2, Bx. 319D, Jonesboro, 72401.

LAKE OUACHITA
ACRES 370   ALT. 578   MAP E-3

Located on the eastern tip of the 48,300-acre lake and surrounded by the Ouachita Mountains, this park is best known for its fishing *(Lake* Ouachita). A 46-slip marina rents boats, motors and party barges. Three *trails,* including a Geo-Float Trail *(Lake* Ouachita), wind around the pine forests of the shoreline. Housekeeping cabins with balconies overlook the lake, and 102 campsites (some "hike-ins") are scattered around the lakeside. Park programs include party barge tours as well as arts and crafts day camps for children (summers). THREE SISTERS SPRINGS: Discovered by homesteader John McFadden and named (possibly for his three daughters) in 1875. Today's park water supply utilizes a combination of the three springs. From 1907 to 1939 it was a heath spa and bottling plant whose "World's Wonder Waters" were shipped nationwide for curing Bright's disease, dropsey, diabetes, high and low blood pressure plus insomnia and kidney stones. The springs still flow. State approved; bring a jug. Events include: Late Apr: Wildflower Weekend. Walks. Programs. *State Park Facilities Chart.* Star Rt. 1, Bx. 1160, Mountain Pine, 71956.

LAKE POINSETT
ACRES 83   ALT. 250   MAP K-4

Located in a forest on *Crowley's Ridge,* the park is oriented toward picnicking and fishing for crappie, bass, catfish and bream on the 640-acre lake. Boat (no motor) rentals. No Swimming. The park has 27 campsites overlooking the lake, and two picnic areas (63 sites with tables and grills). Events: Listed under *Harrisburg. State Park Facilities Chart.* Rt. 3, Bx. 317, Harrisburg, 72201.

LOGOLY
ACRES 345   ALT. 350   MAP H-3

The mineralized water from its 11 springs has been been famous since the turn of the century. Two hotels once stood near the springs; evangelists once held camp meetings here. Today's name was formed from its three landowners' (Longinos, Goodes and Lyles) in 1940, and was kept when sold to the state in

1974 to be made into Arkansas' first environmental education park. The Visitors Center features the history and environment of the area using exhibits, audio-visual displays, movie and slide presentations. Two *trails* with observation platforms and photography blinds wind along the shoreline of the three-acre spring-fed pond and the outer perimeter of the park. Programs range from global ecology to native plants and animals. Six group tent sites, 20 picnic sites. Fishing: bluegill, catfish and bass. *State Park Facilities Chart.* Bx. 245, McNeil, 71752.

LOUISIANA PURCHASE
ACRES 37   ALT. 175   MAP M-3

April 30, 1803. After the ink had dried and the check had cleared, Americans began to wonder just exactly what it was they had bought from Napoleon for three cents an acre ($15,000,000). At the time, President Jefferson only knew that Napoleon was badly in need of money to finance his military campaigns, and that it was in America's best interest to buy a small tract of land near the mouth of the Mississippi River to secure safe passage for shipping. Instead, Napoleon offered the entire area of "Louisiana," which was mostly an uncharted wilderness. Now we know it includes land from Louisiana to Montana, but even by 1815 a survey of the area had barely begun (map, *Why There Is an Arkansas).* Initially the survey in Arkansas began with a "base line" drawn from the mouth of the St. Francis River west to the Arkansas River and a "fifth principle meridian" drawn from the mouth of the Arkansas River north to the Missouri River. Today, a granite marker commemorates the two original *witness trees* accidentally discovered in 1923 that marked the intersection of those two lines. From here (using east-west "standard lines" and north-south "meridian guides") all survey points for the Arkansas area of the Louisiana Purchase were established (in 1819 Arkansas' western *boundary line* included parts of Oklahoma). Of equal significance is the park's conservation of one of the few remaining examples of headwater swamp in eastern Arkansas. This land, which rarely floods yet rarely dries out, supports unique plant and animal populations that once were prevalent before the adjacent region was drained and cleared: swamp cottonwood, bald cypress and tupelo trees as well as the pileated woodpecker, green heron and prothonotary warbler. Wayside exhibits along a 950-foot boardwalk (handicapped-accessible) and a self-guided tour pamphlet explain the history and environment of the park. *State Park Facilities Chart.* 1 Capitol Mall, Little Rock, 72201.

MAMMOTH SPRING
ACRES 62   ALT. 900   MAP I-2

Listed on early 19th century maps as Great Spring, by the turn of the century it was a resort town. In the 19th century the spring was used to power *grists mills,* and in the 20th century it was used for hydroelectricity. Wayside exhibits and self-guided brochures explain its history and environment. "One of the largest, single natural springs in America," it flows at an average of nine million gallons per hour at 58°F. Originating as rain seeping through the flat plains of southern Missouri and converging in an underground river, the actual "flow" cannot be seen because the water emerges 70 feet beneath a 9.5-acre pond. The Spring River *(Float Streams),* formed by its runoff, provides recreation: fishing, boating and swimming. Day Use Only. Picnic Sites. FRISCO DEPOT: This authentically restored 1880s depot serves as the Visitor Center and the Arkansas Tourist Information Center. The depot also houses railroad memorabilia and an HO-scale model train as well as mementos from the town's resort days. MAMMOTH SPRING NATIONAL FISH HATCHERY: One of the oldest national hatcheries, it was built in 1904. Today, using 36 million gal/hr, the constant 58°F water produces fish like largemouth bass, bluegill, sunfish and channel catfish as well as striped bass and walleye. A 10-tank aquarium displays the species raised. SPRING RIVER STATE FISH HATCHERY: Given to the state in 1985 by the Kroger Company of Cincinnati, Ohio, it consists of 36 in-ground silos and 26 concrete raceways that help produce about 300,000 rainbow trout per year. Water flow is about 50,000 gal/min at 54°-62°F. Future plans for other species: smallmouth bass, walleye and pike. SR 342, 2 m. S. *State Park Facilities Chart.* Bx. 36, Mammoth Springs, 72554.

MARKS MILL
ACRES 6   ALT. 235   MAP O-1

This park and battleground monument commemorate the Confederate and Federal soldiers who fought here in the spring of 1864 during the Red River Campaign *(Civil War). State Park Facilities Chart.* One Capitol Mall, Little Rock, 72201.

MILLWOOD LAKE
ACRES 823   ALT. 260   MAP G-2

Called one of the hottest fishing lakes in the South, it is mostly for anglers (Millwood *Lake),* although sightseers have found the area provides a variety of wildlife, including duck, beaver, great blue heron, bald eagle and alligator (in marshes and secluded parts of the lake). Marked boat lanes lead through the submerged timber, and a 1.5-mile nature *trail* winds along the shore's pine forests (some photo/observation blinds). The full-service marina rents boats, motors and party barges. Sand Beach. 114 Campsites (some tent sites). *State Park Facilities Chart.* Rt. 1, Bx. 37AB, Ashdown, 71822.

MORO BAY
ACRES 117   ALT. 100   MAP H-4

Located at a wide horseshoe bend in the Ouachita River *(Float Streams)* and flanked by two lakes (Moro Bay and Raymond), the area is directed toward fishing for bass, bream, white perch and catfish. A short *trail* leads through the pines by Moro Bay. 20 campsites and 2 picnic areas (40 sites with tables, grills). *State Park Facilities Chart.* Star Rt., Jersey, 71651.

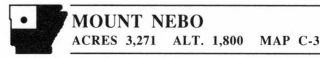

MOUNT NEBO
ACRES 3,271   ALT. 1,800   MAP C-3

Flat-topped as a mesa, Mount Nebo rises 1,800 feet above the *Arkansas River* Valley. The views are spectacular. A resort for steamboat passengers during the 1890s, its climate is usually 10°F cooler than the surrounding countryside. Most of today's cabins, pavilions and bridges were built in 1933 by the CCC, as were some of the 14 miles of unique *trail* systems, which include wet-weather waterfalls, springs, old logging roads and overlooks. Along with a swimming pool said to be the highest in Arkansas, there are two lighted tennis courts, a ball field and bicycles for rent. The park has rustic cabins with stone fireplaces, 25 campsites and 13 "walk-ins" via access trails. CAUTION: The zig-zag approach up the mountain is as spectacular as the park views, but trailers over 15 feet are advised not to make the climb. *State Park Facilities Chart.* Rt. 3, Bx. 374, Dardanelle, 72834.

OLD DAVIDSONVILLE
ACRES 163   ALT. 250   MAP I-3

Said to have been settled on the site of a former Indian village, all that remains of the town that began as Lawrence are legends and "firsts". Established on the banks of the Black River near its confluence with the Spring and Eleven Point Rivers *(Float Streams),* this riverboat town was laid out around a public square in 1815 by John Davidson, who was a representative from Lawrence County in the Missouri Territorial Legislature (Arkansas was a part of Missouri Territory until 1819, *County Profiles).* Davidsonville claims Arkansas' first post office (1817), first courthouse (1818) and first land office (1820). Although archaeological surveys as recently as 1980 have been conducted, little is known about the town except that it flourished until 1829, when the Southwest Trail *(Roads)* was improved and moved a few miles northwest, establishing the new county seat of Jackson, which probably drained away Davidsonville's population (Jackson, in turn, lost the county seat to Smithville in 1837). Along with artifacts found at this site (displayed at the new Visitor Center), the restored town water well is the only physical evidence left among the historical markers locating public buildings. The park has 25 campsites and 10 tent-only sites set under tall oaks near the Black River. Fishing: The river has walleye up to 10 lbs. and Old Davidsonville Lake offers bluegill, catfish and bass. Other features: a self-guided nature *trail* past historic Scott Cemetery and a playground ("Fort Davidsonville," a hollowed-out tree house) said to be the most innovative in the park system. *State Park*

Facilities Chart. Rt. 2, Pocahontas, 72455.

OLD WASHINGTON
ACRES 75 ALT. 265 MAP G-2

National Historic Register. A recipient of the Phoenix Award (one of six chosen nationally) for conservation and preservation, this park preserves and interprets historic *Washington* (1825-1875) through tours of houses and buildings as well as by demonstrations like forging metal at James Black's reconstructed blacksmith shop. Among the variety of sites are: HEMPSTEAD COUNTY COURTHOUSE: Built in 1836, it became the Confederate capitol of Arkansas; restored in 1929. WILLIAMS HOUSE: Built in 1834 as a residence and tavern. GOODLET COTTON GIN: In use from 1883 to 1966, it is believed to be the only operational steam-powered gin in America. HENRY'S CHAPEL: This Methodist Church was built in 1861; used continuously since. MAGNOLIA TREE: Planted in 1839, it is the largest in Arkansas. OTHERS: The town contains what has been called a significant collection of Greek Revival structures. Tours. Extensive Archives. Events and festivals: Early Mar: Annual Jonquil Festival. Arts & Crafts. Folk Music. Jonquils. Mid-May: Annual Washington Antique Show & Sale. Collectibles. Late Oct: Annual Frontier Days. Demonstrations of 19th Century Skills. *State Park Facilities Chart.* Bx. 98, Washington, 71862.

OZARK FOLK CENTER
ACRES 637 ALT. 700 MAP J-1

Recipient of the 1984-85 Phoenix Award given by the Society of American Travel Writers, this unique park presents (seasonally) the music, crafts, songs, dance and humor of Arkansas' Ozark Mountains (1820-1920). In 50 stone and cedar buildings of the complex, including a 1,000-seat auditorium and 300-seat outdoor stage, musicians and artisans perform and demonstrate their arts and crafts. The Ozark Folklore Library has resource materials for the region's folklore and traditions. A conference center for workshops and seminars is provided as well as a 225-seat restaurant and 60 lodging units (color TV and phones) that are arranged facing the woods. Swimming Pool. Events and festivals: Early Apr: Invitational Fiddle Competition. "Contest of Champions." Late Sept: Arkansas State Fiddlers Championship. Mid-Dec: Annual Ozark Christmas (caroling, music and handmade decorations). *State Park Facilities Chart.* Mountain View, 72560.

PETIT JEAN
ACRES 3,637 ALT. 1,100 MAP C-3

Located between the Ozark and Ouachita Mountains, Arkansas' first (1923) state park is set on a mountain top overlooking the *Arkansas River* Valley. Millions of years of erosion cut its terrain into towering bluffs, deep valleys and intricate rock formations. Three hiking *trails* (designated as National Recreation Trails and listed in National Heritage Areas) lead past one of the highest waterfalls in the South, spectacular overlooks, a natural sandstone bridge, a bluff shelter and across a creek. The sandstone outcroppings and canyon hardwood forests are said to be among the finest examples found in the state. Lake Bailey and Roosevelt provide wooded picnic areas, boat rentals and fishing for crappie, bream, catfish and bass. Initially built by the CCC in the early 1930s, Mather Lodge (24 rooms) is said to have the best view of sunset in Arkansas as well as a massive stone fireplace, restaurant, tennis courts and swimming pool. The housekeeping cabins (8 rustic) have fireplaces. The park has 127 campsites divided into four areas. *State Park Facilities Chart.* Rt. 3, Bx. 340, Morrilton, 72110.

PINNACLE MOUNTAIN
ACRES 1,801 ALT. 1,011 MAP D-4

A regional landmark, the cone-shaped peak of this mountain identifies Arkansas' first state park to adjoin a metropolitan area. The park is dedicated to the study and preservation of the environment. "Heavily wooded hillsides, lush lowlands, clear waterways" and spectacular views of the *Arkansas River* Valley are best seen from the seven trails (totalling 41.5 miles) that climb the summit, skirt around the base and wind through the cypress trees along the Little Maumelle River. The 209-mile Ouachita *Trail's* eastern terminus is here. Exhibits explain the Visitor Center's solar heating system, display local fish in an aquarium and show 25 mounted animals in their natural habitat. Park programs focus on topics concerning global ecology. Day Use Only. Lake Maumelle (8,900 acres) has catfish, bass (also hybrid striper), trout and bluegill as well as picnicking, camping and boating (*Arkansas River Parks and Campgrounds,* MAUMELLE). Commercial dock, boats and supplies. Events: Late Mar: Wildflower Weekend. Field Trips. Programs. Early Spring: Wye Mountain Daffodils (seven acres of 30 varieties). *State Park Facilities Chart.* Rt. Bx. 34, Roland, 72135.

POISON SPRING
ACRES 86 ALT. 215 MAP G-3

This park and battleground monument commemorate the Confederate and Federal soldiers who fought here in the spring of 1884 during the Red River Campaign (*Civil War*). *State Park Facilities Chart.* One Capitol Mall, Little Rock, 72201.

POWHATAN COURTHOUSE
ACRES 2 ALT. 529 MAP I-3

National Historic Register, Italianate, 1888. This two-story handmade red brick building houses records (1815-1920) that were left scattered on the floor when it was abandoned in 1963 for the new courthouse in *Walnut Ridge*. Overlooking the Black River, its six-foot windows, eight-foot doors and 18-foot ceilings are original, as is the ornamental pressed-tin ceiling of the courtroom that appears as if it were only adjourned for the day. The delicate woodwork, classic cupola and shades of gray and crimson paint are authentic. Inside rooms have historical artifacts from Lawrence County (1815), which traces its origin to Missouri Territory *(County Profiles)* and to Old Davidsonville *(State Park)*. Grounds: stone jailhouse (National Historic Register, 1871); original and intact. Day Use Only. Not listed on some maps, it is in *Powhatan. State Park Facilities Chart*. Parks & Tourism, 1 Capitol Mall, Little Rock, 72201.

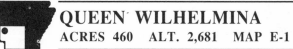

PRAIRIE GROVE
ACRES 130   ALT. 1,080   MAP B-1

National Historic Register. This one-day *Civil War* battle involving over 18,000 Confederates and Federals covered three and a half miles of ground. The Battlefield Museum and Visitors Center has an audio-visual orientation of the Battle of Prairie Grove as well as artifacts and a diorama of the tactics of the *Civil War*. Brochures for a 10-mile self-guided driving tour of the park, along with maps for a one-mile self-guided walking tour, are available at the Visitors Center. On the tours are a collection of structures typical of the 19th century, including the Morrow House (Confederate HQ), Latta House (1834), Borden House (used by Confederate snipers), a schoolhouse and dog-trot cabin. A park historian dressed in a Civil War uniform provides "living history" programs ranging from war stories to lessons on how to fire a musket. No Camping. Events and festivals include: Late Aug: Annual Clothesline Fair. Arts & Crafts. Fiddler's Contest. Square Dance. Nearby Lincoln (US 62, 6 m. W) holds an annual Arkansas Apple Festival in early October: Arts & Crafts. Square Dance. 10K Run. Apple Cider and Dumplings. Local National Historic Register structures: Borden House (pre-1862), US 62, NE of the town. Lake-Bell House (c.1868), Inquire Locally. *State Park Facilities Chart*. Bx. 306, Prairie Grove, 72735.

QUEEN WILHELMINA
ACRES 460   ALT. 2,681   MAP E-1

Located on top of Rich Mountain, which is not only Arkansas' second highest at 2,681 feet *(Magazine)*, but is also called Arkansas' most deadly (due to the number of airplane crashes). The views of the surrounding Ouachita Mountains are spectacular and unobstructed for miles. Replacing the 1896 lodge that burned in 1973 is a modern, 38-room resort with a restaurant, petting zoo and reportedly the world's highest miniature railroad. Hiking trails (including the Ouachita *Trail*) pass by several pioneer homesteads, and lead through one of the state's most scenic areas, where there have been confirmed sightings of cougar and black bear. 40 Campsites. Picnic Areas. *State Park Facilities Chart*. Rt. 7, Bx. 53A, Mena, 71953.

TOLTEC MOUNDS
ACRES 177   ALT. 240   MAP M-1

Built and occupied from about 700 to 950 A.D., these mounds are said to comprise one of the largest and most complex sites in the lower Mississippi Valley. Of the 16 known "inside the moat" mounds, two were 41 and 50 feet tall, and all of them were enclosed on three sides by a six-foot high, one-mile long earthen embankment with outside ditches. The fourth side fronted a pond. Apparently aligned with important solar positions and constructed using standardized units of measurement, the flat-topped mounds supported buildings that were the center of social, political and religious activities for the surrounding Plum Bayou Culture who, unlike their contemporaries, built sturdy houses, farmed, fished and hunted as well as gathered wild plants. Later occupants (1400s A.D.) might have been ancestors of the Quapaw but they did not build the mounds, nor did (as suggested by the amateur who named the mounds) the Toltecs. The Visitor Center contains exhibits and audio-visual programs. Guided Tours Only. The park has no camping or picnic facilities. *State Park Facilities Chart*. #1 Toltec Mounds Road, Scott, 72142.

VILLAGE CREEK
ACRES 7,018   ALT. 400   MAP L-4

Arkansas' largest state park is also one of the newest (1976). Situated in a long, wide valley cut through *Crowley's Ridge* by Village Creek, it has housekeeping cabins with fireplaces and screened porches, 104 campsites, 70 picnic sites, two lakes (electric motors only), tennis courts, a ball field, hiking *trails* and some of the rarest vegetation in the state (like six species of orchids, the Schisandra vine, white walnut, cucumber tree, Kentucky coffee tree and Arkansas' largest known beech tree). Five separate trails lead through the park identifying these specimens, crossing over small streams and hogback ridges, and sometimes following part of the historic Memphis-Little Rock *Road* through Wm. Strong's homestead *(St. Francis, Old)*. Lakes Dunn and Austell have sand beaches and are stocked with bass, bream, crappie and catfish (boat & motor rentals). The Visitor Center exhibits the history, geology and natural environment of the area. *State Park Facilities Chart*. Rt. 3, Bx. 49B, Wynne, 72396.

WHITE OAK
ACRES 662   ALT. 250   MAP G-3

Situated in rolling hills next to a 2,765-acre lake, this park is mostly for fishing (bass, crappie and especially bream) although two *trails* lead from marshland to beech-covered ridges, providing opportunities to see green heron, beaver and deer. 42 Campsites (some on the lake). Boat (no motor) Rental. *State Park Facilities Chart*. Star Rt., Bluff City, 71722.

WITHROW SPRINGS
ACRES 774   ALT. 1,400   MAP A-2

Named for original homesteader (c.1832) Richard Withrow, the spring comes from a small cave at the base of a tall bluff. A wide variety of recreation provides four lighted tennis courts, heated swimming pool, two ball fields and a crossbow range used for national tournaments. Also: canoe and shuttle service for floating and fishing the War Eagle River *(Float Streams)*. Three hiking *trails* lead past a small cave, springs, a 150-foot bluff overlooking the river and countryside, limestone outcroppings and Ozark Mountain plant life. Picnic areas are located along the spring-fed creek. 17 Campsites. 8 Tent Sites. *State Park Facilities Chart*. Rt. 3, Huntsville, 72740.

WOOLLY HOLLOW
ACRES 339   ALT. 500   MAP C-4

Set in the foothills of the Ozark Mountains, this park features its namesake's one-room log cabin (1882) and 40-acre Lake Bennett, which when constructed by the CCC in 1935 was America's first Soil Conservation Service project for studying the effects of water run off. Today it offers boating (electric motors only), swimming and fishing for bass, crappie, bream and catfish. Two nature *trails* (originally laid out by the CCC) lead along the lakeside and through mountain forests. Guided Hikes. No commercial boat dock or supplies. Nine picnic areas along with 20 campsites overlook the lake. *State Park Facilities Chart*. Rt. 1, Bx. 374, Greenbrier, 72058.

TRAILS

There are over 200 defined (blazed and maintained) hiking and nature trails across the state. Many are mentioned under State and National Parks and Lakes as well as Arkansas River Parks and Campgrounds and National Forests (see also Index, Hiking Trails). Information is available from the sponsor or from Trails: c/o Parks and Tourism, 1 Capitol Mall, Little Rock, 72201. The following seven trails are considered backpacking trails although each is accessible at various points for a day's hike or an hour's walk. Mileage is approximate.

ATHENS-BIG FORK
MILES 4.1   MAP E-2

This trail is part of a 19th century postal *road* that once connected Athens (Map F-2) and *Big Fork* (Map E-2). Said to be "truly beautiful," the trail is also unique and strenuous because it travels north-south across the east-west lay of the Ouachita Mountains, resulting in ascents and descents of over 1,200 feet (allow appx. 3.5 hrs.). Motorized vehicles are barred. Access: Athens, SR 246, 2.2 E to Forest Roads or FR 106 from either Bard Springs or Albert Pike Recreational Areas *(Ouachita National Forest)*. Ranger, Box 369, Glenwood, 71943.

BUTTERFIELD
MILES 14.1   MAP B-1

This trail begins and ends at Devil's Den *State Park,* crossing near sections of the *Butterfield Overland Mail* route and passing spectacular overlooks, unique rock formations, old logging roads, caves and creeks, including Lee Creek *(Float Streams).* Equipment Rentals. Superintendent, Devil's Den State Park, West Fork, 72774.

CANEY CREEK
MILES 9   MAP E-1

Located SE of Mena near the Shady Lake Recreational Area in the Ouachita *National Forest,* this trail is characterized by elevations ranging from 940 feet on the Cossatot River *(Float Streams)* to 2,330 feet at Tall Peak, encompassing narrow ridgetops with sandstone outcroppings and broad views as well as narrow year-round creeks with small pools and waterfalls. Forest Supervisor, Ouachita National Forest, Bx. 1270, Hot Springs, 71901.

COSSATOT RIVER
MILES 15   MAP F-2

Recently established by the Natural Heritage Commission and State Parks, this primitive trail is laid out above the Cossatot River *(Float Streams)* for about 15 miles, and is characterized by rugged canyons, waterfalls and dense pine forests (Cossatot River Natural Area, *Umpire).* Trails, c/o Parks & Recreation, One Capitol Mall, Little Rock, 72201.

MAGAZINE MOUNTAIN
MILES 10.6   MAP C-2

Although the longest trail is only 10.6 miles, it is possible to combine several others for longer hikes, which offer lakeside aquatic plants, forests, creeks, beaver dams, bluffs and a climb to Signal Hill, the highest point in Arkansas (2,753 feet). N of Havana. Forest Supervisor, Ozark National Forest, Bx. 1008, Russellville, 72801.

OUACHITA
MILES 209   MAP E-4,3,2+1

This hiking trail traverses the Ouachita Mountains' wide range of scenery and terrain, including upland forests, clear streams, high ridges and wide valleys. Because the mountains run east-west (as opposed to the usual north-south), hardwoods grow on the moist northern slopes, pines on the drier southern sides. The route follows a loosely drawn line from Pinnacle Mountain *State Park* (Map E-4) to south of Williams Jct. (Map E-4), to north of Jessieville (Map E-3) and Sims (Map E-2) through the Ouachita *National Forest* to north of *Mena* near Rich Mountain (Map E-1), then west across the state line into Oklahoma along SR 1 to Talimena State Park. There are numerous access points along the way. Forest Supervisor, Ouachita National Forest, Bx. 1270, Hot Springs, 71901.

OZARK HIGHLAND
MILES 135   MAP B-1,2,3+4

A well-marked trail has been established between Lake Ft. Smith *State Park* (Map B-1) and the Richland Creek Recreational Area in the Ozark *National Forest* (11 miles south of *Snowball* (Map B-4). This cross-country trail is characterized by rough terrain that follows year-round streams across steep ascents and descents providing mountain-top vistas and scenic rock formations. Recreation areas in the Ozark *National Forest* serve as access points. Forest Supervisor, Ozark National Forest, Bx. 1008, Russellville, 72801.

SYLAMORE CREEK
MILES 18   MAP J-1

The entire trail follows the North Sylamore Creek northwest from Sylamore to Barkshed Recreational Area (Ozark *National Forest*). The topography ranges from the low stream zones to higher bluffs and ridges. Along the way are waterfalls, overlooks, a foot bridge across a maidenhead fern bed, springs and a close look at an area struck by a tornado. Forest Supervisor, Ozark National Forest, Bx. 1008, Russellville, 72801.

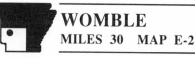

WOMBLE
MILES 30   MAP E-2

This branch of the Ouachita Trail (ABOVE) cuts over forested mountains and follows the Ouachita River *(Float Streams)*. Most access roads are north from *Mount Ida*. Forest Supervisor, Ouachita National Forest, Bx. 1270, Hot Springs, 71901.

WILDLIFE MANAGEMENT AREAS

Set aside for public use, these areas are managed by various (often combined) state and federal agencies as well as private companies working in cooperation with government. While mainly for (and financed by) hunting and fishing, opportunities for other outdoor activities are also available. All management areas are wildlife refuges set in wilderness environments that provide excellent conditions for observation and photography. Some lands lie in spectacular settings offering boating, picnicking, hiking, backpacking and off-road exploration. While primitive, most campsites are unrestricted. Many of these wildlife management areas are mixed with parcels of private property. Be certain the land is public before entering. During hunting seasons, nonhunters should (1) dress in bright colors (day-glo orange hats and vests are ideal), (2) keep a close watch on children, (3) avoid traveling through dense underbrush and (4) be aware that the sound of close gunfire is serious; stay alert and in the open. NOTE: Wildlife management areas are not shown on most maps. Locations described here are relative to a nearby town; area perimeters are partially described by the listed access points. Altitudes listed below are averages. Detailed information about wildlife management areas is available from: Game and Fish Commission, 2 Natural Resources Dr., Little Rock, 72205.

BAYOU DEVIEW
ACRES 4,254   ALT. 240   MAP K-3

Described as "a virtual island of bottomland hardwood timber surrounded by farmland," its primary attraction is waterfowl, although deer and squirrel are hunted. Lake Houge (280 acres) provides very good fishing for bream (1+ lb.) and crappie (2+ lbs.). Camping is restricted to the lake area. Access: W of Weiner, SR 14 & 214.

BAYOU METRO
ACRES 33,700   ALT. 200   MAP N-2

Once one of the largest state-owned wildlife management areas in America (c.1948), this area has been famous for duck hunting since the late 1800s. It also has large populations of deer, squirrel and turkey. Bank fishing from Howell Reservoir offers bream and small catfish. Primarily bottomland, it is laced with sloughs, bayous and canals. Walking and boating are the best (sometimes the only) access. CAUTION: Getting lost is very easy. Unrestricted Camping. Access: E of Pine Bluff, US 79 and SR 88, 11, 276 & 152.

BIG LAKE
ACRES 12,160   ALT. 225   MAP J-5

Notable for having one of the last large tracts of bottomland hardwood remaining in NE Arkansas, it also remains as famous today for duck hunting (over 200 public blinds) as it was at the turn of the century. The southern end contains a unique cypress-tupelo brake that is "outstanding for bird watching." Mallard Lake (300 acres) "has achieved national attention" for its lunker bass (up to 10 lbs), and is said to provide some of the best fishing in the region. A commercial dock (S end of lake) rents boats/motors (Big Lake *National Wildlife Refuge*). Access: W of Blytheville, SR 119, 77, 18 & 181.

BOIS D'ARC
ACRES 5,500   ALT. 250   MAP G-2

Trappers work this area in season. Although some deer and

squirrel are hunted, ducks are the major attraction. The 750-acre Bois D'Arc Lake offers excellent crappie fishing. Alligators are prevalent, mostly at the southern end; some bald eagles have been seen during the winter. Unrestricted Camping. Access: E of Fulton, I-30 and SR 174 & 355.

BUFFALO RIVER
ACRES 16,416   ALT. 1,000   MAP B-3

Said to be the most scenic and the most remote, access is mostly limited to four-wheel drive and hiking. The mixed pine and hardwood forest provides a good habitat for wild turkey, deer and small game. Some black bears have been seen. Best choice for camping is along the Buffalo River *(Float Streams* and *National Parks)*. Access: SE of Jasper, the Buffalo River and SR 123 & 74.

CAMP ROBINSON
ACRES 17,000   ALT. 400   MAP D-4

Actually a three-part complex, it contains a tupelo-cypress swamp and good hunting for fox, coyote, rabbit, quail, deer and duck. The Demonstration Area is a popular meeting place heavily used for dog field trials and training, and provides dog kennels, horse stables, pavilion, camping area, shooting range and archery course. Lake Conway (6,700 acres) is considered "the most productive" for blue gill, bream, lunker bass (up to 8 lbs.), crappie and catfish. Commercial boat docks rent boats and motors. CAUTION: This lake is shallow and littered with stumps and logs. Access: S of Conway, SE *Lake* Conway, I-40 and SR 89.

CANEY CREEK
ACRES 85,000   ALT. 1,000   MAP E-1

Located in the Ouachita *National Forest,* it contains remote and rugged terrain. Portions have been designated as wilderness areas (no vehicles). Bobcat, coyote, fox and black bear are in the area as well as cougar (confirmed sightings). Turkey and squirrel hunting are very good. Fishing in the Cossatot *(Float Streams)* offers smallmouth bass and sunfish; the Little Missouri *(Float Streams)* has trout. Hiking *Trails.* Access: SE of Mena, SR 8, 84 & 246.

CUT-OFF CREEK
ACRES 8,612   ALT. 200   MAP P-3

Unusual for pine tree country, this area is mostly bottomland hardwood (oak and hickory). Popular for hunting squirrel, duck and swamp rabbit, the creek itself is good for catfish, crappie and bream fishing. Camping in designated areas. Access: W of Jerome, Cut-Off Creek, US 165 and SR 35.

DAGMAR
ACRES 7,959   ALT. 200   MAP L-3

Although appearing to be strictly a duck hunting site, a dense hardwood forest makes this area popular for deer hunting also. Miles of bayous and sloughs as well as several lakes like Hickson provide good fishing. 15 campsites. Access: W of Brinkley, I-40 between Bayou DeView and the Cache River.

D. DONALDSON/BLACK R.
ACRES 20,804   ALT. 300   MAP I-3

Although this area is noted for duck hunting, it also has a good squirrel population and some deer. The Black and Little River offer catfish and bass. Also, 17-acre Lake Hubble has good fishing in the warm months; adjacent Lake Ashbaugh stocks bluegill, catfish, crappie and bass. Because of flooding problems, limited camping and picnic areas are available only at commercial boat dock. CAUTION: It is very easy to get lost in the Black River area. Access: E of Pocahontas, US 67, SR 90 and the Black River.

GALLA CREEK
ACRES 2,500   ALT. 350   MAP C-3

One of the smallest and most heavily used areas, its location in the *Arkansas River* Valley among bottomland hardwoods offers good duck, quail and small game hunting. No designated campsites, but nearby Sweeden Island *(Atkins,* Ar.: SR 105, 8 m. S) has facilities. Access: SW of Atkins, SR 324 & 105.

GULF MOUNTAIN
ACRES 10,112   ALT. 1,000   MAP B-4

Called "a remote and mountainous setting for the hunter, the stream fisherman, the nature lover or the weekend camper," this area is one of the most popular in Arkansas. Hunters find quail, turkey, deer and small game; fishing is best for small-mouth bass and bream in the South Fork of the Little Red River *(Float Streams)*. Camping is restricted. Access: W of Clinton, S Fork of the Little Red River, SR 95 &389.

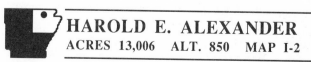

HAROLD E. ALEXANDER
ACRES 13,006   ALT. 850   MAP I-2

One of the newest (1980), it is still little known and lightly used. The Spring River *(Float Streams)* borders a mile of this area, providing good bass fishing and the only public land fronting the river. Deer, quail and rabbit hunting are popular. Camping in designated areas. Access: S of Hardy, Spring River, US 62 & 63 and SR 58 & 354.

HARRIS BRAKE
ACRES 1,200   ALT. 300   MAP D-4

The smallest area in the system, it is crowded during its primary attraction, duck season. The adjoining Harris Brake Lake (1,300 acres) is popular for crappie and bream fishing, and the Fourche La Fave River has large catfish. Camping is restricted to designated areas. Access: SE of Perryville, Fourche LaFave River and SR 9 & 300.

HENRY GRAY/HURRICANE L.
ACRES 16,000   ALT. 200   MAP K-3

Said to have the highest daily visitation of all wildlife management areas, it is popular for deer and duck hunting as well as for family outings. Also: The White and Little Red Rivers (*Float Streams*) cut through this area, an outstanding cypress-tupelo brake is located here, several marked boat trails extend from Glaise Creek, and four lakes dot the area. Along with good quail, rabbit and squirrel hunting there is excellent spring crappie and bass fishing. 26 Campsites. Access: SW of Augusta, White & Little Red Rivers, US 64 and SR 36.

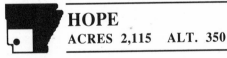

HOBBS MANAGEMENT AREA
ACRES 11,644   ALT. 1,200   MAP A-1

Jointly managed by State Parks, Game and Fish and Natural Heritage Commission, it is the first of its kind in Arkansas. Only 2,400 acres have been developed (Beaver Lake *State Park*), leaving the remainder in its natural state. Steep ridges, oak-hickory forests, springs, sinkholes, overlooks and caves characterize the area, making Hobbs popular with hikers, photographers and bird-watchers (bald eagles and the great blue heron). Fishing and limited hunting. No Camping. Information: State Parks, 1 Capitol Mall, Little Rock, 72201. Access: SE of Rogers, E side of Beaver Lake and SR 12, 303 & 127.

HOPE
ACRES 2,115   ALT. 350   MAP G-2

Small and sometimes crowded, this area is hunted for dove, rabbit and deer. No Camping. WARNING: This property was once a demolition testing area; live explosives may still be present. Access: NW of Hope, SR 4 & 32.

HOWARD COUNTY
ACRES 27,000   ALT. 600   MAP F-1

An intensely managed timber area, the terrain consists of steep hills and valleys typical of the Ouachita Mountains. Good deer country, it also has quail, rabbit and turkey. Adjacent Gillham

and Dierks *Lakes* along with the Upper Saline and Cossatot Rivers (*Float Streams*) offer good fishing. Unrestricted Camping. Access: E side of Gillham Lake, N end of Dierks Lake, SR 4 and Cossatot & Saline Rivers.

LAFAYETTE COUNTY
ACRES 12,430   ALT. 220   MAP H-2

Also managed by the International Paper Company, this is one of the few public hunting areas to charge for deer hunting. No permits are required for rabbit, quail, squirrel or duck. *Lake* Erling (also owned by International Paper Co.) offers excellent fishing for bass, bream, crappie and catfish. Lake Erling Park, "one of the nicest facilities in South Arkansas," has campsites and a boat ramp (S of Walker Creek, SR 53). A large colony of red-cockaded woodpeckers breed here. Camping in the management area is restricted. Access: W of Walnut, W side of Lake Erling and SR 29, 360 & 160.

LAKE GREESON
ACRES 38,000   ALT. 600   MAP F-2

Steep and rugged in most parts, this area offers hunters deer, quail, turkey, rabbit and squirrel. Some trapping is allowed. Adjacent *Lake* Greeson provides campgrounds. Access: SE of Newhope, W side of Lake Greeson, US 70 and SR 369 & 19.

MADISON COUNTY
ACRES 12,974   ALT. 1,680   MAP A-2

Dominated by oak and hickory trees, this area is excellent for deer and squirrel hunting as well as being popular with horseback riding clubs, hikers and backpackers. Numerous springs, sinkholes and caves. The Kings River (*Float Streams*) is along the eastern border. Designated Campsites. Access: SW of Berryville, Kings River and SR 221, 23 & 127.

MT. MAGAZINE
ACRES 120,000   ALT. 1,000   MAP C-2

Located in the southernmost part of the Ozark *National Forest*, this large area provides excellent deer and turkey hunting as well as a 10.8-mile hiking *trail*. The most confirmed sightings of cougar in Arkansas occur here. Magazine Mountain at 2,753 feet is the highest point in Arkansas. Unrestricted Camping. Best access: S from Paris, SR 109, 17 m. S on SR 309.

MUDDY CREEK
ACRES 150,000   ALT. 1,000   MAP D-3

Located in the Ouachita *National Forest,* this area is famous for turkey hunting. Deer and quail populations are also large. Fishing is good at the Fourche La Fave and Ouachita Rivers *(Float Streams)*. Unrestricted Camping. Access: SW of Danville, US 270 and SR 27, 28 & 88.

 ## NIMROD
ACRES 3,634   ALT. 375   MAP D-3

Extremely popular for duck hunting, this area lies inside the Corps of Engineers' Nimrod *Lake* Project. Quail and squirrel hunting are also good. Access: SE of Danville, Nimrod *Lake*.

 ## PETIT JEAN RIVER
ACRES 15,000   ALT. 325   MAP D-3

Much of this area is along the Petit Jean River. Best known for duck hunting, there is a large population of turkey, rabbit and squirrel (hunted from boats). Quail, fox and coon dog trials are popular here. Access: E of Danville, Petit Jean River and SR 7, 154, 10 & 155.

 ## PINEY CREEKS
ACRES 200,000   ALT. 2,000   MAP B-3

Located in the Ozark *National Forest,* this vast area has above average populations of turkey, deer and squirrel, making it very popular with hunters. Big Piney Creek *(Float Streams)* provides additional recreation. Unrestricted Camping. Access: S of Pelsor, SR 7, 27, 16 & 123.

 ## POISON SPRINGS
ACRES 15,000   ALT. 250   MAP G-3

This checkerboard of state and private property mostly surrounds White Oak Lake, and contains the only state forest in Arkansas (mostly Southern pine). Besides deer, quail, squirrel and duck hunting, fishing for crappie, bream, bass and catfish is also popular at 2,676-acre White Oak Lake *(State Park)*. Camping by permit only (Forestry Commission at Camden). Access: SE of Prescott, SR 24, 387, 368, 57 & 299.

 ## R. HANCOCK/BLACK SWAMP
ACRES 3,888   ALT. 175   MAP L-3

At one time proposed as a national natural landmark, this area has "Arkansas' largest, most magnificent cypress and tupelo trees" and "majestic, record-size" oak (upriver, appx. 1 m. from parking lot). Nationally known for duck hunting, it also has a large squirrel population. Most travel is by boat on the Cache River. Camping permitted near parking lot. CAUTION: It is very easy to get lost. Access: county road, E from Gregory.

 ## ST. FRANCIS SUNKEN LANDS
ACRES 16,791   ALT. 225   MAP K-4

Created by the *New Madrid Earthquake* of 1811-12, this area stretches nearly 30 miles from Marked Tree to above Monette (Map J-4) along the St. Francis River in a checkerboard of private-public land. Known for its duck hunting; most use begins at the river. Squirrel and rabbit hunting are also good. No designated camping. Access: N of Marked Tree along roads paralleling both sides of the St. Francis River.

 ## SHIRLEY BAY/RAINEY BRAKE
ACRES 10,500   ALT. 250   MAP J-3

Set at the confluence of the Strawberry and Black Rivers, this area is divided into two geographical sections (Ozark foothills and Delta bottomland) by the Black River. Although primarily hunted for waterfowl, it also has good squirrel, swamp rabbit and deer populations. Well-known for excellent fishing, both rivers offer catfish, bass, bream and crappie. Hill's Slough, Horseshoe Lake and Shirley Bay also provide good fishing. Designated Camping. Best access: SE of Lynn, SR 361.

 ## SULPHUR RIVER
ACRES 16,000   ALT. 250   MAP H-2

Called "some of the wildest country in Arkansas," this area is covered with a dense and swampy river-bottom habitat. While duck hunting is most popular, squirrel and deer are numerous. Trappers work the area in season. Along Sulphur River, Mercer Bayou and at the many "cut-off" lakes there is very good fishing for crappie, bream, catfish and bass. Access: S of Texarkana, Sulphur River, US 71 and SR 237.

 ## SYLAMORE
ACRES 175,000   ALT. 1,000   MAP I-1

Located mostly in the Ozark *National Forest,* the moderate to rugged country of this area offers good deer and squirrel hunting, and is also popular with hikers and campers. The White River *(Float Streams)* has some of the best trout fishing in America. Unrestricted Camping. Access: N of Mountain View (Map J-1) and S of Mountain Home (Map I-1), and by SR 5 & 14 on the east and south.

 ## TRUSTEN HOLDER
ACRES 5,206   ALT. 175   MAP N-3

Adjacent to the SW corner of the White River *National Wildlife Refuge,* primitive and small, this area is mostly accessible only by walking (during wet weather by boat). Popular for deer hunting, there are also turkey and squirrel. Waterfowl are scarce due to the lack of habitat. Designated Camping. Dry weather access: E of Arkansas Post *(National Park),* county road, S from Tichnor. Wet weather access: boat only.

WATTENSAW
ACRES 17,433   ALT. 225   MAP L-2

This is the most popular wildlife management area for deer hunting, and was once known as "an Arkansas deer factory." Relatively uncrowded during other hunting seasons, it offers large populations of squirrel, rabbit and quail. Fishing is good in Wattensaw Bayou for crappie, bass and bream. North of I-40 along the White River is "possibly the largest stand of virgin persimmon and native pecan in East Arkansas" (appx. 300 acres). Because of the mixed upland and bottomland hardwood forest, bird watching is very popular here as well as photography, particularly while floating the Wattensaw Bayou. There are 47 large camping sites. Access: N of DeValls Bluff, White River, US 70 and SR 11 from Hazen.

WHITE ROCK
ACRES 280,000   ALT. 1,600   MAP B-2

A part of the Ozark *National Forest,* this huge area is situated in very rugged terrain that offers scenic and isolated campsites, deer and turkey hunting, a sizable population of black bear and confirmed sightings of cougar. Access: W & SE of Cass, US 71 and SR 103, 215, 23 & 16.

WINONA
ACRES 160,000   ALT. 1,000   MAP D-4

Located in the Ouachita *National Forest,* the rugged mountain terrain, along with lakes and rivers, makes this area popular with hunters, hikers and anglers. Turkey hunting is excellent; quail, rabbit and squirrel, good. *Lake* Sylvia is near the 209-mile Ouachita *Trail. Lake* Winona, Fourche La Fave and Alum Fork Rivers offer good fishing. Unrestricted Camping. Access: W of Williams Jct. SR 9, 10, 155 & 7.

INDEX

MINI-FINDER

Little Red R. 97
Gilbert 36
Gulf Mountain WMA
  129
Leslie 48
Marshall 55
Ozark Highland Trail 127
Ozark National Forest
  111
St. Joe 78
Snowball 80

B–5

Fifty-Six 32
Float Stream
  Little Red R. 97
Greers Ferry Lake 104
Guion 37
Mount Olive 59
Mountain View 60
Ozark Folk Center State
  Park 123
Ozark National Forest
  111
Sylamore Creek Trail 127

C–1

Arkansas River Parks and
  Campgrounds 95
Figure Five 33
Fort Smith 34
Fort Smith National
  Historic Site 34
Greenwood 37
Jenny Lind 45
Ozark Lake 108
Rudy 76
Van Buren 86

C–2

Altus 1
Arkansas River Parks and
  Campgrounds 95
Blue Mountain Lake 101
Booneville 8
Charleston 14
Chismville 14
Clarksville 18
Coal Hill 19
Float Stream
  Mulberry R. 97
Magazine Mountain 53
Magazine Mountain Trail
  126
Mt. Magazine WMA 130
Mulberry 60

Ouachita National Forest
  110
Ozark 63
Ozark Lake 108
Ozark National Forest
  111
Paris 64
Subiaco 82

C–3

Arkansas River Parks and
  Campgrounds 95
Atkins 3
Dardanelle 25
Dover 28
Float Stream
  Big Piney Creek 97
Galla Creek WMA 129
Holla Bend National
  Wildlife Refuge 116
Lake Dardanelle 102
Lake Dardanelle State
  Park 120
Mount Nebo State Park
  122
Ozark National Forest
  111
Petit Jean State Park 123
Pottsville 69
Russellville 76

C–4

Arkansas River Parks and
  Campgrounds 95
Float Streams
  Cadron Creek 98
  Little Red R. 97
Greers Ferry Lake 104
Morrilton 58
Woolly Hollow State
  Park 125

C–5

Float Stream
  Little Red R. 97
Greers Ferry Lake 104
Heber Springs 40
Hickory Flat 41
Pangburn 64
Romance 76
Searcy 79
Woolly Hollow State
  Park 125

D–1

Hartford 40

Ouachita National Forest
  110
Ouachita Trail 127
Queen Wilhelmina State
  Park 124
Sugarloaf Lake 109
Waldron 87

D–2

Blue Mountain Lake 101
Parks 65
Ozark National Forest
  110

D–3

Danville 25
Lake Ouachita 107
Lake Winona 109
Muddy Creek WMA 130
Nimrod Lake 106
Nimrod WMA 131
Ouachita National Forest
  110
Petit Jean River WMA
  131
Petit Jean State Park 123

D–4

Arkansas River Parks and
  Campgrounds 95
Cadron 11
Camp Robinson WMA
  129
Conway 19
Harris Brake WMA 130
Lake Winona 109
Little Rock 48
Mayflower 55
North Little Rock 48
Ouachita National Forest
  110
Ouachita Trail 127
Perryville 66
Pinnacle Mountain State
  Park 123
Winona WMA 132

D–5

Arkansas River Parks and
  Campgrounds 94
Beebe 5
Cabot 10
Carlisle 12
Little Rock 48
Lonoke 52
North Little Rock 48

Scott 79

E–1

Caney Creek Trail 126
Caney Creek WMA 129
Float Streams
  Cossatot R. 99
  Ouachita R. 98
Lake Wilhelmina 109
Mena 57
Ouachita National Forest
  110
Ouachita Trail 127
Queen Wilhelmina State
  Park 124

E–2

Big Fork 7
Caddo Gap 11
Float Streams
  Caddo R. 99
  Little Missouri R. 99
  Ouachita R. 98
Lake Ouachita 107
Mount Ida 59
Ouachita National Forest
  110
Ouachita Trail 127
Parks 65
Pine Ridge 68
Womble Trail 127

E–3

Crystal Springs 25
Hot Springs 42
Hot Springs National
  Park 42
Lake Catherine State Park
  120
Lake Ouachita 107
Lake Ouachita State Park
  121
Lake Winona 109
Ouachita National Forest
  110
Ouachita Trail 127

E–4

Arkansas River Parks and
  Campgrounds 95
Benton 6
Float Stream
  Saline R. 98
Lake Winona 109
Little Rock 48
Magnet Cove 53